Computer Network Topology Design

Computer Network Topology Design

Jocelyn O. Padallan

ARCLER
PRESS

www.arclerpress.com

Computer Network Topology Design

Jocelyn O. Padallan

Arcler Press
4164 Lakeshore Road
Burlington, ON L7L 1A4
Canada
www.arclerpress.com
Email: orders@arclereducation.com

ISBN: 978-1-77956-947-9 (Hardcover)

ABOUT THE AUTHOR

Jocelyn O. Padallan is Associate Professor I from Laguna State Polytechnic University, Philippines and she is currently pursuing her Doctor in Information Technology has Master in Information Technology and Master of Arts in Education from the same University. She has passion for teaching been Instruction and College of Computer Studies - Student Council Adviser at Laguna State Polytechnic University.

TABLE OF CONTENTS

LIST OF FIGURES

PREFACE

Computer networking is the foundation of modern systems of communication and enables trouble-free delivery of information across local, regional, and global geography. From home devices connected to family Wi-Fi to huge enterprise infrastructures extending across continents, the arrangement of a network's design determines its efficiency, reliability, and flexibility. The device setup, channels of communication, and data streams—terms together known as network topology—determine performance, scalability, and security for the most part. An optimized topology not only ensures smooth flow of information but also reduces latency, minimizes congestion, and increases fault tolerance, all critical in today's data-driven world.

As continued technological innovations further expand networking capabilities, the necessity to create topologies suited for specific operating goals has never been greater. Companies must choose between legacy topologies or newer models, balancing such factors as cost, performance, and future expansion. The ideal topology can minimize maintenance, enhance security, and optimize bandwidth utilization, but an ill-designed topology can introduce bottlenecks, vulnerabilities, and operational inefficiencies. Additionally, the increasing prevalence of wireless networks, cloud computing, IoT, and AI-driven systems requires topology strategies that are capable of adapting to evolving needs and the increasingly rapid pace of technology change.

Computer Network Topology Design is a thorough and systematic analysis of the theory, architecture, and realities of designing effective and secure network topologies. The book synthesizes fundamental concepts with advanced design principles, offering practical methods, case studies, and real-world examples. From acquiring knowledge about the basic network models to employing high-end simulation and testing tools, the subject matter spans both theoretical and applied aspects of topology design. Each chapter is designed to build progressively towards expertise, both conceptually and in terms of practical skill.

Chapter 1 is an introduction to computer networks and topologies, including definitions of major network types such as LAN, WAN, and MAN, and descriptions of major components and layouts. It addresses why topology is such a big deal when planning a network, how physical and logical designs differ, and establishes a general overview of the most common forms of topology structure.

Chapter 2 explains basic network topologies like bus, star, ring, mesh, tree, and hybrid. The chapter explains how each topology works, its advantages and disadvantages, and establishes practical scenarios where each is most effective.

Chapter 3 is considering future and upcoming topologies, such as full and partial mesh topologies, daisy chain and backbone configurations, wireless and mobile network topologies. It also touches upon software-defined networking (SDN) and cloud-based topologies like Clos and Fat-Tree, emphasizing their suitability in high-performance and big-data computing environments.

Chapter 4 discusses topology design principles and constraints, explaining goals such as performance, scalability, and reliability. The chapter discusses physical planning, redundancy, bandwidth optimization, and how budgetary, geographical, and scalability considerations influence design choices.

Chapter 5 outlines the methods of network design with the difference between top-down and bottom-up. It outlines the phases in the network design life cycle, the difference between logical and physical diagrams, and the use of tools like Cisco Packet Tracer and GNS3 for design and simulation.

Chapter 6 discusses the relationship between performance and topology in networks. Topics discussed include how topology affects throughput, latency, and packet loss, methods for detecting bottlenecks, load balancing methods, traffic shaping technologies, and simulation as a performance validation technique.

Chapter 7 covers topological security considerations, illustrating how the different configurations influence vulnerability and exposure to attack. It covers segmentation, isolation, and hardening methods that can be integrated into the topology from the outset.

Chapter 8 presents case studies for topology design using real-world examples from enterprise LAN deployments, campus and data center topologies, ISP backbone designs, and cloud service provider topologies such as AWS and Azure.

Chapter 9 introduces simulation techniques and tools in topology, including NS-3, OMNeT++, and Mininet. It explains test and modeling processes, contrasts emulation with simulation, and gives pragmatic exercises for gaining skills.

Chapter 10 discusses nascent trends in network topology, including the needs of 5G and IoT networks, the role played by edge computing, AI-optimized topology, and progress toward quantum and photonic networks. It also considers the continuing evolution of software-defined topologies.

This book is designed to be used by students, IT professionals, and network engineers who require a straightforward and organized explanation of topology design practices and principles. It is equally valuable to beginners building base knowledge as it is to advanced practitioners who want to supplement design techniques with concepts and tools of a higher order. Teachers will find it an excellent teaching aid, while industry specialists can apply its techniques in practical network planning, performance tuning, and security enhancement projects.

CHAPTER 1

INTRODUCTION TO COMPUTER NETWORKS AND TOPOLOGIES

Contents

INTRODUCTION

The phrase computer networks is used to describe the interconnection of more than one computer device for successful communication and data exchange. Essentially, a computer network gives devices a means of sharing information efficiently and effectively. This connection could be in the form of ranging from local area networks (LANs), which operate with computers within a small geographical area, to wide area networks (WANs), which cover large distances and could even reach cities, countries, or even continents. By a network, users can share resources such as files, programs, and Internet access, fostering collaboration and productivity. Furthermore, with increasing complexity and size of networks, so does the need for efficient management systems for optimal performance and security, consistent with the dynamic character of digital communication in our increasingly interconnected world. Effectively, computer networks not only facilitate information exchange but also accommodate various protocols and standards that govern communication. These protocols define how data will be transmitted and received to ultimately arrive at the destination efficiently as well as guarantee integrity and security.

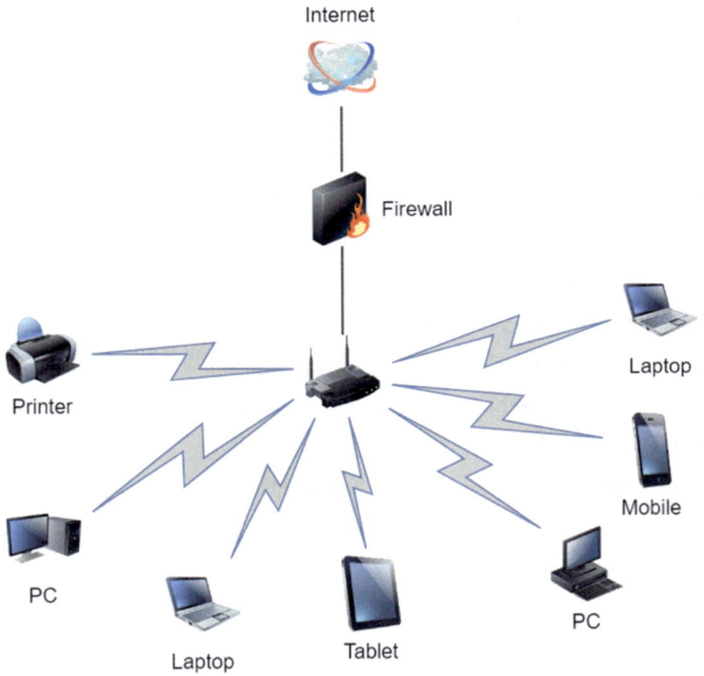

Figure 1.1. *The concept of computer networks encompasses the interconnection of multiple computing devices to facilitate communication and data sharing.*

Source: https://www.guru99.com/images/1/090719_0446_BasicsofCom1.png.

The Transmission Control Protocol/Internet Protocol (TCP/IP) suite, for instance, is inherent to internet communication, defining how data packets are partitioned, transmitted, and reassembled along many nodes. Understanding such protocols will be critical to address issues related to network latency, bandwidth, and reliability. Advancements in technology have resulted in the evolution of such standards on a constant basis, driven by mounting needs for efficient connectivity, thereby marking a significant interdependence between network evolution and technological evolution. Further, the advent of concepts such as Software-Defined Networking (SDN) signifies a paradigmatic shift in the structure of networks as well as their management. As asserted, traditional IP networks are typically plagued with complexity and configuration complexity, which may complicate effective management (Kreutz et al., 2014). With the use of SDN principles, decoupling the control and data planes simplifies network functions, enabling flexibility and responsiveness. This reform enhances resources management and policy enforcement capabilities as well as facilitating the creation of networking technologies in line with changing needs. Thus, the ongoing progression of computer networks is a dynamic interplay between the basic theories and innovative practices, repeatedly reshaping the digital communication and infrastructure landscape (Zhu et al., 2017) (Figure 1.1).

Explanation of Computer Networks

Computer networking is simply an examination of the intricate interconnection that enables data and communication between devices. A computer network, on its most basic level, consists of numerous interlinked computers and resources sharing data using a shared medium. This system is not merely based on hardware and software but also involves communication protocols that determine how data is transmitted and accepted. Such protocols, such as TCP/IP, establish the guidelines upon which data are routed efficiently and messages remain intact. On the aspect of network topology, the arrangement of devices that are linked also influences performance and reliability. Different topologies, such as star, ring, and mesh, are different approaches toward network arrangement that are differently efficient and robust under differing operating conditions. When comparing network topologies, effectiveness, and scalability, as well as fault tolerance, become critical concerns. For instance, a star topology with many nodes and the central hub connecting them is easy to administer and maintain. The disadvantage is that it contains a point of failure, meaning a crash of the central hub can cripple the entire network. By way of contrast, a mesh topology adds an element of robustness since multiple paths are available for data transmission, hence protecting network operation when some of the connections fail. Robustness is more than just structural design; it also matters where one considers external attacks that could undermine network integrity. As has been suggested in earlier studies, robust models of network robustness do require close examination, but good metrics with the right balance of complexity and utility are still in short supply. This issue emphasizes the significance of ongoing investigation in network resilience, especially against cyberattacks and natural disasters (Kooij et al., 2008). Moreover, the role of multidisciplinary research on computer networks should not be overlooked. Interdisciplinary work among disciplines such as computer science, sociology, and physics can yield results that enhance greater knowledge of network dynamics and behavior. Sociophysics, on the other hand, attempts to bring social phenomena and models of networks in a bid to explain how interactions of people can be simulated by computer networks. The major challenge is still how to make such models catch up in the real world without being computationally cumbersome. Tightening the links makes prediction stronger, thus developing networks that not only function optimally but are also robust to varied challenges. Ultimately, an in-depth comprehension of computer networks involves not just technical knowledge but also appreciation of the intricate social structures underlying their operation (Sobkowicz, 2025) (Figure 1.2).

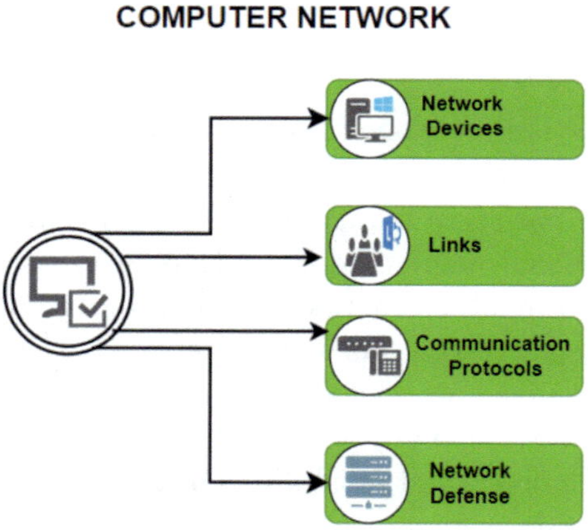

Figure 1.2. *The computer networks.*

Source: https://media.geeksforgeeks.org/wp-content/uploads/20240611150843/Key-components-of-computer-network.png.

Importance of Computer Networks in Modern Society

Computer networks nowadays are the cornerstones of communication, possessing the ability to transfer data thousands of miles away in mere seconds. This revolutionized both personal and business communication. With individuals banking increasingly on digital media for day-to-day activities—starting from working remotely to learning online—the importance of safe and efficient networking increases day by day. Notably, network topologies such as tree and mesh have been enhanced, developing more robust communications systems. They have allowed organizations to provide distributed simulations that can optimize operational capacity and model complex environments, demonstrating the use of efficient computer networks in a broad array of fields, from defense to urban planning (Barrett et al., 2004). Moreover, computer networks play a critical role in facilitating collaboration and innovation. By interconnecting individuals and institutions across the globe, such networks facilitate cooperation and sharing of information, thus empowering experts, and scientists to tackle controversial topics in concert. Network topology and analysis and synthesis study, for instance, have assumed a central role in the understanding of the complex interactions that govern the online space (Vahdat et al., 2006). Scientists now use systematic approaches, such as the dK-series of probability distributions, to measure and replicate the complexities existing in various network arrangements. Not only do these analyses provide our understanding of existing structures but also promote design and performance of future networks and enable technological progress and economic development. Finally, incorporating computer networks into our daily lives has profound implications for information management and security. Since the society is becoming more dependent on these networks for storing and passing sensitive data, protection from cyber-attacks is very important. Efficient data management systems facilitated by advanced topologies of networks make it possible to transfer information more securely while maximizing the bandwidth and limiting latency. This is of great importance in industries like medicine and finance, where integrity in data is very critical. With the growth of computer networks, they not only facilitate organizational operational needs but also influence policies and practices in relation to security and privacy, bringing to the forefront their ultimate importance within the fabric of modern society.

Overview of Network Components

In computer networking, several units work in coordination to facilitate communication and sharing of data. The fundamental components of any network include routers, switches, and access points, each having distinct roles to play. Routers have a significant function in relaying data packets from one network to another, acting as traffic controllers that direct information along the most optimal routes. Switches operate at a lower layer, connecting devices within the same segment of the network and ensuring data is delivered only to the destination device. Access points extend the network by connecting wireless devices, bridging the gap between wireless and wire-based infrastructure. This understanding of these fundamental building blocks gives insight into how they combine to create an integrated network infrastructure that can service multiple applications. Other components, such as firewalls and network interface cards

(NICs), are also crucial to the overall performance and security of computer networks. NICs enable devices to communicate over a network by providing the hardware interface necessary, as dictated by the specific network protocol in use. This enables the free interaction of devices, from desktops and laptops to servers. Firewalls, on the other hand, are essential in protecting networks from external unauthorized access and cyber-attacks.

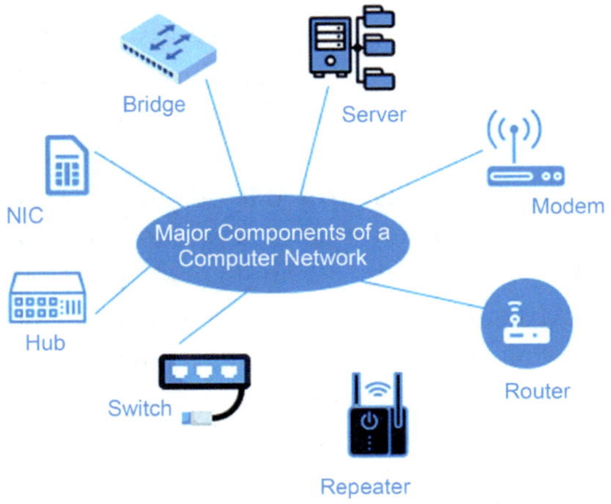

Figure 1.3. *An overview of network components.*

Source: https://prepbytes-misc-images.s3.ap-south-1.amazonaws.com/assets/1681284624186-1%20%2812%29.png.

As a filter of security, firewalls examine incoming and outgoing traffic based on pre-defined security rules. Together, NICs and firewalls guarantee not only the functionality of the network but also its strength against possible attacks and intrusions, which underscores the importance of secure networking practices for organizations nowadays. As technology progresses, the capability and complexity of network components also grow, creating capable components such as graph neural networks (GNNs). Whereas traditional networking components are worried about connectivity and information sharing, GNNs represent a new trend dealing with challenges related to data management in non-Euclidean forms. This advancement is particularly remarkable in scenarios where there are intricate relationships between nodes within a network, allowing for enhanced data handling and analysis. By integrating these new elements into the network infrastructure, organizations can benefit from greater flexibility and performance, paving the way for aggressive applications in various applications such as data mining and machine learning. This balancing of diverse components directs towards the ongoing evolution of computer networks, with the necessity for flexibility in design and implementation, as highlighted in existing research on network architecture innovation (Mildenhall et al., 2021) and (Wu et al., 2020) (Figure 1.3).

1.1. TYPES OF COMPUTER NETWORKS

Computer network heterogeneity comes from the diversity of requirements and purpose they are programmed to serve and hence the variation in categorization along size, topology, and application dimensions. Local Area Networks (LANs) are the smallest in scope and are usually located within a specific geographical area such as a single building or campus. LANs accommodate high-speed data transfer in a short distance and are utilized heavily in domestic dwellings, educational institutions, and small businesses. Conversely, Wide Area Networks (WANs) stretch large geographical distances, connecting multiple LANs over regional, national, or international distances. WANs offer communication through leased telecommunication lines or satellite transmissions, offering broader connectivity required in multinational corporations. Being aware of these fundamental types helps to explain how various networks offer unique roles in our increasingly interconnected world. Another crucial categorization of computer networks is their topology, that is, the organization of different components present in the network. Common topologies include star, ring, bus, and mesh. The star topology has gained prominence in most modern-day networks since it is centralized where all the nodes are connected to a single hub or switch, allowing for more fault tolerance since failure in one node does not impact the network. On the other hand, a ring topology connects every node to two nodes in a loop, which is easier for data transportation but becomes troublesome upon failure in one node. Awareness of such topological structures is not only necessary for network design but also pre-empts problems of management, upkeep, and scalability in networks in systems, as contended in the analysis of Software-Defined Networking (Singla, 2024). Besides, there are specialized classes of networks to deal with particular applications and requirements, such as Personal Area Networks (PANs) and Metropolitan Area Networks (MANs). PANs are typically applied for near-range personal appliances to enable straightforward communication among laptops, mobile phones, and peripheral devices such as printers. They are a classic example of the new trend of connectivity in personal technology, typically employing Bluetooth or Wi-Fi protocols. At another level, MANs provide interconnection of networks within a city, basically providing high-speed internet connectivity and other services over an area greater than that of a LAN but less than that of a WAN. The flexibility and strategic utilization of various types of networks underscore the physical and performance challenges in rolling them out, particularly the intersection between increasing bandwidth demand and network engineering innovation (Sinnen, 2007) (Figure 1.4).

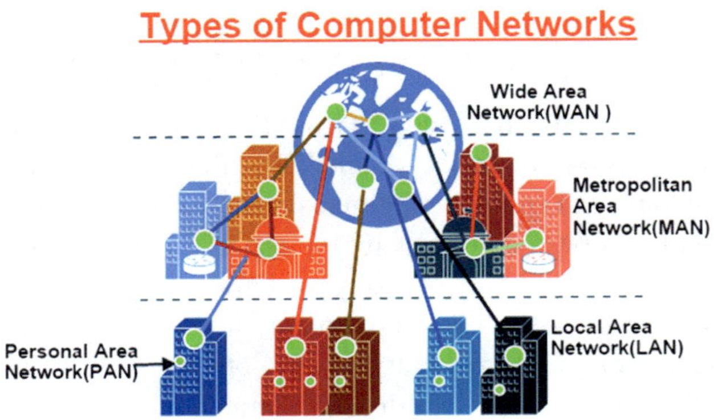

Figure 1.4. *Types of computer networks.*

Source: https://www.brainwareuniversity.ac.in/blog/wp-content/uploads/2019/03/CN.png.

1.1.1. Local Area Network (LAN)

In computer networking, the Local Area Network (LAN) is a principal component in the communication of devices over a small geographical location, typically spanning to one building or campus. Through this setup, data transmission at high speeds as well as resource sharing is facilitated, and therefore it is an integral infrastructure for personal and organizational use. A LAN typically employs a technology such as Ethernet or Wi-Fi to connect various devices, such as computers, printers, and servers. The topology of a LAN is of different types—most notably, star, ring, or bus topologies—each offering its own advantages in network efficiency as well as fault tolerance. Moreover, its scalability enables organizations to grow their network infrastructure as per needs, which is extremely necessary in the dynamic work environments of the present times. Security is one of the cornerstones of LAN design, especially considering the increasing sophistication of threats to data privacy and integrity that rise day by day. Adequate security measures such as firewalls and intrusion detection systems are critical in safeguarding sensitive data flowing over the network. As documented in existing literature, various intrusion detection methods have been employed to address these issues and are collectively categorized into Signature-based Intrusion Detection Systems (SIDS) and Anomaly-based

Intrusion Detection Systems (AIDS) (Khraisat et al., 2019). Both attempt to enhance network security but are fundamentally distinct in their operational mechanisms. SIDS employ known intrusion models, while AIDS focus on abnormal behavior deviations. The choice between these systems can greatly influence the extent to which a LAN is able to resist threats and defend against unauthorized access, particularly in data-intensive communities. The modularity of modern LANs also allows them to easily integrate new technologies, such as blockchain platforms like Hyperledger Fabric. This characteristic allows firms to enhance their working models with powerful security and performance. Fabrics design is particularly well-positioned to realize distributed applications on a permissioned network, facilitating secure transactions without relying on native cryptocurrencies (Androulaki et al., 2018). This flexibility makes evident the growing convergence between traditional networking and leading-edge technologies, positioning LANs as central features in the adoption of new solutions. Such alignment not only facilitates communication but also facilitates greater potential for more sophisticated applications to be integrated into local networks, exemplifying how LANs continue to evolve in an increasingly integrated technological world (Figure 1.5).

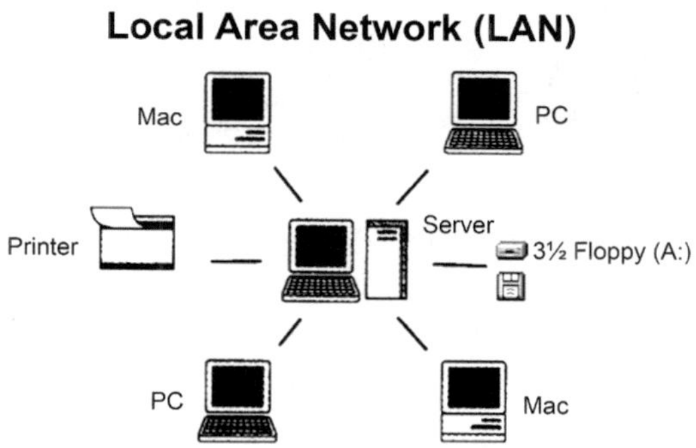

Figure 1.5. *The local area network (LAN).*

Source: https://www.mbaskool.com/2015_images/stories/may-images/kum-lan.jpg.

1.1.2. Wide Area Network (WAN)

The architecture of a Wide Area Network (WAN) facilitates connectivity over extensive geographical distances, making it a pivotal component of modern communication systems. Unlike Local Area Networks (LANs), which operate within confined spaces such as offices or campuses, WANs can connect users across cities, countries, or even continents. This expansive reach is supported by various transmission mediums, including leased lines, satellites, and fiber-optic cables, allowing WANs to deliver consistent and reliable data transfer. Additionally, WANs enable diverse connections, from enterprise resource planning systems to internet access for remote users, thus fostering collaboration and operational efficiency in various sectors. As organizations continue to expand their reach, the underlying architecture of WANs becomes increasingly critical in ensuring seamless communication and data sharing across different locations. The performance and reliability of a WAN are contingent on the technologies and protocols employed within its infrastructure. Protocols such as Frame Relay, Asynchronous Transfer Mode (ATM), and Multiprotocol Label Switching (MPLS) play an essential role in managing data transmission traffic and optimizing bandwidth utilization across a WAN.

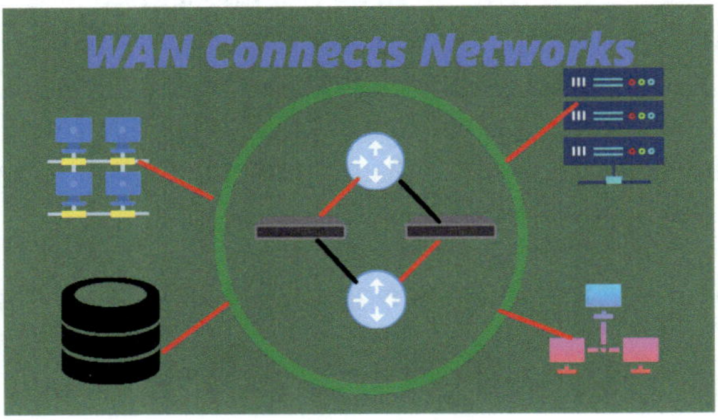

Figure 1.6. *The architecture of a wide area network (WAN).*

Source: *https://www.cspsprotocol.com/wp-content/uploads/2021/05/What-is-WAN.png.*

Each protocol serves distinct purposes, whether it is to facilitate high-speed data transfers, manage varying types of service levels, or enhance routing efficiency. These technologies can be configured to accommodate specific organizational requirements, which is crucial as businesses evolve and adapt to new digital demands. Moreover, the implementation of edge computing, as exemplified in cutting-edge research, signifies a noteworthy trend where data is processed closer to the source, thereby enhancing response times and alleviating bandwidth costs ((Shi et al., 2016)). This intersection illustrates the adaptability of WAN technologies in meeting contemporary challenges. Security concerns also emerge as significant factors in WAN implementations, necessitating robust strategies to protect sensitive information traversing vast networks. As the sophistication of cyber threats escalates, organizations are compelled to adopt comprehensive security measures such as Virtual Private Networks (VPNs), encryption, and firewalls to safeguard data. The secure transfer protocols ensure that information remains confidential and integral alongside the WANs performance needs. Furthermore, the integration of blockchain technologies within WAN frameworks enhances security and data integrity, as highlighted in advances like Hyperledger Fabric, which promotes a permissioned environment for secure transactions ((Androulaki et al., 2018)). By marrying innovative technologies with established WAN protocols, organizations can create more resilient networks capable of addressing the evolving landscape of cybersecurity threats while maintaining efficient communication pathways (Figure 1.6).

1.1.3. Metropolitan Area Network (MAN)

In computer networks, a Metropolitan Area Network (MAN) is an intermediate layer that links multiple Local Area Networks (LANs) across a specific geographical area, for example, a city or a large campus. Limited by its intermediate geographic coverage area, typically between 5 and 50 kilometers, a MAN facilitates high-speed data transportation and more sophisticated communication between various networks. This is particularly useful for multi-site businesses, as it allows them to possess a common network topology without the redundancy associated with Wide Area Networks (WANs). MANs using fiber-optic technology are capable of enhancing data transport rates and bandwidth significantly, thereby meeting business requirements that require rapid data exchange and high-quality connectivity features. In this context, MANs are of invaluable application in the development of urban networking infrastructure. Beyond mere connectivity, the architecture of a MAN supports a variety of applications and services that provide the foundation for modern communications. These networks are of significant relevance in environments where high data throughput is required, for example, universities, large businesses, and public service providers. With the change in the consumption pattern of digital content and the increasing need for bandwidth, the use of MANs has risen proportionally. The architecture typically employs more than one topology, including star, ring, and mesh, to provide flexibility and an effective networking system. Flexibility allows business organizations to select a topology that would best meet their operating need and growth trend. With proper utilization of the right topology, organizations can get the maximum out of their network performance and enable possible future growth. The impact contributed by technology advancements in further enabling MAN capabilities cannot be overstated. The newest innovations, especially those related to deep learning and high-precision recognition models, have transformed the interaction of MANs with leading-edge technologies like the Metaverse. These advancements enriched the portfolio of data services and applications supported by a MAN, bridging the physical-virtual gap for users. The potential support of virtual currencies and deeper user interactions within a MAN is indicative of a broader trend towards creating immersive connectivity experiences. As various sectors, ranging from education to entertainment, trend towards increased deployment of networked environments, the significance of MANs as supporting infrastructure grows. They not only demonstrate the strong potentials of current communication technologies but also ground the potential future innovations in networked interactions, capturing the nature of current metropolitan connectivity (Hamid et al., 2022; Park et al., 2022) (Figure 1.7).

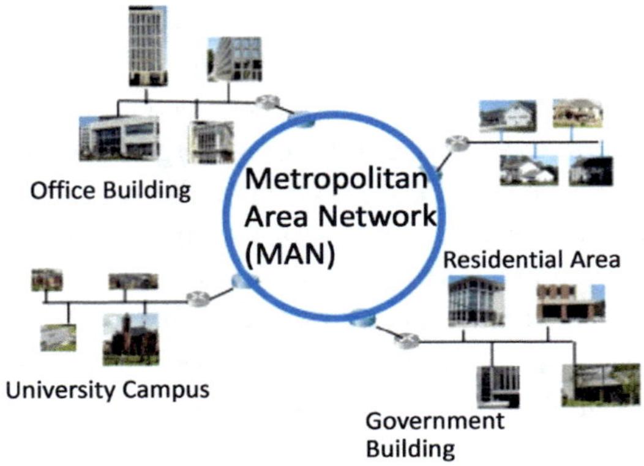

Figure 1.7. *A metropolitan area network (MAN).*

Source: https://ars.els-cdn.com/content/image/3-s2.0-B9780128133651000023-f02-05-9780128133651.jpg.

1.2. NETWORK PROTOCOLS

In the realm of computer networks, network protocols form the basis for efficient communication between devices. The protocols are standardized sets of rules that facilitate the sharing of data to ensure information is conveyed efficiently and accurately across heterogeneous systems. There are different families of protocols, each specified for specific network operations, such as the Transmission Control Protocol (TCP) for assured data transfer, and the Internet Protocol (IP) for routing of packets. The performance and design of a network are based on knowledge of the functions and the layers of such protocols. As networks increase in complexity, the need for robust protocols becomes more necessary; not only should they facilitate data exchange, but also should enforce security, reliability, and error handling operations, since the reliance on networks for business and private communication increases. One field of recent focus in network protocol studies is the enhancement of Peer-to-Peer (P2P) networks, which are founded upon decentralized networks. New approaches, such as self-organizing protocols using local knowledge of network nodes, are being researched to improve the reliability of such networks towards failures. In a recent study, two similar self-organizing schemes were evaluated that employed node interaction and Edge Clustering Coefficient (ECC) measures for improving connectivity as well as reliability in dynamic overlays.

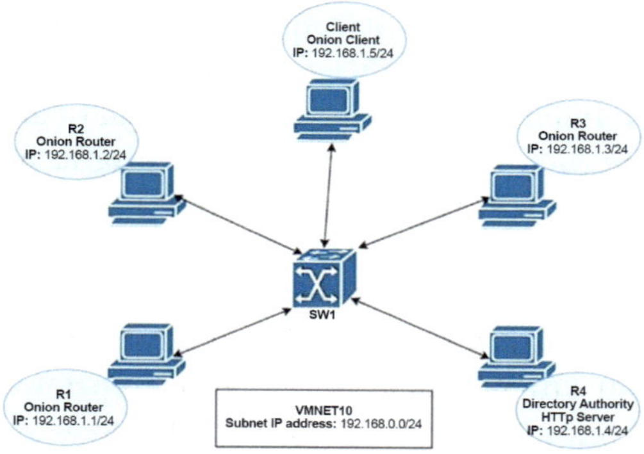

Figure 1.8. *The network protocols.*

Source: https://infraon.io/blog/wp-content/uploads/2023/01/1629873089173-1.jpg.

These methodologies have shown potential simulation output on various network topologies, verifying that properly designed protocols can significantly enhance the functionality of peer-to-peer communications to make more stable and robust networks possible, eventually adding to the overall background of network structure and design procedures (Ferretti et al., 2015). Ethernet, the prevailing networking technology, continues to develop and upgrade, its core becoming the focal point of Local Area Networks (LANs) and extending its influence to industrial use. Its popularity stems from factors such as cost-effectiveness, flexibility, and backward compatibility that have rendered it attractive in different environments, ranging from telecommunication to multimedia. However, the diverse use of Ethernet presents serious challenges, especially regarding the quality of service (QoS) demands of the protocol. Mapping Ethernet protocols to specific contexts requires proper knowledge of application-specific requirements. By examining Ethernet enhancements intended for transport, embedded systems, and multimedia, researchers introduce the manner in which altered network protocols are able to adapt to the unique requirements of each domain, thereby enhancing performance and maximizing utilization of resources in next-generation computing environments (Feller et al., 2010) (Figure 1.8).

1.2.1. Definition and Purpose of Network Protocols

In the context of computer networks, protocols are regulatory structures that define the conventions and rules of communication between computers. As a sequence of standardized procedures, network protocols facilitate data exchange, permitting data to flow safely and efficiently across several systems. Network protocols include everything from error correction and data compression to management of connections. Every protocol has specific functions that it is responsible for, such as the Transmission Control Protocol (TCP), which guarantees the delivery of data, and the Internet Protocol (IP), which addresses and routes packets of information. When they follow these common practices, different hardware and software components can convey a common vocabulary so that networks with different topologies can interoperate with each other. The function of network protocols extends beyond mere communication; they become essential in ensuring a safe and reliable network. They allow devices to share resources effectively, manage bandwidth, and guarantee data integrity. In today's ever-connected world, where system breakdown and data exposure can have disastrous consequences, robust protocols become the necessary choice. For instance, fault-tolerant protocols aid in the creation of network disruption resilience by facilitating fast recovery in systems. A classic example is the RAIN project with a focus on fault-tolerant interconnect topologies and communication protocols for securing data exchange in hostile environments. The work serves to demonstrate that properly designed protocols enhance network service availability and reliability to ultimately allow seamless user experience. In addition, as network technologies evolve, the role of protocols also becomes increasingly sophisticated, charting the way in integrating new innovations while being compatible with existing infrastructure. Emerging protocols are picking up on current concerns, such as the need for enhanced security components against cyber threats, which (Bohossian et al., 1998) brings out in the presentation of fault-tolerant designs using off-the-shelf components to construct fault-tolerant distributed computer systems. These new approaches illustrate the way protocols can evolve as the dynamic nature of network requirements brings about changing needs. Further, the development of protocols that accommodate several application needs ensures that when organizations adopt new technologies, they do so in consonant structure, hence preserving the workings of communications and data transfer within highly complicated networking structures.

1.2.2. Protocols courants (TCP/IP, HTTP, FTP)

The underlying internet protocols are required to enable communication among various devices and networks. Transmission Control Protocol (TCP) and Internet Protocol (IP) collectively are referred to as TCP/IP, and it is the core of internet communications. TCP provides reliable transmission of data between devices and handles the establishment, maintenance, and termination of the connection. This protocol ensures the order of delivery of data packets and the absence of duplication, making it critical for applications that demand accuracy, like file transfer and email. IP addresses each machine on the network with a unique identifier that allows routing to navigate the expansive vistas of interconnected computers. These protocols cooperate to facilitate data exchange and have a significant influence on the design and functioning of modern computer networks. TCP/IP is not the sole protocol employed; additional application-layer protocols add usability and value to the internet. One of the best-known protocols is the Hypertext Transfer Protocol (HTTP), which manages the transfer of hypertext documents and enables web browsing, the activity now so prevalent in contemporary society. HTTP simplifies the communication between web browsers and servers to enable users to request and retrieve web pages comfortably. HTTP is a request-response protocol in which browsers send requests for resources and servers respond with the content requested. The evolution of HTTP to HTTPS aims at security via encryption and integrity of data in web communication. Consequently, HTTP and its derivatives are significant regarding how individuals obtain and interact with information on the Internet, putting the data's availability and security in a continuous balancing act. File Transfer Protocol (FTP) is another essential protocol that allows files to move across devices on a network. Unlike HTTP, which is optimized for web pages, FTP is optimized for file upload and download handling and therefore is a critical tool for web designers and IT administrators who handle server content. FTP uses a client-server architecture, supporting users in remote connection to a server, directory navigation, and easy exchange of files. Its support for active and passive connections via the dual-mode architecture makes it compatible with various network configurations. As attacks online continue to evolve, technologies such as FTP adapt to include security features that assist in ensuring data integrity and confidentiality, with better versions such as Secure File Transfer Protocol (SFTP) emerging to provide secure alternatives. As explicated in the literature, FTP and associated protocol resilience is central to functionality in an increasingly interconnected and security-driven digital world, wherein a robust cyber-attack defense is imperative (Khraisat et al., 2021; Khraisat et al., 2019) (Figure 1.9).

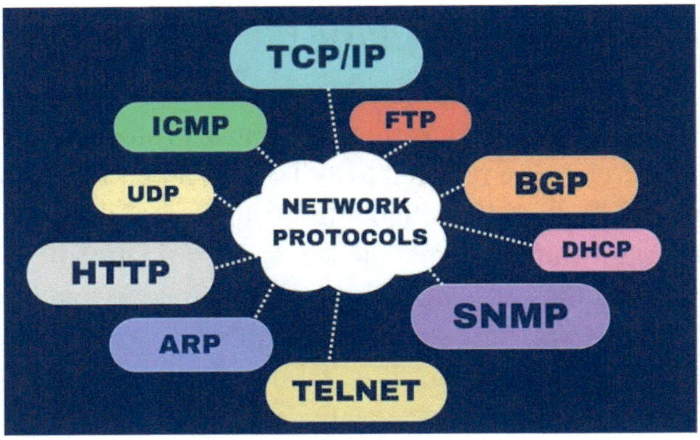

Figure 1.9. *Common protocols.*

Source: https://www.whatismyip.com/static/f13c11cfc592e0aa643a05e3680ab54f/network-protocols.webp.

1.2.3. Role of Protocols in Data Transmission

In the field of computer networks, protocols are fundamental guidelines that dictate how data is transmitted and accepted among various systems. They are now indispensable for the role of making communication efficient, effective, and secure. In establishing a common language that different systems can use, protocols make different hardware and software systems compatible with each other. This connectivity is particularly vital in an era that is rapidly dominated by the Internet of Things (IoT), where millions of devices need to communicate with one another without any glitches. Essentially, protocols define rules of error detection, compression of data, and encryption, which are crucial for the integrity and confidentiality of data in communication. With emerging technology, the role of protocols has evolved significantly, particularly with the advent of mobile edge computing (MEC). MEC is revolutionizing data transmission by moving processing close to the user and therefore reducing latency significantly. Through protocols that support MEC architectures, data transmission becomes even more efficient as it allows real-time processing of data at network edges such as base stations and access points. This shift not only optimizes performance but also maximizes the energy consumption of mobile devices. Accordingly, protocol creation and optimization targeted at MEC has emerged as a significant research area addressing topics such as joint radio-and-computational resource management within this novel paradigm of mobile computing (Mao et al., 2017). Moreover, edge computing protocols are becoming increasingly important since they address bandwidth issues, response time, and privacy. By making data processing occur at the edge of networks, such protocols alleviate bandwidth expense and data breach issues. For instance, edge computing protocols can address local data processing and storage as well as protect data through encryption mechanisms that accommodate broadly applicable applications ranging from smart homes to collaborative city-wide initiatives. These are within a larger trend toward decentralized computing models, which rely on sound protocols for maintaining system integrity and performance (Shi et al., 2016). The role of data transfer protocols under these circumstances is not only tactical but strategic, playing a key role in the roll-out of modern network structures (Figure 1.10).

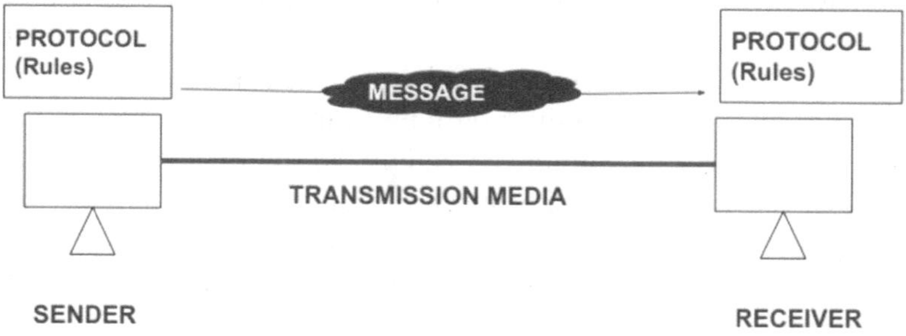

Figure 1.10. *Role of protocols in data transmission.*

Source: https://media.geeksforgeeks.org/wp-content/uploads/20210219161108/protocol.png.

1.3. NETWORK TOPOLOGIES

The advanced study of network topologies is critical in determining the performance and effectiveness of computer networks. Various configurations, such as star, ring, mesh, and tree topologies, are applied for specific reasons depending on the unique requirements of a network. Each topology possesses strengths and weaknesses regarding scalability, fault tolerance, and data transmission speed. For example, while a star topology facilitates the addition of nodes with ease and prevents failure risks by segmenting links, a mesh topology offers more than one path among nodes, enhancing redundancy as well as reliability. The decision on topology significantly influences the overall performance and fault tolerance of a network and therefore demands an accurate evaluation of the effects of every setup on data flow and management strategies within different situations. Recent studies highlight the important performance disparities between different network topologies, especially in high-throughput-demanding applications like data centers and high-performance computing (HPC) systems. In order to systematically compare their performance, frameworks for evaluating throughput based on both synthetic and experimentally-obtained traffic matrices have been suggested. This two-part comparison approach allows for a fine-grained understanding of the differences in handling worst-case traffic patterns and their scalability under tight conditions among different topologies. These tests confirm that some topologies demonstrate excellent consistency in performance under different traffic patterns, which is highly desirable in applications that need durability and competence in processing data. Generating these frameworks is important in creating a quantitative foundation for network structure optimization in problematic environments, which will eventually influence design decisions and network operations (Godfrey et al., 2016). Furthermore, the higher-order concepts of spectral graph theory bring forth new perspectives on how to maximize networks' topology towards dynamical process. Summits highlight the significance of spectral gaps within Laplacian matrices regarding synchronizability as well as random walker minimization between nodes in networks. Certain configurations of networks, defined as entangled networks, are proven to be highly efficient and show resilient performance under synchronizability as well as solution capacity, such as searchability in situations of congestion. The relationship of such networks to the Ramanujan and Cage graphs implies higher structural effectiveness that can be tapped into in order to identify approximate solutions to many computational issues. The use of such results in practical applications thus not only expands the theoretical platform for network design but also offers opportunities for more efficient and reliable computer network architecture.

1.3.1. Network Topology Definition

Network topology specifies the organization, structure, and interconnection of various elements in a computer network. This significant term encompasses both the physical and logical structure of the network. Physical topology specifies the real position of cables, computers, and other equipment, while the logical topology describes the manner in which the data is transmitted throughout the network. Through determining how the elements are related, network topology plays the crucial role in defining performance, scalability, and fault tolerance. Understanding topology well allows networkers to optimally design to accommodate the different uses so that the network can handle the loads imposed by users and devices onto it effectively. With the progress of technology, the significance of topology is highlighted even more and requires more study and research to form today's networks. The most used types of network topologies are star, bus, ring, and mesh, each having its pros and cons. All devices, for instance, are connected to a single central hub in a star topology, which is simple to troubleshoot but represents a point of failure. Conversely, a bus topology connects all devices with a single line of communication, which is cost-effective but performance degenerates with the number of devices. Ring topology, wherein each device is connected to two others, allows for clean delivery of data packets but suffers if any of its connections is interrupted. Finally, mesh topology with numerous paths between devices offers redundancy and reliability but at greater cost and complexity. Understanding these configurations is essential for network engineers who must streamline data streams without weakening strong, effective systems. As technology's horizon continues to advance, so too does the use of network topology in emerging frameworks like edge computing. Edge computing demands a unique topology approach, as it aims to process data closest to the source, rather than simply employing centralized data centers. The elevated usage of Internet of Things (IoT) devices, in addition to real-time data processing needs, tends to require innovative topological structures that prioritize low-latency links and dynamic asset relocation. Additionally, the integration of these sophisticated topologies into common frameworks is challenging in terms of security, management, and interoperability. Thus, a general understanding of network topology is required not only for traditional structures but also for adherence to contemporary trends such as edge computing, eventually culminating in the establishment of efficient, scalable, and resilient networks (Zhu et al., 2017; Shi et al., 2016) (Figure 1.11).

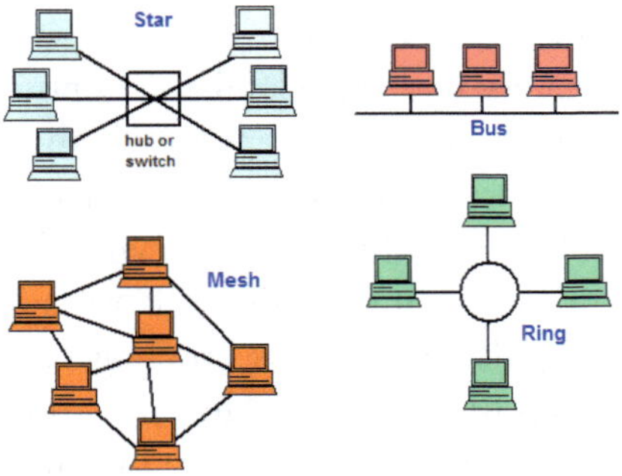

Figure 1.11. *Network topology refers to the arrangement.*

Source: https://i.pcmag.com/imagery/encyclopedia-terms/network-topology-topology.fit_lim.size_1050x.gif.

1.3.2. Common Types of Topologies (Star, Bus, Ring)

In computer networks, topologies are critical to describing how different devices communicate and exchange information with one another. One of the most common is the star topology, in which all the nodes are connected to a single switch or hub. It is easy to administer a network and has a visible point for fault tracing. When one link fails in a star topology, it will not affect others, and hence fault tolerance is enhanced. Moreover, centralized management allows for easier addition or removal of devices with less interruption. Star topology is widely utilized in small and large network scenarios due to the fact that it is highly scalable and provides reliable performance, thus making it a preferred option in stable and uncomplicated network design situations. Star topology ought to be realized in an organization which appreciates the ease of upkeep and operation efficiency. Alternatively, the bus topology presents a different setup in which all devices are connected to a single communication line called the bus. It is straightforward and cheap, particularly for small networks, as it requires less cable than other topologies. But its reliance on a single cable at the center can make it very difficult. If the main cable is broken or faulty, the whole network will be halted, which poses a high-risk factor. When more devices are connected, the system can also degrade as a result of more traffic and collisions. Despite these drawbacks, the bus topology is nevertheless a great candidate for some applications, especially in temporary installations like LANs where cost concerns are a priority in general. Such setups require an understanding of both the pros and cons of bus topology to efficiently design networks. Lastly, the ring topology presents a fascinating configuration in which all devices relate to two others in a closed-loop configuration. Data transmissions in a ring topology move unidirectionally or bidirectionally through each node until it reaches the target destination. This setup can provide consistent transfer of data with assured performance, as every node checks the data prior to forwarding. Once more, as in the case of bus topology, ring topology is susceptible to disruptions; if one node fails, it would bring down the entire network unless one uses a dual ring or other fault tolerance solutions. Even with these shortcomings, ring topologies are still useful in situations where there is a need for continuous data flow and their orderly design enables efficient data management, which increases the network's overall efficiency. Thus, it is important to evaluate the merits and demerits of ring topology to make an informed decision on the best network design for particular organizational requirements.

1.3.3. Advantage and Disadvantage of Each Topology

In the context of computer networks, topologies determine the organization of nodes and links and have significant implications for performance, reliability, and scalability. There are specific strengths and weaknesses of each topology that influence design decisions in the network. For instance, the star topology is widely utilized because it is simple and easy to manage and facilitates effective troubleshooting and centralized management. But its dependence on a single point of contention is dangerous; when this point fails, the entire system collapses. But mesh topologies enhance redundancy and dependability with redundant connections between nodes and create a solid structure against failure. But the complex nature of such a network can lead to higher cost and more difficult demands on maintenance. Therefore, information on these special attributes assumes significance for network managers wishing to optimize performance at a low cost. Further, bus topology, which consists of linear coupling of nodes onto a common line of communication, offers the advantage of lower cost for less extensive networks. Its advantages are ease of setup and minimal cabling requirements, and hence, it represents a preferred solution for temporary setups or small local structures. Bus topology does, however, have some significant disadvantages, mainly in terms of scalability and fault tolerance; failure of the main cable can impact the entire network, with devices being taken offline. It is therefore essential that network planners weigh these features when considering the bus topology as an option for their implementation. It is essential to consider how different topologies affect the design of a network as a whole and helps in selecting the best possible structure that best meets the specific needs of the organization. Decentralized topologies, such as hybrid systems and peer-to-peer designs, provide additional challenges and benefits. By dispersing control among nodes, these topologies are ideal for systems that require constant availability of service. They also provide higher data privacy and integrity since they inherently possess no single point of failure, which aligns with the results showcased in current studies on decentralized systems (Danezis et al., 2017). The disadvantages include higher system complexity and the problems of maintenance and data consistency in the nodes. Furthermore, not all applications may require decentralized frameworks, and this may result in unnecessarily incurred costs in network management (Cervelló Pastor et al., 2008). Hence, addressing these pros and cons carefully is still required for the effective use of decentralized topologies in modern network architectures.

1.4. NETWORK ARCHITECTURE

Understanding network architecture is central to studying how computer network's function and evolve. Network architecture, simply put, is the general organization of a network, including its hardware, software, protocols, and transmission media, which collectively govern data transmission and communication among devices. The architecture could have significant impact on performance, scalability, and reliability. For example, various topologies such as star, mesh, or ring topologies specify the way the devices are interconnected and influence overall network efficiency. As more organizations are shifting towards decentralized architectures for increased flexibility, it becomes critical to address bandwidth allocation, latency, and fault tolerance issues. Thus, in-depth study of the network architecture not only provides an understanding of the current technologies but also directs the development of state-of-the-art network solutions. Besides, the advent of Information Centric Networking (ICN) highlights an essential shift in network structure to support content availability regardless of location. ICN architecture allows routers to cache highly popular content along the path to the users, thus speeding up and enhancing efficiency by cutting down on constant data retrieval from remote servers.

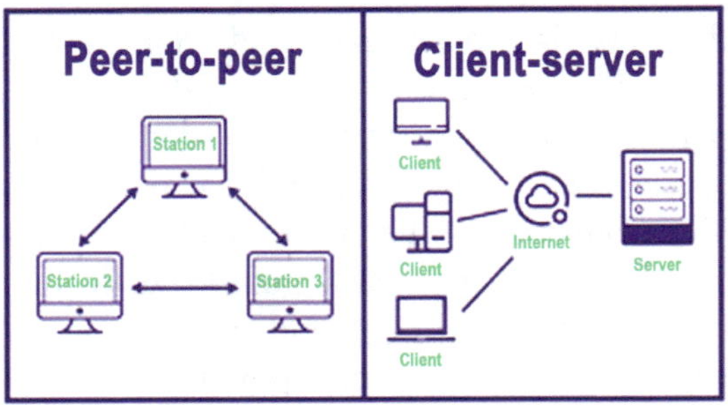

Figure 1.12. *The network architecture.*

Source: https://encrypted-tbn0.gstatic.com/images?q=tbn:ANd9GcT8oqjDtAmkWPVpMgGKrNa2QZrLDt9Sz3yVdw&s.

Experiments confirm the effectiveness of various caching schemes, such as First In First Out (FIFO) and Least Recently Used (LRU), across various network models, such as sensor networks and ISP networks, as being most effective in Universal Caching (UC) ((Panigrahi et al., 2016)). This achievement shows the fluidity of network structure and its ability for data dissemination maximization. As new architectures are in the process of being built, traditional paradigms of data routing are being replaced and rewritten increasingly. Parallel to these developments, neuromorphic computing also began to shed light on new network architectures in the making. For instance, the Spiking Temporal Processing Unit (STPU) presents a new framework which simulates synaptic response functions more realistically for biological neural networks. In comparison to conventional architectures based on linear computations, the STPU exploits temporal coding, a paradigm that effectively emulates the dense connectivity of human thinking ((Aimone et al., 2017)). Aside from increasing the efficiency of computations, this approach also opens new avenues for applications such as speech recognition, which capitalize on the versatility of neural-inspired designs. By incorporating elements of biological systems, network design can evolve to become more adaptive and efficient in fulfilling the nuanced requirements of modern computing environments. Altogether, the convergence of these revolutionary architectural concepts is revolutionizing the computing world and making computer networks more useful (Figure 1.12).

1.4.1. Definition of Network Architecture

Network architecture plays a critical role in the field of computer networks because it provides a comprehensive description of network system design, implementation, and administration. Network architecture literally refers to the physical layout and working mechanism of a network and serves as a master plan that dictates how the elements of a network talk to and interconnect with one another. This architecture can be implemented through various topologies, which dictate the physical or logical arrangement of devices and links within a network. Considering scalability, reliability, and performance, network architecture determines the path in making decisions for the appropriate networking technologies and protocols. An established network architecture, thus, not just enhances overall efficiency but also addresses potential issues that could accompany network growth and evolving user requirements. The evolution of data centers underscores the need for robust network infrastructure in enabling sophisticated ICT solutions. According to literature, data centers have shifted from being passive infrastructure elements to critical drivers of information and communication technology (ICT) innovation. The network fabric of data centers is particularly vital as it enables data transmission and data interconnectivity among servers, storage devices, and end-users. Modular data centers (MDCs), for instance, are a design paradigm that enhances resilience and flexibility under hostile environments by amplifying fault tolerance. Efficiency in such MDCs is highly reliant on the architectural decisions made in their network designs, which are assessed through extensive failure analyses and simulation methods like the Monte-Carlo approach. Such analysis ensures the stability of the network structure, thus influencing the operational effectiveness of the entire data center (Asghari et al., 2017). Network topology is a component of what constitutes network structure since it directly influences throughput and level of performance in different applications. Topologies such as mesh, star, and tree structures are different and have varying attributes that affect the efficiency and reliability of data transmission. Recent research works on different topologies emphasize the importance of throughput performance benchmarking across diverse traffic patterns. The results of such studies extend beyond theory of knowledge, in that they provide architects with real-world insights about the interdependencies between some design parameters and scalability and resiliency. For instance, performance analysis based on synthetic and actual traffic matrices reveals stress points within specific network configurations. This analytical approach assists in guaranteeing optimum network design in the management of diverse workloads, pointing to the essential link between cautious network architecture and effective performance outcomes (Godfrey et al., 2016) (Figure 1.13).

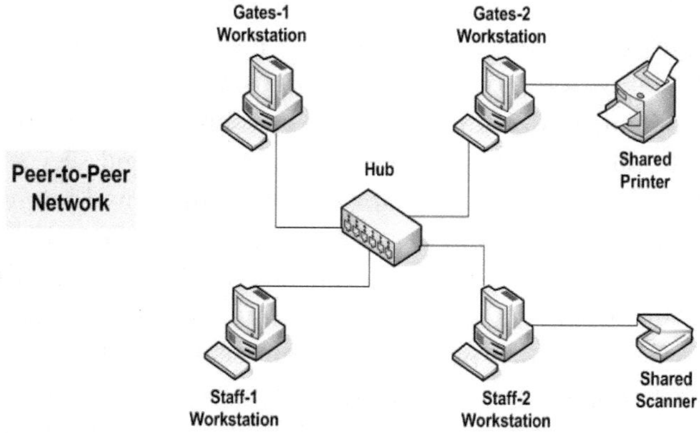

Figure 1.13. *Network architecture is crucial in the realm of computer networks.*

*Source: https://miro.medium.com/1*v8vgd0FFgJy_fBUmxbOBgg.jpeg.*

1.4.2. Client-Server Versus Peer-to-Peer Architecture

Both the client-server and peer-to-peer architectures in computer networks hold varying data exchange and resource-sharing paradigms. A central server that manages resources and services for efficient access control, security, and ease of maintenance characterizes the client-server architecture. It is best used in organizations, where scalability and systematic management of the systems is the priority. Under this architecture, clients ask for services from the server, who receives such requests processed and delivers necessary data or services. This hierarchical scheme is generally better in performance and reliability, especially for those applications which require strong integrity of data and centralized control. Under peer-to-peer (P2P) architecture, a decentralized approach is encouraged where each node in the network acts as a client and server. Resources and data can be shared instantaneously between nodes so that collaborative processes are possible without the need for central management. This structure has advantages in applications where there is a need for high redundancy and availability because nodes involved can join or leave the network without causing a disruption to the overall system. P2P's flexibility is also evident in its application in file sharing and decentralized applications, where end-user donations provide resource distribution. Nevertheless, the lack of central administration brings about problems related to data security and homogeneity, leading to skepticism of the efficiency of sensitive data exchange across the network. The choice between client-server or peer-to-peer architectures relies on specific use cases and organizational needs. In cases requiring high-security protocols and enforcing strong control over data, client-server models are typically more preferred since they possess a formalized structure. On the contrary, however, the emergence of technologies such as IoT, as highlighted in the example of fog and edge computing, illustrates the potential for P2P models to manage large networks of cooperating devices with ease. The growing demand for systems to balance performance versus resource sharing implies a shift towards the exploration of hybrid architectures that can leverage the advantages of both models. Lastly, understanding the meaning of such design choices is vital in the creation of scalable and optimized computer networks, particularly with the continuous technology evolution (Verbraeken et al., 2020; Yousefpour et al., 2019) (Figure 1.14).

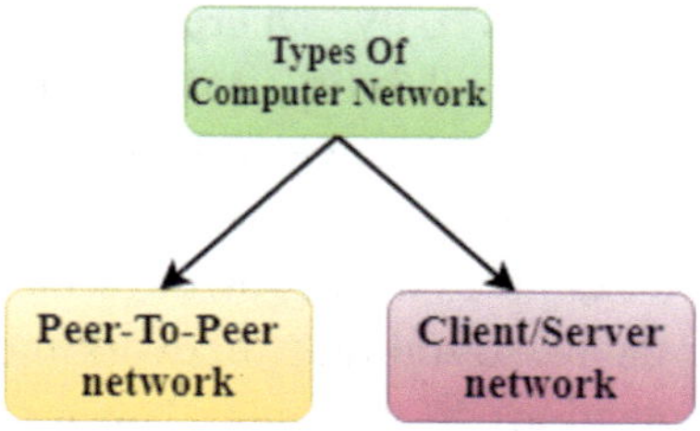

Figure 1.14. *Two types computer-network-architecture.*

Source: https://blog.able.com.pg/wp-content/uploads/2023/07/computer-network-architecture.png.

1.4.3. Role of Architecture in Network Design

The network design model of architecture plays an important part in enabling efficient communication and data exchange among computer networks. A well-defined architecture serves as the foundation upon which physical as well as logical parts of a network are built. This includes the selection of appropriate hardware, for example, switches and routers, as well as topological setups that determine structure and relationship among connected systems. Various topologies, such as star, ring, bus, and mesh, all have distinct strengths and weaknesses that influence performance, scalability, and reliability. Through thoughtful integration of these selections of topologies into the network infrastructure, network designers can optimize resource usage, eliminate latency, and enhance overall network performance. Interestingly, an unambiguous architectural design also facilitates easy troubleshooting and subsequent expansions, thus underlining the importance of robust network architecture in the bigger picture of computer networks. Additionally, the role of architecture extends beyond technology demands to encompass security and manageability in network architecture. As schools become more inclined to adopt advanced network solutions to facilitate their operations, the importance of a robust architecture becomes ever more paramount. The need for secure, scalable networks can be observed in a variety of circumstances, particularly in circumstances involving the transfer of sensitive information, such as within research and education settings. An effective network infrastructure must encompass security characteristics unique to its setting while being compliant with evolving regulation. For instance, features such as VLAN segmentation, firewalls, and intrusion detection can be integrated seamlessly into the design architecture in order to shield against new threats. The potency of such integration is exemplified in projects like the secure campus network concept at the East Africa University, where strategic architectural design enabled strengthening security, availability, and overall performance in various departments (Abdi et al., 2024). Also, network design allows for sensitivity to emerging technologies and changing organizational needs. As networking continues to change—for example, with growth of cloud computing, Internet of Things (IoT), and big data—so too must network models. Frameworks that are adaptive allow organizations to accommodate new technologies without redesigns, thereby efficiently leveraging current infrastructure. For example, the use of custom-designed architecture, such as Software-Defined Networking (SDN), offers a dynamic network management approach that can respond to shifting requirements in real-time. Flexibility is crucial to provide business continuity and competitiveness in the extremely fluid technology landscape. Therefore, the architectural role in network design not only serves current functionality but also future-proofs against the inevitable development that continually redefines how networks operate (Awais et al., 2025).

1.5. NETWORK SECURITY

Network security involves technologies and policies that are employed to protect networked environments against cyber-attacks and ensure the confidentiality, integrity, and availability of data. Considering increasing trends in remote work and evolving cyber threats, organizations find it challenging to provide effective security governance. Research has shown that endpoint security management and network security boundary breaches are among the significant concerns to be addressed by organizations. By recognizing these challenges, businesses are better placed to embrace robust security controls that take into account the challenges of remote working environments. The equilibrium between technical controls and human-centered security controls has more become essential, emphasizing the imperative to define all-inclusive frameworks that cater to both the technology and organizational aspects of security (Mahimalur, 2025). For network security, safeguarding data communication by various topologies comes to the forefront. mbracing approach toward protecting their online assets (Figure 1.15).

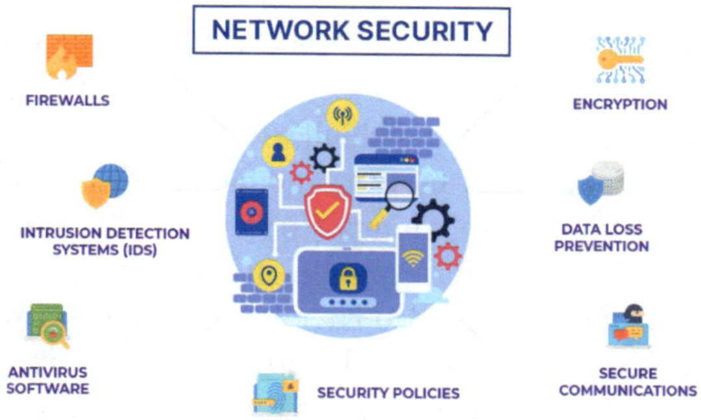

Figure 1.15. *Network-security.*

Source: https://www.extnoc.com/learn/wp-content/uploads/2022/02/Network-Security.jpg.

Different network topologies, such as star, mesh, and bus, have unique security threats and challenges. For instance, in star topology, the central hub is a single point of failure, so protecting this side from potential attacks is key. Besides, with increasing growth and interconnectedness through cloud computing, the proliferation of shadow IT, or unauthorized programs and devices, makes it difficult to secure. Organizations are then tasked with deploying adaptive governance systems that evolve in line with their network topologies. These systems must facilitate compliance checks as well as cultivate a security culture among teams so that all the members can value the role that they undertake in maintaining network security (Mahimalur, 2025). Moreover, the application of secure practices within network infrastructure significantly reduces the likelihood of data breaches and cyberattacks. Security hardening processes, like strict access controls and regular vulnerability scans, are core elements in securing network defenses. Database configuration and design, like in PostgreSQL, can have similar effects on total security and performance. Proper memory allocation, query optimization, and security measures put a strong network environment that can defy a multitude of threats. By emphasizing the integrated security systems based on optimal configurations and continuous monitoring, organizations are able to enable their networks not only to protect sensitive data but also to maintain their operational efficiency. By realizing the interconnectedness of network topology and security process, firms are able to achieve an all-e

1.5.1. Importance of Network Security

Computer network and topology development has revolutionized the platform of information sharing, but the rapid pace at which the technology is developing is raising extremely serious concerns regarding network security. As organizations increasingly rely on cloud services and connected devices, the threat of cyber-attacks becomes more pronounced. Firms employ innovative technologies like the Internet of Things (IoT) and cyber-physical systems to enhance operational efficiency, for example, in Industry 4.0 projects (Xu et al., 2018). However, the technologies also have loopholes that can be exploited by cyber attackers. Without stringent security protocols, sensitive information can be hacked into and lead to financial loss and reputational harm. The demand for network security systems therefore extends beyond traditional IT boundaries to organizational culture, risk management methods, and compliance with regulatory requirements, and hence makes a compelling case for investment in all-encompassing security solutions. In addressing the role of network security, preventive action and implementation accordingly must be emphasized. Organizations must adopt a multi-layered security policy comprising firewalls, intrusion detection systems, and encryption mechanisms to safeguard data along with network infrastructures. Furthermore, ongoing employee training and education in secure procedures are of paramount importance since human mistakes remain a significant reason for security violations. As systems grow more interdependent, the kind of cyber threats is developing into ever more sophisticated forms. Thus, companies cannot wait until the eleventh hour; they have to proactively secure their defenses through a security-centric approach to network design. Strategic alignment not just protects confidential information but preserves business continuity, ultimately generating organizational resilience against potential cyber threats. Finally, in today's globally connected world, it becomes necessary to consider the international implications of network security. Cyber threats are not of isolated organizations but can propagate through networks and affect industries and even nations in general. It is therefore important that there is collaboration between governments, industry players, and cybersecurity experts to develop effective measures to counter the threats. Besides, the advances in newer technologies such as artificial intelligence and machine learning create opportunities as well as problems for network security. Therefore, the stakeholders need to do more to engage in ongoing discussions regarding the best practices and innovative methods in the area of cybersecurity, as well as are also further dictated by such programs like Made-in-China 2025 to seek industrial innovations (Zhu et al., 2017). Lastly, the interplay between network security and technological advancement underlines the need for a concerted effort to protect the integrity and reliability of computer networks during our era of technology.

1.5.2. Mutual Threats to Network Safety (Malware, Hacking)

Among network threats, malware and hacking are two of the most harmful and malicious. Malware is a wide variety of malicious program categories that are designed to infiltrate, damage, or disable computers and networks. The most common forms of malware are viruses, worms, Trojan horses, and ransomware. These different forms of malware function in various ways, but their primary goal is often the same: to disrupt normal operation or steal sensitive data. The wide deployment of Internet of Things (IoT) devices has increased the vulnerability of networks to these threats since every connected device is a potential entry point for malware attacks (Kammara et al., 2018). In addition, a successful malware attack can result in compromising essential systems, which translates to significant monetary loss and reputation damage to individuals and organizations. Hacking, the unapproved access to computer systems or networks, also represents another major network security threat. Professional hackers, who are frequently referred to as black hat hackers, exploit vulnerabilities in network security for gaining unauthorized access to confidential information or disrupting the services. The motives for hacking are very much varied, ranging from financial gain to ideology. Various techniques are exploited by hackers, including phishing, SQL injection, and denial-of-service attacks. These techniques exploit vulnerabilities in both hardware and software defenses, emphasizing the importance of taking very robust security measures. As more companies rely on digital infrastructures, the hacking risk becomes increasingly important, and incidents worldwide have demonstrated the catastrophic potential of such attacks (Nyagudi et al., 2013). Countering these common threats requires an integrated approach to network security that encompasses technology, policy, and user education. Companies must spend money on advanced security software that will detect and eliminate malware before it can cause harm. Software patches and updates must regularly be brought up-to-date so that vulnerabilities hackers can exploit are erased. Additionally, organizational security-aware culture is the solution; employees should be educated on how to detect phishing and unauthorized access attempts. This multi-faceted strategy ensures both malware and hacking operations are greatly reduced, improving overall network resiliency. As dangers posed by sophisticated cyber attackers continuously rise, pro-active measures need to be taken to ensure the integrity and usability of computer networks (Kammara et al., 2018).

1.5.3. Strategies for Enhancing Network Security

In the current digital environment, ensuring good network security is paramount to ensuring information system availability and integrity. Decentralized systems serve effectively to do so, distributing power across different constituents rather than authoritatively on one point. This structure minimizes the vulnerability threat connected to centralized systems as each constituent operates independently but harmoniously. Decentralized architecture naturally enhances privacy, integrity, and availability but at the cost of the need to have a careful understanding of the trade-offs involved, notably increased system complexity and the potential for adversarial activity within the network. Designers must get past these challenges while balancing their approach with axioms borrowed from cryptography and distributed systems, so that the final architecture is resistant to both external attacks and internal configuration faults (Danezis et al., 2017). Another important method for enhancing network security is the use of Information-Centric Networking (ICN), in which one places emphasis on the content itself over the location mechanism. Since one can request content in terms of its identification and not its address, ICN shifts the paradigm towards more efficient and secure data retrieval procedures. The decentralized ICN paradigm enables effective content dissemination between heterogeneous topologies of networks, particularly in community networks where scalability and adaptability are essential. The approach not only improves the utilization of resources but also protects the system against Denial of Service (DoS) attacks by dispersing traffic across a number of nodes. Enhancing ICN systems through such developments as multi-stage Bloom filters serves to further mitigate scalability challenges, offering a more secure platform for handling heterogeneous traffic within dynamic environments (Carrea et al., 2016). Finally, the use of a robust firewall and intrusion detection system (IDS) is an essential element in any network security strategy. Firewalls are the initial line of defense since they manage incoming and outgoing traffic based on predefined security policies, thereby denying unauthorized access while allowing legitimate communication. Concurrently, IDS technologies complement this system since they provide real-time monitoring and analysis of network traffic, identifying potential threats or anomalies that eluded traditional defenses. The dual role of firewalls and IDS not only assists in enhancing malicious activity identification but also facilitates adaptive security planning. Through ongoing updates to rules and analysis based on emerging threats, corporations are better equipped to defend their networks. Together, these methods create a multi-dimensional defense system critical to the protection of digital assets within the dynamic landscape of network risks.

1.6. UPCOMING TECHNOLOGIES IN NETWORKING

The computer networking landscape is being transformed by emerging next-generation technologies which are claimed to enhance connectivity and data transfer. One of the critical research areas is the development of quantum networking, where principles of quantum mechanics are utilized to make communication faster and more secure. Different topologies and network architectures that reduce latency and optimize performance, particularly in distributed quantum systems, have been investigated by researchers. The comparative analysis of gate execution methods illustrates the relative benefits of quantum teleportation protocols over traditional approaches, presaging a shift towards more efficient network structures. As illustrated in recent papers, employing smaller nodes with larger input-output (I/O) bandwidth significantly increases the performance of quantum calculations, ultimately turning quantum networking into a revolutionary force in the area of communication technology (ACM. et al., 2007). In addition to quantum networking, machine learning and AI are also becoming central components of next-generation networks. These enable adaptive learning algorithms that provide enhanced network performance, security, and management. By processing vast amounts of network data, machine learning algorithms can predict and stop impending disruptions, creating more robust systems. Apart from this, AI-enabled automation for networking can automate such processes as network traffic management, fault identification, and network configuration. This innovation is keeping up with expanding network topologies that are becoming increasingly complex and dynamic due to the integration of heterogeneous devices and services. The convergence of these technologies highlights the need for establishing secure frameworks that will be capable of supporting intelligent networking solutions and enhancing system efficiency overall (Liu et al., 2007). In addition, the emergence of Internet of Things (IoT) devices has necessitated the development of networking technologies that can accommodate the exponential growth of connected devices. Key measures to handle the resultant traffic and data complexity are the application of edge computing and software-defined networking (SDN). Edge computing decentralizes processing power to allow data to be processed close to the source, where latency and response times are minimized. Similarly, SDN enables more efficient and flexible handling of network resources by separating controlling logic from the physical hardware. Programmatic network control offers more network condition and variable demand flexibility. In this case, new technologies make it possible to have more scalable and optimized topologies, thus making smart cities and networked ecosystems on the basis of end-to-end IoT device communication a reality (ACM. et al., 2007).

1.6.1. Overview of Current Trends (IoT, 5G)

In the contemporary computer network environment, IoT is a key phenomenon revolutionizing connectivity. Internet of Things refers to the network of devices connected to one another that share data and interact with each other autonomously, establishing enhanced automation and efficiency in various fields. It enables real-time monitoring and control through the technology, an aspect that has far-reaching impacts on industries such as health, agriculture, and smart cities. The intersection of IoT with the latest networking technologies has led to advancements like smart domestic appliances and wearable health monitors, which are the paragon of data-driven insight. Further, more widespread usage of IoT products compels a reconsideration of network infrastructure to prioritize scalability-driven solutions that can support the unprecedented volumes of data generated by such networked devices. Concurrent with the innovations in IoT, technology in 5G is a behemoth leap in mobile telephony that provides quicker data speeds, reduced latency, and the capacity to network exponentially more devices. Rollout of 5G has enhanced the architecture of IoT systems so that devices can talk to one another smoothly and send information more securely. As seen, fifth generation (5G) mobile networks have come to the stage of commercial deployment, providing consumers with new offerings and improved user experience as well as a variety of new opportunities to various industries (Cheng-Wang et al., 2023). The capacity of 5G network infrastructure to handle vast amounts of data is crucial for applications requiring real-time processing, such as autonomous cars and intelligent grid networks. As 5G use for business grows, it lays the groundwork not only for more IoT potential but also for the exploration of new concepts like the metaverse, which relies on this new generation of connectivity. Development of networking technology is also underway toward the next wireless comms generation, that is, the future sixth generation (6G). This second stage aims to bridge the deficiencies and challenges of 5G with the aim of providing even broader network capabilities, improved spectrum efficiency, and enhanced user experience. While the groundwork for 6G is being debated, a renewed interest in extended application scenarios, technical specifications, and innovative architectures is emerging (Cheng-Wang et al., 2023). The potential of these innovations transcends connectivity, since they offer a model for high-end environments, such as the metaverse, that seek to offer immersive and interactive experiences within virtual shared spaces. But with so much opportunity lies a cost in privacy, scalability, and security that must be overcome if the potential hidden within these next-generation networks is to be realized to the full. Therefore, the trends for IoT and 5G open up to a revolutionizing era in computer networking with opportunities and challenges in equal measures.

1.6.2. Impact of Emerging Technologies on Networking

Within the environment of computer networks and topologies, emerging technologies such as the Internet of Things (IoT) and cloud computing have profoundly influenced the manner in which devices communicate and share data with each other. The integration of these technologies has created a never-before-seen explosion in network complexity as devices grow to be more dependent on each other and demand the free flow of data. This expansion has facilitated the development of intelligent cities and increased manufacturing ability, such as in initiatives like Industry 4.0 and Chinas Made-in-China 2025. These projects point toward robust networking solutions able to maintain the intricate interdependencies between systems and devices. Furthermore, the integration of these technologies is requiring network protocols to evolve in order to address needs for scalability and efficiency, and consequently impact the performance and reliability of networks in the future (Xu et al., 2018). With evolving networking paradigms, machine learning (ML) and artificial intelligence (AI) are becoming the focal points in enhancing network performance and resource management. With the ability to analyze vast volumes of data, AI programs can predict traffic trends, detect anomalies, and set up networks by themselves. Such capabilities enhance network operational efficiency, thereby reducing downtime and operational costs for companies. Interestingly, AI-driven approaches are becoming increasingly central in securing networks from advanced cyber-attacks. The convergence of networking and AI facilitates the development of self-sustaining networks, which can heal themselves and make decisions independently. This evolution not only streamlines network operation but also facilitates real-time dynamism in adjustment to changing circumstances, hence bolstering the resilience of network infrastructures against changing threats (Zhu et al., 2017). Finally, the rapid evolution of 5G technology is a gigantic leap in networking, fundamentally altering the connectivity dynamics. With higher bandwidth, lower latency, and increased capacity, 5G networks enable the mass proliferation of next-generation applications in areas such as autonomous vehicles, telemedicine, and augmented reality. Such heightened connectivity can be bolted onto current IoT devices, and it can be used to expand the scale of smart networks that exchange and respond in real time. Moreover, such advancements are expected to drive a shift toward network slicing where every slice may be tailored to meet the specific needs of every application. The implications of 5G are more than mere speed; they reflect a revolutionary shift in the data transmission and processing mode, which demands re-examination of existing networking strategy and architecture end-to-end in a bid to harvest the optimal benefits of these new technologies (Xu et al., 2018).

1.6.3. Future Prospects for Computer Networks

Computer network development is rapidly moving toward an integrated world with great promise due to the introduction of new technologies. Among the most significant developments is the foreseen introduction of sixth-generation (6G) mobile communication systems with the goal of overcoming fifth-generation (5G) technology's limitations. As outlined by recent research, 5G already transformed user experience and introduced new services but is confronted with some challenges that need further innovation (Cheng-Wang et al., 2023). The discussion about 6G today is not only about more speed and reliability but also about dreaming up entirely new usage scenarios and network topologies that could revolutionize global communication standards. Continued investment in research and development will be crucial in ensuring such next-generation networks are efficient, secure, and capable of handling increasing data requirements of the current society. In addition to wireless communication innovation, the incorporation of artificial intelligence (AI) and machine learning into computer networks can transform network operation and management. The emergence of deep learning as an innovative technology enables networks to shift from traditional physics-based models to advanced data-based models. As noted in current reviews, deep learning has already demonstrated great success in many areas, including compensation for errors and data processing in optical metrology systems (Zuo et al., 2022). By employing extensive datasets and high-performance algorithms, networks can offer better-informed decision-making, real-time problem-solving, and enhanced security mechanisms. The impact of AI on network operations promises a future where the systems are capable of dynamic adjustments based on changing conditions, thereby minimizing downtime, and optimizing overall performance. Further, the rise of the Internet of Things (IoT) has a profound impact on the future of computer networks with both opportunities and challenges. With trillions of connected devices, the need for robust network architectures capable of supporting this expansion is necessary. This increasing interconnectivity allows for innovative application across a wide range of industries, from smart homes to industrial automation. But with this expansion are issues surrounding data security and privacy that must be addressed ahead of time through the encouragement of advanced encryption techniques and secure channels of communication. As hinted by present discussions in the industry, the future chances of success for computer networks will largely be based on the cooperation among industry participants, researchers, and policymakers in developing comprehensive strategies that ensure operational efficiency and user trust.

SUMMARY

The examination of computer networks and topologies testifies to the vulnerable dance between functionality and structure. The fundamental components of network topology play a significant role in affecting the efficiency of data transmission and the network's robustness. With the complexity of the networks, ensuring that they remain reliable under every conceivable operation condition is essential. The concept of robustness as shown illustrates the network's strength in resisting failures and attacks without compromising performance. In addition, the construction of new metrics, including elasticity, offers a rich avenue for studying network resilience by overcoming the accuracy-versus-complexity compromises in network models (Kooij et al., 2008). Preparing for the increasingly networked world, understanding these phenomena is crucial to the design of systems that can learn and thrive as challenges evolve. Furthermore, the realization of optimal network topologies involves a multidisciplinary approach that combines sophisticated mathematical concepts and empirical techniques. The application of spectral graph theory provides valuable insights into how to tune network configurations, particularly concerning synchronizability and information diffusion. The role of spectral gaps to enhance the performance of networks can give rise to the design of entangled networks, which are valuable models to achieve target dynamic features. This strong theoretical-practical correlation demonstrates the necessity for ongoing research in network topology. With an emphasis on these mathematical foundations, computer scientists are able to develop solutions that not just enhance current infrastructure but also look ahead and prepare for future requirements and challenges. Ultimately, studying the structure of computer networks and topologies is necessary for the present and future of technology. With each of these elements separated, we see that making intelligent design choices is the way to operational excellence. Network system construction is driven by the dual imperative of adaptability under stress and resilience in diverse conditions. By applying innovative models and metrics to evaluate network properties like elasticity, stakeholders can achieve long-term sustainability and resilience in their infrastructures. With further development underway, the constant reevaluation of theory and actual practice will provide the foundation for building the robust networks capable of addressing the complexities of today's digital environments.

With the discussion of network topologies and their application within computer networks, several significant aspects illustrate the usability and complexity of these networks. Network coding as a topological inference method is one of the key concerns. This technique facilitates a more efficient approach to analyzing network structures through the relationship it establishes between receivers and nodes. By applying probes to collect information and performing basic coding operations, researchers can better identify tree and directed acyclic graph (DAG) topologies. What is demonstrated here is that network coding not only possesses the capability to facilitate topology discovery but even to enhance overall network performance. Hence, acquiring knowledge of such dynamics is the principle for building robust networks to deal with fluctuating operating environments, finally making communication efficient in complex networks (Buchbinder et al., 1998). Another important topic covered is performance measures that are connected to network topologies, particularly in high-throughput environments like data centers and high-performance computing (HPC) networks. The comparison of various topologies through a two-faceted benchmarking framework demonstrates how they sustain throughput with varied traffic matrices. Quantitative research of this type facilitates worst-case performance scenarios comparisons, providing valuable insight into how topologies accommodate scalability and heterogeneous workloads. The absence of comprehensive head-to-head comparison across various topological forms accentuates the need for systematic comparison methods, thereby enabling network designers to make topology choices in accordance with their own performance requirements (Godfrey et al., 2016). Lastly, synthesizing theoretical and practical knowledge in network topologies underscores the importance of continuous research in the area. The blending of simulation techniques with active and passive inference methods not only enhances the theoretical foundations but also renders it applicable in practice. In network performance and reliability optimization, understanding the limitation and benefits of different topologies becomes imperative. With the evolution of technology comes the approach taken in navigating the intricacies of networks. This ongoing dialogue between practice and theory serves to advance the understanding of network topologies, readying researchers and practitioners to better address contemporary challenges in computer network design and deployment (Buchbinder et al., 1998; Godfrey et al., 2016).

REFERENCES

1. Abdi, A. H. H., Audah, L., Omar, A. M., & Abdiaziz, M. J. (2024). Design and simulation of a secured enterprise network architecture for all departments at East Africa University (EAU), Somalia. *2024 4th International Conference of Science and Information Technology in Smart Administration (ICSINTESA).* https://www.semanticscholar.org/paper/b7a1ed9ecf00d774b8b3dd1aa65a048fb4c22b50 (accessed on 9th September 2025).
2. Aimone, J. B., Carlson, K. D., Donaldson, J., Follett, C., et al. (2017). A digital neuromorphic architecture efficiently facilitating complex synaptic response functions applied to liquid state machines. http://arxiv.org/abs/1704.08306 (accessed on 9th September 2025).
3. Androulaki, E., Barger, A., Bortnikov, V., Cachin, C., Christidis, K., De, A., Enyeart, D., et al. (2018). Hyperledger Fabric. https://doi.org/10.1145/3190508.3190538 (accessed on 9th September 2025).
4. Asghari, V., Cheriet, M., Lemieux, Y., Moghaddam, H., et al. (2017). A Monte-Carlo approach to lifespan failure performance analysis of the network fabric in modular data centers. http://arxiv.org/abs/1401.7528 (accessed on 9th September 2025).
5. Awais, M., Kim, Y., Yoon, T., Choi, W., & Lee, B. (2025). A lightweight neural network for denoising wrapped-phase images generated with full-field optical interferometry. *Applied Sciences.* https://www.semanticscholar.org/paper/8b12f4cf42897e9073c2f1e0809472f3e8b74db7 (accessed on 9th September 2025).
6. Barrett, B., & Gottschalk, T. (2004). Advanced message routing for scalable distributed simulations. https://core.ac.uk/download/4892847.pdf (accessed on 9th September 2025).
7. Bohossian, V., Bruck, J., Fan, C. C., LeMahieu, A., et al. (1998). Computing in the RAIN: A reliable array of independent nodes. https://core.ac.uk/download/4873622.pdf (accessed on 9th September 2025).
8. Buchbinder, E. I., Buchbinder, I. L., Ivanov, E. A., Kuzenko, S., et al. (1998). Active topology inference using network coding. https://core.ac.uk/download/pdf/147979172.pdf (accessed on 9th September 2025).
9. Carrea, L., Logothetis, M., Moscholios, I., Vassilakis, C., et al. (2016). Scalable bloom-filter based content dissemination in community networks using information centric principles. https://core.ac.uk/download/46598398.pdf (accessed on 9th September 2025).

10. Cervelló Pastor, C., & Machado, R. (2008). Deliverable JRA1.1: Evaluation of current network control and management planes for multi-domain network infrastructure. https://core.ac.uk/download/187264911.pdf (accessed on 9th September 2025).

11. Danezis, G., Halpin, H., Isaakidis, M., Troncoso, C., et al. (2017). Systematizing decentralization and privacy: Lessons from 15 years of research and deployments. http://core.ac.uk/download/141515178.pdf (accessed on 9th September 2025).

12. Estrin, D., Gupta, S., & Helmy, A. (2002). The STRESS method for boundary-point performance analysis of end-to-end multicast timer-suppression mechanisms. http://arxiv.org/abs/cs/0208023 (accessed on 9th September 2025).

13. Feller, F., Gunreben, S., Kohn, M., Mifdaoui, A., et al. (2010). Ethernet–A survey on its fields of application. https://core.ac.uk/download/12040594.pdf (accessed on 9th September 2025).

14. Ferretti, S. (2015). Self-healing protocols for connectivity maintenance in unstructured overlays. http://arxiv.org/abs/1506.04512 (accessed on 9th September 2025).

15. Gad, A. G. (2022). Particle swarm optimization algorithm and its applications: A systematic review. *Archives of Computational Methods in Engineering, 29*, 2531–2561. https://doi.org/10.1007/s11831-021-09694-4 (accessed on 9th September 2025).

16. Gao, J., Gu, X. D., Lin, Y. Y., Ni, X., et al. (2015). Ricci curvature of the internet topology. http://arxiv.org/abs/1501.04138 (accessed on 9th September 2025).

17. Godfrey, P. B., Jyothi, S. A., Kolla, A., Singla, A., et al. (2016). Measuring and understanding throughput of network topologies. http://arxiv.org/abs/1402.2531 (accessed on 9th September 2025).

18. Hamid, K., Iqbal, M. W., Arif, E., Mahmood, Y., Khan, A. S., Kama, N., Azmi, A., et al. (2022). K-Banhatti invariants empowered topological investigation of bridge networks. *Computers, Materials & Continua, 73*, 5423–5440. https://doi.org/10.32604/cmc.2022.030927 (accessed on 9th September 2025).

19. Kammara, T. T. (2018). Management and security of IoT systems using microservices. https://core.ac.uk/download/215414662.pdf (accessed on 9th September 2025).

20. Kayan, H., Nunes, M., Rana, O., Burnap, P., & Perera, C. (2022). Cybersecurity of industrial cyber-physical systems: A review. *ACM Computing Surveys, 54*, 1–35. https://doi.org/10.1145/3510410 (accessed on 9th September 2025).

21. Khraisat, A., & Alazab, A. (2021). A critical review of intrusion detection systems in the internet of things: Techniques, deployment strategy, validation strategy, attacks, public datasets and challenges. *Cybersecurity, 4.* https://doi.org/10.1186/s42400-021-00077-7 (accessed on 9th September 2025).

22. Khraisat, A., Gondal, I., Vamplew, P., & Kamruzzaman, J. (2019). Survey of intrusion detection systems: Techniques, datasets and challenges. *Cybersecurity, 2.* https://doi.org/10.1186/s42400-019-0038-7 (accessed on 9th September 2025).

23. Kooij, R., Schumm, P., Scoglio, C., Sydney, A., et al. (2008). ELASTICITY: Topological characterization of robustness in complex networks. http://arxiv.org/abs/0811.4040 (accessed on 9th September 2025).

24. Kreutz, D., Ramos, F. M. V., Veríssimo, P. E., Rothenberg, C. E., Azodolmolky, S., & Uhlig, S. (2014). Software-defined networking: A comprehensive survey. *Proceedings of the IEEE, 103*, 14–76. https://doi.org/10.1109/jproc.2014.2371999 (accessed on 9th September 2025).

25. Liu, R., Strawderman, W., & Zhang, C. H. (2007). Complex datasets and inverse problems. *Tomography, Networks and Beyond.* http://arxiv.org/abs/0708.1130 (accessed on 9th September 2025).

26. Mahimalur, R. K. (2025). Implementing security governance for remote work: Challenges and best practices. *Information & Computer Security.* https://www.semanticscholar.org/paper/02f016b8f0a8746975292931e3e56d62ca6348f9 (accessed on 9th September 2025).

27. Mao, Y., You, C., Zhang, J., Huang, K., & Letaief, K. B. (2017). A survey on mobile edge computing: The communication perspective. *IEEE Communications Surveys & Tutorials, 19*, 2322–2358. https://doi.org/10.1109/comst.2017.2745201 (accessed on 9th September 2025).

28. Maurer, A., & Tixeuil, S. (2012). Parameterizable Byzantine broadcast in loosely connected networks. http://arxiv.org/abs/1301.3996 (accessed on 9th September 2025).

29. Mildenhall, B., Srinivasan, P. P., Tancik, M., Barron, J. T., Ramamoorthi, R., & Ng, R. (2021). NeRF. *Communications of the ACM, 65*, 99–106. https://doi.org/10.1145/3503250 (accessed on 9th September 2025).

30. Nemoto, K., Itoh, K. M., Van Meter, R., Szymanski, T., Thaker, D. D., & Munro, W. J. (2007). Arithmetic on a distributed-memory quantum multicomputer. http://arxiv.org/abs/quant-ph/0607160 (accessed on 9th September 2025).

31. Nyagudi, N. M. (2013). Post-Westgate SWAT: C4ISTAR architectural framework for autonomous network integrated multifaceted warfighting

solutions Version 1.0: A peer-reviewed monograph. http://arxiv.org/abs/1401.6379 (accessed on 9th September 2025).

32. Panigrahi, B., Rath, H. K., Sengottuvelan, S., Shailendra, R., et al. (2016). Performance evaluation of caching policies in NDN–an ICN architecture. http://arxiv.org/abs/1612.00352 (accessed on 9th September 2025).
33. Park, S., & Kim, Y. G. (2022). A metaverse: Taxonomy, components, applications, and open challenges. *IEEE Access, 10*, 4209–4251. https://doi.org/10.1109/access.2021.3140175 (accessed on 9th September 2025).
34. Shi, W., Cao, J., Zhang, Q., Li, Y., & Xu, L. (2016). Edge computing: Vision and challenges. *IEEE Internet of Things Journal, 3*, 637–646. https://doi.org/10.1109/jiot.2016.2579198 (accessed on 9th September 2025).
35. Singla, N. (2024). Configuration of complex networking using secure software defined network system. *Communications on Applied Nonlinear Analysis*. https://www.semanticscholar.org/paper/cfe4ced1a4d5e3366ecfad2a468e85fd724f5e4f (accessed on 9th September 2025).
36. Sinnen, O. (2007). *Task Scheduling for Parallel Systems*. https://www.semanticscholar.org/paper/25f199c09540ca8000b6b50ad99fc7da47eaad88 (accessed on 9th September 2025).
37. Sobkowicz, P. (2025). Modelling opinion formation with physics tools: Call for closer link with reality. https://core.ac.uk/download/pdf/6280726.pdf (accessed on 9th September 2025).
38. Vahdat, A., Bu, T., Krioukov, D., Dorogovtsev, S. N., Erdős, P., Fraigniaud, P., Gkantsidis, C., et al. (2006). Systematic topology analysis and generation using degree correlations. http://arxiv.org/abs/cs/0605007 (accessed on 9th September 2025).
39. Vellanki, R. B. (2025). PostgreSQL configuration: Best practices for performance and security. *European Journal of Computer Science and Information Technology*. https://www.semanticscholar.org/paper/6001a03dba4b4801c1d4e749a8b7b64a1b7a349f (accessed on 9th September 2025).
40. Verbraeken, J., Wolting, M., Katzy, J., Kloppenburg, J., Verbelen, T., & Rellermeyer, J. S. (2020). A survey on distributed machine learning. *ACM Computing Surveys, 53*, 1–33. https://doi.org/10.1145/3377454 (accessed on 9th September 2025).
41. Wang, C. X., You, X., Gao, X., Zhu, X., Li, Z., Zhang, C., Wang, H., et al. (2023). On the road to 6G: Visions, requirements, key technologies, and testbeds. *IEEE Communications Surveys & Tutorials, 25*, 905–974.

https://doi.org/10.1109/comst.2023.3249835 (accessed on 9th September 2025).

42. Wang, Y., Su, Z., Zhang, N., Xing, R., Liu, D., Luan, T. H., & Shen, X. (2022). A survey on metaverse: Fundamentals, security, and privacy. *IEEE Communications Surveys & Tutorials, 25*, 319–352. https://doi.org/10.1109/comst.2022.3202047 (accessed on 9th September 2025).
43. Wu, Z., Pan, S., Chen, F., Long, G., Zhang, C., & Yu, P. S. (2020). A comprehensive survey on graph neural networks. *IEEE Transactions on Neural Networks and Learning Systems, 32*, 4–24. https://doi.org/10.1109/tnnls.2020.2978386 (accessed on 9th September 2025).
44. Xu, L. D., Xu, E., & Li, L. (2018). Industry 4.0: State of the art and future trends. *International Journal of Production Research, 56*, 2941–2962. https://doi.org/10.1080/00207543.2018.1444806 (accessed on 9th September 2025).
45. Yousefpour, A., Fung, C., Nguyen, T. N., Kadiyala, K., Jalali, F., Niakanlahiji, A., Kong, J., et al. (2019). All one needs to know about fog computing and related edge computing paradigms: A complete survey. *Journal of Systems Architecture, 98*, 289–330. https://doi.org/10.1016/j.sysarc.2019.02.009 (accessed on 9th September 2025).
46. Zhu, J. Y., Park, T., Isola, P., & Efros, A. A. (2017). Unpaired image-to-image translation using cycle-consistent adversarial networks. https://doi.org/10.1109/iccv.2017.244 (accessed on 9th September 2025).
47. Zuo, C., Qian, J., Feng, S., Yin, W., Li, Y., Fan, P., Han, J., et al. (2022). Deep learning in optical metrology: A review. *Light Science & Applications, 11*. https://doi.org/10.1038/s41377-022-00714-x (accessed on 9th September 2025).

CHAPTER 2

BASIC NETWORK TOPOLOGIES

Contents

INTRODUCTION

For computer networking, an understanding of the fundamental concepts of network topologies is vital in developing efficient systems. Network topology refers to the configuration of various elements of a computer network, including nodes and lines, and can significantly influence the efficiency and dependability of data transmission. Different topologies, such as star, bus, and ring, have their own strengths and vulnerabilities depending on the specific requirements of the network. For instance, star topology may provide simplicity and ease of troubleshooting, while bus topology tends to be cheaper for small networks. The increasing complexity of modern computer distributed systems calls for detailed examination of such topologies, as proper configuration can enhance efficiency and reduce operating costs, as in Kaur (2024). Understanding these various configurations is most significant to network administrators and engineers in order to optimize computational efficiency. Moreover, network topologies are more than simple designs; they consist of two significant types: physical and logical topologies. Physical topology refers to the physical layout of different network components and connects nodes in real setups, while logical topology deals with data transmission in the network regardless of the physical layout. This is important in comprehending how data is processed and transmitted using networks of diverse shapes. For instance, a star physical topology can be logically a bus if the data transfer is simulated in an identical fashion to that of a bus network. This nuance allows for more sophisticated designs considering both material physical limitations and the logical data transfer, thereby enhancing the system's performance and reliability as a whole. As expounded in Kaur (2024), this complex interplay between physical and logical topology is the basis for good network design practices. Lastly, the relevance of network topologies echoes across an array of applications, including fields in biomedical research, in which network form can interpret complex interdependencies between objects. For example, in drug discovery, network topologies aid link prediction, which calculates the likelihood of connecting two non-adjacent nodes, and such provides informative data regarding potential interactions among different biomedical entities. Such application corroborates that high-level understanding of network topologies is not a theory; it has real-world applications that can drive innovation and facilitate breakthroughs in numerous areas. As, quoted, suggests, methods learned from investigating such topological forms may improve prediction along with boosting connectivity patterns in networks, which underlines the need for a strong understanding of network design principles while pursuing the development of fields based on complex data interconnectivity.

Definition of Network Topology

Network topology is simply defined as the organization or structure of the different elements in a computer network, describing the relationship between nodes and links. The phenomenon plays a central role in physical and logical networking, not just defining the data transmission efficiency but also the scalability and stability of the networks. In real-world use, various topologies—star, ring, bus, mesh, and hybrid—are each characterized by certain special features that make them so uniquely strong or weak. A star topology with a central hub for all peripheral nodes is simple to install and troubleshoot but susceptible to a single point of failure, for instance. Mesh topology provides dependable redundancy but at the expense of greater implementation as it involves more cabling and complexity. An appreciation of these differences allows for wise choices in network topology and management concepts. The effect of network topology extends beyond merely having to set it up; it also affects network performance and behavior under different operating conditions. Hierarchical topologies, for example, are often a key part of enterprise networks with structured access points that can minimize management complexity and enhance security.

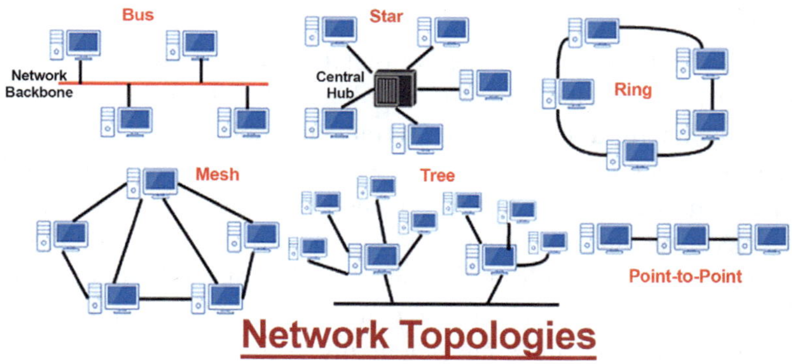

Figure 2.1. *Definition of network topology.*

Source: https://i1.wp.com/www.vidyagyaan.com/wp-content/uploads/2017/10/network-topology.png?resize=550%2C247.

Additionally, with technology such as Software-Defined Networking (SDN) that is evolving in networks, the dynamic topology configuration has become a reality. SDN introduces a new paradigm with the control and data plane decoupling in offering greater agility and programmable network control. As documented in Kreutz et al. (2014), this distinction paves the way for developing and using new abstractions in networking, thus making the complexity inherent in traditional network designs more manageable. In this regard, the definition of network topology therefore is not limited to physical designs but equally involves strategic implications that drive technological innovations. Also, with cloud computing, the use of network topology has increased with adaptive and dynamic design surfacing. Topologies must encompass applications that are based on the cloud and dynamically adapt as a function of use and availability, further reinforcing complicated existing definitions. Hybrid approaches that utilize both physical and virtual components emphasize this advancement, necessitating careful examination of how resources are provisioned and maximized. Examining the performance of hybrid configurations in such networks usually requires sophisticated simulation tools, like CloudSim, that provide valuable insights into managing the resources and allocation methods under varying demands, as seen in Rodrigo et al. (2010). The network topology definition thus finds itself serving as an essential building block in the fragmentation and application of cutting-edge networking solutions, with emphasis on the requirement of flexibility and future-oriented directions in an increasingly dynamic world of technology (Figure 2.1).

Importance of Understanding Network Topologies

Understanding network topologies is crucial in the management and design of robust network systems. Network topology refers to a description of how various elements of a network are arranged, including nodes, links, and devices. Understanding various topologies such as star, ring, bus, and mesh is vital as each one of them has its advantages and disadvantages that affect performance, scalability, and maintenance. For instance, a star topology, while simply serviced and scalable, relies on a single point of failure at the hub. A mesh topology does, however, offer greater redundancy and reliability in terms of interconnecting links but potentially at greater complexity and cost. Therefore, these subtleties in understanding enable network administrators to make rational decisions about network topology that align with organizational requirements and constraints. In practical application, as in the newer Internet of Things (IoT) and cloud computing, awareness of network topologies assumes an even broader significance. The more intertwined networks get, the more their connectivity must be maximized to maximize data transport and minimize latency. For example, multiple topologies will influence the efficiency of data transfer in IoT implementations where numerous devices send and receive data simultaneously. An optimally chosen topology can enhance data processing ability and resistance to disruption. Moreover, the ongoing convergence of converging technologies necessitates self-tuning networks that are dynamic to responding demand. Consequently, knowledge of network architectures not only guides current network strategy but also enables stakeholders to forecast future evolution in network management and technology uptake (Thomas, 2019). In addition, simulation tool hands-on practice can profoundly improve network topology understanding. Instructional environments, like the Computer Protocol Simulation System, allow learners to observe protocols in action under multiple topologies and connect theoretical and practical. This kind of experiential learning familiarizes learners with the complexity of the TCP/IP protocol suite and reinforces their understanding of physical layout and impact on network performance. It focuses on the way different protocols function at various levels of the network organization and encourages insights into how network topologies impact communication efficiency. This effective blending of theory and practice ultimately fosters analytical skills needed in solving real-world networking problems (Xu et al., 2014). The appropriateness of understanding network topologies thus profoundly resonates both in educational and professional aspects of network management.

2.1. WHAT IS NETWORK TOPOLOGY?

Network topology is a description of the structure and connectivity of the various elements of a network, including nodes and links, which in turn define the structure and behavior of a network. It is important to understand network topology because it has a direct impact on the performance, scalability, and reliability of networked systems. The topology can be represented with physical topology, which represents the physical shape of equipment, and logical topology, which denotes how data travels over the network independent of its physical shape. Familiarity with these topological characteristics in full will help network planners in making decisions regarding how to deploy with confidence, enabling them to optimize for performance at the cost of cost and complexity. There are several network topologies, and each provides a different set of strengths and weaknesses to meet different networking needs. Some of the common topologies are star, bus, ring, and mesh. For instance, a star topology has all the nodes attached to a central hub, which can be simply regulated and controlled. However, a mesh topology provides more redundancy and reliability through interconnecting nodes that assist in creating a decentralized framework. Each topology's decision is based on a specific set of applications and requirements, leading organizations to choose topologies that are most beneficial to their operating goals and constraints. Understanding these different configurations is key to understanding successful network performance. Furthermore, the importance of network topology extends beyond its application to connectivity alone; it is crucial in examining the movement of data as well as identifying potential bottlenecks or vulnerabilities in the system. For example, the application of correlation networks has revolutionized the interpretation of complex biological information, such as gene expression, as described by the Weighted Gene Co-expression Network Analysis (WGCNA) method (Langfelder et al., 2008). These methods not only provide insights into system function but also facilitate the design of networks to allow for data integrity and security. Consequently, a thorough investigation of network topology contributes to the overarching objective of enhancing operational efficiency across various disciplines, emphasizing the essential nature of understanding these foundational concepts in network design and analysis (Figure 2.2).

Figure 2.2. *Network topology refers to the arrangement and interconnection of various elements within a network.*

Source: https://www.motadata.com/wp-content/uploads/2024/01/Blog-Inner-Best-Practices-for-Choosing-Network-Topology-1.png.

2.1.1. Explanation of Network Topology Concepts

It is important to understand network topology in order to develop and improve wired and wireless networks. Network topology refers to the setup of multiple elements of a computer network, including nodes, links, and the way they share information with one another. This design blueprint directly affects the performance, reliability, and scalability of a network. Topologies may be of different types, including star, ring, bus, and mesh, each having its own merits and demerits. For example, the star topology with its central core connecting all nodes is easier to manage and troubleshoot but eliminates the possibility of network failure since one node's failure does not have an impact on the other nodes. By defining the manner in which devices are connected to one another, network topology is a major concept within the science of networking and its application in other areas. Star topology also has simplicity and efficiency in LAN and wireless networks. In star configuration, all network devices are connected to a central hub or switch, through which data can move among them freely. As noted by studies through Cisco Packet Tracer, the star topology offers greater performance in wireless networks due to the fact that it consists of a minimal design and fault tolerance aspects. When one of the connections is lost, the others are not affected, significantly enhancing the strength of the overall network. The growing pervasiveness of Wi-Fi technology in today's networks also demonstrates the star topology's relevance, as it effectively supports wireless connectivity and is conducive to managing and monitoring network resources. Such use offers relevant applications to the relevancy of studying and implementing network topologies in network design. Another applicable topology in wireless communication is the Wireless Body Area Network (WBAN), utilized in a specialty application of medical monitoring. In a WBAN, sensors are deployed across a patient's body, sending vital health information wirelessly to a receiving device, such as a computer or mobile phone. Network performance and sensor node functionality in this setting become critical factors, as timely and accurate reporting of health information is crucial for patient tracking. The interconnection of nodes can utilize a number of topological structures for effective data transmission. As is treated in studies that investigate WBAN applications, network topology is critical to the optimization of performance of these healthcare monitoring systems. Focusing on the communication between and arrangement of the sensor nodes in the network, the design can optimize monitoring efficacy, with better patient care and outcomes as a consequence, indicating the indispensable role of topology in specialized areas such as WBANs.

2.1.2. Types of Network Topologies

Within the context of networking, a basic understanding of topologies is necessary in building effective networks. Some of the most used topologies include the star, ring, bus, and mesh topologies. The star topology uses a central node as a connection point between all the peripheral nodes, offering ease of management and failure containment. Unlike this, ring topology is a closed-loop system where each node is connected to two others with data one-way flow. This method minimizes collision but is negatively impacted by the loss of one node. On the other hand, a bus topology places all nodes on a master cable, which can lead to simplicity in installation but has less fault tolerance, as any issue in the master cable delays network communication. All topologies lead to varying strengths and weaknesses, which influence their usability according to respective operating needs. Modifying the classical topologies, modified structures have emerged because of added complexity in use of networks. For instance, dual-active-bridge converters are typical of sophisticated topologies that rely on multiple primary cells, such as transformers and active bridges. Such refinements offset the weak points characteristic of standard designs to allow for best performance under various operational modes. Analysis shows that technological improvements in network topologies demand flexibility in design to satisfy specific electrical characteristics and performance needs. Therefore, innovations in the topological domain not only exhibit technological advancements but also reflect the needs of current markets. Innovations such as these create avenues for establishing a delineated framework, forming an enhanced comprehension of the laws governing operation within manipulated systems, as exemplified in scholarly contexts in relation to DAB topologies (Li et al., 2023). The integration of new topologies is not only specific to electrical engineering but also extensible in fault diagnosis of system-of-systems. A new approach is constrained in the Bayesian network-based probabilistic ensemble learning framework (PEL-BN) that responds to the shortcomings of single diagnostic models. Using a robust framework encompassing several structural characteristics of topologies, the method achieves an improved fault identification and resolution accuracy in multifault situations—an area that increasingly becomes more significant for purposes of using it in modern industry. In addition, PEL-BN selectively incorporates models with improved diagnostic performance, thereby adhering to the intricate nature of networked systems (Yu et al., 2019). This comingling of topology and diagnostic methodology illustrates the interdependent connection between function and design, emphasizing the critical role of topology not only in connectivity, but also in operational resiliency (Figure 2.3).

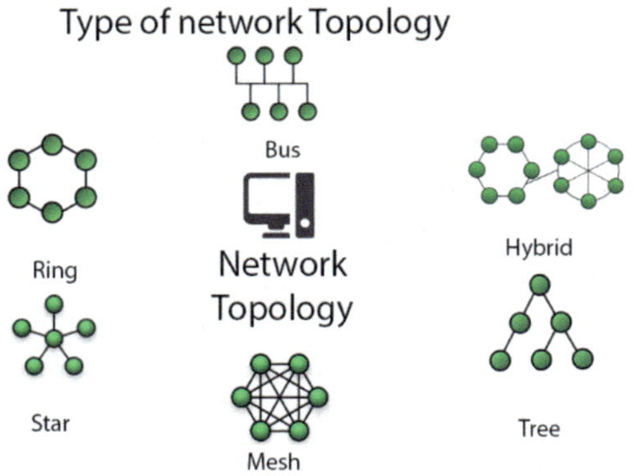

Figure 2.3. *Types of network topologies.*

Source: https://www.vedantu.com/seo/content-images/e75a287b-79fa-4c7b-adf2-ce8a82744dc0.png.

2.1.3. Role of Topology in Network Design

The role of topology in network design is critical in that it prescribes how different nodes are connected and share data with one another. A well-thought-out topology can enhance efficiency, reliability, and scalability of a network. An illustration is a star topology, where all nodes are connected to a central hub, which allows for ease in introducing and removing devices without impacting the entire network. Conversely, a mesh topology offers redundant paths to data transfer that can improve fault tolerance significantly. Redundancy is valuable in those situations where uptime is crucial because it implies that even when there is one failure, the system will not break down. Thus, topology choice has a significant effect on network performance and fault-tolerance and must be given due consideration during the design process. Also, network topology implications go beyond connectivity to encompass security and management concerns. In topologies like hierarchies, for instance, traffic can be effectively prioritized and monitored, which is important in maintaining cybersecurity measures. With ever-increasingly sophisticated networks, understanding data flow through various topologies facilitates deploying appropriate security interventions to limit unauthorized input and data breaches. This is particularly fitting in delicate applications such as financial transactions or exchanges of health data, where confidentiality and integrity take precedence. By systematically considering the place of topology in such contexts, designers can achieve a balance between usability and security that will give confidence to the users and stakeholders. Finally, with the development of technology, emerging trends such as cloud computing and Internet of Things (IoT) pose challenges to traditional network topologies and require innovative design methods. In such architectures, flexible and adaptable topologies, such as hybrid topologies which benefit from both star and mesh structures, become increasingly important. These new architectures support dynamic resource allocation and flexible connectivity, successfully responding to changing levels of demand. Furthermore, application of cutting-edge technology, such as Software-Defined Networking (SDN), can optimize traffic handling and optimize network agility. Consequently, dynamic topology development not only decides how networks are constructed but also influences the broader ecosystem where these systems reside, showing continued applicability of topology to network construction.

2.2. STAR TOPOLOGY

The star topological structure is the most popular network design with a centralized topology in which all nodes are linked to a single centralized switch or hub. This kind of design allows for efficient data transmission as messages are routed directly from the source to the hub and then to the destination, thereby minimizing transmission delay. One of its most striking strengths is the ability to easily remove and add devices without affecting the network, which offers a huge degree of flexibility in dynamic environments. Additionally, the centralized nature makes management of the network easier with improved monitoring and troubleshooting due to the concentration of points of connection. The robust infrastructure enables a neat hierarchy of data flow, which is critical in high-reliability systems like in fire alarm control systems at energy storage stations, where traditional architectures are not capable of coping with single-point failures and channel-sharing faults (Liu et al., 2025). Despite its numerous benefits, the star topology has its drawbacks as well. The reliance on a single key node means that if this node collapses, the whole network may be able to be shut down, with the single point of failure risk. This is particularly valuable in situations where uptime is crucial as lost connectivity can cause operations to be extremely difficult.

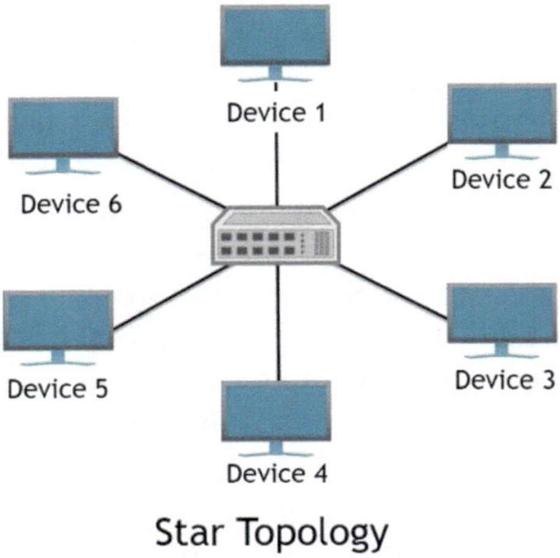

Figure 2.4. *The star topology emerges as a prominent network design.*

Source: https://circuitglobe.com/wp-content/uploads/2019/06/star-topology.jpg.

Moreover, the switch at the center must be of a high capacity to handle the load of data from all the devices connected to it, which could mean lots of hardware investment, such as switches with higher throughput capacity. When it comes to scalability, devices are easily added, but there might still be physical and cost constraints to manage when the network expands beyond a certain extent. Balancing these considerations is key to maximizing performance without sacrificing robustness and operation integrity (Nadezhkin et al., 2024). The integration of star structure within hybrid systems ensures its versatility and capacity to overcome some of the drawbacks of traditional installations. Merger of various topological structures, such as bus and tree configurations, enables networks that can be tailored to needed specifications, thus enhancing reliability and flexibility. For example, in the previously discussed fire alarm control systems, utilization of a hierarchical redundant elastic multi-dimensional network allows star topology to utilize the strength of localized quick response while combining with other topologies to facilitate global resource scheduling and dependable information collection (Liu et al., 2025). These multi-protocol designs usher in smart upgrades and sophisticated deployment techniques, which make the star topology not only practical but necessary in modern network planning, particularly in mission-critical applications (Figure 2.4).

2.2.1. Description of Star Topology

In the context of network topologies, the star topology is one of the most prevalent configurations due to its effectiveness and simplicity in managing devices that are networked together. In a star topology, all nodes, for example, computers, printers, and servers, are connected directly to a single master device, for instance, a hub or switch. This central hub is the point of regulation from and through which all data transfer occurs, facilitating communication between the devices. The setup facilitates simple troubleshooting and efficient data processing since any malfunction or communication breakdown can be easily identified by checking the central hub. As the literature would suggest, star topology is most beneficial in an environment where maintainability and reliability are of utmost concern, in that it is a default in most modern networking environments (Jiang, 2015). The dynamics of operation within a star topology are responsible for its popularity and effectiveness. Unlike other topologies, such as bus or ring topologies, the star model allows for the isolation of the devices so that the failure of one node does not result in the failure of the entire network. This aspect enhances the overall reliability of the system to ensure continuous use even with single component failure. Furthermore, star topology enjoys scalability; it is simple to introduce new devices as they can be directly connected to the core hub without interrupting current network designs. Network managers are able to add more resources smoothly, a characteristic that aligns with evolving organizational demands. Mostly, the star design depicts a robust model for managing diverse network demands while maintaining operational stability (Freeman, 2005). Moreover, the technological advancements and the inclusion of high-speed data protocols have served to further augment the functionality of star topology in contemporary networking. The central switch or hub can support large amounts of data traffic, which translates to more throughput and efficiency. This is particularly important where distributed processing is involved and the computing processes are distributed across various nodes that still talk to each other via the core device. The stars topology is adaptable to the facilitation of modern internet protocols and packet-switching technologies necessary for optimal data transportation. With the ever-growing and expanding networks, the star topology remains a viable and efficient option, particularly in business organizations where reliability, scalability, and administration ease are a priority (Jiang, 2015).

2.2.2. Advantages of Star Topology

Star topology is widely known to be very fault-tolerant and easy to maintain, with evident advantages that make it a popular choice in network configuration. The devices are all connected to one central hub or switch, creating a structure that minimizes points of failure. In the event of a failed cable or device failure, only the affected node is compromised while the rest of the network is still intact. This characteristic enhances dependability, thus being very suited in scenarios where uptime is of major importance. Additionally, the ease of the star topologies means simple troubleshooting since issues can be isolated to individual nodes without retracing through different connections, which easily get complex with other types of topologies. Scalability is also a major advantage in star topology so that networks can grow without complications.

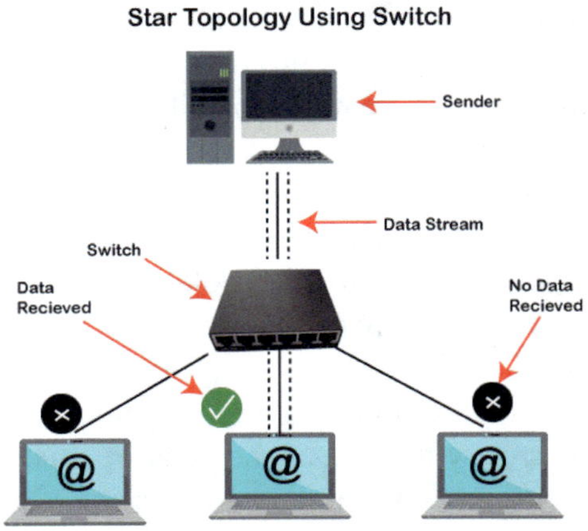

Figure 2.5. *The topology is widely recognized for its robustness and ease of management.*

Source: https://www.sify.com/wp-content/uploads/2024/08/star_topology_switch_javatpoint.jpg/.

When additional devices need to be integrated, they are easily brought in with the central hub without disrupting the present configuration. This is very important in organizational settings, where user numbers tend to fluctuate over time. As a result, network administrators can effectively respond to evolving needs by adding or removing devices as the case may be without experiencing major downtime or reconfiguration costs. Hierarchical topology also allows for better bandwidth allocation and control, so that data flows freely and efficiently across the network. In terms of overall performance, star topology can offer greater speed and efficiency than other topologies. Since each device is wired directly to the center hub, data packets can flow rapidly from device to device without disruption from data transmitted by other nodes. This reduces the latency and enhances the networks throughput, particularly in heavy-usage environments. Centralized control provided by the hub also tends to make network monitoring and management easier, allowing security measures and performance optimizations to be deployed. Overall, these advantages make star topology a desirable choice for various applications, achieving a point of balance between performance, reliability, and scalability, which are important parameters when dealing with network infrastructures (NF'iz et al., 2024; Li et al., 2024) (Figure 2.5).

2.2.3. Disadvantages of Star Topology

One significant disadvantage of star topology arises from its reliance on a central hub to function effectively. In this configuration, all nodes are connected individually to the hub, and if this central device experiences failure, the entire network is rendered inoperative. Such dependence on a single point of failure can lead to substantial downtime, creating challenges for businesses or institutions that rely heavily on network availability. The impact of a hub failure can be far-reaching, particularly in environments where constant connectivity is crucial. Thus, the centralization of control in star topology poses risks that can disrupt operations and delay communication between users, which may not be ideal for organizations that require robust and reliable networking solutions. Additionally, the cost implications of implementing a star topology can be more significant than other network designs. Each node needs a dedicated cable that connects to the central hub, which can lead to increased expenses, especially in large networks with numerous devices. Moreover, high-quality cables and a more advanced hub or switch are often required, further driving up the budget. The expense associated with the physical infrastructure of star topology may deter smaller organizations or those with budget constraints from adopting this design. While the performance benefits of star networks may justify the investment for some, the financial drawbacks present a substantial barrier that should be carefully considered in the context of overall network requirements and resources. Finally, star topology can encounter limitations related to network scalability. Each time a new device is added to the network, additional cabling and possibly a more powerful central hub become necessary to accommodate the new connections. This requirement can lead to complications in managing the network, especially in rapidly growing environments where changes are frequent. Moreover, as the number of devices increases, the hub may become a bottleneck if it cannot handle the increased traffic efficiently. These potential scaling issues indicate that while star topology can initially appear advantageous, its long-term adaptability may not meet the evolving demands of a growing organization. Thus, while implementing a star configuration may offer immediate benefits, the challenges associated with scalability warrant careful examination, especially in light of future networking needs (Ahmed, 2022; Lin et al., 2022) (Figure 2.6).

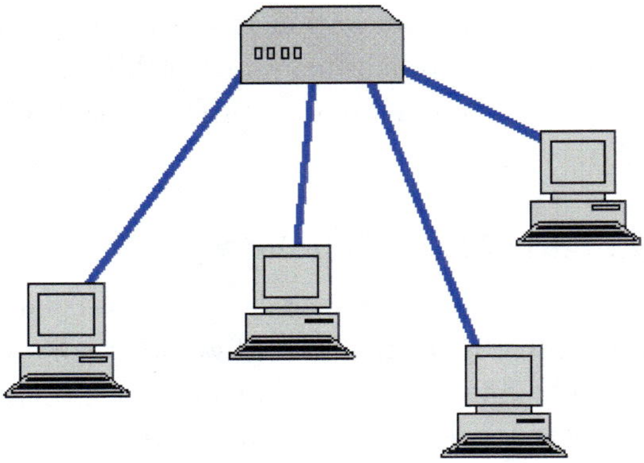

Figure 2.6. *One significant disadvantage of star topology.*

Source: https://qph.cf2.quoracdn.net/main-qimg-f59cf9d7cd73d595d163ddeb2810b453.

2.3. BUS TOPOLOGY

Bus topology is also the most straightforward type of computer network architecture where one has a single cable in the center, usually referred to as the bus, connected to various nodes. All nodes in the network are connected to the central cable in a way that data transmission and communication are easily facilitated. The ease of bus topology configuration leads to reduced costs since there is minimal cabling and simpler setup procedures. It is most effective in the case of small local area networks (LANs), where its straightforward structure facilitates efficient information sharing without employing sophisticated routing protocols. This structure has its downfalls, though. The fact that it relies on a single cable also means that any error or physical damage to the bus renders the entire network useless, thereby isolating all the devices connected to it from communicating with one another. In terms of scalability, bus topology suffices for small-scale implementations but becomes an issue when scaled to larger networks. Overall performance suffers as additional devices are attached to the bus because the data collisions also rise, leading to a slower speed of communication. Furthermore, fault-tracing faults is made complex because the network administrators need to inspect the physical bus for faults. This configuration is one case of cost-reliability trade-off and is most appropriate for specific applications where budget is a major concern. Bus topology may still be sufficient in small offices or temporary configurations for which scalability requirements are low. However, organizations that expect future expansion prefer more reliable configurations that eliminate the susceptibility of a single point of failure. Emerging developments in networking technology have made it important to compare other topologies, like bus topology, with contemporary requirements. New concepts like smart grids utilize cutting-edge computational systems that require more stable network models, making it difficult to utilize outdated bus configurations. While simplicity is offered in bus topology, by studies it has been proven that, for example, in instances of high-performance applications like smart substations, other topologies like star, ring, and mesh can offer better reliability and network capacity of performance. These technologies address fundamental performance issues, such as congestion and flow control, which are increasingly relevant in sophisticated networking environments. Therefore, though bus topology remains a viable alternative for some purposes, its disadvantages can drive users towards more sophisticated topological solutions for the aim of guaranteeing resilience and efficacy (NF'iz et al., 2024; Lin et al., 2022) (Figure 2.7).

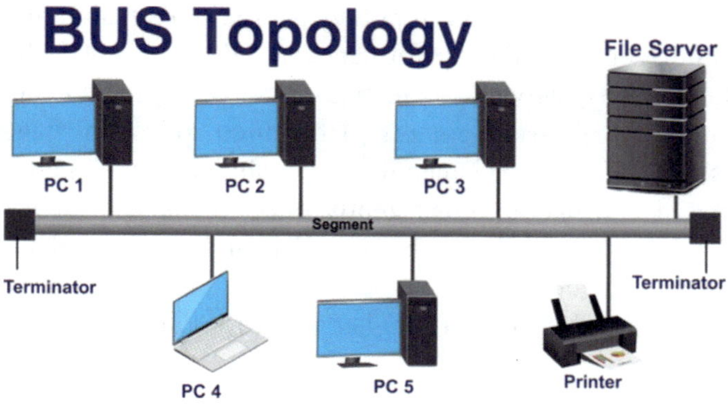

Figure 2.7. *Bus topology.*

Source: https://www.shutterstock.com/image-vector/bus-topology-diagram-network-illustration-600nw-2446474157.jpg.

2.3.1. Description of Bus Topology

Bus topology, a simple network architecture, employs a single bus cable, to which all network nodes, or devices, are connected. It is a design of simplicity and frugality, and one that lends itself particularly to small networks. The nodes communicate with each other by sending data across the bus, which is not only a data transmission medium but also a data collision detection medium. Each device must receive data packets with its own address and can send packets on the bus. Though it possesses good characteristics, bus topology has its demerits; cable failure in the middle can disable the entire network, so it is very important to maintain its integrity to ensure successful operation. Bus topology's functioning behavior makes it an excellent performer and a safe one under varying loads. In situations where data traffic is high, possibilities of data collision also heighten, which disrupts network throughput. But the employment of terminators at both bus ends can avoid signal reflection, thereby making the communication more efficient. Also, the ease of adding or deleting nodes with minimum interference makes it even more desirable. Where rapid deployment and simple maintenance are needed, bus topology offers a fundamental architecture upon which more advanced topologies can be developed or added. Its flexibility is its worth in most applications, especially localized or temporary network settings. While the physical design of bus topology conveys obvious advantages, the underlying disadvantages need to be taken into account. Specifically, its vulnerability to a single cable leaves the network at risk; if the bus cable were compromised, the entire system would fail, leading to potential downtime and greater maintenance requirements. Apart from this, bus topology also exhibits scalability constraints where high node counts lead to performance loss due to bandwidth constraints. To avoid these issues, network architects prefer using redundancy protocols or mixed topological arrangements. Utilization of sophisticated control mechanisms is also seen to enhance the survivability of such networks so that they can continue to operate consistently even in the face of variability. In the case of building networking needs, understanding these elements of bus topology still remains crucial, as can be determined from most recent research on network system architectures (Dragi et al., 2015; Olivares et al., 2014).

2.3.2. Disadvantages of Bus Topology

One of the primary reasons in identifying the strengths of bus topology is that it is easy and cheap. Bus topology uses a single primary central cable, or bus, to which all network devices are connected, so it is relatively easy to install and implement. This straightforward design cuts way down on the amount of cabling needed compared to more complex topologies, that is, star or tree architectures. Thus, installation costs at the beginning are less, something that can particularly benefit small organizations or people who have limited financial resources. Fixing a fault is also typically simpler since any issue can typically be traced to a single component of the bus, thereby being easier and quicker to fix without rewiring and changes in setup. Another significant advantage of bus topology is its simplicity in scalability, with the ease of adding new devices to the network. As companies grow and become more established, having the ability to add more computers or workstations without too much interruption is valuable. Adding new devices to expand the network in bus topology is merely a matter of adding additional devices to the existing bus, which usually entails minimal configuration readjustment. This in-built flexibility enables the network to be molded to suit evolving needs without needing a complete redesign or significant investment in new infrastructure. Such flexibility is especially useful in dynamic environments, where network usage is in a continuous state of flux, and provides a degree of responsiveness to total operating efficiency. Lastly, bus topology can deliver decent performance in applications in which network utilization is reasonably light. Due to its nature, bus topology accommodates simple data transmission, which can be optimized within a setting where there are fewer users for the network. Efficient management guarantees that the network becomes efficient with regard to communication speed, particularly in setups that do not cater to heavy data traffic. However, one needs to acknowledge that although bus topology is quite ideal for small networks, its efficiency gets lower as data loads and users rise. Yet, in specific applications, such as in case of temporary setup or mini office environments, bus topology's advantages in terms of simplicity, low cost, and moderate scalability present it as a viable consideration in the overall discussion of network design (FNF'iz et al., 2024; Lin et al., 2022).

2.3.3. Drawbacks of Bus Topology

Bus topology, while it facilitates a straightforward design and minimal complexity in implementation, has overpowering drawbacks that can undermine network performance and reliability. Its worst limitation is the fact that it is based on the utilization of a single central communications bus, or bus, meaning that if the bus fails, the whole network is compromised. This failure point can cause prolonged downtime since fixing the issue can take considerable effort and technical expertise. Further, network load buildup from several machines can lead to data collisions, causing network delay or even shutting down of the network entirely. Users can see annoying delays as simultaneous transmissions have the potential to jeopardize overall efficiency, such that bus topology is not suitable for large networks that require high data throughput. One other weakness of bus topology is related to scalability and maintenance problems. While it can accommodate an initial small group of devices quite well, expansion of the network often involves adding terminating resistors and careful planning to prevent signal-quality deterioration. As devices are appended to the bus, performance is degraded by increased traffic and potential data collisions. This limitation discourages organizations from expanding the networks or introducing new equipment without anticipating future troubles. Furthermore, debugging is more complex since determining the devices connected to a shared bus entails careful examination of the entire network, which may lead to prolonged network downtime that affects productivity. Finally, the cost implication of bus topology cannot be overlooked. Although the initial cost of the installation may appear economical compared to other topologies, over time the long-term cost can be considerable in terms of ongoing maintenance and the potential need to upgrade or replace network cables. Further, as technology varies and new developments occur, older cabling standards can make themselves obsolete, creating other problems of maintenance and compatibility. Smart grids and other modern infrastructures are likely to require more robust networking solutions since the failure of bus topology in recent network communication standards reviews, for example, with respect to smart substations (Lin et al., 2022), has demonstrated. Thus, enterprises seeking effective and sustainable networking solutions might discover that the limitations of bus topology impose constraints on their functional ability and performance.

2.4. RING TOPOLOGY

Of all the various network topologies, ring topology stands out in terms of structure and modes of operation. In ring topology, each device is linked to two devices, a closed loop or ring-like connection being formed. The structure permits data to pass in one direction only, and it reduces the potential for packet collision since data packets are sent in one direction around the ring. The data, after being sent, travels through all devices that it is interfaced with until reaching the destination. This stable channel of data enables efficient communication but can also bring severe vulnerabilities, mostly due to the fact that it relies on the ability of each node to pass information correctly. Failure of one device will make the entire network fail, which differentiates ring topology from fault-tolerant designs such as star or mesh topology. Ring topology puts extremely high emphasis on bandwidth and latency if one considers performance. Because every node in the ring decides on data incoming to it before forwarding it, the total delay will grow with each additional device in the ring. This delay is a significant factor in the design of efficient networks; therefore, proper consideration must be accorded to the total node count to achieve tolerable levels of performance. Ring topology may achieve high data transfer rates in certain applications, such as in fiber optic networks, because it experiences minimal signal degradation with distance. However, the incorporation of new functionalities, such as the ones in photonic crystal operations, highlights potential enhancements in ring configurations. These advancements focus on accelerating transmission operations with less physical space needs by network devices, thereby reducing the issues of the typical ring topologies (Tamer et al., 2023). Furthermore, the employment of ring topology is ubiquitous in many areas, indicating its diversity and versatility. In networks, it can be used in LAN environments where cheap solutions are needed, and network traffic is minimal. Also, the similar ring structure of ring topology has found application in fields like computer architecture, where circular data buses make data transfers optimal and backup delays minimized. Equally significant is the research on functionalities indigenous to buckybowls towards network topology structures, a convergence of chemistry and computational networking topologies (Chen et al., 2025). With ongoing research progress, synthesis of ring topologies with new materials and technologies holds out the promise of a high-performance index, capability longevity, and wider range of practical utilization in modern communication systems (Figure 2.8).

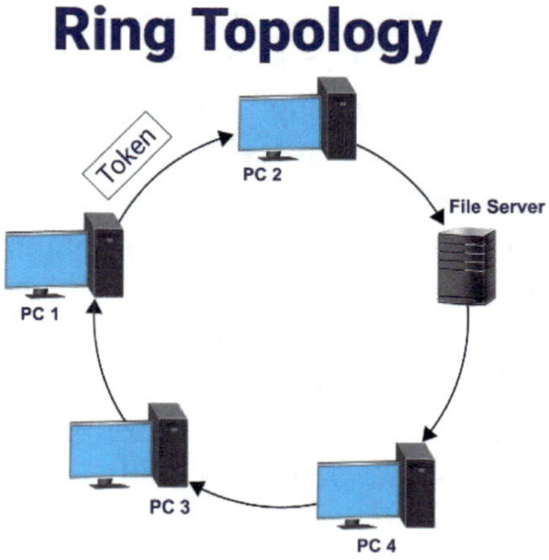

Figure 2.8. *The ring topology.*

Source: https://static.vecteezy.com/system/resources/previews/048/802/841/non_2x/ring-topology-diagram-icon-it-is-a-type-of-network-topology-vector.jpg.

2.4.1. Description of Ring Topology

Ring topology is characterized by the unique structure, such that a closed loop of connections between each node or device exists. Unidirectional or bidirectional data flow is supported by the structure, where signals can circulate in the network without interruption. Unlike bus or star topologies, ring structures do not require a hub for distributing data. Instead, each node functions as a repeater, re-transmitting signals to enhance data transmission quality for longer distances. This setting might reduce the chance of data collisions, which is an excellent feature when data transfer is mission-critical. However, if an individual node or link is cut off, the entire network can be compromised and even lead to network disruption. Therefore, although ring topology might offer effective performance and scalability, it also requires redundancy and failure management systems to be accorded close monitoring. The ease of implementation of a ring topology is also emphasized through the ability to implement it in most networking setups. Local area networks (LANs), for instance, employ the use of this topology due to its minimal configuration and ease of installation. The data packets that travel around the ring are intended to reduce delay of transmissions, a characteristic highly beneficial in systems where data consistency is an essential issue. Moreover, breakthroughs like the provision of dual rings enable higher fault tolerance. In these systems, whenever a segment of one ring fails, the other can readily take its place so that operation does not cease. This versatility has had it applied in modern technologies, like wireless networks where data transmission focus and requirement for fast links are essential (Tamer et al., 2023). The development of processing speed proves the robustness of this topology, making it an industry favorite in the network designer's toolkit. Its advantages come with corresponding detriments to ring topology that need attention. One significant concern is the overall vulnerability to failures; a ring break can lock up data traffic throughout the entire network. This threat calls for an advanced understanding of network management and potential countermeasures, particularly in mission-critical applications. Further, as more nodes are added, the time to transmit data around the ring increases, creating potential latency issues. Where there are growing demands on data, network performance will be hindered if not well controlled. Therefore, while ring topology is an appealing structure for certain networking applications, its limitations must be well documented and controlled to maximize reliability and efficiency in applications (Chen et al., 2025).

2.4.2. Advantages of Ring Topology

Of all network topologies, ring topology possesses several advantages that render it easily adaptable to real-world situations. The simpleness of design is one of the greatest advantages, and it allows for easy setup and installation as opposed to intricate systems like mesh topology. In ring topology, each device is only connected to two devices to form a circular path through which data flows. This ring connection schema provides effective data movement as each data packet travels through the ring to its destination. Consequently, traffic in the network is reduced under normal operating conditions, and thus, overall performance could be enhanced. Also, the determinism of data movement in ring structure facilitates fault tracing due to the fact that identifying a specific fault in the loop could be easier, hence fewer downtime conditions in network availability. One of the strongest points of ring topology is its immunity to network failure, though under specific conditions. Under normal configurations, a ring break can bring down the entire network; nevertheless, with the inclusion of dual rings or token passing protocol, this threat can be effectively managed. With the provision of data transmission in both directions or via redundancy schemes, the network remains operational even under node failure. This characteristic is especially valuable in mission-critical applications where availability is of the highest importance, such as banking or healthcare environments. Furthermore, the constant packet transmission times inherent within ring topology can provide guaranteed data transmission that is important for applications requiring synchronization, such as online gaming or video conferencing. Generally, ring topology's flexibility of design provides strength uniquely suited to high-use applications. Lastly, the cost-effectiveness of using a ring topology provides businesses with the space to optimize their networking investments. The minimal cabling needs in relation to bus or star topologies serve to decrease the cost of materials and lower the installation costs. In addition, because ring topologies are easy, bare-bones networking equipment is typically all that is needed, further decreasing the overall expenses. This cost advantage is most desirable for small and medium companies that may not be capable of sustaining big budgets for network configurations. Enhanced network performance, dependability, and affordability make ring topology a good choice for organizations looking to establish efficient communication systems. Because firms are always seeking to improve the efficiency of their operations, the advantage of ring topology still rings true and is sensible in the broader context of network design (Ozawa et al., 2019; Yu et al., 2018) (Figure 2.9).

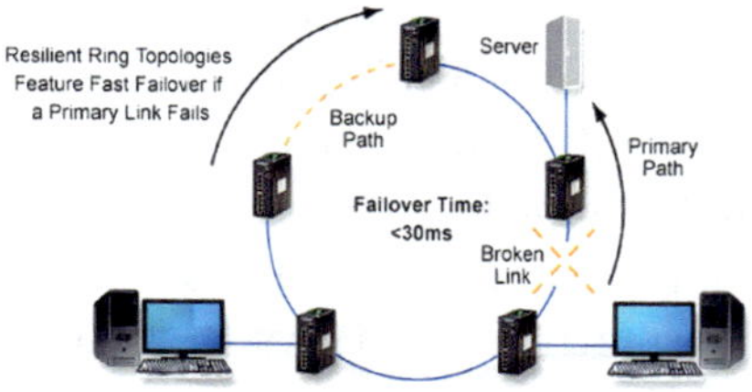

Figure 2.9. *Advantages of ring topology.*

Source: https://www.black-box.de/_AppData/cms/Default%20pages/TechInfo/BBE/Resilient-Ring-Topologies.jpg.

2.4.3. Disadvantages of Ring Topology

Ring topology, easy as it is, has several critical disadvantages that might be precluding its efficiency in network systems. The most critical disadvantage is that it relies on a single point of failure; if one node or network cable fails, the entire network will be disabled. This lack of redundancy means that maintenance and repair will be particularly frustrating, as network managers will need to locate and replace the defective component in order to reestablish connectivity.

In addition, this linear communication flow also means increased latency, as data packets will need to pass through each node sequentially, which can mean slow operation with high traffic levels. In all cases where highest availability is prioritized, such as in sophisticated smart grids, this one point of failure makes it a significant disadvantage, emphasizing the requirement of more fault-resilient topological structures (Lin et al., 2022).

Second, scalability of ring topology is typically cited as another disadvantage. When it becomes necessary for the network to grow—whether through the inclusion of new devices or geographical extension thereof—network administrators will be faced with significant issues. Each new device installed on the ring can potentially cause latency and interfere with the network as a whole when installed.

Also, rebuilding a ring network takes more than introducing new nodes; in most instances, it means shutting down the network temporarily to rebuild properly, and this can be a business-stopping exercise. Unlike more versatile topologies, such as star or mesh, where expansions are possible without breakage, ring topologies need to be planned and managed with care, particularly in environments undergoing a shift towards rapid technology jumps and expandable designs (Кулаков et al., 2020).

Besides, the performance degradation associated with higher nodes in a ring topology can render its real-world application less effective. Each extra node creates an extra need for extra data token flow, and this has the potential to lead to traffic congestion and delayed data transfer. This particularly occurs in scenarios where high data transfer rate demands are experienced, such as in data centers or bandwidth-intensive applications. Such performance problems are then exacerbated by the inherent flaws of ring topology, including its vulnerability to data collisions and requirement for error detection in continuous data transmission. Therefore, while ring topology offers an inexpensive and simple means of dealing with small-scale limited networks, it has only disadvantages in more complex or demanding networking scenarios (Lin et al., 2022; Кулаков et al., 2020).

2.5. MESH TOPOLOGY

In network topology, mesh topology is significant in terms of offering redundancy and reliability in network architecture. The design has several connections of one device to the others in a web-like structure. It provides for the fact that if one connection is disrupted, there are other paths available to carry on the communication, significantly enhancing the strength of the network in terms of resilience. This characteristic is especially useful in critical use, like military or emergency communications, where continuous service is critical. Yet, while the fault-tolerant advantages of mesh topology are obvious, the complexity of network operation and higher costs in terms of cabling and installation can be a stumbling block. Hence, organizations should carefully weigh the benefits with the disadvantages while making a decision to adopt or not adopt a mesh topology as part of their network designs. Besides its fault tolerance, mesh topology also encourages better performance due to its dedicated channels, which also lead to less latency in data transmission. The numerous points of connection allow efficient routing of the data as devices communicate to one another directly without a central device to manage the flow. Decentralization can greatly improve network performance overall, especially in areas where the population is highly populated. Further, technologies such as spatial and frequency division multiplexing can be applied to further optimize the flow of data in mesh networks. Nevertheless, it has to be mentioned that it could require advanced routing protocols and topological mapping to manage such a complex structure, adding even more to the burden of network administrators. Therefore, while the performance advantage is enticing, complexity of operation cannot be disregarded. The emergence of advanced algorithms has already provided a marked shift in the way mesh topologies can be optimized and implemented in today's networking environments. Automatic mesh generation technology is one such technology, which enhances the geometric processing capabilities of networks. Surface meshes, for example, are a requirement to accurately represent and transfer three-dimensional geometric figures, which are crucial in robotics and computer graphics. Such surface meshes with the help of hardware-accelerated rendering are capable of handling complex data sets in a simpler and more simplified manner. Besides, with the incorporation of deep learning methods such as those seen through developments in the mode of Neural Vector Fields (NVF), optimization and automatic adaptation are done to enhance not only fidelity but also mesh structure quality ((Wang, 2024; Yang et al., 2023)). With these technologies continually improving, the future of network design with mesh topology becomes brighter by the day, opening new avenues to efficiency and performance in data-intensive applications (Figure 2.10)..

Figure 2.10. *Mesh topology.*

Source: *https://images.shiksha.com/mediadata/images/articles/1708600057phpvcrpB7.jpeg.*

2.5.1. Description of Mesh Topology

Mesh topology is a complicated but very effective network topology that links multiple devices, or nodes, to one another directly in order to form a failure-free network. In the full mesh topology, all nodes are linked to every other node, providing multiple paths for data transmission. This redundancy does not just make the network more reliable but also decreases latency significantly, as data packets can take the most efficient path to the destination. In a partial mesh topology, however, not all nodes are interconnected but only a limited number, which accomplishes a balance between complexity and resource utilization. The choice to adopt full or partial mesh will practically be driven by the unique needs of an organization, such as size of the network, traffic pattern, and finances. The complexity of mesh topology provides powerful data handling and mobility; it is, however, with high challenges. The number of links in a full mesh can be so great that it creates greater cabling and maintenance expenses and additional administrative effort in dealing with the large node configuration. Further, while fault tolerance is greater since failure of one node will not typically interfere with the network as a whole—since each node is linked to every other node—difficulty in recognizing and diagnosing issues can grow. For dynamical traffic demands networks, adaptive techniques and configurations generally become inevitable due to the need for maintaining optimal performance. All of these points necessitate a careful cost-benefit analysis to determine the feasibility of mesh topology across various applications from small networks to complex infrastructures. Mesh topology is particularly critical in modern applications where reliability and performance are the top priorities, including data centers and mission-critical communication networks. The configuration supports a high volume of data traffic management and packet delivery integrity. Furthermore, the ongoing innovation in network technologies, such as the development of mesh networking in wireless environments, indicates the adaptability of the topology. As networks evolve even further, particularly with the increasing application of self-supervised learning and intricate network geometries to sort data, the principles behind mesh topology—such as direct connection and redundancy—remain relevant. These regulations can offer suggestions for improving traffic management and resource allocation programs, and hence pave the way for advanced applications in complex network systems (Gao et al., 2025; Allard et al., 2023).

2.5.2. Benefits of Mesh Topology

Mesh topology, a more complex network design, has a variety of unique advantages that set it apart from typical designs. Maybe the most significant of these is its inherent redundancy and fault tolerance. With mesh networking, each node can link to multiple other nodes, so when one connection fails, data can still be routed via others. This capability greatly enhances network reliability and downtime reduction, an even bigger consideration in environments where uninterrupted access to data is critical. The functional relevance of this advantage is particularly evident in applications with leading-edge technologies such as TCP/IP over fiber optic networks, where the integration of such technologies can achieve high performance and reliability, underscoring the benefits of using a mesh topology (Alghafari et al., 2024). Another major advantage of mesh topology is that it is very scalable. As companies grow, so do their networking needs. Mesh topology allows for the addition of new nodes without disturbing the initial network configuration. Any new device can be added in order to connect to any other node, which makes expansions and changes to the network simple. This flexibility makes it possible to handle growing numbers of devices and traffic without decreasing performance. In addition, this topology will be able to support greater demands imposed on the system, such as in studies of fiber optic technologies that prove to be agile in mesh configurations when incorporated in complicated infrastructure arrangements (Alghafari et al., 2024). Being capable of adjusting according to transforming requirements implies that mesh networks are able to grow in tandem with organizational development, thus maintaining long-term sustainability. The same high-end performance in the mesh topology can be applied to improved data transmission performance as well. With multiple paths through which data can flow between nodes, a mesh network will reduce latency while increasing throughput. In contrast with other topologies, where data must go through a linear path, mesh structures can engage in simultaneous communication between nodes with different nodes, leading to higher transmission rates and increased overall efficiency. This advantage is most pronounced in systems that base their operation on fast data transfer, such as those used in next-generation underwater information networks. In these applications, a stable power supply system, researched through powerful optimization algorithms, emphasizes the applicability of mesh structures in harsh environments and thus further endorses the advantages of this topology to emerging networking projects. This combination of reliability and speed puts mesh topology at or near the top choices for a wide variety of modern network applications.

2.5.3. Disadvantages of Mesh Topology

Mesh topology usage, while offering a set of advantages like redundancy and fault tolerance, possesses certain drawbacks in-built into its use which influences its application towards practical network design. One such significant drawback is that it takes a very complicated installation process and configuration process. As each device in mesh topology needs to be connected with all other devices, the connections rise exponentially as the network size increases. This increased sophistication not only complicates setup but also takes a lot of time and technical expertise to manage effectively. This implies that organizations with limited technical knowledge can find it difficult to install a mesh network, which can lead to possible inefficiencies during the setup phases as well as normal network upkeep. Furthermore, the cost implication of adopting mesh topology cannot be overlooked. The extent of cabling and hardware required to establish a highly linked network renders the topology very expensive compared to such topologies as bus or star topologies. Each additional link is an added resource, which could increase both capital costs and operational costs in the future. Organizations can also be constrained by budgets when considering such a network topology's long-term sustainability. Consequently, for organizations with lesser financial capacity, the viability of investing in a mesh topology may be restricted, leading them to cheaper networking alternatives that would potentially be more ideal within their budget. In addition to issues regarding cost and complexity, mesh topology can result in issues of network performance and efficiency. As the number of devices within the network increases, the potential for network congestion significantly increases. This congestion can lead to bottlenecks and make it difficult to process the data across the network. When real-time data transfer is a must, such as in smart safety systems for building construction (Li et al., 2021), the performance constraints inherent in a mesh topology can detract from the operational efficiency. Thus, mesh topology's limitations—along with technology requirements and budget considerations—warrant careful consideration for organizations looking at implementing it as part of their network infrastructure (Figure 2.11).

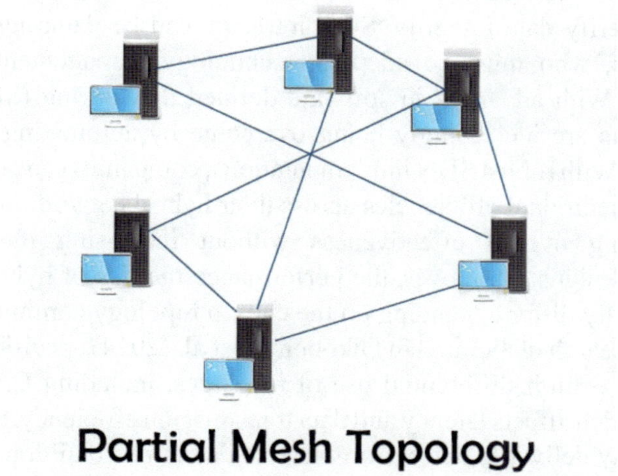

Figure 2.11. *The implementation of mesh topology.*

Source: https://itrelease.com/wp-content/uploads/2021/06/Partial-Mesh-Topology.jpg.

2.6. HYBRID TOPOLOGY

Hybrid topology, which is the consolidation of two or more different networking topologies, offers special advantages by leveraging the strengths without adopting the weaknesses of the individual designs. Hybrid topologies, as implemented in actual applications, can integrate parts of star, ring, bus, and mesh designs and thus achieve flexibility and redundancy in network architecture. This ensures that it becomes simpler for organizations to customize their network infrastructure to meet individual requirements of operations with support for growth and scalability better. Also, hybrid networks achieve maximum performance and dependability because they can re-route information along an alternative pathway, with functionality still being intact if a segment is lost. Through the integration of various topologies, organizations can make their networks conform to the unique requirements of their operating environments and realize a compromise between cost-effectiveness and performance levels required. One important consideration for implementing hybrid topologies is the sophistication of their design and management. The integration of multiple topologies can lead to high operational overhead with more sophisticated network management tools to ensure trouble-free working. For instance, wireless networks with hybrid topologies, as described in Shigapov et al. (2025), must account for individual layers, that is, perceptual and processing levels, to protect and verify data integrity. Such intricacy can be daunting for network administrators, who must be adept at technology management in multiple architectures. With advances in software-defined networking (SDN), though, these problems are increasingly being overcome by automating much of the management. With robust SDN implementations, companies can achieve greater control and operational efficiencies across their hybrid network infrastructures, thus improving overall effectiveness without increasing the dangers of complicated designs. Moreover, the performance metrics of hybrid topologies can substantially differ depending on the chosen topology combination and the hardware. Research elaborated in Oikonomou et al. (2024) specifies that certain hybrid setups exhibit differential use of resources, including CPU and RAM utilization, which affects latency and data transmission efficiency. Simple hybrid topologies may deliver better performance under some conditions, while more complex configurations may offer flexibility with compromise on connection reliability. Choice of elements and topologies in hybrid frameworks is hence crucial to gain optimal network performance. Through their understanding of the inherent strength and weakness of different topologies, network engineers can design hybrid networks with high data rates and reliability on purpose, thereby enabling organizational communications infrastructure to keep up with changing technology trends (Figure 2.12).

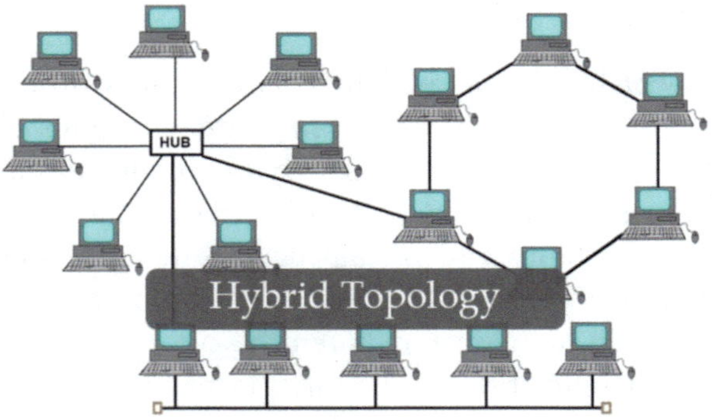

Figure 2.12. *Hybrid topology.*

Source: https://itrelease.com/wp-content/uploads/2020/07/What-is-hybrid-topology.jpg.

2.6.1. Description of Hybrid Topology

Among the various network topologies, hybrid topology is a versatile and dynamic configuration that integrates aspects of several network designs, such as star, ring, and bus topologies. The adaptability helps organizations tailor their network infrastructure according to singular needs, enhancing performance and resource utilization. Hybrid topology frequently facilitates blending of various networking technologies to accommodate disparate communication protocols and standards in an integrated system. For instance, some segments of the network might utilize star topology for reliability and ease of management while nodes in other segments could be in bus arrangement for simplicity and cost-effectiveness. This integrated approach to designing networks enables organizations to reap respective advantages of these topologies while eschewing respective disadvantages of employing any one of them. Hybrid topologies' flexibility accommodates improved scalability, a critical aspect of growing organizations. As an organization expands, its networking needs tend to shift, and it requires an architecture that can expand or contract with relative ease. In hybrid configurations, it is usually easy to insert or remove nodes in a network without completely rearranging the existing network setup. This flexibility is essential in high-traffic applications where the demand for additional bandwidth or more sophisticated data-processing capabilities is continuous. Hybrid topologies are therefore typical to industries that require stable networking systems as well as room for future growth, such as healthcare and telecommunications. The intersection of multiple topological structures generally leads to a most effective communication path and improved data traffic handling, which ultimately means increased productivity across the organization. In addition to that, hybrid topology can also increase fault tolerance and network reliability. By employing multiple topologies underneath, organizations can offer redundant data transmission paths, decreasing the possibility of single-point failure further. For example, if a section of the network operating in a bus topology is faulty, redundant paths through a star topology section can still run without major outages. This feature is particularly critical in mission-critical environments, as exemplified by recent innovation in health technologies, where data flow integrity is critical (Gupta et al., 2020). Moreover, as evident in the evolving telecommunications landscape, technological convergence in a merged network has the ability to lead to greater provision of services and customer satisfaction, facilitating firms to remain in the race in an increasingly digitizing marketplace (Koontz et al., 2008).

2.6.2. Advantages of Hybrid Topology

The hybrid topology, which combines elements of the star and bus topologies, provides a wealth of benefits that place network design and performance ahead of others. The major advantage is its flexibility, with support for many organizational requirements as well as many devices and architectures. The flexibility not only makes it easier to scale but also allows customization in terms of the individual needs of an organization. Therefore, with growth in business, more nodes can be added without drastically reconstructing the current setup. Since hybrid topology supports various topology arrangements in a single network, it effortlessly deals with different technological implementations, thus being highly appropriate in dynamic environments where demands tend to keep changing. Another strong reason why hybrid topology is appealing is its fault tolerance ability.

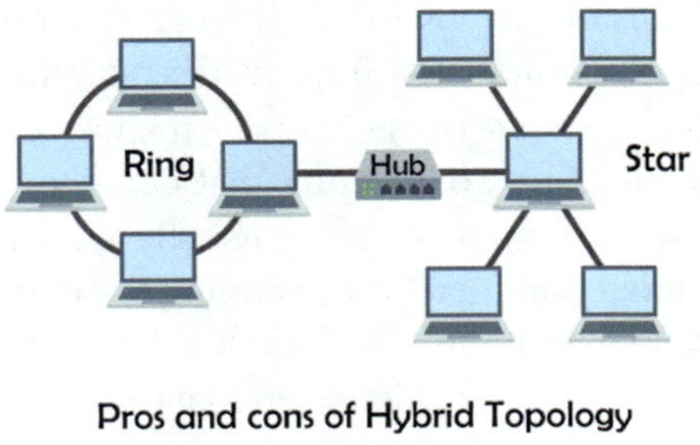

Figure 2.13. *The hybrid topology, which integrates elements of both star and bus topologies.*

Source: https://itrelease.com/wp-content/uploads/2021/06/Pros-and-cons-of-hybrid-topology-1024x683.jpg.

Since it encompasses a number of topological structures, it is better fault isolating than purely linear or centralized configurations. In case a part of the network fails, other parts can continue operating uninterruptedly, thus minimizing network downtime. This matters in scenarios where high availability is critical, such as data centers or business networks that rely on uninterrupted service. Also, the structure can be configured with redundancy features to further enhance reliability. As organizations increasingly address the complexities of their operational environments, fault tolerance from hybrid topology is a key factor in ensuring seamless communication and operations. The hybrid topology also has an advantage with respect to resource use and management, particularly as it brings together multiple operating models and technologies. By leveraging the strengths of multiple topologies, hybrid networks can optimize bandwidth usage and reduce latency, so data can move undisturbed across the network. Hybrid architectures also facilitate the integration of specific technologies, such as the Internet of Things (IoT), which benefit particularly from the flexibility of the architectural design. For instance, the application of IoT in intelligent load balancing and proactive resource management finds direct application in hybrid networks, as has been compared across research on the integration of computational units and energy networks (Shotov, 2025). By efficient management of data as well as energy resources, hybrid topology not just improves efficiency but also leads to cost savings in network functioning (Figure 2.13).

2.6.3. Disadvantages of Hybrid Topology

The hybrid topology, as it stands at the juncture of star and bus networks, has some disadvantages that can make it complicated to implement and maintain. One of the most important issues is the increased complexity in its composition, which requires sophisticated network management features. The challenge of complexity can lead to issues with fault isolation and troubleshooting, since identifying the cause of faults can involve tracing various components and their relationships within the network topology. Besides, as the network expands, coping with such complexity can even be an overbearing burden calling for more resources and more skill. Such operational problems may discourage organizations from using a hybrid topology, particularly small ones with fewer IT resources. Another major disadvantage of hybrid topologies relates to the cost implications of applying them. Several topologies being merged means that companies will have to invest in various networking hardware and software solutions for them to accommodate the varied protocols and architectures. This requires an increase in setup expenditures at the initial stages, making hybrid topologies economically inefficient for cost-conscious organizations. Further, the need for technical hardware and specialists also translates into recurring expenses in the long term, bringing about a significant economic burden. Most organizations may weigh these fixed costs against what they consider the benefits of greater performance, thus deeming simpler topological solutions as more suited to their specific needs. Scalability and reliability are critical matters stemming from the constraints of hybrid topologies. As a business grows and network demands grow, a hybrid topology would theoretically struggle with appropriately scaling. The interdependence between different forms of networks can create bottlenecks particularly if expansion for scaling is conducted via physical infrastructure. These bottlenecks have the potential to severely impair network performance, most significantly during periods of highest use, thus diminishing the advantages which the hybrid setup would theoretically provide. The complexity of the hybrid setup also increases the risk of failure; a failure in one area can seriously undermine the entire network. This weakness creates red flags for companies in which uptime is critical, and as such, many are considering alternate topologies that provide higher reliability guarantees as they continue to build out networking capabilities (Figure 2.14).

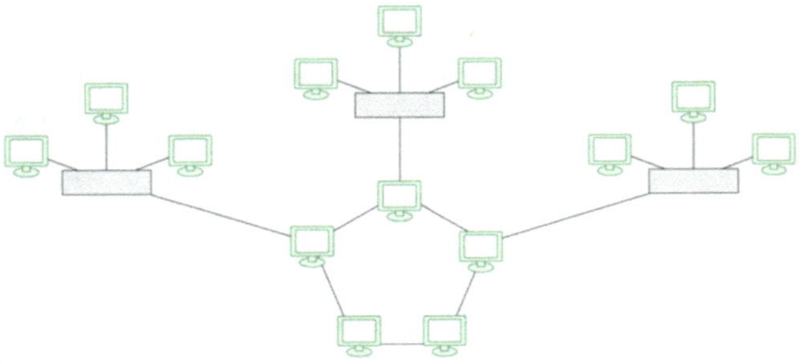

Figure 2.14. *Disadvantages of hybrid topology.*

Source: https://media.geeksforgeeks.org/wp-content/uploads/20230526072928/Hybrid-Topology-1-660.png.

SUMMARY

In Conclusion, the examination of basic network topologies highlights their central role in defining efficient networks of communication. This examination identifies the need to make the appropriate choice of topology according to specific organizational needs and circumstances. From mesh to bus and star topologies, each structure has special strengths and limitations, and it is therefore crucial that network planners fine-tune their choice against desired levels of performance. Understanding of factors such as scalability, fault tolerance, and cost is necessary when one incorporates such topologies. As observed in various studies, optimized network configuration can significantly enhance performance and reliability, affirming the role of stringent analysis in making decisions. The ongoing development of networks necessitates that designers tap into past experiences and meet the needs of today by drawing lessons from history, as evidenced by the ongoing developments in network design tools like Library of Networks, which aims to bridge the gap of design capability and comparative analysis (Chatterjee et al., 2025). Furthermore, as technology advances and redefines the landscape of networking, the application of basic topologies must adapt to new paradigms such as software-defined networking (SDN). SDN architecture's programmability offers dynamic reconfiguration and improved control and has a critical influence on how traditional topologies are used. Research with simulators like Mininet has demonstrated variations in performance for common topologies, facilitating the selection of topology based on real-time measurements of performance (Nikolaos et al., 2024). Examination of the measurement metrics of latency, CPU, and RAM usage emphasizes the necessity of continuous evaluation and modification in network configuration. Thus, knowledge about how straightforward topologies is integrated into models of SDN will provide network administrators with the capability to make their work more efficient and reliable, upholding the significance of well-known topologies in contemporary networking contexts. Ultimately, the study of straightforward network topologies is a foundation for the learning of more advanced networking ideas. By strengths and weaknesses, designers can develop plans that not only meet existing networking requirements but also set bases for future advancements. Additional research and development in the field are needed as companies try to implement networks that are dynamic as well as robust. Integration of tools that facilitate simpler design and analysis is vital for ongoing network topology development. When industry standards evolve, the value of fully understanding fundamental topologies will continue to increase, and it will affect teaching methods, employment policies, and the overall digital environment. Therefore, devoting time to fully learn these foundation principles implies that subsequent network endeavors are informed, efficient, and successful, ultimately leading to more resilient forms of communication networks against an ever-evolving technological landscape.

In examining basic network topologies, a fundamental element that emerges is the classification of models that govern data movement and network performance. Star, ring, mesh, bus, and hybrid topologies provide different models for connecting devices in a network. A model of star topology involves the existence of a central hub that facilitates communication among nodes connected to it, which enhances performance but creates a point of failure. Conversely, the ring topology has a circular design where each device connects to two other devices with an assured path of data transfer. Each topology has its own set of distinct advantages and disadvantages, making the choice process significant based on factors such as scalability, fault tolerance, and cost-effectiveness. The utilization of topological configurations has consequences that extend beyond physical representation to influence network reliability and operational efficiency. An appropriately structured network topology will significantly enhance data integrity and efficiency as well as minimize the potential for interruptions. Here, the mesh topology is special in the redundancy it offers since each node is able to link with multiple others, creating backup routes for data and assistance towards fault tolerance. Further, hybrid topologies also offer organizations the advantage of leveraging a mix of several structures to adapt to changing operational requirements and environments. Therefore, understanding the implications of such configurations is critical in the optimization of networks, particularly in providing continuous communication and exchange of information. In addition, advancements in technology in recent times have led to new considerations regarding the translation of topological concepts into a myriad of other disciplines, including photonic systems and decision support models. For example, recent research in photonic networks illustrates the application of topological characteristics to enhance wave propagation and manipulate light in intricate modes, mimicking essentially the fundamental topologies of traditional networks. Similarly, black box decision system debates highlight interpretability and transparency across complicated networks, as scientists are under pressure to classify approaches well while technology evolves at a breakneck speed. These intersections depict the use of network topologies not only in traditional data networks but also in other technical scenarios, with the necessity for ongoing examination and usage in the field (Ozawa et al., 2019; Guidotti et al., 2018).

REFERENCES

1. Al Barazanchi, I., Razali, R., Hashim, W., Alkahtani, A. A., Abdulshaheed, H. R., Shawkat, S. A., & Jaaz, Z. A. (2021). WBAN system organization, network performance and access control: A review. *2021 International Conference on Engineering and Emerging Technologies (ICEET)*. https://www.semanticscholar.org/paper/4806860a7478f4e0c4d2057362b4f7d8afcd6852 (accessed on 9th September 2025).
2. Alghafari, R., Sofyana, S., Retriani, V., Nurfadillah, A., & Aribowo, D. (2024). Penerapan TCP IP fiber optic menggunakan topologi mesh pada aplikasi Cisco Packet Tracer. *Jurnal Teknik Mesin, Industri, Elektro dan Informatika*. https://www.semanticscholar.org/paper/d5113ae252d9c3ad72c9e34059ef9067b7b2c484 (accessed on 9th September 2025).
3. Allard, A., Serrano, M., & Boguná, M. (2023). Geometric description of clustering in directed networks. *Nature Physics, 20*, 150–156. https://www.semanticscholar.org/paper/8328c5e140a368ebd753d6a3579b6b43f00158db (accessed on 9th September 2025).
4. Androulaki, E., Barger, A., Bortnikov, V., Cachin, C., Christidis, K., De, A., Enyeart, D., et al. (2018). Hyperledger Fabric. https://doi.org/10.1145/3190508.3190538 (accessed on 9th September 2025).
5. Borsboom, D. (2017). A network theory of mental disorders. *World Psychiatry, 16*, 5–13. https://doi.org/10.1002/wps.20375 (accessed on 9th September 2025).
6. Calheiros, R. N., Ranjan, R., Beloglazov, A., De Rose, C. A. F., & Buyya, R. (2010). CloudSim: A toolkit for modeling and simulation of cloud computing environments and evaluation of resource provisioning algorithms. *Software Practice and Experience, 41*, 23–50. https://doi.org/10.1002/spe.995 (accessed on 9th September 2025).
7. Chatterjee, A., Green, C., & Thottethodi, M. (2025). Library of networks: An online tool for design and analysis of network topologies. *2025 IEEE International Symposium on Performance Analysis of Systems and Software (ISPASS)*. https://www.semanticscholar.org/paper/60dbe24c47692c43644151f4e3b1588059b7f893 (accessed on 9th September 2025).
8. Chen, Y., & Zhang, L. (2025). Buckybowl-based nanocarbons: Synthesis, properties, and applications. *Accounts of Chemical Research*. https://www.semanticscholar.org/paper/bb7acaa38509ebf35854e2da5bb6abf59e942925 (accessed on 9th September 2025).

9. Dragičević, T., Lu, X., Vásquez, J. C., & Guerrero, J. M. (2015). DC microgrids—Part II: A review of power architectures, applications, and standardization issues. *IEEE Transactions on Power Electronics, 31*, 3528–3549. https://doi.org/10.1109/tpel.2015.2464277 (accessed on 9th September 2025).

10. Fa'iz, N. F., Irfawan, D. R., Putri, A. W., & Hidayatullah, S. (2024). Arsitektur jaringan menggunakan topologi tree. *Merkurius: Jurnal Riset Sistem Informasi dan Teknik Informatika*. https://www.semanticscholar.org/paper/5cf1652ac1f551a540514ff50b27dd58108ea70f (accessed on 9th September 2025).

11. Forouzesh, M., Siwakoti, Y. P., Gorji, S. A., Blaabjerg, F., & Lehman, B. (2017). Step-up DC–DC converters: A comprehensive review of voltage-boosting techniques, topologies, and applications. *IEEE Transactions on Power Electronics, 32*, 9143–9178. https://doi.org/10.1109/tpel.2017.2652318 (accessed on 9th September 2025).

12. Freeman, R. (2005). *Enterprise Networks II: Wide Area Networks*. https://www.semanticscholar.org/paper/be374701d3ac1a4b2fd9c08e99bf0c6e8a85cc21 (accessed on 9th September 2025).

13. Gad, A. G. (2022). Particle swarm optimization algorithm and its applications: A systematic review. *Archives of Computational Methods in Engineering, 29*, 2531–2561. https://doi.org/10.1007/s11831-021-09694-4 (accessed on 9th September 2025).

14. Gao, B., Liu, W., Liu, G., Nie, F., & Huang, J. (2025). Multi-level resource-coherented graph learning for website fingerprinting attacks. *IEEE Transactions on Information Forensics and Security, 20*, 693–708. https://www.semanticscholar.org/paper/4166cdd7d94ba272e4aac82dca48a6a1ee66de6f (accessed on 9th September 2025).

15. Guidotti, R., Monreale, A., Ruggieri, S., Turini, F., Giannotti, F., & Pedreschi, D. (2018). A survey of methods for explaining black box models. *ACM Computing Surveys, 51*, 1–42. https://doi.org/10.1145/3236009 (accessed on 9th September 2025).

16. Gupta, D., Rodrigues, J., & Castillo, O. (2020). Special issue on intelligent biomedical data analysis and processing. *Intelligent Decision Technologies, 15*, 13–17. https://www.semanticscholar.org/paper/7ab4416cf6bcc4dc8ce257f42fe97ab347aee818 (accessed on 9th September 2025).

17. Jiang, R. (2015). A review of network topology. https://www.semanticscholar.org/paper/3fc7f1160db45f15caa1e64a9d273ec02fa23602 (accessed on 9th September 2025).

18. Kaur, K. (2024). Overview of network topology. *International Journal for Multidisciplinary Research.* https://www.semanticscholar.org/paper/ffa9db12edb7f40eabdb9b6d5264017b632e5331 (accessed on 9th September 2025).
19. Khairyansyah, S. R., Amalia, D. S., Aditya, S., Sah, A., & Aribowo, D. (2024). Teknologi WI-FI menggunakan topologi star. *Mars: Jurnal Teknik Mesin, Industri, Elektro dan Ilmu Komputer.* https://www.semanticscholar.org/paper/9e4ec3be3e702135ddce3e438c7a5e3b246c0644 (accessed on 9th September 2025).
20. Koontz, W., Glenn, C., & Indelicato, M. (2008). Incorporation of broadband access technology in a telecommunications engineering technology program. https://www.semanticscholar.org/paper/30b12c536c4abbf46cf500674a3e485fec7bee90 (accessed on 9th September 2025).
21. Kreutz, D., Ramos, F. M. V., Veríssimo, P. E., Rothenberg, C. E., Azodolmolky, S., & Uhlig, S. (2014). Software-defined networking: A comprehensive survey. *Proceedings of the IEEE, 103*, 14–76. https://doi.org/10.1109/jproc.2014.2371999 (accessed on 9th September 2025).
22. Küchler, J., Vulić, K., Yao, H., Valmaggia, C., Ihle, S. J., Weaver, S. M., & Vörös, J. (2025). Engineered biological neuronal networks as basic logic operators. *Frontiers in Computational Neuroscience, 19.* https://www.semanticscholar.org/paper/6a54422c7fed68c70ffc5a03f0b6f03f07c9bba1 (accessed on 9th September 2025).
23. Langfelder, P., & Horvath, S. (2008). WGCNA: An R package for weighted correlation network analysis. *BMC Bioinformatics, 9.* https://doi.org/10.1186/1471-2105-9-559 (accessed on 9th September 2025).
24. Li, J., & Tang, F. (2021). Computer aided intelligent safety measures for building construction based on internet information system. *2021 5th International Conference on Electronics, Communication and Aerospace Technology (ICECA).* https://www.semanticscholar.org/paper/b45837186675295b49c96e18a2e718cf0df89238 (accessed on 9th September 2025).
25. Li, L., Xu, G., Sha, D., Liu, Y., Sun, Y., & Su, M. (2023). Review of dual-active-bridge converters with topological modifications. *IEEE Transactions on Power Electronics, 38*, 9046–9076. https://doi.org/10.1109/tpel.2023.3258418 (accessed on 9th September 2025).
26. Li, X., Liu, W., Yang, X., Zhang, H., Wang, G., & Wang, X. (2024). Topology synthesis of hybrid on-load tap changer in ultrahigh voltage (UHV) transformer with fast arcless switching. *Journal of Engineering.*

https://www.semanticscholar.org/paper/1fc0e2a0a288f01edd312b80cb5acba727d70695 (accessed on 9th September 2025).

27. Liang, W., Li, Z., Zhang, H., Wang, S., & Bie, R. (2015). Vehicular ad hoc networks: Architectures, research issues, methodologies, challenges, and trends. *International Journal of Distributed Sensor Networks, 11*. https://www.semanticscholar.org/paper/fff4ebab4d2a72789f150d78ec3e4be4b0bac00e (accessed on 9th September 2025).
28. Lin, Y., Ruan, X., Li, J., Huang, X., & Yang, D. (2022). Construction of intelligent substation-optimized networking communication network based on source-network-load interaction environment. *Journal of Environmental and Public Health, 2022*. https://doi.org/10.1155/2022/4730233 (accessed on 9th September 2025).
29. Liu, Y., Li, S., Ding, W., & Qiao, W. (2025). Design of elastic multi-dimensional network topology architecture for fire alarm control systems in electrochemical energy storage stations. *2025 6th International Conference on Electrical, Electronic Information and Communication Engineering (EEICE)*. https://www.semanticscholar.org/paper/497ca4b3f04c47cfc46836f9d9ceb010686c9db5 (accessed on 9th September 2025).
30. Lu, T., & Chen, F. (2011). Multiwfn: A multifunctional wavefunction analyzer. *Journal of Computational Chemistry, 33*, 580–592. https://doi.org/10.1002/jcc.22885 (accessed on 9th September 2025).
31. Mostafa, T. S., Kroush, S. A., & El-Rabaie, E. S. M. (2023). Photonic crystal circuitry and its impact on wireless networks. *International Journal of Wireless and Ad Hoc Communication*. https://www.semanticscholar.org/paper/e7fb4b3546cf1b05f8198e8050c6d46602eca7ab (accessed on 9th September 2025).
32. Nadezhkin, V., Nadezhkina, S. A., Zolkin, A., Burakova, A. V., & Zhuravleva, I. V. (2024). Improvement of transportation process management effectiveness: Assessment and analysis of network topologies. *E3S Web of Conferences*. https://www.semanticscholar.org/paper/4a25db44080bae6042317fa5ffa9eca32c46519d (accessed on 9th September 2025).
33. Oikonomou, N. V., Oikonomou, D. V., Stergiou, E., & Liarokapis, D. (2024). Comprehensive analysis of software-defined networking: Evaluating performance across diverse topologies and investigating topology discovery protocols. *Journal of Engineering Research and Sciences*. https://www.semanticscholar.org/paper/c446ce353d5a0db90769801e30dd045fbb58fc05 (accessed on 9th September 2025).

34. Olivares, D., Mehrizi-Sani, A., Etemadi, A., Cañizares, C. A., Iravani, R., Kazerani, M., Hajimiragha, A. H., et al. (2014). Trends in microgrid control. *IEEE Transactions on Smart Grid, 5*, 1905–1919. https://doi.org/10.1109/tsg.2013.2295514 (accessed on 9th September 2025).

35. Ozawa, T., Price, H. M., Amo, A., Goldman, N., Hafezi, M., Lü, L., Rechtsman, M. C., et al. (2019). Topological photonics. *Reviews of Modern Physics, 91*. https://doi.org/10.1103/revmodphys.91.015006 (accessed on 9th September 2025).

36. Sherson, T. W. (2019). *Distributed Convex Optimization: Based on Monotone Operator Theory*. https://www.semanticscholar.org/paper/f92759b125dfb3c95476e2566bb678f48220612b (accessed on 9th September 2025).

37. Shigapov, A., Ilmushkina, A. A., & Yusupova, A. S. (2025). Self-organizing wireless IIoT networks with security priorities. *Ekonomika i upravlenie: problemy, resheniya*. https://www.semanticscholar.org/paper/f98eb409a825f02528f5bf47807c18773bee58ff (accessed on 9th September 2025).

38. Shotov, A. (2025). Architectural models for integration of mining installations into existing IoTcontrolled HVAC systems. *The American Journal of Engineering and Technology*. https://www.semanticscholar.org/paper/eea698cb43d2a0912d03a59ea58bec9fbcd38131 (accessed on 9th September 2025).

39. Son, J., & Kim, D. (2023). Applying network link prediction in drug discovery: An overview of the literature. *Expert Opinion on Drug Discovery, 19*, 43–56. https://www.semanticscholar.org/paper/4e774bfe638376a6f326ce9c9c1c93a41473c254 (accessed on 9th September 2025).

40. Wang, Y. (2024). Research and implementation of isosurface extraction algorithm based on Flexicubes. *Highlights in Science, Engineering and Technology*. https://www.semanticscholar.org/paper/0ae55aa7f8fe8324dfabdc2168e4f20a35e24155 (accessed on 9th September 2025).

41. Xu, X., Liu, Y., Wang, J., & Si, T. (2014). Exploration and reform on TCP/IP protocol analysis experiment under simulation system. https://www.semanticscholar.org/paper/221f21d4a5547fbe3d41f76bdb161fac4c8b8c81 (accessed on 9th September 2025).

42. Yang, X., Lin, G., Chen, Z., & Zhou, L. (2023). Neural vector fields: Implicit representation by explicit learning. *2023 IEEE/CVF Conference on Computer Vision and Pattern Recognition (CVPR)*. https://www.semanticscholar.org/paper/57176225fb96ff4f5845400e50895f7a2f73df49 (accessed on 9th September 2025).

43. Yu, B., Yin, H., & Zhu, Z. (2018). Spatio-temporal graph convolutional networks: A deep learning framework for traffic forecasting. https://doi.org/10.24963/ijcai.2018/505 (accessed on 9th September 2025).
44. Yu, W., & Zhao, C. (2019). Online fault diagnosis for industrial processes with Bayesian network-based probabilistic ensemble learning strategy. *IEEE Transactions on Automation Science and Engineering, 16*, 1922–1932. https://doi.org/10.1109/tase.2019.2915286 (accessed on 9th September 2025).
45. Zhang, Z., Pang, H., Georgiadis, A., & Cecati, C. (2018). Wireless power transfer—An overview. *IEEE Transactions on Industrial Electronics, 66*, 1044–1058. https://doi.org/10.1109/tie.2018.2835378 (accessed on 9th September 2025).
46. Zheng, Z., Zhang, T. J., Zhen, H., Li, M. H., & Cai, C. X. (2023). Research on reliability analysis of underwater constant current supply system in mesh topology model. *2023 IEEE 11th Joint International Information Technology and Artificial Intelligence Conference (ITAIC), 11*, 1628–1633. https://www.semanticscholar.org/paper/9326b5bd4997051969a8535a7c3c076cce362b80 (accessed on 9th September 2025).
47. Zhu, H., Chen, S., Yu, Y., Zhao, H., Zhang, J., & Yi, R. (2023). Research status and prospects of key technologies for electric energy router. *2023 6th International Conference on Electronics Technology (ICET).* https://www.semanticscholar.org/paper/cdf44098f16c4e60c51ddf232a60ba5027e8adc1 (accessed on 9th September 2025).

CHAPTER 3

ADVANCED AND EMERGING TOPOLOGIES

Contents

INTRODUCTION

Research into next-generation and future topologies is a growing imperative in today's engineering disciplines because of widespread technological advancement and growing requirements for high-performance systems. With networked environments becoming more complex, the demand arises for new paradigms capable of merging different technologies without intricacies. Scholars and practitioners look towards new paradigms that will optimize resource allocation, enhance performance, and reduce latency. This need is further addressed by initiatives such as FABRIC, providing an integrated research facility designed to enable experimental work on a range of domains, including networking and security, thereby allowing exploration into future topologies and their implications on various applications (Baldin et al., 2019). The transition to wide band-gap materials from conventional silicon devices in power electronics and electrical engineering represents a milestone in progress. Gallium nitride (GaN) and silicon carbide (SiC) devices are the best example of the technology direction towards high-performance, more dependable power conversion technology. Such materials not only allow for the production of converters with significantly reduced power losses but also introduce new operation efficiencies that are not possible with existing technologies. Production of power converters from such novel materials is part of a bigger revolution in engineering where integration of novel materials and designs is key to ensuring maximum system performance and enabling sustainability in energy use (Escolano et al., 2019). The interface between various future topologies and advanced materials offers an interesting venue for study and application. The deeper researchers and engineers delve into these technologies; the clearer is the potential to develop resilient infrastructures that support scalable and adaptive systems. For instance, the intersection of network design and high-performance computing through advanced topologies can lead to data processing power achievements and machine learning algorithm utilization. This convergence of disciplines not only enhances the efficiency of isolated systems but also brings us to a new era of interdisciplinary complementarity, leading ultimately to a more cohesive and streamlined technological landscape. The ongoing research in these disciplines promises significant breakthroughs that will shape the engineering and applied sciences of the future.

Definition of Topology

Topology, in its turn, as a mathematical discipline is dealing with the investigation of spatial properties and structures that are invariant under continuous deformation, say, stretching or bending. The theory of open and closed sets is the defining feature of topology, which is used to construct building blocks for the definition of topological spaces. Spaces are thus constructed in terms of the interrelationships between points, constructing a topological structure independent of usual geometric structures of distance and angle. Consequently, topology has widespread applications in many fields such as computer science, robotics, and data analysis. The versatility of topological techniques makes it easier to investigate intricate structures, and researchers can determine fundamental characteristics and relationships that may otherwise not be evident under the use of traditional methods of analysis. This flexibility in understanding spatial structure makes topology such an important area of study, particularly where conventional techniques would flounder in the face of novel and emergent uses. Topology's newer branches are increasingly cutting into the areas of cutting-edge technologies, particularly material science, and mobile computing. Lattice structures, for instance, which constitute a core focus in material science, are starting to be recognized for their promise to shake up engineering uses.

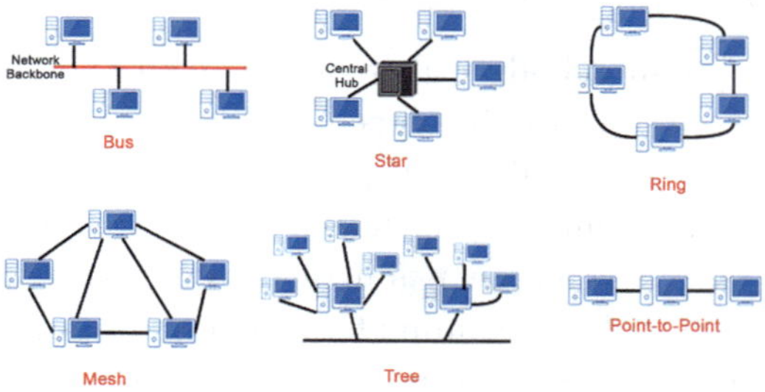

Figure 3.1. *Topology.*

Source: https://i0.wp.com/systemzone.net/wp-content/uploads/2017/09/network-topology.png?resize=600%2C318&ssl=1.

Their adequate assessment is required; recent literature has demonstrated that current definitions of lattice structures are narrow and therefore it was suggested that there needs to be a systematic redefinition including the connections between unit cells and their tessellation properties. This redefinition not only renders the definition of lattice structures more transparent but also widens their application areas towards weight optimization as well as in energy-saving manufacturing processes. This conflict between theoretical advances and empirical use reflects the significance of robust topological structures to enable novel solutions in various scientific endeavors (Helou et al., 2017). Topology is the foundation on which mobile edge computing (MEC) emerges as a paradigm shift aimed at maximizing computational power at network edges, in mobile computing. Legacy cloud architectures have at times struggled to deliver low-latency applications the performance they require, opening up a movement towards the utilization of edge resources for computation. Topology in this context plays a significant role in choreographing the interplay between wireless communication and computation to enable efficient utilization of resources that are limited. Today, research is ongoing to join these two domains, and this has led to innovative resource management and network architectures.

Through solution for problems such as mobility management and privacy, the field of MEC is a firm realization of topological concepts that are not only likely to bring improved technical performance but also appeal to visions of future technology environments such as 5G and the Internet of Things (Mao et al., 2017). Once topological ideas develop, they can have the power to transform our understanding and utilization of complex systems across many arenas (Figure 3.1).

Importance of Topology in Mathematics and Science

Topology is a base system in both mathematics as well as other scientific fields where scientists are able to examine space properties that are invariant under continuous transformations. Mathematics as a discipline is also used to describe other concepts like continuity, compactness, and convergence with wider implications towards the comprehension of complex systems. For instance, topology possesses the tools to examine the structure of networks, a relatively new area of study in contemporary science. Social, biological, or technological networks possess intricate relations which are best analyzed with topological techniques. The interdependence between networks, such as in cascading failures as referred to in HINT (Heterogeneous Interdependent Networks), is merely one of the many ways topological methods widen our knowledge of network vulnerability and resilience (Conti et al., 2015). Topology, thus, not only extends mathematical theory but also gives valuable information about real-world things. New topologies, therefore, increasingly demonstrated their importance in scientific research, particularly in fields like materials science and physics. The self-assembly study at the nanoscale, for example, emphasizes how topology determines nanoparticle organization into complex structures. Having the geometrical organization and interaction between the particles in hand can assist in developing functional materials with unprecedented properties. A computational model of cooperative self-assembly demonstrates how topological principles are employed to investigate the growth of complex networks with simplexes and bridge the gap between mathematical concepts and practical applications (Andjelkovic et al., 2017). The integration also underscores the usability of topology in advancing the boundaries of scientific knowledge as well as its potential of revolutionizing various sectors through enhanced material design and engineering protocols. In addition, the use of topology in cutting-edge scientific inquiry is enriching our ability to model and comprehend phenomena at more than one scale. From cell networks that expose cellular interactions to intricate relationships in ecosystems, topological models provide a window through which interdependence can be explored. Such explorations have dramatic implications for areas like climate modeling and epidemiology, where the stability and dynamics of interdependent systems determine results. The ability to characterize and analyze these interactions through topological techniques enables researchers to predict behavior and identify key thresholds in systems. In light of these advancements, it is apparent that topology is not merely some abstract piece of mathematics; it actually impacts our understanding of reality and the strategies we develop for solving fundamental scientific challenges.

Overview of Advanced and Emerging Topologies

With advancing technology, the need for complex and emerging topologies has prompted massive research and development in different sectors. Advanced topologies tend to employ intricate architectures that provide efficiency along with improvements in data transmission. For example, emerging wireless technology such as cognitive radio and ultra-wideband (UWB) has been key to maximizing use of the spectrum by being adaptive to environments as well as interference, hence enabling various users to operate interchangeably over a frequency. This adaptability is core in modern telecommunications, promising more reliable and flexible communications systems. The intricate interdependence between such technologies and regulatory frameworks forms a vital component in their successful utilization, as elaborated in the context of the SPORT VIEWS project that cites implications for market competition and technology uptake (Pujol et al., 2025). Second, embedding new emerging topologies into networking infrastructures represents a move towards more dynamic and robust infrastructures. Infrastructures like the FABRIC research infrastructure capture this trend by offering a programmable network infrastructure that can host a vast range of applications. By interconnecting customized testbeds for cloud research and well beyond 5G technologies, FABRIC facilitates experimental research to push the limits of what can be done in distributed computing, machine learning, and cybersecurity. Such centers not only enrich the body of research but also bring together academia, industry, and governments to collaborate, thus promoting innovation required to overcome challenges of the future in technology (Baldin et al., 2019). Lastly, due to the convergence of intricate topologies and the growth of data-driven applications, the need for scalable and flexible network solutions becomes increasingly evident. With digital transformation accelerating, organizations are being forced to leverage topologies that are capable of handling huge amounts of data in high-performance modes without compromising efficiency. The transition to software-defined networking (SDN) and network functions virtualization (NFV) is indicative of a dramatic shift in the networking arena, enabling agility and programmability far superior to those of traditional architectures. With the introduction of these new topologies, organizations can optimize resources, enhance user experience, and protect themselves against emerging cyber threats. Thus, the study of futuristic and new topologies is driving technological innovation, enabling systems to perform in a world that is constantly changing (Figure 3.2).

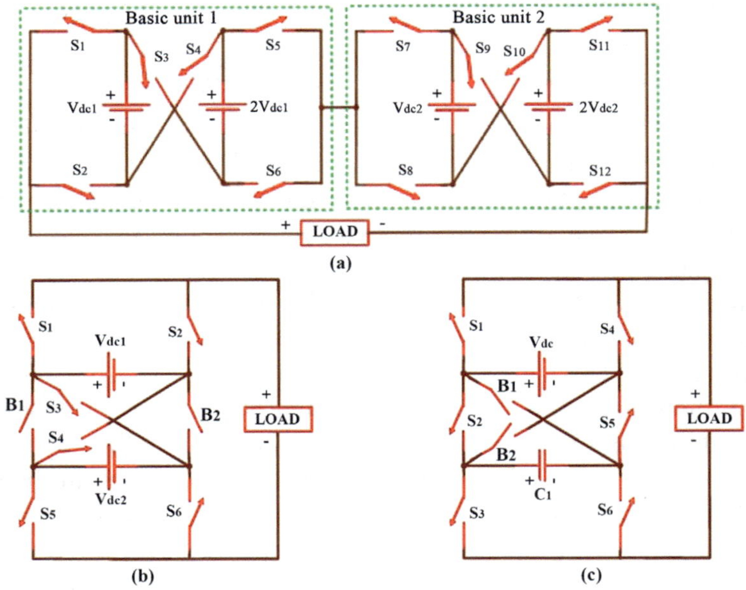

Figure 3.2. *An overview of advanced and emerging topologies.*

Source: https://ars.els-cdn.com/content/image/1-s2.0-S1110016823009511-gr16.jpg.

3.1. HISTORICAL CONTEXT OF TOPOLOGY

The development of topology as a mathematical discipline can be traced back to the end of the 19th and beginning of the 20th century when its origins began showing itself through the work of mathematicians such as Georg Cantor and Henri Poincare. Cantor's introduction of set theory gave the foundation for the understanding of the nature of infinity and continuity, which paved the way for the study of topological spaces. Poincare's work, particularly his text on algebraic topology under its contemporary title, extended the discipline to encompass such concepts as homology and fundamental groups. It was not only an era of transition into abstract mathematics but the era in which topology came into existence as an essential framework to comprehend space's nature irrespective of fixed geometric form. As these ideas unfolded, they came to have influence on other disciplines, including physics and computer science, affirming the interrelatedness of topology with new disciplines. The 20th century witnessed an explosive expansion of the variety and applicability of topological thought, significantly influenced by developments in other mathematical fields, that is, set theory, logic, and analysis. After World War II, mathematicians like Paul Cohen and John Nash added significantly to the field, proving the relevance of topology to applications in the real world, ranging from game theory to mathematics foundations.

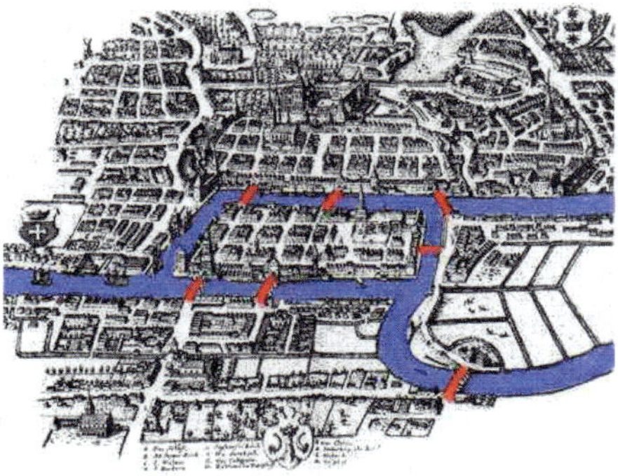

Figure 3.3. *Historical context of topology.*

Source: https://mathshistory.st-andrews.ac.uk/Diagrams/Konigsberg_colour.jpeg.

The creation of definitions like homotopy and manifold theory made further research into the internal structure of various spaces and their role in scientific applications possible from cosmology to biological modeling. These advancements paved the way for more affluent algebraic foundations of topology, providing a framework within which thoughts such as category theory began to flourish, pushing further the debate on higher topological construction and its relevance to various scientific issues. Progress in topology encountered new fields such as quantum mechanics and complex systems, forcing scientists to re-examine classical assumptions of space and dimension. The last decade has witnessed the arrival of quantum automata in demonstrating the capabilities of quantum dynamics in illuminating our understanding of cellular interactomics as intricate interactions between biomolecular entities and their cascades of signaling (Baianu et al., 2010). In addition, the use of Complex Agent Networks (CANs) for simulating phenomena such as the HIV epidemic is the broader range of application of topological methods over traditional mathematics, which affects public health interventions and policies (Mei et al., 2009). This development is evidence not just of the history of topology but also of its ability to evolve and deliver insights into disparate scientific environments, lending strength to the idea that sophisticated and nascent topological theories will go on to influence our understanding of complicated systems (Figure 3.3).

3.1.1. Origins of Topological Concepts

The origins of topological concepts date back to the intersection of mathematics and theoretical paradigms that sought to redefine space and structure. Topology emerged primarily out of the exploration of geometry and set theory, with its origins lying in the work of mathematicians in the 19th century, such as Henri Poincare and Georg Cantor. When mathematicians began exploring the invariants of space through continuous alteration, they acknowledged that there must be a new lexicon for characterizing form and shape. This assisted mathematicians in moving beyond the utilization of traditional Euclidean definitions in favor of more theoretical concepts that would become the cornerstone of the science of topology. Within a broader epistemological context, the advances set the stage for understanding not just geometric space, but also abstract spaces like function spaces and their attributes, which continue to be of importance in modern mathematical and scientific discourse. Surprisingly, topological concepts are not restricted to mathematics but have implications in areas like biology and technology, and hence follow an interdisciplinary investigation of their contribution to society. For instance, topological ideas have been found extremely beneficial in the examination of complicated systems within the life sciences. Current research efforts in cell interactomics, as outlined in recent reviews, represent a convergence of traditional states and quantum evolution with an outlook for elucidating the interactions of molecules reminiscent of topological shapes (Baianu et al., 2010). This intersection points to the dynamic, intertwined nature of biological life forms, whereby topology is not just a mathematical construct, but a necessary instrument for understanding life's complexity. In line with this, the evolution of topological concepts has profound implications, enhancing our understanding of physical as well as abstract events in a wide range of domains. Furthermore, technological implementation of topology has triggered new arguments over its use in social construct determination and critique. The deployment of topology as a theoretical framework for understanding the interplay between technology and society points out the malleability of these concepts within contemporary debate. As indicated by digital technology studies, a topological approach facilitates an open-ended understanding of how techno-processes are intertwined with socio-cultural processes and demonstrates the capacity to invert typical deterministic explanations of technology (Marres et al., 2025). This new storyline facilitates critical approaches, making it easier for researchers to appreciate the intricate interplay between technical and social change. Therefore, the origins of topological concepts are directly related to their ability to direct and transform our comprehension of complex systems and to render sophisticated and future topologies more applicable in the contemporary interconnected world (Figure 3.4).

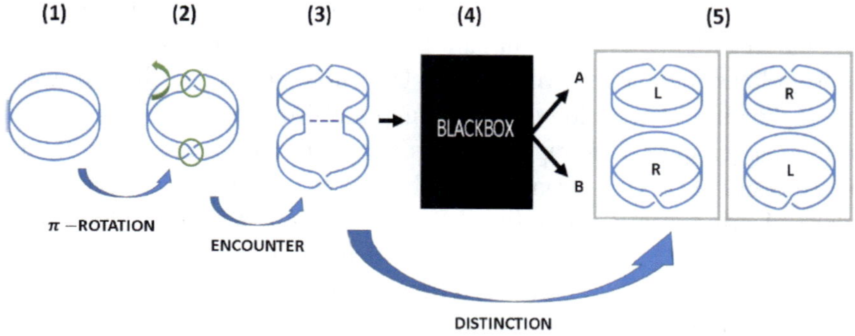

Figure 3.4. *The origins of topological concepts.*

Source: https://www.mdpi.com/symmetry/symmetry-13-00581/article_deploy/html/images/symmetry-13-00581-g001.png.

3.1.2. Key Figures in the Development of Topology

The development of topology, one of mathematics' and its application's central areas of study, has been significantly shaped by the contributions of leading mathematicians down the centuries. One of them is Henri Poincare, commonly referred to as the father of topology. His pioneering work in the late 19th century established core concepts such as homology and homotopy that served as the foundation for subsequent breakthroughs in the field. Poincare's insight into space's conserved properties in continuous transformations created new avenues for understanding complex structures. Not only did the intellectual framework influence pure mathematics but was also applied practically in the sciences, attesting to the profound impact of his work on the course of topology's development. Another key contributor to the field is David Hilbert, who at the start of the 20th century further solidified the foundations of topology. Hilbert created the theory of a topological space, going beyond Euclid's geometry in exploring more abstract spaces. His famous Hilbert's Hotel paradox proved the seemingly impossible nature of infinite sets, thus proving the conventional wisdom wrong and challenging further research into the nature of mathematical infinity. In creating the concept of continuity and compactness in different mathematical contexts, Hilbert extended the scope of topological inquiry, influencing generations of mathematicians. His rigorously established techniques have persisted, influencing the development of modern topology and its cross-disciplinary applications, underscoring the practical relevance of early theoretic work. As the relevance of topology in today's debate reaches more fields, ongoing academic research into the origins of its pioneers is still needed. For instance, topological relations with modern technologies illustrate how traditional knowledge is still dominant in science and technology innovations. Recent applications, such as in naval vessels' electric power distribution systems, illustrate the utility of topology in addressing real-life issues, including efficient energy management and storage. The chronology of emergent technology from refined electric sensors to the creation of kinetic energy storage is founded upon topological principles, highlighting how early pioneers such as Poincare and Hilbert have created a legacy which persists through new technologies. Such confluences highlight the relevance of analyzing past contexts while creating innovation within the realm of topology, offering gates through which to explore and apply in the future.

3.1.3. Development of Topological Theories

Topological theories have undergone fierce revolutions in their history as they have been influenced by various scientific paradigms and technological advances. It was the interaction between architecture and structural engineering that resulted in the understanding of tectonics as a theory that went beyond mere structural stability from the past. The integration of morphogenetic theories and digital media transformed the relationship between form and structure. As quoted in the institution of digital tectonics, contemporary architectural design employs such theories to generate responsive forms that sensibly respond to their environmental context. This transformation shows how topological theory has evolved from limiting definitions towards practices that embrace fluidity and complexity, reflecting corresponding shifts in the practice of architecture as a field. These advancements create new avenues of architectural expression that blend both structural functionality and aesthetic appeal, indicative of the ongoing advancement in the way that we perceive and apply topological principles. Additionally, the use of high-level topological theory transcends the realm of architecture into other areas of science such as quantum physics. Quantum Chromodynamics (QCD), for instance, shows a strong theoretical basis that accounts for the complexities of strong interactions over a wide range of phenomena of nuclear physics to quark-gluon matter behaviors. The intertwined development of old-school theoretical ideas of yesteryears with fresh ideas like holographic images and duality concepts is reflective of the flexibility of knowledge across disciplines. This interweaving not only further enriches our understanding of high-energy physics but also encourages reevaluation of topological theories along mathematical lines. The creation of such theories displays an inherent interdependence between abstract theoretical concepts and their applications to experiment, the result of a dynamic dialogue between theory and observation that enriches both. Current controversy surrounding topological theories involves new ideas that question traditional meanings and suggest new applications. The trend towards the investigation of architecture in morphogenetic terms underlines the dynamically adaptive character of architecture, which necessitates a re-thinking of conventional paradigms in design. As outlined by contemporary studies, the integration of digital design strategies gives rise to a re-definition of tectonics as a dynamic morphogenetic process, thereby enhancing architectural responsiveness to environmental stimuli. This paradigm requires an interdisciplinarity, combining insights from digital technology with aesthetic vision and structural coherence. Ultimately, the construction of topological theories is a culmination not merely of a chronological order of thought but of an ongoing conversation that reflects the richness of a more interconnected world, pushing against the union of creativity and scientific rigor in future explorations of advanced and emergent topologies (Figure 3.5).

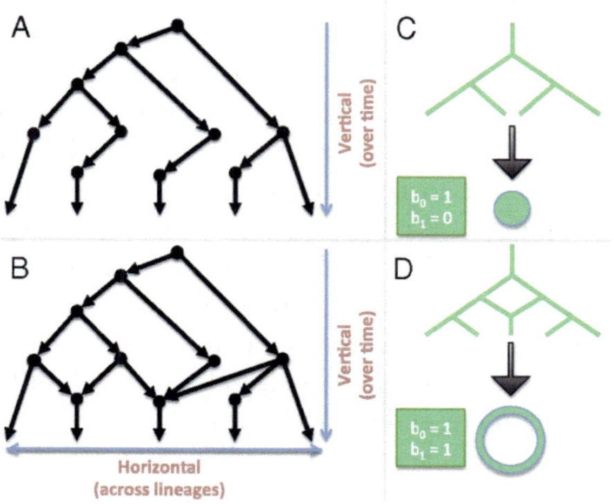

Figure 3.5. *Evolution of topological theories.*

Source: https://www.pnas.org/cms/10.1073/pnas.1313480110/asset/ce30e9df-d595-4520-a68a-74f3c6f151d1/assets/graphic/pnas.1313480110fig01.jpeg.

3.2. FUNDAMENTAL CONCEPTS IN TOPOLOGY

In the exploration of fundamental concepts in topology, one must appreciate the intricacies of how topological spaces are defined and explored. A topological space inherently comprises a set equipped with a topology, which is a collection of open sets that satisfy specific axioms. These axioms include the closure under arbitrary unions and finite intersections, allowing for a robust framework to analyze continuity, convergence, and connectedness within mathematical structures. As topological spaces serve as the foundational building blocks of topology, they facilitate the examination of numerous properties such as compactness and separation axioms. Such concepts are pivotal as they cross-pollinate with various fields, including analysis and algebra, broadening their applicability in the search for understanding complex systems. By grounding advanced topics such as homotopy and homology within these fundamental concepts, one can appreciate the rich and interconnected tapestry that topology offers.

While traditional topological concepts set the stage, emerging topologies continue to redefine our understanding of spatial relationships and mathematical properties. For instance, the increasing complexity of networks necessitates novel approaches in topology, particularly in graph theory where nodes and connections symbolize relationships among various components. In this context, graph topology allows researchers to model interactions and detect vulnerabilities within complex networks, especially in the realm of cybersecurity. Utilizing graph theory, it becomes feasible to develop robust recovery techniques that ensure network resiliency against advanced persistent threats (APTs). Such methodologies are integral to not only managing network survival but also to provide nuanced responses based on dynamically changing topologies in the presence of attacks, thus establishing a new frontier for topological application and research (Shamir et al., 2017). Furthermore, the advancement of technology has brought forth specialized topologies that cater to high-demand applications in power electronics and industrial systems. Multilevel converters exemplify this trend, representing sophisticated power-conversion systems designed to enhance performance in demanding contexts. With varied circuit topologies and modulation methods, these converters manage power quality while addressing critical technical issues pertinent to industry applications. Understanding the fundamental principles of these topologies equips engineers with the knowledge necessary to implement and innovate within the sector. By bridging theory and real-world practice, emerging topologies not only enhance efficiency but also encourage continued research and development aligned with cutting-edge advancements in engineering and technology (García et al., 2009). Such developments accentuate the dynamic nature of topology, marking its significant evolution from foundational concepts to applications that shape modern infrastructures (Figure 3.6).

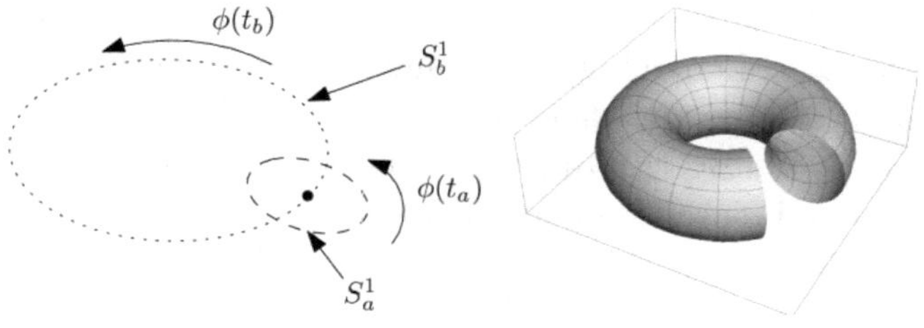

Figure 3.6. *Fundamental concepts in topology.*

Source: https://media.springernature.com/lw685/springer-static/image/chp%3A10.1007%2F978-3-030-73449-7_6/MediaObjects/479542_1_En_6_Fig14_HTML.png.

3.2.1. Open and Closed Sets

The open and closed set ideologies form the building blocks of topology and influence the construction and analysis of mathematical spaces. Open set, defined standardly by possessing a neighborhood around every one of its points, is areas where locally defined limits do not apply. This concept broadens the definition of continuity because functions that perform smoothly in open sets can be analyzed without the inconvenience of boundary points. Nevertheless, closed sets, as sets that contain all of their limit points, provide us with vital information regarding convergence and closure properties of topological spaces. The duality of closed and open sets not only facilitates understanding of topological structures but also serves as the basis for generalizations to advances in such areas as metric spaces and more abstract algebraic systems. The analogy between open and closed sets can be depicted through the usual topology on real numbers, where intervals are used as the primitive building blocks for continuity and convergence definition. In this regard, it is evident that open sets can be expressed as unions of open intervals, whereas closed set intersections correspond to closed sets. This duality provides the concept of compactness in the sense that a set is compact if it can be covered by finitely many open sets, effectively reducing open and closed sets. This characteristic is particularly relevant in greater topological work, when one examines sets with very complex structures, such as in functional analysis and algebraic topology. The examination of compactness and its relation to open and closed sets provides valuable insight into significant implications for mathematical modeling and theoretical demonstration. Recent works in the topology of various structures, such as polyrings, also further consider delicate interplay among open and closed sets. Research shows that the Zariski topology on such algebraic objects captures unique features that blur the traditional distinction between openness and closedness in topology. The non-discrete Zariski topology of infinite polyrings, for instance, illustrates how closed sets realize as nowhere dense subsets of bigger spaces, capturing an intriguing region of overlap of algebra and topology. These findings verify the use of open and closed sets not only in classical geometry and analysis but also in wider mathematical theories, including those involving idempotent ultrafilters as well as more general algebraic topologies (Saveliev et al., 2018) and (Rejzner et al., 2011). Not only do these researches expand the range of topology, but also improve our understanding of the algebraic foundations of sophisticated mathematical structures (Figure 3.7).

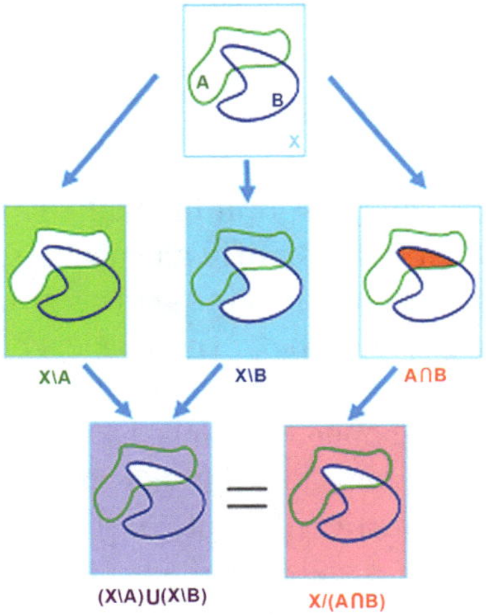

Figure 3.7. *The concepts of open and closed sets form foundational elements in topology.*

Source: https://calculus123.com/images/d/df/Intersection_of_closed_sets.png.

3.2.2. Continuity and Homeomorphism

Homeomorphism and continuity are both included in the definition of the fundamental concepts of topology, which is pivotal in theoretical and practical mathematics. Topological continuity refers to those functions that preserve sequence limit points so that points close to one another in one space remain close to one another in another. A continuous function maps open sets in the domain to open sets in the codomain, and this allows mathematicians to transition smoothly from a topological space to another. This principle forms a basis for more advanced forms and their functionality in various mathematical frameworks. Maintaining continuity is crucial for the derivation of topological properties where mathematicians can analyze the underlying relationship between various topologies and their respective transformations. Homeomorphism is one step further in the investigation of continuity in that it gives a bijective mapping between topological spaces and retains their characteristics. Essentially, two spaces are homeomorphic if one can be molded into the other without tearing or gluing, which means that their topological characteristics are retained. Homeomorphism is a fundamental concept in the differentiation of topological spaces since homeomorphic spaces, although they are geometrically different, have identical properties like connectivity and compactness. The implications of homeomorphism extend beyond simple topology, opening the door for a variety of other fields of mathematics and its applications, such as those that occur in knowledge graph embeddings, which utilize continuous maps to assist in dynamic information systems (Cao et al., 2024). Alongside this, continuity and homeomorphism have tremendous implications for a wide array of other fields of science, including revealing extensive insight into the structure of many mathematical entities. Specifically, topology's influence can be observed in psychology, as topological concepts provide models for understanding complex human behavior and relational processes. By the application of topological concepts like those embodied by Kurt Lewin's theory of persons, researchers can achieve a nuanced understanding of psychological processes, replicating the global qualitative character of conduct. Thus, the strict meanings and applications of homeomorphism and continuity, not just alone but also as applied, do not only enhance our knowledge about abstract mathematical structures but also develop interdisciplinarity, which illuminates other fields of study, and dispatch more researchers into new fields of inquiry (Bartłomiej et al., 2020).

3.2.3. Compactness and Connectedness

In the realm of topology, connectedness and compactness are cornerstones of comprehension that define the world of topological spaces. Compactness, which is a property where spaces are able to retain some favorable properties under continuous maps, is what ensures the convergence of sequences and coverings to be finite. It is critical to analysis in both classical and emerging topological spaces. For instance, several conclusions in functional analysis rely on compactness of operators, illustrating how compact spaces facilitate the use of powerful mathematical tools. The usefulness of the concept extends to lattice gauge theories, where compact spaces enable rigorous definitions and computation to be achieved, which allow physicists to efficiently simulate complex systems, as illustrated in Creutz (2022). This relationship of compactness with numerous diverse mathematical structures instills better comprehension of theoretical principles and their applicability to the world. Connectedness exists, however, as an antithesis to compactness by emphasizing the cohesiveness of a space as a unit, resisting random separation into independent subsets. A topological space is connected if it cannot be decomposed into two separated, non-empty open sets, which creates an intuition of continuity in much of mathematics and physics. It is particularly applicable when learning manifold theory and algebraic topology, offering insight into the nature and behavior of higher-dimensional shapes and spaces. Besides, connectivity also plays a critical role within the new domains of quantum computing, where coherence between qubits needs to be maintained to guarantee the successful execution of quantum algorithms.

Figure 3.8. *The concepts of compactness and connectedness.*

Source: https://open-images.acast.com/shows/661ce685f50b790017037391/1718948090739-ab934f4874e203b9ed4051b3eb008993.jpeg?height=750.

Under the noisy intermediate scale quantum (NISQ) era, topological connectivity is known to enhance techniques against error and promote computing reliability since it highlights the relevance of this property in present research as presented in Bharti et al. (2022). The relationship between compactness and connectedness becomes even more fascinating when one sees them working in other fields of mathematics and physics. For example, the Heine-Borel theorem that links compactness with closedness and boundedness in Euclidean space illustrates how compact spaces are both connected and amenable to real analysis. Conversely, while certain small spaces are linked, yet others are not, revealing that these concepts, while dependent upon one another, exist independently in certain instances. The examination of complex patterns, such as fractals, reveals fascinating findings in which connectedness appears in contradictory ways, in many cases in opposition to conventional definitions. Other interdisciplinarity breakthroughs, especially in the quantum field theories, also reinforce the relative nature of compactness and connectedness as imperative in establishing stable foundations for understanding the universe at its most primitive level, translating the space between mathematical theory and use to an ever-decreasing space (Figure 3.8).

3.3. ADVANCED TOPOLOGICAL STRUCTURES

The finding of higher-order topological structures is of far-reaching implications in many sciences, particularly in cellular and biomolecular interaction sciences. A quantum automata concept has been framed, which includes normal cell cycling and division under a modular framework. This finding brings the phenomenon of quantum interactomics, which combines biomolecular interactions and complex cascades of signaling to shed light on processes like neural plasticity and brain development. By conceptualizing cellular interactomics as a mix of classical states driven by Boltzmann statistics and metastable quantum states, scientists create new directions for approaching consciousness and memory establishment—essential processes during initial brain growth. Such an approach not only improves our understanding of fundamental biological processes but also provides a basis for developing novel therapeutic strategies, particularly in the context of neurodevelopmental illnesses and cancer therapy (Baianu et al., 2010). Moving to electrical engineering, the emergence of soft electronics underlines how complex topological structures are capable of revolutionizing traditional circuit designs. Traditional circuits are stiff, imposing limitations on the uses of bioelectronics and in environments with water. To offset this, the entry of droplet circuits provides a new remedy, where liquid metal droplets form the central components of a self-healing and flexible electrical circuit. These circuits operate in aqueous conditions and take advantage of conductive materials such as carbon nanotubes to facilitate electron transport through quantum tunneling effects. The topology is able to support parallel electron transport and multi-point connectivity while minimizing the circuit break issue. The implications of such a venture extend revolutionary applications, including room temperature quantum computation and higher nerve-machine interfaces, hence merging the idea of topology with technological advancements in the real world (Liu et al., 2018). Therefore, the conjoining of advanced topological constructs across domains highlights interconnection between emerging paradigms in science. The cellular interactomics modeling in the novel represents a deeper understanding of essential biological functions, paving the way for future medical advancements. Simultaneously, droplet circuitry points to the significance of adaptability and flexibility in modern electronic design, particularly within systems of bioengineering. As these technologies arise, they unsettle traditional paradigms and promote a multidisciplinary approach to solve complex scientific questions. The future of next-generation topologies and emerging topologies has the potential to revolutionize biological knowledge as well as technological innovation, culminating in a better understanding of life and the advent of next-generation electronic systems (Baianu et al., 2010; Liu et al., 2018).

3.3.1. Manifolds and Their Applications

Manifolds are a central concept in numerous fields of science and engineering, as evidenced by their application in higher topologies. Manifolds are mathematical objects that are locally Euclidean in nature and facilitate the generalization of concepts such as curves and surfaces. This flexibility allows for the description of complex systems over a broad variety of fields from robotics and computer graphics to cosmology. Here, the geometry and intrinsic curvature of manifolds contribute to optimal algorithmic optimization and design. Let us consider the example of robotics. Manifold learning algorithms enhance the capability of path planning and sensor fusion, showcasing how topology can be employed to optimize machine performance. This confluence of application and geometry shows not only the beauty of manifolds in theory but their applicability in technological innovation and scientific discovery in reality. Aside from robotics, manifolds are also shown to play a growing significant part in additive manufacturing, more specifically in aerospace use. The advent of metal additive manufacturing has transformed the design and manufacturing of parts. Manifolds, in this case, can be used to help engineers make geometry-to-functionality correlations of parts. Capability to create delicate and light structures is a chief pillar of modern aerospace design, perfectly complementing manifold properties that achieve optimal material distribution and minimal weight. As explained, these potentialities comprise substantial cost and lead-time reductions via integrated manufacturing routes where delicate internal geometries facilitated by manifold design principles enhance heat transfer in high-performance items like rocket engines (Blakey-Milner et al., 2021). These developments underscore manifold theory's relevance in aerospace engineering's management of evolving needs. Additional exploration of manifold use finds their applicability in biological systems, more specifically via advancement in single-cell RNA sequencing (scRNA-seq) technologies. Gene expression analysis at the single-cell level is only achievable by sophisticated mathematical frameworks, and manifolds provide the necessary structure to grasp high-dimensional biological data. For this, manifold assumption suggests that the data lies on a lower-dimensional manifold embedded in a high-dimensional space and, therefore, scientists can discover patterns and cellular hierarchies in an effective manner. The integration of manifold-based approaches in the RNA-seq pipelines has played a significant role in improving data processing and analysis, and consequently, in offering improved biological insights and understanding of complex processes such as development and disease status (Malte et al., 2019). With science continually evolving, the application of manifolds in theoretical and applied science is promising to yield additional breakthroughs in areas where it is critical to understand the topology of data (Figure 3.9).

Figure 3.9. *The concept of manifolds plays a pivotal role in various scientific and engineering domains.*

Source: https://www.honiron.com/wp-content/uploads/2017/02/Oil-Production-Manifold-1000x480.jpg.

3.3.2. Algebraic Topology and Homotopy Theory

The interplay between Algebraic Topology and Homotopy Theory is the leading motif of contemporary mathematical research, bringing its paradigms and methods to bear on a wide range of disciplines. Algebraic Topology is primarily concerned with the study of topological spaces using algebraic tools, that is, through interlinking algebraic structures, such as groups, with topological properties. This characterization allows mathematicians to distinguish and classify spaces based on their intrinsic properties and gain significant leverage for other studies in geometry and analysis. Homotopy, another essential component of this study, emphasizes continuous deformation of functions. Homotopy theory leverages this concept, enabling the exploration of deeper connections between spaces that are continuously deformable into one another, thereby unlocking insight which can be greater than traditional geometric appreciation. Since the last few decades, breakthroughs in computer algorithms have driven innovations in the subject of Algebraic Topology and Homotopy Theory, with spectacular advances in most applications. Techniques such as numerical polynomial homotopy continuation, Groebner basis methods, and moment/sum-of-squares relaxations have emerged as powerful tools that can tackle very complex problems in these fields. Specifically, these techniques have proven capable of solving the power flow equations that form the basis of electrical engineering and thus showing the applications of mathematical theory in real contexts. Specifically, while traditional methods generally prevail with their recognition of enduring high-voltage solutions, they generally lag as concerns low-voltage scenarios, which are no less significant in ensuring system dependability. Advances in computational techniques aim to correct these shortcomings, expanding our insight and potential in Algebraic Topology and Homotopy Theory beyond the theoretical boundaries to engineering technology and systems applications (Mehta et al., 2015). The need for further research in Algebraic Topology and Homotopy Theory is also highlighted by scholarly conferences and workshops, which provide a forum for collaboration between mathematicians and applied scientists. The Stanford Symposium on Algebraic Topology is an example of this, which demonstrates active participation and exchange of ideas between leading figures in the field, serving as a spur to new avenues and applications. Such cross-disciplinary conversation does not just shed light on central ideas, as with the scholarship on influential mathematicians like Gunnar Carlsson, Ralph Cohen, and Ib Madsen, but instead shows how those mathematical frameworks can be applied to a range of disciplines ranging from data analysis, robotics, to even quantum computing (Kahle et al., 2013). With continued interest by scholars on new and emerging topologies, the blending of theory and practice mirrors the rich energies of mathematical inquiry to provide promising breakthroughs in the future combining abstraction and usability.

3.3.3. Topological Groups and Why They Matter

In the evolving field of mathematics, topological groups are a significant blend of topology and abstract algebra that provides a highly efficient device for the study of symmetrical objects. As a category of groups with a topology, topological groups enable both algebraic operations and topological properties to be investigated at once. The duality offered by this relationship allows for the exploration of continuity under the operations of the groups and results in observations which are crucial in a wide range of mathematics as well as physics. Topological groups play particularly significant roles when used in such fields as harmonic analysis and functional analysis, where the interaction between group theory and topology assists in understanding more complex systems and processes. As scientists venture deeper into the networks, the possibility of creating new mathematical theories based on the properties of topological groups becomes more apparent.

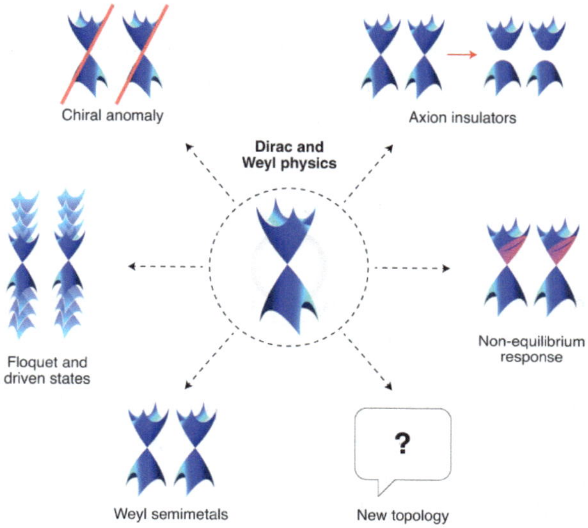

Figure 3.10. *Topological groups and their significance.*

Source: https://media.springernature.com/m685/springer-static/image/art%3A10.1038%2Fs41563-020-00820-4/MediaObjects/41563_2020_820_Fig1_HTML.png.

Topological groups possess one of the most intriguing characteristics in that they are capable of modeling the dynamics within many applications, from urban planning and intelligent cities. The combination of IoT and AI technologies has emerged as the driving force in producing intelligent solutions to urbanization challenges. For instance, Eshrat et al. (2023) provides an elaborate explanation of how geospatial data management following principles analogous to those found in topology can provide more effective urban planning by providing new means of analyzing and visualizing big data. These applications emphasize the significance of understanding underlying topological structures that govern relationships in spatial data sets, thereby facilitating urban planners to optimize resource deployment and improve the overall quality of life for inhabitants in densely populated regions. Furthermore, the theoretical advancements in topological concepts contribute significantly to evolving the future of data management, as expressed in modern-day literature. As explained in Breunig et al. (2020), topology is now a crucial tool for the management of geospatial data, bridging modeling, visualization, and analysis in increasingly complex urban environments. The achievements within the discipline, particularly the integration of Geographic Information Systems (GIS) with Building Information Modeling (BIM), highlight the potential of topological theory in facilitating sophisticated analysis of spatial relationships and structures. These developments outline a transformational potential for topological groups in reimagining smart technologies, as they afford fresh horizons of perception into and agency over the data that drive modern infrastructures, ultimately transforming how we interact with our worlds (Figure 3.10).

3.4. EMERGING TOPOLOGIES IN MODERN RESEARCH

The research on new topologies in recent research has now begun redefining existing paradigms in some industries, but largely in telecommunications and technology. Paradigm shifts have occurred as scientists make use of advancements in areas such as spectrum policy, universal wireless systems, and cognitive radio. For instance, the SPORT VIEWS initiative is highlighting key findings on how novel radio technologies, such as Ultra-Wideband (UWB) and Software Defined Radio (SDR), can enhance market competitiveness, and address evolving communication needs. Not only are these technologies an evolution in hardware, but they also call for a rethinking of regulatory models that govern electromagnetic spectrum usage, which can directly influence economic growth and innovation. This e-gory between technological innovations and policy-making is a vivid demonstration of the reality that new topologies are not merely technical designs but critical determinants of systemic change in our communication system (Pujol et al., 2025). For energy systems, innovation in new topologies, particularly in battery storage technology, has sweeping implications for sustainable development. Vanadium Redox Flow Battery (VRFB) is a new energy storage technology, particularly for the smart grid. Renewable energy technologies, such as solar and wind power, lead the charge these days, and the need for efficient storage increases manyfold. The new features of VRFB, including scalability and long-term lifespan, represent a significant milestone in the evolution of our energy grid. Research on the operating efficiencies and structural designs of such batteries allows for their capacity to mitigate the issues of intermittency for renewable energy sources. Adaptability and resilience, in the realm of a sustainable economic model, are characteristics that highlight that these new battery topologies are not just possible but inevitable to utilizing most of green energy (Guarnieri et al., 2016). In addition, the complementarity of different research fields is propelling the development of hybrid systems that adopt principles from more than one field and thus expanding the diversity of future topologies. This interdiscipline allows for new approaches not obtainable in standalone studies. The combination of knowledge from telecommunications and energy storage, for example, can allow for more interconnected systems with the possibility of optimizing resource allocation and reliability in grid management. The synergy between technologies on the cusp foretells a time when complex issues are addressed by convergence and synergy of expertise. While scientists continue to push beyond the limits, upcoming progress in such emerging topologies will not only be foundation for technologies but also drivers towards sustainable and resilient infrastructures in an increasingly interconnected world.

3.4.1. Digital Topology and Applications

Digital topology is a fresh and emerging field of topological research as such, and it is concerned with the structure and properties applicable in digital space and particularly those applicable to computer science and network topology. Its theoretical aspects pave the way to new applications in interdisciplinary fields such as data networks and computer security. Through discrete mathematics, digital topology facilitates the understanding of the network structure of digital data and how it interacts in network topologies. For instance, building and understanding complex networking frameworks rely heavily on the idea of digital topology, which allows it to efficiently handle packets of data and simplify communication flow. With growing demand for higher-level digital infrastructures, the integration of these topological concepts is increasingly important to address the challenges associated with large-scale networks and contribute directly to performance as well as security mechanisms. Recent advances in network infrastructure are the finest testimony to the actual applications of digital topology in reality. Fabric is a significant milestone toward a dynamic research center that encompasses elements of digital topology. Through its provision of richly programmable network capabilities, it connects various testbeds, enabling researchers to find novel uses in many disciplines, including machine learning and distributed computing. This broad network foundation is of most use to researchers who want to experiment and tune algorithms in changing environments in which typical network structures are not sufficient. Filling in the gaps of research in addition to conventional methods, FABRIC creates a better understanding of how digital topology will enable experimental design and results to be optimized, thereby stimulating innovation. Scholars can establish solid systems that address adequately the growing computational demands of contemporary digital applications through such work, confirming theoretical topology's cooperation with practical application. Ethernet technology is another influential example of the utilization of digital topology principles. Over the course of the last decades, Ethernet has evolved to become a standard component of local area networks, and its influence has extended to other areas like telecommunications and multimedia. The flexibility of Ethernet is the key to its universality of use, and it is a desirable choice for many technological contexts. However, since Ethernet is being implemented in different fields, special adaptations are necessary to meet the specific requirements of each application. Acknowledging these specific adaptations with the digital topology idea not only enhances performance but also quality of service in various contexts. As the complexities of contemporary applications grow, a deeper comprehension of digital topology can inspire further innovation in Ethernet technology, thereby establishing it as a cornerstone in local and broader network infrastructure (Baldin et al., 2019; Feller et al., 2010) (Figure 3.11).

Figure 3.11. *Digital topology and its applications.*

Source: https://img.freepik.com/premium-photo/visual-representation-network-topology-with-various-devices-connected_1314467-90171.jpg.

3.4.2. Topological Data Analysis (TDA)

Topological Data Analysis (TDA) is a revolutionary method for the analysis of complex datasets, characterized by its ability to reveal underlying structures that may not otherwise come to light using normal analytical means. Through the application of principles of algebraic topology, TDA is able to transform data into a space that is topological in character, and thus be analyzed based on its shape. This approach has been particularly useful across a variety of fields, from material science to social media studies, where finding complicated relationships is critical. In research focused on the density anomalies of liquid silica, TDA proves its worth by describing the one-dimensional topology of the -Si-Si- network at critical temperature transitions, emphasizing its applicability to glassy materials and glass-liquid phase changes (Nakano et al., 2022). Such findings represent the kinds of ways that TDA can shed light on messy phenomena by offering a novel vantage point from which researchers may interpret multi-dimensional data. Social media sites offer a special case for using TDA in the political sphere, where interactions may be measured quantitatively to understand larger socio-political processes. By employing Persistent Homology, scientists have come up with ways of examining retweet patterns, which effectively identify different types of political clusters, which include Nuclear, Bipolar, and Multipolar Constellations. This is not an exercise in classification; it is a work towards probing deeper into understanding the mathematical constructions underpinning political discourse and algorithmic social media engagement (Rocha et al., 2024). By employing Gaussian functions to characterize such topological structures, the work offers additional insight into phenomena such as political personalism and polarization, which form the cornerstone of contemporary political science. As such, TDAs use in political analytics is therefore an indication of its generalizability and potential to make effective contributions to social science studies. The ability of TDA to express and quantify relationships between datasets is not just an analytical tool but a vehicle for cross-disciplinary inspiration. The evolution from classical network analysis to a topological one enables scientists to go beyond mere correlation and into the universe of shape and structure, inviting richer insight into complex data interactions. As has been observed through the exploration of various datasets, including political networks, TDA allows researchers to hypothesize about the existence of long-standing topological attributes, suggesting that similar patterns will be found in various datasets and domains (Rocha et al., 2024). The possibility of generalizability suggests that the future of TDA and its attempts to account for various phenomena is promising, ultimately leading to theory development and applications in the real world. By incorporating TDA into conventional research practices, researchers can open up new avenues of investigation that connect mathematics, data science, and social research, informing our understanding of the data-driven world.

3.4.3. Quantum Topology and Its Consequences

Quantum topology has picked up serious steam in recent years as researchers probe the intriguing interplay of topological structures and quantum mechanics. Quantum topology explores the topological nature of quantum states, where the geometry of space plays a crucial role in defining physical phenomena. Topological concepts in quantum, such as braids and knots, may help to clarify some insight regarding the behavior of quantum systems, particularly in the context of quantum computing. As quantum technologies were being established, establishing how topology influences quantum states and their dynamics becomes increasingly important. By investigating the quantum protocols and their topological basis, researchers hope to leverage such findings for future advancements in quantum computing, resulting in fascinating applications in numerous areas of scientific activity. Quantum topological practical applications are achieved by innovations like Noisy Intermediate-Scale Quantum (NISQ) computers, a landmark in quantum computing research.

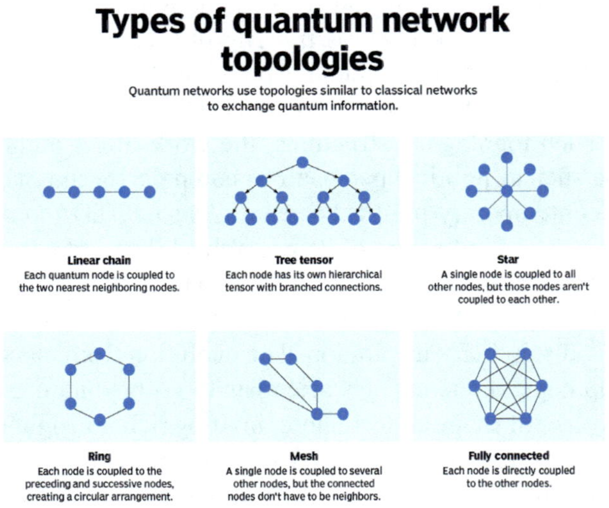

Figure 3.12. *Quantum topology and its implications.*

Source: https://www.techtarget.com/rms/onlineimages/types_of_quantum_network_topologies-f_mobile.png.

Despite limitations such as noise and coherence times, these proofs of concept demonstrate the effectiveness of quantum algorithms when appropriately compiled to take advantage of topological aspects of qubit arrangements. Current work has considered the evaluation of quantum system architecture, performance benchmark definition, and communication topology between qubits (Abhari et al., 2019). By examining various implementations of devices—superconducting qubits, trapped ions, and so forth—physicists push the bounds of our understanding of the challenges and possibilities of large-scale quantum computer design. Not only does this understanding guide hardware design, but it also enables the creation of groundbreaking software optimizations that are fine-tuned to the underlying topological character of the subject qubits. The uses of quantum topology are not just with respect to the practical applications of quantum computing. The examination of topological properties within the wider context of general relativity provides an intriguing set of theoretical principles, namely with respect to the nature of spacetime. In terms of the unimodular theory of gravity, researchers have found complex solutions to Einsteins equations that reflect profound connections between topology and gravity (Linde et al., 1998). Examining these solutions, one may regard them as an indication of a path integral that composes the structure of spacetime in a more integrated manner. Compatibility of these solutions by quantum measures raises essential questions about the universes topology built-in implications for quantum gravity nature. These investigations not only improve our understanding of the underlying physics but also enhance the interaction between mathematics and theory since they reunite disparate disciplines of knowledge (Figure 3.12).

3.5. APPLICATIONS OF ADVANCED TOPOLOGIES

Applications of advanced topologies have become critical in enhancing the efficiency and flexibility of modern electrical systems. In particular, the integration of distributed generation, electric vehicles, and energy storage into conventional distribution systems has transformed their operation from passive to active control systems. This calls for revamping the topological architectures on which power distribution is dependent. Hybrid AC/DC system development is the best illustration of this trend, given that configurations of this type ensure improved energy management through the integration of the natural direct current (DC) nature of new devices and resources. Through the study of the development of AC distribution systems, it is clear that adopting innovative topologies not only maximizes energy flow but also enables ancillary services critical to a decarbonized energy future, highlighting the invaluable role advanced topologies have in addressing current energy needs (Barragán et al., 2019). In computing, Network-on-Chip (NoC) embodies a quintessential use of advanced topological concepts. As with more sophisticated chiplet multiprocessors comprising hundreds or thousands of cores, conventional NoCs are incapable of addressing increasing on-chip communication requirements. Broadcast and multicast traffic in conventional networks can pose scalability constraints, bringing about performance degradation. To surmount such constraints, researchers introduced Wireless Network-on-Chip (WNoC) architectures, which rely on a single broadband channel that is available to all the cores. This new topology is designed to enable low-latency communication and improve the efficiency of broadcast and multicast operations over the inherent limitation of wired NoCs. Hence, the integration of such evolved topologies like WNoC ensures that multiprocessor systems keep pace with increased demands for efficient inter-core communication (Cavall et al., 2016). Furthermore, the study of topological complexity extends to other fields where complex networks have to be optimized. Telecommunications, for example, calls for topological configurations as part of network construction with fault-tolerant networks being capable of holding mixed traffic patterns and evolving user demands. As systems are becoming increasingly interdependent, topological design becomes a top priority when it comes to keeping networks reliable and fault-tolerant against failures and hacker intrusions. The installation of new routing schemes and network configurations is an evident manifestation of improved topological implementations, facilitating better data stream and low latency between diverse platforms. By embracing such groundbreaking topological methodologies, companies can enhance their operational efficiency to the fullest, paving the way for breakthroughs in future technology and communication infrastructure. The applicability of advanced topologies thus extends far and wide, touching many areas and shaping the future of interconnected systems.

3.5.1. Topology in Computer Science

Topology has increasingly been making significant contributions to computer science, primarily through its applications in data analysis, robotics, and network engineering. Topological data analysis (TDA) is a new field that uses concepts of algebraic topology to extract insightful features from complex data sets. By encoding data into geometric objects, TDA allows scientists to identify patterns that are hard to identify with usual statistical methods. For instance, in machine learning, analysis of shapes in data space can enhance model interpretability and robustness, detecting clusters or outliers responsible for better decision-making processes. Additionally, the mathematical roots of TDA also apply in robotics, particularly for the case of motion planning and interaction with physical spaces, adding to the bridge of topology and technological advancement in computational fields. In robotics, advanced topologies make intricate structures such as 3D trusses possible to be manufactured effectively using robotic spatial extrusion. As mentioned in earlier work, planning extrusion steps and movements for structures with unconstrained topologies has been extensively addressed ((Garrett et al., 2019)). This work introduces a hierarchical planning framework with the capability to decouple sequential and motion planning. This is a reaction to the complexity of three-dimensional structures as well as prolonged planning periods traditionally involved with such endeavors. Thus, the use of topology in conjunction with robotics not only optimizes fabrication processes but also represents a step forward in methodological application of automation. Moreover, opening up to open-source algorithms here can make advanced planning tools available to everyone, hence offering greater scope for real-world applications across all manufacturing sectors. Topology's versatility is not just confined to robotics but extends to the design and optimization of Industrial Wireless Sensor Networks (IWSNs) as well, which are critical for today's automated industries. The utilization of topological principles enables systematic ordering of the sensor nodes, enhancing the network's connectivity and reliability ((Aslam et al., 2018)). These networks are paramount in oil and gas, as well as automobile manufacturing industries, where they are applied in real-time monitoring and control. IWSNs have challenges of environmental complexities and operational risks despite their advantages of flexibility and scalability. A good grasp of these topological forms is needed in order to design robust standards and protocols that reduce vulnerabilities while optimally maximizing performance. Finally, the study of topological constructs in these networks has the potential to reveal new solutions that solve existing constraints and ensure the resilience of industrial systems in the future.

3.5.2. Applications in Physics and Cosmology

The synergy between advanced topologies and their uses in physics and cosmology is more and more dominant, especially in fields such as high-energy physics (HEP). With changing computational methods, the ability to simulate intricate physical systems and explore vast amounts of data greatly improves. The HEP field has seen the need to establish advanced computational models for processing the growing demands of data throughput and volume. Such projects as the HEP Forum for Computational Excellence (HEP-FCE) accentuate the importance of software efficiency and IA enhancement. By creating work groups for Applications Software, Software Libraries and Tools, and Systems, HEP-FCE aims to chart the current status and future directions in computational approaches and thereby develop a roadmap that is consistent with the rapid evolution of computational technologies as well as the theoretical underpinnings of high-energy phenomenon (Asai et al., 2015). In addition to the applied applications in computational physics, new avenues in our conceptual thinking on quantum theories are also provided by upcoming topologies. The topos method, for instance, revolutionizes the foundations of quantum mechanics with the suggestion that physical values can be expressed, not as simple real numbers but as collections of real intervals describing unsharp values. This abstraction enables a new form of flexibility within the realm of quantum structures, unifying classical and quantum paradigms. The meeting of order theory, particularly domain theory, with the topos framework indicates how advanced mathematical concepts can be employed to shed light upon our understanding of particle physics and spacetime. With the use of these topological methods, research into new quantum space and space-time models can significantly redefine current cosmological theory, opening up further understanding of the very nature of reality itself (Barbosa et al., 2011). The implications of these higher-level topological models extend even beyond theoretic argument; they fundamentally impact experimental physics and our approach to the study of cosmological phenomena. The refinement process of computational models, stimulated by advanced topological knowledge, makes it standard practice to predict and simulate a wide variety of results for particle collider experiments. This synergy of computational power and topological thinking not only refines our predictive powers but also sheds light on experiment design to investigate fundamental questions about the universe. As researchers integrate these techniques, they are destined to uncover new physical laws, a deeper comprehension of cosmic evolution, and contribute significantly to the discussion on fundamental forces. In this fast-evolving setting, the interrelation of innovative topologies and physics becomes the foundation for addressing the sophisticated challenges of contemporary science (Asai et al., 2015) (Figure 3.13).

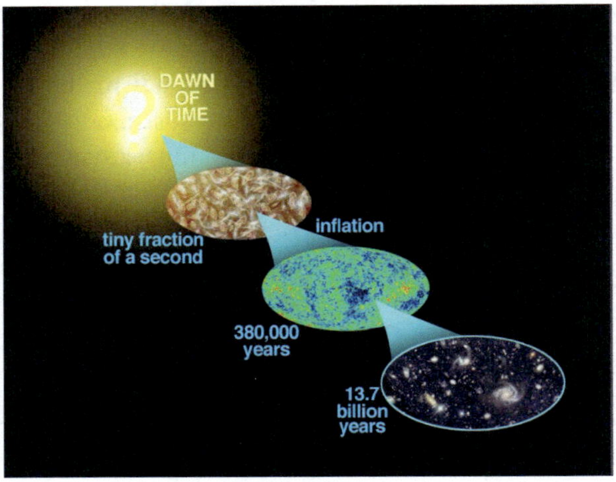

Figure 3.13. *Applications in physics and cosmology.*

Source: https://www.physics.drexel.edu/~vogeley/Cosmology/cosmos.jpg.

3.5.3. Role in Biological Systems and Ecology

The exploration of biological systems through the lens of emerging topologies reveals a multidimensional dialogue between cellular machinery and ecological interactions. At the molecular level, cell interactomics reveals how cells communicate and differentiate to form multicellular organisms. This dynamic signaling is not merely a background mechanism; it embodies the laws of quantum automata, which explain reversible processes akin to regular cell cycling and division. These quantum interactomics findings illustrate the manner in which cells develop by going through metabolic states and multi-stable manifolds to enable organisms to react to environmental stimuli. Understanding these cellular dynamics offers a rich foundation for the research of larger ecological systems because they account for the molecular causes of organismal development, behavior, and interactions in ecosystems, proposing that life is intimately coupled with the principles of complex systems dynamics and therefore offers a rich dimension to ecological research (Baianu et al., 2010). The patterns that emerge in the interactions of cells also carry over into the evolutionary narrative and support a deeper understanding of adaptation and diversity. The investigation of developmental genetics, particularly in the model organism Drosophila, yields analogs in gene regulatory functions among seemingly disparate forms of life, for example, protostomes and deuterostomes. This functional homily concept is a reason to reexamine evolutionary paths and highlights the notion that complex environmental contexts often evolve through the evolution of more simplified ancestral states. These conceptions contradict traditional philosophy of bilateral evolution and urge scientists to consider how these simple genetic patterns influence ecological functions in organisms. The implications are significant, with the determination of simpler ancestor characters having the potential to redefine conservation plans and ecological restoration projects, pointing to the conservation of not just species but also the genetic architectures that uphold diversity (Davidson et al., 2002). At the same time, quantum dynamics' role in cell-cell interactions provides a new perspective on processes like carcinogenesis, where cancer cells exhibit dramatic genomic instability and diversity that depart from normal cell behavior. The dynamics of cancer cell interactomics that can radically shift over generations call for new modeling paradigms to improved understand the mechanisms and plasticity of cancer. As knowledge in quantum interactomics makes evident the principles that govern cell behavior, they have the potential to significantly influence therapy regimens and clinical trial design. This emerging understanding is crucial to the resolution of the problems introduced by cancer resistance to therapy, providing a multi-faceted approach that brings together complex biological processes with advanced modeling techniques. Thus, this nexus of quantum dynamics in cell behavior and ecological significance provides a rich soil for continued investigation, with the major balance of molecular stability and dynamic change in biological processes (Baianu et al., 2010).

3.6. CHALLENGES AND CONTROVERSIES IN TOPOLOGY

The field of topology, while rich in theory and practical application, is not immune from controversy and difficulties. A significant one is that there is conflict between classical topology and newer trends based on more advanced frameworks. Classical topological concepts such as continuity and compactness often clash with emergent paradigms that accommodate non-Euclidean thinking. This tension leads to mathematicians questioning the validity and applicability of traditional principles when confronted with advanced topological structures.

The evolution of mathematics brings about the necessity for revisioning traditional conventions, which makes it essential to embrace the complexity caused by new topologies. Therefore, the controversy regarding the validity of classical rather than contemporary methods is an axis of disagreement in mathematics. Another challenge of topology comes from its interdisciplinary character, particularly in disciplines such as computer science and biology. The molecular clock theory, for instance, refers to the involvement of topological theories with biology in describing the history of development of living organisms, and several controversies regarding evolutionary rate fluctuations and the methods used in dating divergences of species.

Current molecular clock techniques like maximum likelihood and Bayesian approaches reflect the intricate interconnections between different domains because they involve topological information as well as an ability to grasp biological complexity. Such reliance on each other complicates the study of topology even further by introducing involved issues which seek exhaustive and collaborative approaches from different scientific fields. Consequently, the cross-breeding of topology with other disciplines challenges the coherence and consistency of the topological principles when applied outside classical situations and contributes to a broader controversy regarding its future. Finally, the coping with emergent technologies and computational methods is another sophistication level of the discipline of topology.

With growing popularity of computational topology, mathematicians are confronted with the issues created by large data sets as well as the algorithmic encoding of topological entities. The union of topology and computation, with all its potential to enrich scholarship, raises significant issues regarding interpreting data as well as the translatability of topological concepts. Algorithmic accuracy and efficiency problems can lead to ongoing disputes in the mathematics community about the adequacy of traditional topological models when it comes to dealing with real-world issues. As scientists are confronted by such issues, it becomes increasingly important to create robust methodologies that are not only respectful of traditional topological axioms but that also embrace the potential offered by new developments, enabling the further evolution of topology in a constantly changing scientific climate.

3.6.1. Outstanding Problems in Topological Studies

The field of topological research keeps expanding in richness with problems that pose new solutions, particularly when automated manufacturing processes are at stake. One significant open problem concern planning extrusion sequences and robot movement for trusses possessing unconstrained topologies. Current procedures are not capable of automating these processes efficiently, as exemplified in the stringent definition of the extrusion sequence and motion planning (SAMP) problem. A research paper has proposed a novel hierarchical planning framework that addresses the complexity of 3D configurations in architectural-scale trusses. By decoupling sequence planning from motion planning, it attempts to offer efficient solutions to various constituents such as end-effector poses and joint configurations. Resolution of these problems advances robotic design, as well as profoundly influencing the future of bespoke architectural design and materials science, emphasizing a strong confluence between topology and actual application (Garrett et al., 2019). Enhanced topological understanding is also key to optimizing energy storage systems, especially in how it applies to renewable energy integration. One such intriguing open question exists in the domain of Vanadium Redox Flow Batteries (VRFBs), which are being highly interrogated for their suitability in smart grids. The complexity of their architecture and performance properties is an extant rich domain for exploration via topological lenses. Studies have indicated that VRFBs possess several strengths, including scalability and longevity in terms of energy, with significant shortcomings that work against their mass commercial adoption. The study of these characteristics from a topological point of view can bring new insight into the design and effectiveness of such systems. The resolution of these outstanding issues might thus facilitate innovation not only in the energy storage technology but also be amenable to the broader objective of integrating more sustainable processes into electrical grids (Guarnieri et al., 2016). The intersection of topology and robotics and energy systems is a potential for thrilling innovation. Both fields are confronted with open issues that go beyond traditional mathematical environments, which require interdisciplinary solutions. The problem of SAMP in robotic extrusion, for instance, presents challenges not only computational but also requiring very deep understanding of spatial relations and structural stability, which are topological concepts per se. Similarly, the development of VRFB technologies can benefit significantly from advances in topological analysis, particularly as they relate to the requirements and conditions of actual instances. As scientists move forward to meet these challenges, the potential for breakthroughs that enable both theoretical and applied applications grows increasingly likely. Thus, exploring such open issues can not only advance specific disciplines but also elevate the discourse on complex topologies and their possibilities for transformation in society (Figure 3.14).

Figure 3.14. *The realm of topological research is increasingly rich with challenges that beckon for innovative solutions.*

Source: https://www.quantamagazine.org/wp-content/uploads/2021/10/Spheres_2880x1620_Lede.jpg.

3.6.2. Debates on the Foundations of Topology

Within mathematics, topology is a core subject that is entwined with many controversies regarding its theoretical foundations and ramifications. At the center of controversies are point-set topology and algebraic topology, both with distinct methods of dealing with continuity, compactness, and convergence. This bifurcation has also instigated debate regarding the philosophical importance of topology, with researchers struggling with whether topology prioritizes the abstract character of space or the tangible character evident in math objects. This critical examination of such variations not merely illuminates mathematics but also raises interdisciplinary questions concerning how topology intersects with physical science and computer science, where its ideas have diverse uses. As the field of study continues to progress, knowing about these early controversies is at the heart of forming theoretical and practical topological notions within modern research frameworks. Equally important is the history of the development of topological thinking, particularly how the participants of the early stages left the reader prepared for methodology today. Mathematicians such as Henri Poincaré and Felix Klein were instrumental in creating the fundamental principles of topology, often struggling with notions of dimension and spatial arrangement. Their research precipitated a reconsideration of preconceptions regarding mathematical objects, countering norms and inviting an intellectual mobility akin to today's debates in psychosocial studies. The conflation of internal and external views in topology, balancing personal experience against societal invention, mirrors arguments in psychosocial fields questioning the distinctions between the self and the other (TW et al., 2015). This historicized viewpoint provides contemporary mathematicians and scientists with a deeper understanding of the relevance of their work, broadening the conversation on bleeding-edge and emerging topologies. Scholarship in recent decades has further complicated these questions by introducing concepts from other intellectual groups, foreshadowing a shift towards a more transdisciplinary framework for understanding topology. By exploring topology from multiple vantage points, researchers engage with complex issues in urban studies and political economy, recognizing how spatial processes create social realities. For example, local analyses of urbanization demonstrate how topology does account for our comprehension of socio-spatial relations and thereby erases boundary lines between traditional urban and suburban environments (Addie et al., 2016). As the field matures, the integration of disparate theoretical models opens richer understanding of topology's origin, encouraging ongoing exploration of the tension between mathematical abstraction and real-world application. Within these disputes, contemporary topology not only relocates its presumptions but elevates its responsiveness to addressing multi-faceted challenges to an increasingly more networked, increasingly more intricate world.

3.6.3. Ethical Considerations in Topological Applications

In the field of topological utilization, moral concerns are increasingly significant, especially with evolving technology leading to more and more complex interrelated systems. For instance, in wireless sensor networks, efficient versus secure becomes a significant consideration. Such networks, typically powered by finite energy sources, can be penalized by security measures like encryption and authentication if the balance between these variables and power consumption is not found. Research has highlighted that the absence of strong security makes sensors susceptible to attacks such as denial of sleep, which significantly reduces their operational lifespan. Thus, ethical use of such networks requires critical analysis of energy efficiency and security measures so that technological advancement does not unintentionally generate increased vulnerabilities or operational failures, as highlighted in energy-aware protocols (Udoh et al., 2019). Expanding even more into future technologies, the ethical challenge of integrating autonomous systems into defense and law enforcement planning is especially pertinent. The deployment of lethal autonomous weapons raises a challenge that blurs operational effectiveness with ethical accountability. The requirement for the systems stems from the increasing heterogeneity of hybrid threats facing security forces with both criminal and military components. However, the ethical issues in employing machines that can make life-and-death choices need to be examined seriously. It is essential that these systems are empirically based so as to fulfill legal requirements as well as gain the confidence of people. As pointed out in the Westgate Terrorist Attack forums, the implications of using hybrid-capability weapons underscore the importance of ethical principles in creating autonomous capabilities for genuine security objectives (Nyagudi et al., 2013). Additionally, the interfacing of topological applications with ethics usually calls for consideration of implications to privacy and data protection in the age of global connectivity. With advancing technology, the ability to keep and process huge amounts of data becomes more important, and it creates ethical issues related to consent and ownership of personal data. Optimization and methods that improve connectivity in topological science can inadvertently lead to surveillance and privacy loss if not properly regulated. It is thus crucial to have an ethical framework focusing on user consent and data security to establish trust in these systems. The stakeholders need to consider not just technological advantages associated with topologies, but also the potential social implications on conventions and individual rights. The present discourse of such issues is appropriate for ethical technology design for use in the upcoming topological applications.

SUMMARY

In Conclusion, the research on new and advanced topologies proves the major role played in improving network performance and efficiency across various applications. With evolving technology, the increasing demand for precise time synchronization, particularly in smart grid deployments, proves the necessity for new solutions. Conventionally used protocols like the Network Time Protocol (NTP) typically do not satisfy the demanding requirements of accuracy for current applications, with their tolerance often being only 1 millisecond for key components of the critical infrastructure like Phasor Measurement Units (PMUs). The concept of clock synchronization using gossip algorithms is a notable development, resolving issues of dense networking and poor bandwidth, while having strong guarantees of time synchronization among the network elements. These achievements highlight the need to develop future network structures to meet contemporary needs, demonstrating that continued research is crucial to fostering technological potential for real-time applications (Khandaker et al., 2017). Moreover, the evolution of Industrial Wireless Sensor and Actuator Networks (IWSAN) represents the revolutionary potential of wireless technologies within the industrial landscape, particularly signifying the era of Industry 4.0. The implementation of wireless actuators and sensors encourages record levels of interconnectivity, enabling synchronizations across a number of processes—stretching from manufacturing stages through asset tracking and coordination of mobile robots. To this end, however, adoption of the same technologies calls for a keen comprehension of their compromise and constraints on performance. Evaluation of the diverse capabilities of current wireless solutions allows engineers to select the most appropriate technology for their specific application, thereby optimizing deployment and managing infrastructure expense. This fundamental wireless technology evaluation further highlights that success with integration hinges on aligning network topologies to industrial applications, allowing flexibility to drive innovation (Poorter et al., 2020). Finally, the future of network design lies in mastering and implementing high-level topologies that cater to dynamic and heterogeneous applications. As industries continue towards integrated systems, the significance of selecting elastic, scalable networks cannot be overestimated. The findings and innovation covered in this essay indicate the necessity for continuous enhancements in topological designs, particularly in designing synchronization mechanisms which are crucial for real-time operational efficiency. Future breakthroughs in wireless communication and smart grid technologies will necessitate re-examination of present topologies, stimulating innovation in performance and connectivity. Prioritizing research and development guarantees stakeholders address not only current needs but also future issues, reaffirming their commitment to establishing a responsive and resilient network infrastructure.

The topic of advanced and emerging topologies is very extensive and encompasses a plethora of systems that are becoming more and more defined by their decentralized characteristics. Such systems are characterized by multiple authorities controlling various components, which enhances privacy and fault tolerance. Decentralization of authority also comes with challenges, particularly where balance is to be achieved between complexity and functionality. Designers must balance among different system design components carefully so that decentralization advantages such as improved integrity and availability are gained without excessively introducing complexity. This necessitates a solid background in cryptography, distributed systems, and mechanism design to create scalable privacy-preserving systems capable of adapting to the evolving need for technology. The decentralization implications reach far beyond visual architectural design; it also calls for a strategic perspective on privacy and security in the applications of today (Danezis et al., 2017). New topologies are also taking a great impact on the future of architectural construction and fabrication methodologies. Robotic extrusion of space, for instance, has entirely redefined design and construction of intricate structures, particularly in the matter of 3D trusses. But the challenge of automatically planning the extrusion sequence and robot motion for structures with unconstrained topologies has become increasingly apparent. Work on this subject has created a full framework that robustly models the sequence and motion planning (SAMP) problem. Utilizing a Constraint Satisfaction Problem (CSP) formulation, the framework allows effective planning by isolating sequence and motion so that it makes it easier to generate complicated structures while minimizing runtime bottlenecks. This innovation not only offers computational benefits but also serves as a baseline model for future algorithmic innovation within the discipline (Garrett et al., 2019). Briefly, it is apparent that decentralized systems and advanced fabrication methods like robotic spatial extrusion are at the forefront in terms of architectural and technological advancement. The overlap of decentralized design philosophies and new fabrication techniques mirrors the need for innovative solutions to complex system control. While scientists and practitioners develop new approaches, integrating information from a variety of fields will be an integral part in addressing unique challenges presented by these next-generation topologies. The ongoing examination of these interconnected subjects will undoubtedly bring about a greater acknowledgment of how to effectively face the difficulties and opportunities that arise at the intersection of technology and design, towards more resilient, adaptable buildings in contemporary and future design work.

REFERENCES

1. Abadal Cavallé, S., Alarcón Cot, E. J., Cabellos Aparicio, A., González Colás, J., et al. (2016). Scalability of broadcast performance in wireless network-on-chip. https://core.ac.uk/download/81578757.pdf (accessed on 9th September 2025).
2. Abhari, A. J., Alderete, C. H., Linke, N. M., Martonosi, M., et al. (2019). Full-stack, real-system quantum computer studies: Architectural comparisons and design insights. http://arxiv.org/abs/1905.11349 (accessed on 9th September 2025).
3. Addie, J. D., & Keil, R. (2016). 'It's not going to be suburban; it's going to be all urban': Assembling post-suburbia in the Toronto and Chicago regions. https://core.ac.uk/download/79498194.pdf (accessed on 9th September 2025).
4. Adorno, T. W., Adorno, T. W., Arlow, J. A., Benjamin, J., Benjamin, J., Benjamin, J., Bhabha, H., et al. (2015). Temporal drag: Trans disciplinarity and the 'case' of psychosocial studies. https://core.ac.uk/download/42136007.pdf (accessed on 9th September 2025).
5. Alahi, M. E. E., Sukkuea, A., Tina, F. W., Nag, A., Kurdthongmee, W., Suwannarat, K., & Mukhopadhyay, S. C. (2023). Integration of IoT-enabled technologies and artificial intelligence (AI) for smart city scenario: Recent advancements and future trends. *Sensors, 23*, 5206–5206. https://doi.org/10.3390/s23115206 (accessed on 9th September 2025).
6. Andjelkovic, M., Suvakov, M., & Tadic, B. (2017). Hidden geometries in networks arising from cooperative self-assembly. https://core.ac.uk/download/pdf/197924216.pdf (accessed on 9th September 2025).
7. Asai, M., Bauerdick, L., Borgland, A., Calafiura, A., et al. (2015). High energy physics forum for computational excellence: Working group reports (I. Applications software II. Software libraries and tools III. Systems). http://arxiv.org/abs/1510.08545 (accessed on 9th September 2025).
8. Aslam, N., Cao, Y., Hussain, S., Khan, I., et al. (2018). A critical analysis of research potential, challenges and future directives in industrial wireless sensor networks. https://core.ac.uk/download/96885354.pdf (accessed on 9th September 2025).
9. Baianu, I. C., & Glazebrook, J. F. (2010). Categorical ontology of complex systems, meta-systems and theory of levels: The emergence of life, human consciousness and society. https://core.ac.uk/download/pdf/332869.pdf (accessed on 9th September 2025).

10. Baldin, I., Deelman, E., Griffioen, J., Lehman, B., et al. (2019). FABRIC: A national-scale programmable experimental network infrastructure. https://core.ac.uk/download/322493913.pdf (accessed on 9th September 2025).
11. Barbosa, R. S., & Doering, A. (2011). Unsharp values, domains and topoi. http://arxiv.org/abs/1107.1083 (accessed on 9th September 2025).
12. Barragán Villarejo, M., Demoulias, C., Gómez Expósito, A., Mauricio Ferramola, R., et al. (2019). Ancillary services in hybrid AC/DC low voltage distribution networks. https://core.ac.uk/download/288002607.pdf (accessed on 9th September 2025).
13. Bharti, K., Cervera-Lierta, A., Kyaw, T. H., Haug, T., Alperin-Lea, S., Anand, A., Degroote, M., et al. (2022). Noisy intermediate-scale quantum algorithms. *Reviews of Modern Physics, 94*. https://doi.org/10.1103/revmodphys.94.015004 (accessed on 9th September 2025).
14. Blakey-Milner, B., Gradl, P., Snedden, G., Brooks, M. J., Pitot, J., López, E., Leary, M., et al. (2021). Metal additive manufacturing in aerospace: A review. *Materials & Design, 209*, 110008–110008. https://doi.org/10.1016/j.matdes.2021.110008 (accessed on 9th September 2025).
15. Breunig, M., Bradley, P. E., Jahn, M., Kuper, P. V., Mazroob, N., Rösch, N., Al-Doori, M., et al. (2020). Geospatial data management research: Progress and future directions. *ISPRS International Journal of Geo-Information, 9*, 95–95. https://doi.org/10.3390/ijgi9020095 (accessed on 9th September 2025).
16. Cao, J., Fang, J., Meng, Z., & Liang, S. (2024). Knowledge graph embedding: A survey from the perspective of representation spaces. *ACM Computing Surveys, 56*, 1–42. https://doi.org/10.1145/3643806 (accessed on 9th September 2025).
17. Collado Escolano, A., Gálvez, E., Lumbreras Carrasco, D., Mon González, M., et al. (2019). Efficiency analysis of wide band-gap semiconductors for two-level and three-level power converters. https://core.ac.uk/download/286456302.pdf (accessed on 9th September 2025).
18. Conti, M., Das, S. K., Silvestri, S., Sturaro, A., et al. (2015). Towards a realistic model for failure propagation in interdependent networks. http://arxiv.org/abs/1510.08380 (accessed on 9th September 2025).
19. Creutz, M. (2022). *Quarks, Gluons and Lattices*. https://doi.org/10.1017/9781009290395 (accessed on 9th September 2025).
20. Danezis, G., Halpin, H., Isaakidis, M., Troncoso, C., et al. (2017). Systematizing decentralization and privacy: Lessons from 15 years of research and deployments. https://core.ac.uk/download/141515178.pdf (accessed on 9th September 2025).

21. Davidson, E. H., & Erwin, D. H. (2002). The last common bilaterian ancestor. https://core.ac.uk/download/4879593.pdf (accessed on 9th September 2025).

22. De Poorter, E., Famaey, J., Hoebeke, J., Seferagić, A., et al. (2020). Survey on wireless technology trade-offs for the industrial internet of things. https://core.ac.uk/download/299792107.pdf (accessed on 9th September 2025).

23. Dokshitzer, Y., Field, R. D., Green, M. B., Shifman, M., Peloso, M., Shifman, M., & Shifman, M. (2006). Persistent challenges of quantum chromodynamics. https://core.ac.uk/download/44114781.pdf (accessed on 9th September 2025).

24 Feller, F., Gunreben, S., Kohn, M., Mifdaoui, A., et al. (2010). Ethernet–A survey on its fields of application. https://core.ac.uk/download/12040594.pdf (accessed on 9th September 2025).

25. García Franquelo, L., Kouro, S., León Galván, J. I., Martín Prats, M. A., et al. (2009). Multilevel converters: An enabling technology for high-power applications. https://core.ac.uk/download/286564367.pdf (accessed on 9th September 2025).

26. Garrett, C. R., Huang, Y., & Mueller, C. T. (2019). Automated sequence and motion planning for robotic spatial extrusion of 3D trusses. http://arxiv.org/abs/1810.00998 (accessed on 9th September 2025).

27. Gattozzi, A., Herbst, J. D., Ouroua, A., Pratap, S., et al. (2025). Rotating machine technologies for integration of pulsed and high-power loads in naval electric power systems. https://core.ac.uk/download/211340371.pdf (accessed on 9th September 2025).

28. Guarnieri, M., Mattavelli, P., Petrone, G., Spagnuolo, G., et al. (2016). Vanadium redox flow batteries: Potentials and challenges of an emerging storage technology. https://core.ac.uk/download/80155277.pdf (accessed on 9th September 2025).

29. Helou, M., & Kara, S. (2017). Design, analysis and manufacturing of lattice structures: An overview. *International Journal of Computer Integrated Manufacturing, 31*, 243–261. https://doi.org/10.1080/0951192x.2017.1407456 (accessed on 9th September 2025).

30. Kahle, M. (2013). Topology of random simplicial complexes: A survey. http://arxiv.org/abs/1301.7165 (accessed on 9th September 2025).

31. Khandaker, M. A., Parvez, I., Parvez, Z., Pinto, R., et al. (2017). A gossip algorithm-based clock synchronization scheme for smart grid applications. http://arxiv.org/abs/1707.08216 (accessed on 9th September 2025).

32. Linde, A., Linde, A., Linde, A., Linde, A., Linde, A., Vilenkin, A., Vilenkin, A., et al. (1998). Instantons and unitarity in quantum cosmology with fixed four-volume. https://core.ac.uk/download/25240092.pdf (accessed on 9th September 2025).

33. Liu, J., & Ren, Y. (2018). Liquid metal enabled droplet circuits. http://arxiv.org/abs/1803.10511 (accessed on 9th September 2025).

34. Luecken, M. D., & Theis, F. J. (2019). Current best practices in single-cell RNA-seq analysis: A tutorial. *Molecular Systems Biology, 15*. https://doi.org/10.15252/msb.20188746 (accessed on 9th September 2025).

35. Mao, Y., You, C., Zhang, J., Huang, K., & Letaief, K. B. (2017). A survey on mobile edge computing: The communication perspective. *IEEE Communications Surveys & Tutorials, 19*, 2322–2358. https://doi.org/10.1109/comst.2017.2745201 (accessed on 9th September 2025).

36. Marres, N. (2025). On some uses and abuses of topology in the social analysis of technology (or the problem with smart meters). https://core.ac.uk/download/9656943.pdf (accessed on 9th September 2025).

37. Mehta, D., Molzahn, D. K., & Turitsyn, K. (2015). Recent advances in computational methods for the power flow equations. https://core.ac.uk/download/83233595.pdf (accessed on 9th September 2025).

38. Mei, S., Quax, R., Sloot, P. M. A., Wang, H., et al. (2009). Complex agent networks explaining the HIV epidemic among homosexual men in Amsterdam. http://arxiv.org/abs/0812.1155 (accessed on 9th September 2025).

39. N/A. (2017). *SciTech News, 71*(2). https://core.ac.uk/download/83050022.pdf (accessed on 9th September 2025).

40. Nakano, K., & Tirelli, A. (2022). Topological data analysis for revealing structural origin of density anomalies in silica glass. http://arxiv.org/abs/2208.06378 (accessed on 9th September 2025).

41. Nyagudi, N. M. (2013). Post-Westgate SWAT: C4ISTAR architectural framework for autonomous network integrated multifaceted warfighting solutions version 1.0: A peer-reviewed monograph. http://arxiv.org/abs/1401.6379 (accessed on 9th September 2025).

42. Oxman, R. (2010). Digital tectonics as a morphogenetic process. http://hdl.handle.net/10251/6959 (accessed on 9th September 2025).

43. Pfender, J., Seah, W. K. G., & Valera, A. (2019). Content delivery latency of caching strategies for information-centric IoT. http://arxiv.org/abs/1905.01011 (accessed on 9th September 2025).

44. Pujol, F. (2025). Regulatory and policy implications of emerging technologies to spectrum management. https://core.ac.uk/download/pdf/7304707.pdf (accessed on 9th September 2025).
45. Rannala, B., & Yang, Z. (2013). Molecular clock dating. https://core.ac.uk/download/79498072.pdf (accessed on 9th September 2025).
46. Rejzner, K. (2011). Fermionic fields in the functional approach to classical field theory. http://arxiv.org/abs/1101.5126 (accessed on 9th September 2025).
47. Rocha, I. (2024). Persistent homology generalizations for social media network analysis. http://arxiv.org/abs/2404.19257 (accessed on 9th September 2025).
48. Saveliev, D. I. (2018). Hindman's finite sums theorem and its application to topologizations of algebras. http://arxiv.org/abs/1810.01947 (accessed on 9th September 2025).
49. Shamir, A., Ek, B., Alcaraz, C., Alcaraz, C., Lin, C. T., Lee, C. Y., Dijkstra, E. W., et al. (2017). Preventing advanced persistent threats in complex control networks. https://core.ac.uk/download/214842241.pdf (accessed on 9th September 2025).
50. Skowron, B., & Wójtowicz, K. (2020). Throwing spatial light: On topological explanations in Gestalt psychology. *Phenomenology and the Cognitive Sciences, 20*, 537–558. https://doi.org/10.1007/s11097-020-09691-1 (accessed on 9th September 2025).
51. Udoh, E., & Udoh, E. (2019). An energy aware and secure MAC protocol for tackling denial of sleep attacks in wireless sensor networks. https://core.ac.uk/download/305119264.pdf (accessed on 9th September 2025).

CHAPTER 4

TOPOLOGY DESIGN PRINCIPLES AND CONSTRAINTS

Contents

INTRODUCTION

The topology design principles and constraints are the realm of the foundational building blocks that govern the evolution and optimality of complex systems. Topology in network and engineering design is the configuration of various elements and interactions. As designers and engineers look for creative solutions, understanding principles of successful topology becomes essential. This observation not only allows for the design of efficient systems but also accommodates the limitations set by physical reality, technology, and computational power. Through the recognition of these two aspects, practitioners can better handle the nuances of design processes and engineer functional yet efficient solutions. The notion of controlling geometrical contradictions in design is to highlight the importance of topology in promoting novel problem-solving paradigms in engineering applications and thereby making it a vital area of study. In modern-day fields of engineering, uniting theoretical aspects with practical needs is the cornerstone of efficient topology design. As is clear from the recent advancements in optimization systems, the use of Computer-Aided Innovation (CAI) and Product Lifecycle Management (PLM) presents a robust method to solve design conflicts. Through the usage of these pairings, methods are developed to manage density distributions, thus allowing designers to solve geometrical conflicts with ease (Cascini et al., 2009). Such conflict resolution capacity not only aids the optimization of particular design activities but also affects system performance overall. Thus, the relationship between design constraints and guidelines is two-pronged: it acts both as a guideline and as a foundation through which engineers can design while keeping in mind the realities they're designing for. Additionally, how critical it is to understand physical infrastructure in topology design cannot be overstressed. Through approaches that integrate theoretical modeling and empirical observation, one derives invaluable insights into designing systems, particularly for network architecture. The representation of physical connectivity as an annotated graph highlights the manner in which raw connectivity and bandwidth are provided under realistic constraints (Alderson et al., 2005). With data from suitable projects, such as from Abilene and the Rocket fuel project, it has been demonstrated how this analytical approach is able to identify latent patterns and problems in network architectures. The ability of such methods to accommodate other design objectives, such as enhancing system resilience, is a testament to the extreme significance of a thorough examination of topology design guidelines in a period of increased technological complexity.

Definition of Topology Design

Topology design is of importance to the development and optimization of network topologies, which form the backbone of communication and data processing in most industries. By simple definition, topology design is the configuration of a network's components, like nodes, links, and their interconnectivity, to adequately meet some operational demands and constraints. This topology has a significant effect on the reliability and performance of a system since it decides how data travels and how resources are allocated. If spatial and logical topologies are both considered, then topology design covers a number of factors such as scalability, fault tolerance, and latency. By creating appropriate models, network architects strive to create systems not only working but that are responsive to evolving technological contexts and user aspirations, something comparable to the adaptive behaviors that develop in biological systems, as posited by research into Digital Ecosystems (Briscoe et al., 2011). In addition, the analytical topology design model goes from static configurations to encompass dynamic relationships and adaptive mechanisms. This involves determining the need for self-organizing and adaptive networks, consistent with the ecological rules which apply to the development of Digital Ecosystems.

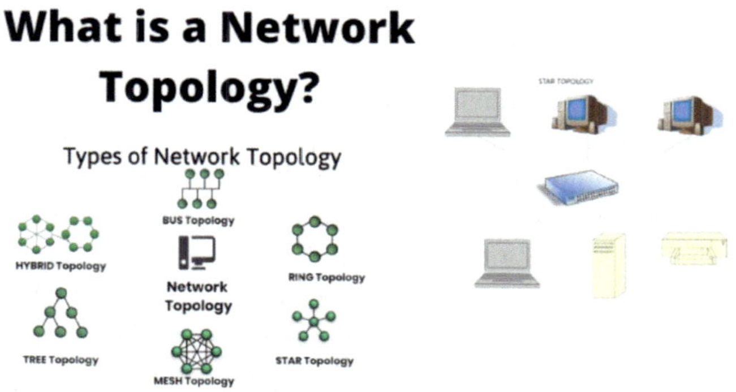

Figure 4.1. *Topology design plays a crucial role in the establishment and optimization of network structures.*

Source: https://www.electrical4u.com/wp-content/uploads/What-is-a-Network-Topology.png.

These allow for ongoing optimization of network structure through local and global interactions between nodes in order to enhance overall system responsiveness and efficiency. For instance, within such networks, agents can be transferred and reconfigured in real-time to adapt to change, better manage resources, and enhance the capability to process data. The adoption of peer-to-peer network frameworks further depicts this refinement, whereby groups of nodes function and interact in an effective manner to solve domain-specific problems. Thus, topology design is not only an infrastructure building block of network structure but also a facilitator of innovation and adaptability in digital communication spaces (Benatallah et al., 2005). Lastly, topology design concepts function to influence the application of theoretical concepts in practical environments. With the explicit identification of constraints and objectives of a network, topological design techniques can be used by designers to make systems adapt to individual users' requirements while retaining resiliency against disruptions. These principles steer the processes under which data integration and interactions among communities are constructed, eventually towards more productive and efficient peer networks. Continuous monitoring and feedback mechanisms also enable re-alignment and re-evaluation of network designs so that they remain relevant and operational with the passage of time. With the continuous evolution of the art of topology design, its integration with concepts borrowed from ecosystem systems will increasingly play a crucial role in creating dynamic, adaptive, and sustainable network designs that can ride through the relentless flux of digital ecosystems (Figure 4.1).

Importance in Network Architecture

In network design, it is essential to realize the interaction of the topology principles and constraints to come up with sound communication systems. The level of complexity in modern networks, fueled by their multi-dimensional interdependencies and interactions, requires a rigorous approach to their design and implementation. With increasingly advanced systems, the proper selection of architectural frameworks becomes increasingly vital in order to guarantee robustness and flexibility. Also, the issues brought by very advanced technological infrastructures point out the theory of "robust but fragile" trade-offs; while complexity can enhance how the system works, it can also bring about weaknesses that must be taken care of in good ways. This dualism reflects the necessity to integrate an organized method that harmonizes both the network architecture requirements and constraints and assisting systems to stay resilient to unexpected challenges while being able to sustain their functionality in varying environments (Alderson et al., 2010). Topology design is cornerstones in the construction of efficient network architectures. They establish strategic node and link placement and play a direct role in system performance, reliability, and scalability. Through examination of various topologies, such as star, mesh, and tree-based topologies, designers are able to ascertain the implications of each structure on data transmission and fault tolerance. These decisions are not only motivated by theoretical models but are also informed by empirical evidence collected from real-world implementations. Recent studies illustrate that the majority of characteristics of the Internet that are generally attributed to self-organization stem from deliberate design choices supporting the operation and resilience of the networks (Alderson et al., 2005). As such, a deeper understanding of principles of topological design is invaluable in designing networks responsive to current and future requirements, ensuring longevity and adaptability. Moreover, the constraints that network architects are working with cannot be ignored, since they as well influence the behavior and functionality of the network. These constraints can be of technological, regulatory, or financial origin, each of which impacts the choice of topology as well as overall architecture. To deal with the complex environment is to be acutely aware of how such constraints are capable of directing design choices, forcing the architect into balancing some characteristics over others. To this end, finding a balance between innovation and practical constraints in this regard is essential. At the end of the day, the value of creating good network designs is that they can accommodate both the design principles and the pragmatic constraints in which they find themselves, thus enabling the building of robust, flexible infrastructures well positioned to cope with the needs of an increasingly dynamic digital environment (Alderson et al., 2010).

Overview of Principles and Constraints

The design of topology for the majority of networks is inherently influenced by a sequence of principles that promote efficiency and performance. Such principles are optimization characteristics that involve minimizing resource utilization while providing connectivity. In communication networks, for example, topology control algorithms are crucial in ensuring that the structure supports the dynamic nature of network nodes and their interactions. With the networks dynamically being altered by node additions, deletions, or migrations, the algorithms must learn to incrementally adapt to such advancements. Consistency takes precedence; the designers must hence ensure that any topology change does not compromise its connectivity or overall functionality. It is thus through these that one achieves maximum output as well as constructs solidity in the ever-changing tech landscape (Hollick et al., 2017). Other than fundamental principles, constraints also play a vital role in designing topology. Constraints can be either based on performance parameters, like bandwidth limits or delay limits, or physical constraints related to the environment where the network operates. Whether one is dealing with electric power transmission systems or with communication networks, the design must collaborate with these constraints cleverly in order to come up with a practicable and efficient topology. For instance, use of a decision support system in electrical transmission power demonstrates how constraints affect design choices and define how engineers design and deploy their systems. The choice-making process is significantly facilitated by methods that are within the constraints without sacrificing in finding optimal design solutions (Duffy et al., 2001). Further, integrating advanced methods that combine principles and constraints is essential in efficient topology design. For instance, visual programming and specification languages offer a stable platform for specifying both structural elements and the required consistency properties of complex topologies. This approach can facilitate the construction of incrementally controlled topology algorithms to enable practitioners to specify and control consistency and optimization features in a dynamic manner. In realistic applications, such as re-engineering well-accepted algorithms, this balance of principles and constraints is critical. The ability to generate advanced graph transformation rules that meet these demands highly impacts reliability and effectiveness of network operations, and thus underscores the importance of strategic design in applications (Hollick et al., 2017).

4.1. FUNDAMENTAL PRINCIPLES OF TOPOLOGY DESIGN

It is most crucial to know the physical infrastructure and constraint in the topological design space. The simplest approach of examining connectivity as an annotated graph is one of the key principles of modern network design. Through this way, network planners can get a hold of how raw connectivity interacts with bandwidth and other higher-layer requirements of the TCP/IP protocol suite. The empirical results from tests such as Abilene and Rocket fuel reflect the usefulness of such a graph-based perspective, providing router-level variation insights. Also, this perspective enables the inclusion of design objectives, such as common router-failure robustness improvements. Hence, a complete comprehension of statistics and graph theory is required in order to address both structural and operational problems of existing networking scenarios, thus forming the basis of effective topology design (Alderson et al., 2005). Another vital principle of topology design is that of recognizing the inherent trade-offs between complexity and robustness. Maximally evolved systems, whether biological or technological, must balance supplying high connectivity with how to deal with potential fragilities of complexity. These forces working together become evident when considering network-centric technology, where architecture will dictate a system's overall reliability. Recent developments in distributed control theory show how network technologies can reduce such challenges, postulating that robust and vulnerable systems have to be designed considering both characteristics. This concept compels engineers and designers to perpetually work between the robust and fragile duality, hence the need to build topologies that will be resilient against operational stresses yet also responsive to uncertainties (Alderson et al., 2010). Lastly, the incorporation of design constraints also establishes the landscape of topology design. Constraints aren't just formed by physical problems, such as hardware capability and economics, but regulatory and environmental factors that must be taken into consideration in any network deployment. Topology design must address these various constraints to create systems not only that function but also that can survive. The challenge facing designers is to create imaginative solutions that respect these limitations yet retain scope to push the boundaries of what is technologically feasible. In looking at all constraints holistically through a systems approach, topology designers can foster not only optimal but resilient systems, setting the stage for innovation in network structure and connectivity as a whole in the future (Alderson et al., 2005) (Figure 4.2).

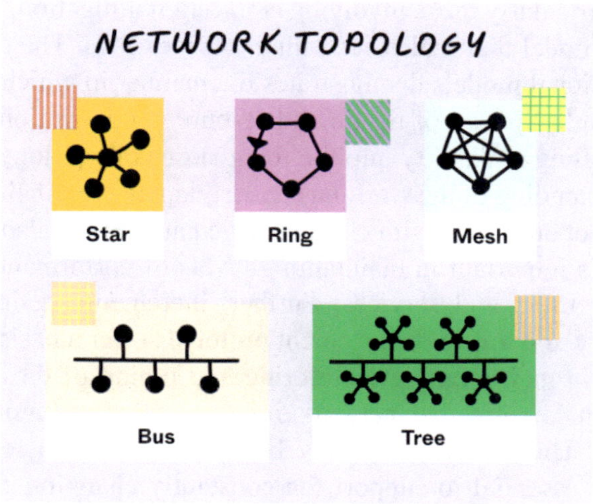

Figure 4.2. *Fundamental principles of topology design.*

Source: https://cdn.sanity.io/images/599r6htc/regionalized/79f4f39c79671f2f882b7039cbccc0d562f40b41-1440x1212.png?w=1440&h=1212&q=75&fit=max&auto=format.

4.1.1. Scalability

The scalability principle of design is most critical in topology design since it is one of the most basic rules that dictate how well a network may grow and adapt to increasing demands. A well-designed topology needs to be able to handle incremental growth as well as periodic usage spikes without penalizing too much on performance. Scalability not only impacts the physical structure of network devices but also the technologies and protocols employed. When scalability is being considered, service discovery in the context of distributed systems becomes something that must be taken into account. In learning how service discovery acts as a third-generation naming system, designers are able to more effectively plan scalable solutions. This step enhances operational qualities of network performance so that the system can be kept sound when additional services and endpoints are added (Hartel et al., 2007). Moreover, the advent of Software-Defined Networking (SDN) has revolutionized scalability processing in network topologies. Due to its dynamic nature, SDN provides the capability to dynamically allocate resources and routes, thus enhancing the scalability of a network significantly. By segregating SDN protocols into distinct interfaces, it is possible for designers to utilize these protocols strategically to tackle traffic and congestion—a capability crucial to scalability. Traffic engineering applications, particularly those involving congestion mitigation, are maximized by an adaptive model that scales according to user needs. The convergence of SDN with traditional models demonstrates the manner in which contemporary practice is scalable by way of traffic and resource optimization (Burgo et al., 2017). Incorporating scalability into the foundations of topology design entails profound understanding of the workings underlying network behavior. An ideal topology must not only cope with current usage patterns but also explore future demands. This is important in maintaining levels of performance as networks expand in both users and services. Further, incremental gains achieved in service discovery and traffic management protocols offer a basis for scalability enhancement. Through ongoing monitoring and tuning of these components, designers can make sure that network infrastructures are agile and able to support growth. Ultimately, scalability being prioritized in topology design fundamentals is essential to support the constantly changing environment of network technologies and needs (Figure 4.3).

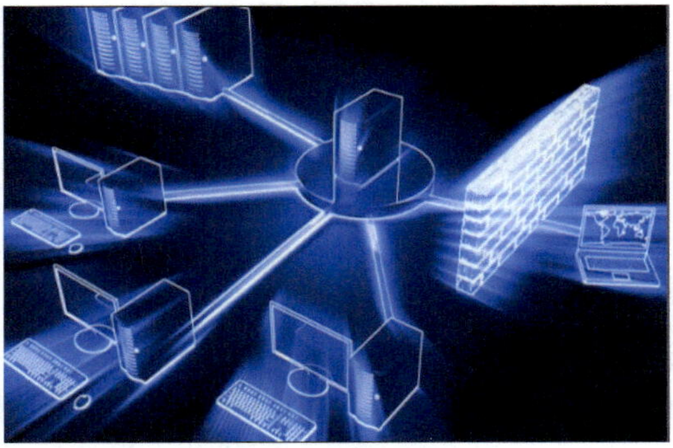

Figure 4.3. *The concept of scalability.*

Source: https://images.squarespace-cdn.com/content/v1/54c2b1afe4b0688a881a6e01/d5dfc804-962c-49b4-b55b-4967e8ddaf4e/Why+network+scalability+is+important+for+your+SME.jpg.

4.1.2. Redundancy

Redundancy is an important aspect of principles of topology design that influences both complex system reliability and robustness. In engineering and technology, redundancy can be revealed through the availability of duplicate components or routes that ensure continued operation in the event of failure. This preventive action is not the sole buffer against potential malfunctions; rather, it permits adaptive solutions to unforeseen adversity in system environments. Thus, redundancy enhances system robustness, allowing organizations to maintain functional continuity while optimizing performance in varying circumstances. On scrutiny of these frameworks in topological terms, redundancy can easily be seen as being compatible with functional efficiency and structural integrity as well since redundancy shields against threats of single points of failure and promotes incentives for innovation in design. The concept of redundancy extends beyond duplication to encompass the subtle notion of degenerate systems, which are characterized by partial redundancy rather than complete duplication of elements. Such systems possess a unique capability for innovation and flexibility, demonstrating that topology design principles can lead to evolutionary outcomes.

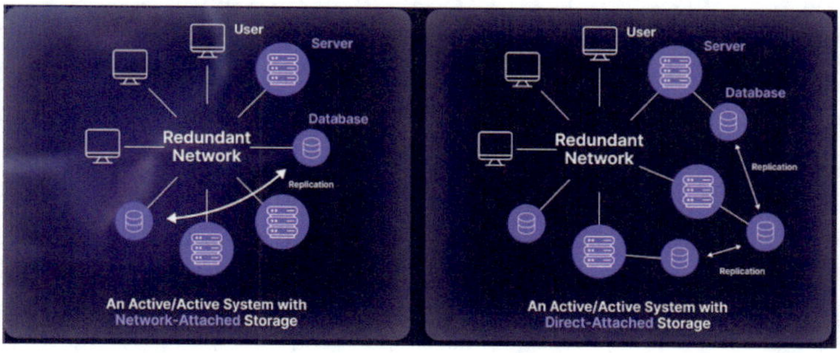

Figure 4.4. *Redundancy.*

Source: https://www.emnify.com/hs-fs/hubfs/Image-network-redundancy-2_1x.webp?width=881&height=443&name=Image-network-redundancy-2_1x.webp.

Redundant systems, as exclusively redundant, actually turn out to be restrictive to evolvability, while degenerate systems are likely to result in increased evolutionary flexibility. This is largely due to the fact that degeneracy allows for multiple functional outcomes under fixed conditions, thereby facilitating that systems can fit more readily to environmental changes. These results encourage the merit of considering both redundancy and degeneracy in topology design since they are not only relevant to engineering but also address the biological realm, which operates in complex sets of interlinked functions and adaptable mechanisms (Bender et al., 2009). Further, examining redundancy from the biological system perspective adds a rich dimension to the study of principles in topology design. Highly complex biological networks are characterized by resilient yet supple structures which have been optimized and developed over an extended span of history. Unlike technological networks that seek to optimize performance through the maximum establishment of redundancy, biological networks exhibit a clear set of principles based on contingency and historical constraint. Notably, biological redundancy tends to produce harmony in which strength is paired with the potential for novelty and creativity. Structural limitations observed in biological systems are evidence of a natural evolution of redundancy, allowing a diversified and robust architecture (Cancho et al., 2002). Thus, recognizing redundancy, evolvability, and robustness in interaction with one another not only enhances our understanding of design principles, but also provides us with vital understanding regarding the constraints and capabilities that will be present within engineered and biological systems (Figure 4.4).

4.1.3. Modularity

The concept of modularity is pivotal in understanding the design and functionality of complex systems, particularly in relation to topology. Modularity refers to the degree to which a systems component can be separated and recombined, promoting adaptability and resilience in both biological and technological contexts. In engineered structures, modular design facilitates ease of reconfiguration and optimization, enabling designers to meet evolving requirements efficiently. This structural flexibility parallels natural systems where modularity is observed in evolved biological networks, which often consist of interchangeable units that confer robustness to varying environmental challenges. The capacity for modules to adapt and reorder themselves is critical for maintaining system stability and function under different constraints, showcasing the value of modularity in achieving overall system efficiency. Additionally, modularity impacts the performance and reliability of complex systems, a fact that becomes increasingly relevant as interconnectedness in technology and biology grows. The trade-off between robustness and fragility becomes apparent in modular designs, where the resilience provided by modularity can inadvertently introduce vulnerabilities. For instance, while the separation of functions into distinct modules helps isolate failures, it can also lead to increased complexity and potential points of failure if not properly managed. This robustness-fragility dichotomy suggests that while modular systems can adapt and thrive under stress, careful consideration must be given to their architecture and inter-module dependencies. Understanding these dynamics is essential for optimizing designs that balance adaptability with stability, a challenge seen in advanced engineering and ecological systems. The role of modularity in systems design extends towards creating universal laws applicable to various fields, as expressed in the quest for managing complex "systems of systems." This search highlights the necessity for coherent and integrative methods to study and harness the potential of modular designs in diverse domains, ranging from biology to network-centric technologies. Increasing understanding of modularity and its implications can drive innovations in distributed control systems and adaptive infrastructure. To achieve this, researchers are challenged to synthesize fragmented theoretical frameworks that capture the essence of modular interactions, enhancing predictive capabilities for system behavior. Ultimately, embracing modular design principles fosters innovation while highlighting the importance of building systems capable of adaptation and resilience in the face of constraints, aligning closely with the evolving needs of biological and technological landscapes (Cancho et al., 2002; Alderson et al., 2010) (Figure 4.5).

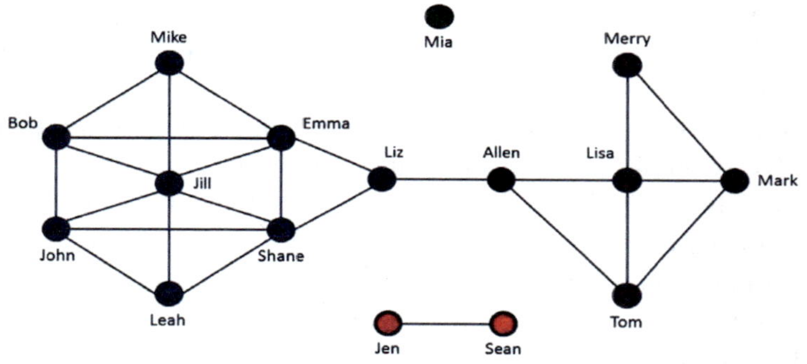

Figure 4.5. *The concept of modularity.*

Source: https://i.ytimg.com/vi/2_Q7uPAl34M/maxresdefault.jpg.

4.2. TYPES OF NETWORK TOPOLOGIES

Research into network topologies reveals a range of structures, each with particular benefits and drawbacks that govern their use in specific conditions. Traditional categories involve star, bus, and ring topologies, each with different means of data conveyance and connectivity. Star topologies, in which a single node facilitates exchanges between peripheral devices, are renowned for simplicity and ease of fault isolation. But these benefits usually come at the cost of the central node being a single point of failure. Bus topologies, while inexpensive, can be bandwidth-constrained by increasing network loads. Ring topologies, however, with their ordered way of moving data along the ring, suffer from scalability and fault tolerance problems in that the failure of any node would bring down the whole network. As companies grow and become more mature, an understanding of these topological models becomes part of well-informed design decision. How network topologies have been represented has experienced considerable advancement in recent years with empirical research intertwining with theoretical models. The addition of first-principles constraints into topology generation modeling's is significant because it allows more representative network architecture to be generated. For instance, the understanding of the physical form of a network as an annotated graph facilitates the ease of insight into its connectivity and bandwidth availability since these are economically decided, for example, routing technology and link price. By the addition of practical constraints into the design process, network engineers can model real-world conditions affecting the performance and reliability of varied topologies more realistically. It promotes a greater chance of successful planning, ultimately culminating in pre-planned network topologies that are compatible both with the organizational goals and infrastructure limitations, exhibiting the importance of topological aspects in present-day network architecture, as hypothesized in research emphasizing the imperative of adequate modeling (Byers et al., 2007). Empirical observations corroborate the merit of incorporating first-principles models within topological design through the illustration of the intricate relationship between constructs and practice. With a data-driven process on the basis of experience from existing Internet Service Provider (ISP) systems, for example, Abilene, these processes facilitate an improved comprehension of the variations that are incorporated into real-world connectivity outcomes. This analytical approach not only enhances network topologies' resilience but also allows for strategic maneuvering over unforeseen issues of operation, for example, router failures. Furthermore, it provides a foundation for solving additional design needs, for example, to provide fault tolerance and reduce resource deployment. With the passage of time and progressive research, the balancing of theoretical insight and ground realities will enlighten paths for innovative topological designs that simultaneously satisfy efficiency and resilience standards, ultimately driving the evolution of topological thinking in modern network ecosystems (Alderson et al., 2005).

4.2.1. Star Topology

Star topology is one of the most popular network configurations in current communication systems, boasting many merits that align with the concepts of topology design. Computers here are linked to a central switch or hub, facilitating speedy data exchange as well as ease in management. Centralized connections automatically simplify fault-tracing since issues can be reduced to locating issues with individual nodes rather than having to scan the whole network.

Secondly, this setup is easy and adaptable to scale; additional devices can be integrated by merely plugging them in the hub without significant modifications to already deployed infrastructure. Star topology not only supports expansion but also maximizes performance, as every node is autonomous, reducing the risk of network congestion, a factor integral in settings that provide audio-visual information services, as indicated from the Distributed Computation and Communication Group of Columbia University (Suda et al., 1986).

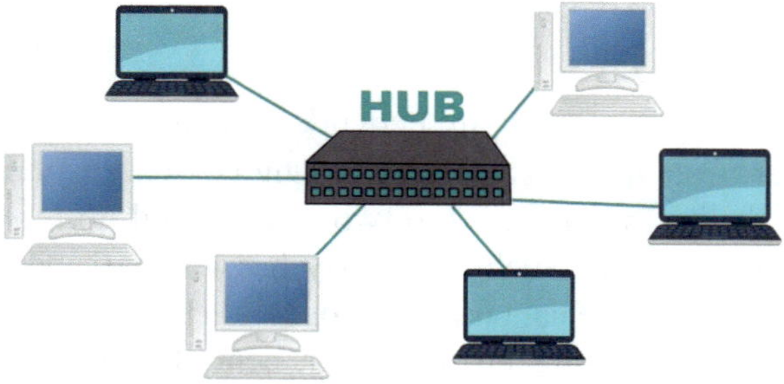

Figure 4.6. *Star topology.*

Source: https://educatecomputer.com/wp-content/uploads/2024/04/Star-Topology-Diagram.webp

However, the operation of a single hub does present some weaknesses that need to be taken into account in using star topology. Specifically, the overall reliability of systems relies on the integrity of this central node; when the hub is compromised, communication among all devices connected to it ceases, rendering the network unusable. This consideration makes redundancy and failover capability an important part of design planning. For example, establishing dual hubs or more routes would help offset single points of failure to provide around-the-clock connectivity. Additionally, organizations will need to balance the expense of sturdy hub gear and subsequent installation challenges against the operational gains through a star topology. Due to the swift revolution in network technology, bringing these factors into play alongside real-world limitations can dramatically affect the impact of topology design (Byers et al., 2007). In terms of performance, star topology is the best in terms of higher bandwidth utilization, especially where data-intensive operations are needed, such as exchange of multimedia information. The design inherently minimizes data collision because it permits more than one node to transmit data to the hub at a time, promoting optimal channels of communication. Theoretically, modeling network behavior for a star topology can leverage empirical knowledge and theoretical understanding to hone design situations.

Understanding network traffic patterns and the consequent effect on latency and capacity can give information for strategic upgrade. By incorporating considerations of the constraints faced by Internet Service Providers such as router configurations and budgetary constraints, network designers can design robust star topologies that not only function well but also adapt to evolving demands of multimedia integration and other emerging technological solutions (Byers et al., 2007) (Figure 4.6).

4.2.2. Ring Topology

Of the ever-changing situations in network design, ring topologies are a highly desirable structure considering its unique node connection. In its configuration, a device is connected to two devices and no more, forming an unbroken path of data flow. Such a property has a benefit when it comes to stable delivery of data where data travels in one direction only, thereby limiting the occurrence of packet collision. However, central nature of this structure also has some severe disadvantages. For instance, if one of the nodes fails, it can collapse the entire network, pointing towards a basic flaw inherent in ring topologies. This vulnerability indicates how far-reaching is the consideration of redundancy and fault tolerance in actual implementations, a concern that recurs through discussions of good topological design principles. Moreover, ring topology integration can be tightly related to specific applications of communication networks. For example, within the optical telecommunication network environment, ring structures present unique challenges such as the Synchronous Optical Network Ring Assignment Problem (SRAP) and the Intra-ring Synchronous Optical Network Design Problem (IDP). Both require the establishment of new design techniques, such as graph partitioning techniques with underlying capacity constraints. New algorithms and objective functions have been obtained from modern research that can optimize these configurations to enhance their operating efficiency and reliability. This is how ring topology can cope with evolving telecommunications needs, such as increased bandwidth and more dependable service ability, as shown through some research studies (Pelleau et al., 2009). With network needs increasingly becoming diversified, ring topology's flexibility encourages its use in any technology environment, mostly in the area of Ethernet networking. Developed initially for local area networks (LANs), Ethernet has evolved considerably since to meet the needs of diversified application areas such as industry, avionics, and multimedia. Ethernet evolution in such environments shows how ring topology can provide an effective platform for data transfer that is backward compatible and scalable. The evolution, however, testifies to the need for solutions that are maximized to address peculiar service requirements that accompany such environments.

Thus, the interconnection of ring topology and Ethernet illustrates broader design constraints and principles, emphasizing requirements for flexibility and quality of service while installing diversified network structures (Feller et al., 2010) (Figure 4.7).

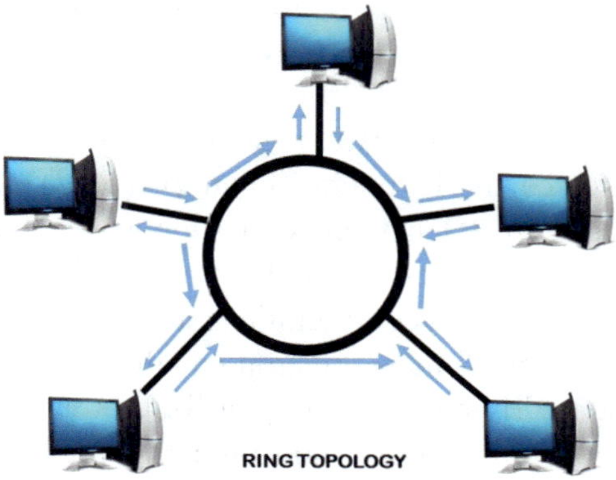

Figure 4.7. *Ring topology.*

Source: https://fossbytes.com/wp-content/uploads/2016/03/Ring-topology.jpg.

4.2.3. Mesh Topology

Mesh topology paradigm is at the heart of design principles and constraints that govern current network architecture. Based on how every node is linked to many nodes, the mesh topology provides support for fault-tolerant and reliable data transmission. Through this kind of design, there are no single points of failure, enhancing the networks resilience without causing disruption in operation whenever some of the connections fail. Redundancy that is built into meshed configurations is particularly useful in situations where it is necessary to achieve high availability, such as telephony and data networks for enterprise use. Bypassing faulty paths is a characteristic that is useful in actually rerouting data, which is critical in a situation where network performance and dependability matter most to user satisfaction and efficiency (Alderson et al., 2005). Moreover, the mesh topology is very flexible and can easily be adopted in numerous applications, from local area networks to wide area networks. The complexity and additional expenditure involved in the implementation and management of mesh networks are also commonly criticized. With every additional link, there comes additional cabling and a more complicated configuration protocol, which can lead to the issues of scalability and overhead. Budget constraints can be most restrictive for small organizations or under circumstances where budget constraints are harsh. Accordingly, the same must be weighed against the performance desired of the networks, which demands care and foresight at the design stage to satisfy both budgetary constraints as well as operational requirements (Bahrebar et al., 2015). In actual deployment, hybrid topologies typically emerge by mixing ideas of meshes with other architecture to achieve a middle ground between redundancy, cost, and performance. Clustering techniques brought in help optimize the physical infrastructure to enable more efficient resource allocation under the constraints presented by real applications. For instance, the Through-Silicon Via (TSV) technology enhances inter-layer connections in 3D networks to support the purposes of a mesh topology in response to area overhead and loss of yield issues (Bahrebar et al., 2015). Integrating cluster-based configurations in mesh structures facilitates the preservation of the topology's inherent strong qualities while responding to the economical parameters driving technology utilization in the more competitive markets. This strategic convergence shows the ongoing development of mesh topology in the broader area of topology design principles, pointing toward the need for innovation as much as pragmatism in modern networking designs (Figure 4.8).

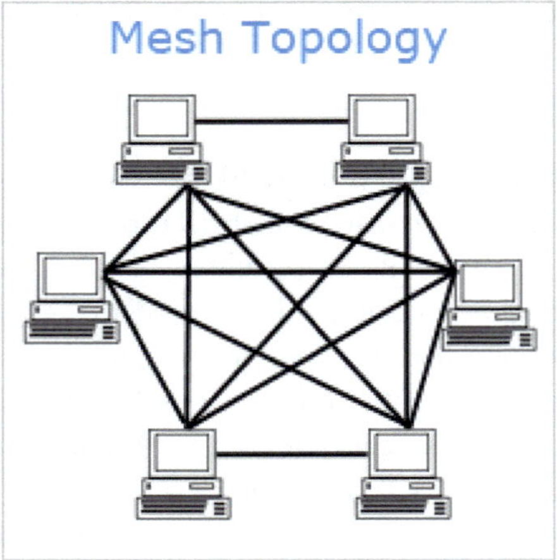

Figure 4.8. *The concept of mesh topology.*

Source: https://www.computerhope.com/jargon/m/mesh.png.

4.3. DESIGN CONSTRAINTS IN TOPOLOGY

Design constraints in topology are a fundamental concept in the comprehension of network behavior under various operating conditions. Design constraints usually arise due to a need for reliability, optimality, and peak performance under uncertainties, such as noise in signal processing. In structural design of noise-canceling networks, for instance, it is apparent that architectures evolve to counteract environmental and internal oscillations. Because networks are bound to face diverse input conditions, the employment of cost-effective mechanisms is of paramount concern. Research indicates that network architecture must develop to be sparser and hierarchical as input correlations increase, reflecting the inherent design principles of biological entities, for example, the intricate vasculature in animals and plants (Dunkel et al., 2018). This topological perspective on evolution reveals how design constraints shape robust systems that are able to maintain performance under different conditions. In addition to noise tolerance, design constraints arise from the requirement for functional integration within complex systems. Service discovery, a crucial attribute of distributed systems, is a fitting example of these constraints because it calls for user accessibility and efficiency of operation within a complex architecture. Service discovery might be thought of as a third-generation naming system that must contend with problems regarding component-to-component communication, data access, and service performance. Investigating state-of-the-art approaches allows one to identify gaps and possible improvements, namely concerning the processing mechanism of functionality and performance (Hartel et al., 2007). A perceptive understanding of these limitations leads to building better methods to integrate services, enhancing overall system reliability and usability. Implications of design limits also transcend technical needs; they greatly affect user experience and operational viability. As networks become increasingly complex, integrating various components has to be accomplished with proper regard for both structural strength and functional capacity. For instance, the structured nature of networks that are controlled by the type of noise represents a trade-off between beauty in a network's structure and operation needs. To address these complexities, designers must focus on developing topologies that are both efficient but also adaptive to different scenarios. This dual focus on beauty and functionality highlights the importance of adopting a holistic approach to welcoming limitations as challenges to creative innovation in the field of topology design. Ultimately, good solutions need to alleviate the tension between design limitation and performance needs to create systems that perform well with a variety of challenges.

4.3.1. Cost Factors

Under the field of topological design principles, the consideration of cost is the major driver in deciding the structuring of the formation of networks. Economic value in the realization of some topological designs is in the limelight in deciding the scalability and adequacy of neural networks, particularly for minimizing operational costs. High-performance on-chip communication networks are critical in providing efficient information delivery, which is aptly illustrated in neuromorphic computing environments. However, attaining this equilibrium of performance against cost-effectiveness is made complex, as designing for accommodating high degrees of connectivity without incurring significant costs demands innovative sensitivity to resource availability and technological sophistication.

Figure 4.9. *The domain of topology.*

Source: https://www.guru.com/blog/wp-content/uploads/2023/05/network-design-cost.jpg.

The determination of this interplay of design fidelity and cost, therefore, is what directly determines the feasibility of applying advanced technologies within specific applications, marking the limits of functional performance and economic viability within large systems. Along with that, network cost inputs also tend to extend beyond sheer short-term cost and involve other economic inputs in terms of infrastructure construction and maintenance. When looking at the Internet's connectivity protocols, for instance, physical infrastructure awareness entails an examination of the costs of router technology and investments in links. Effective design has to consider these parameters in the interest of delivering network systems adequate bandwidth within cost constraints. The integration of graph theory and statistical techniques allows designers to come up with effective topologies that deliver maximum connectivity for lowest cost. Cost considerations, therefore, are not merely a function of initial design but a continuous function to determine operational strategy and scalability in the future, encouraging a sustainable approach to technology deployment for networking infrastructure (Alderson et al., 2005). Finally, the calculation of Total Cost in designing topology involves a check of both short-term expense and long-term sustainability. Emerging technologies, such as non-volatile memory systems, offer promising developments that can enhance computational efficiency alongside the alleviation of cost concerns in neuromorphic designs. These innovative solutions potentially ease some of the economic constraints through enhanced integration densities along with computation resource reduction. However, the efficient realization of these technologies also demands proper understanding of the communication requirements behind large-scale designs. As observed in the research on next-generation intelligent computing, however, the question is not merely one of cost-effectiveness in adopting new solutions but how such solutions accommodate existing systems. The pertinence of the matter of cost factors underscores the necessity of an end-to-end approach to topology design, combining performance and economic viability to attain efficient and sustainable network solutions (Manohar et al., 2018) (Figure 4.9).

4.3.2. Physical Limitations

The concept of physical limitation is integral to the examination of topology design feasibility and performance in network infrastructure. Physical limitations are caused by a variety of factors including material properties of used materials, geographical properties of service regions, and technological properties of networking equipment. For instance, the material properties of optical cables and copper wires limit transmission speed and range. Accordingly, designers must take note of these physical factors with care as they create network topologies that tradeoff between performance and realism. Condensing these constraints into design decisions can lead to improved reliability and quality of service, such that networks cannot just meet current demands but also scale up to accommodate future demands. Hence, the understanding of physical limitations of network elements plays a key role in maximizing topology design to enable improved user experience and operational effectiveness. Further, economic conditions involved with physical constraints play a significant role in topology design ideas. The cost of physical infrastructure deployment and maintenance can act as a regulatory regime specifying design alternatives. For instance, redundant paths in network planning might increase reliability but at an increased operational cost by means of additional hardware and support requirements. In contrast, minimalist planning could save on initial cost but potentially at the expense of a preference for efficiency over robustness and possibly leading to bottlenecks. Scientists have proposed that statistical models and graph theory can reconcile these physical and economic constraints, and they could gain information about good design approaches that maximize functionality in budgetary limits. This also ultimately facilitates navigation of quality, performance, and cost trade-offs necessary to obtain sustainable network designs in spite of physical constraints (Alderson et al., 2005). Also, the effects of physical limitations become most evident in large network structures, for example, those employed by giant Internet Service Providers (ISPs). Understanding these limits facilitates the development of models that can efficiently model the intricate network of interconnected devices and how they share information. For example, creating algorithms that work with real-world information helps to construct more accurate physical connectivity models, which, when viewed in terms of an annotated graph, provides valuable information on bandwidth distribution and connectivity bounds between routers. This empirical approach helps increase the understanding of the Internet's underlying topology and helps researchers discover solutions to problems like router-level map variability. Therefore, by identifying and taking into account physical limitations in network design, experts can innovate to bring about solutions that give prominence to strength, effectiveness, and scalability under real operation conditions (Alderson et al., 2009).

4.3.3. Performing Requirements

The topological nature of performance requirements is at the core of topology design, particularly when addressing distributed system operational complexities. Performance requirements include factors such as latency, throughput, and fault tolerance that significantly impact topological structure choice and optimization. For instance, minimum latency is critical for real-time processing needs in applications and, therefore, network topology choice becomes system performance-centric. In this vein, service discovery is a critical component in the process of identifying and capitalizing on services in a distributed system. Realizing the complexity of service discovery systems can be better understood within the context of understanding how the systems operate, as it provides insight into how topology influences performance as a whole. Understanding these requirements helps develop systems not only that meet but also adapt with changing operational requirements (Hartel et al., 2007). During research in performance requirements, recall is made of the communication complicities in emergent technologies. For instance, in neuromorphic computing, integration of non-volatile memory enables high-density designs that enable avoiding many of the traditional CMOS design constraints. But the challenge is building robust on-chip communication networks enabling the flexible, large-fanout connectivity necessary for effective neural computation. Such requirements, as presented in the literature, highlight demands for new design styles to accommodate efficient information transfer among processing units. The evolving of these requirements calls for thorough examination of various architectures so communication protocols can be optimized for both speed and scalability. Thus, the alignment of topology with performance requirements becomes a revolutionary aspect in realizing advanced computing systems (Manohar et al., 2018). Also, the influences of performance requirements are not only limited to intrinsic computational capabilities; instead, they extend into long-term viability and capacity of systems to develop. Along with technology advancement also come the performance requirements for different operating environments. This flexibility calls upon designers to remain as much as possible attuned to future trends and technologies, thereby ensuring that topological decisions not only meet today's performance requirements but also anticipate future requirements. Successful topology design must therefore include principles that enable scalability, flexibility, and adaptability to change. By integrating these factors into the design process, engineers can create more robust systems that not only satisfy today's demands but also evolve over time based on available technology and user needs. Such forward thinking in performance requirement analysis solidifies the paradigm of sustainable topology design in a rapidly changing world (Figure 4.10).

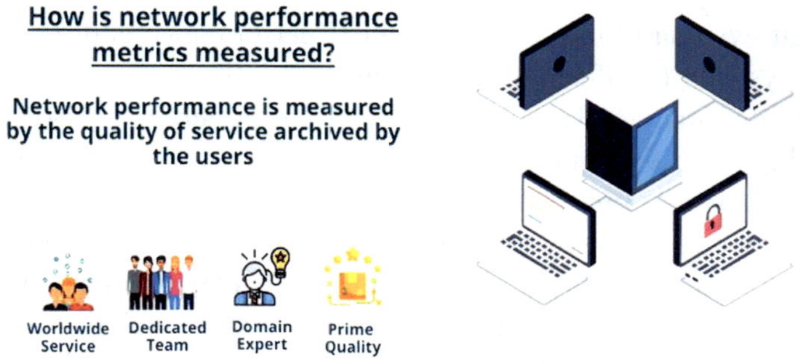

Figure 4.10. *Performance requirements.*

Source: https://networksimulationtools.com/wp-content/uploads/2021/12/Network-Perfromance-Metrics-Evaluation.jpg.

4.4. IMPACT OF TECHNOLOGY ON TOPOLOGY DESIGN

The integration of advanced technologies in topology design has transformed the field at its foundation, allowing for intricate approaches to enhancing design efficacy. Computer-Aided Innovation (CAI) systems have become the focal point of design, allowing designers to manage topological optimization's intricacy. CAI systems are capable of detecting geometrical contradictions, a key element in design, with the convergence of CAI and Product Lifecycle Management (PLM). This type of synergy in technology allows designers to manage density distributions within a contradictory pair, creating topological solutions that effectively address these geometrical complications. Through these advanced methodologies, designers can attain more customization and accuracy within their models, significantly impacting the overall performance and feasibility of the final products (Cascini et al., 2009). Moreover, the advent of solid freeform fabrication (SFF) technology has exposed the field of topology design to new possibilities with its capacity to create complicated structures on numerous different scales. The capability aids in creating components with tailored mesostructures, such as those implemented in aerospace, where honeycomb-arranged wings are optimized for stiffness and strength. The challenge of integrating design elements over various scales demands new techniques that reduce iterative redesign occurrence to optimize development. An example is a multiscale design approach relying on sets, which eliminates adjustments made in one level from not being achieved in the remaining system effectively, showing the integration of technology into traditional design processes that eventually improves functional performance and dependability in complex systems (Madhavan et al., 2007). Briefly, technology combined with topology design not only makes new solutions possible but also introduces complexity layers in themselves. With designers implementing optimization systems to resolve contradictions and create components with intricate geometries, they must also pay attention to the constantly changing constraints introduced by such technologies. The ability to design on micro, meso, and macro levels compels the designer to be holistic-oriented such that innovations in one area do not negatively impact others. This paradigm shift is a reflection of an increased appreciation for the interplay between technological innovation and design principles and calls for flexibility in a dynamic world. Therefore, the application of these technologies is vital in contemporary topology design since they offer windows for efficiency and performance enhancement (Cascini et al., 2009; Madhavan et al., 2007).

4.4.1. Advances in Networking Equipment

Networking hardware development is heavily influenced by technological innovation, pushing the boundary of topology design principles. As companies increasingly rely on wireless networking technologies, they grapple with reconciling market turbulence and organizational formats that allow for technological innovation. This concept becomes central when thinking about developing dynamic network topologies that can adapt to wireless technologies' dynamic forces. Using mobile networking principles, organizations can provide more precise analysis of their infrastructure needs, and hence, they are more responsive when it comes to deploying network resources. Application of such advanced systems not only encourages efficiency but also scalability, which causes the network to grow and reshape in real-time whenever there is a shift in operational requirements (Coster et al., 2009).

Figure 4.11. *The evolution of networking equipment.*

Source: https://media.licdn.com/dms/image/v2/C4E12AQEOtrxb4IfdPA/article-cover_image-shrink_600_2000/article-cover_image-shrink_600_2000/0/1520157079113?e=2147483647&v=beta&t=XX838r9NZlcJJxZW_b0M89IUnva598DOJ-CaF8a4Q2sA.

Furthermore, the invention of power line communication technology adds yet another dimension of complexity and possibility to networking hardware design. Historically, this technology has been of great interest to researchers and industry alike, and so on, which has called for investigation into its narrowband and broadband systems. With the richness of network topologies, the inclusion of power line communication within a pre-existing infrastructure provides certain advantages in terms of reliability in data transmission and the efficient utilization of already existing infrastructures. With enhanced characterization of the channel and advancements in physical layer performance, one can integrate such technologies seamlessly within contemporary network architectures, thereby revolutionizing the constraints primarily associated with traditional networking methods (Cano et al., 2016). Lastly, the strategic application of both power line communication networks and mobile networking technology heralds a topological revolution in design principles. As firms take steps towards an avalanche of impending emerging technologies, it becomes clear that adherence to stringent design constraints is crucial to enduring growth and performance. The interaction among various approaches to communication facilitates the optimum use of resources, resulting in networks that not only survive better but also are more capable of meeting the requirements of diverse applications. In the future, with the growth of the field, constant research and enhancements would be needed to make networking hardware catch up with changing technological environments as well as physical environment limitations (Figure 4.11).

4.4.2. Influence of Cloud Computing

Cloud computing has profoundly transformed the context of network topology design by introducing new paradigms into resource allocation and management. Cloud computing offers flexibility that enables dynamic deployment of resources by organizations, as per their needs, resulting in better performance and cost-effectiveness. Allocation of resources in traditional topologies is normally static, making it hard to respond to fluctuating requirements or sudden system failures. However, cloud infrastructure provides the ability to move workloads between servers and network facilities in the event of faults, thus enhancing resilience by minimizing downtime. This is particularly significant for application in advanced infrastructures since, as illustrated in existing works employing integer linear programming to determine the optimal deployment of server resources to facilitate failure-free and failure-prone scenarios, as illustrated in Buysse et al. (2014). The embracement of cloud computing also necessitates the reconsideration of performance engineering practices in distributed systems. Existing seminars, such as GI-Dagstuhl Seminar 16394, highlight the necessity of pushing performance awareness into cloud operations, especially given that organizations are increasingly embracing DevOps practices. The rapid move towards performance-aware DevOps identifies the interdependence of software engineering, performance engineering, and cloud computing on one another. Bridging these domains allows for not only a better understanding of system behavior but also the identification of performance anomalies, which are vital for maintaining the quality of service in cloud environments. Besides, promoting research collaboration between practitioners and researchers in these fields can yield novel solutions that promote system resilience and efficiency, thereby solving the complex issues of performance within cloud computing environments as studied in Jamshidi et al. (2017). Strategic deployment of cloud computing concepts in topology design can also yield significant resources savings, particularly in sparse networks with numerous server locations. Relocation strategies, when implemented correctly, allow for more effective utilization of both network and server resources. The correct deployment of maximum settings of resource allocation and the implementation of failure-dependent recovery models will allow organizations to thrive despite the uncertainty that exists in network management. Reduction of the resources' dimensions, as indicated in European-scale network case studies, verifies that cloud options not only make systems more reliable but also allow for cost-effective scalability. This focus on efficiency becomes even more important as organizations increasingly want to maximize their infrastructure investment while keeping themselves robust to failures, further delineating the effect of cloud computing on modern topology design principles as expounded in Buysse et al. (2014).

4.4.3. Role of IoT in Topology Choices

The explosive growth of the Internet of Things (IoT) has transformed topology design considerations in network design significantly. Traditionally, topology design required single-source analysis, where bandwidth and latency demands were the key drivers. The mature diversity of devices and applications introduced by IoT, nonetheless, demands multi-faceted consideration for choosing topology. With networks growing increasingly complex with increasingly interconnected devices, architecture must accommodate varied operation profiles like legacy data streams and novel sensor data flows. The creation of efficient network topologies thus demands a comprehensive understanding of the special requirements of IoT applications, leading to the deployment of hybrid or dynamic topologies that can optimize resource allocation, ensure higher reliability, and reduce latency, thereby achieving improved performance across various environments. Energy efficiency thus becomes a paramount concern among the topology choices under the control of the IoT. With networked sensors gaining momentum, sheer device count necessitates prudent energy consumption choices and operational lifespan. Most IoT devices are designed to function through low-energy consumption protocols, but large-scale deployment of millions of such devices exerts an overarching influence on bulk energy utilization. To this effect, used topology should be able to support energy-efficient structures to guarantee reduced wastage of energy during network operation. Adaptive topologies can be used to facilitate efficient dynamic energy management, with the ability to make real-time adjustments based on network load and device status. Hence, along with promoting cost-effectiveness, this strategy also aligns with longer-term sustainability goals, thereby aligning with the requirement of energy-efficient designs for contemporary IoT infrastructure (Anabi et al., 2019). As IoT technology continues to evolve further, a focus on security implications is increasingly significant in topology design. Each device that is networked in an IoT system has potential vulnerabilities that need to be addressed carefully through wise topology considerations. Selecting the appropriate topology directly influences the ease of enacting and managing security throughout the network. For example, a mesh topology can enhance resiliency and threat confinement through direct node-to-node communication, thus limiting exposure from compromised devices. Hierarchical topologies, on the other hand, can facilitate central security but may bring about single points of failure. Thus, with growing network evolution by way of IoT integration, the topology choice must include comprehensive risk assessment and security measures to carry out robust protection from evolving cyber-attacks (Brintrup et al., 2024) (Figure 4.12).

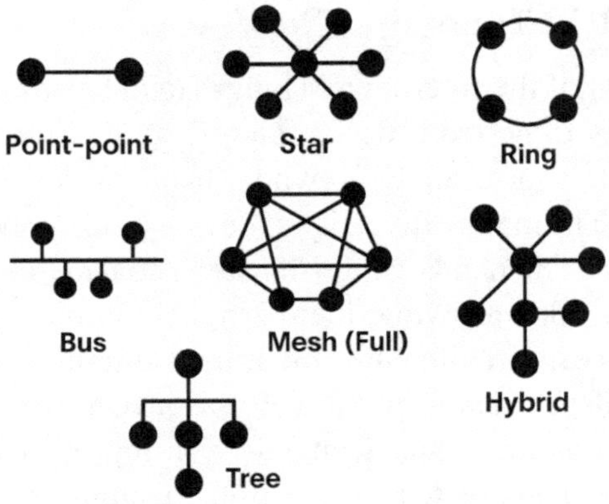

Figure 4.12. *Role of IoT in topology choices.*

Source: https://www.engineersgarage.com/wp-content/uploads/2025/07/Screenshot-2025-07-15-at-1.30.41%E2%80%AFPM.jpg.

4.5. BEST PRACTICES FOR TOPOLOGY DESIGN

In topological design, the utilization of efficient communication routes is the key to achieving maximum performance in interacting systems. Among the trends being worked on is leveraging the use of Through-Silicon Via (TSV) technology, which enables more data transfer in 3D stacked forms. By supporting greater speed and bandwidth while simultaneously reducing power consumption for inter-layer communication, TSVs present a futuristic solution for cutting-edge designs. Their use, however, has some drawbacks, particularly with respect to area footprint and yield loss. To best address these issues, best practices advise selective minimization of the TSV count using router clustering in a topology. Clustering allows multiple routers to be served with a single TSV pillar, facilitating a cost-effective design at the expense of functional integrity. Also, simulations verify that restructuring mesh topologies using cluster routers offers better performance-cost ratio, essential to successful chip design and implementation (Bahrebar et al., 2015). Another key aspect of topology design best practices involves the incorporation of decision support systems that facilitate the engineering process. For example, the Design Engineering Knowledge Application System (DEKAS) is designed to aid UK utility organizations in designing electrical power transmission protection systems. Intelligent decision support tools are utilized by topological designers to use case-based reasoning (CBR) to aid in informed design decisions. Not only does this make the design process easier but also enhances the ability to make realistic decisions through reliance on past experience. The efficient use of such systems in real-world applications indicates the potential in applying advanced decision-making structures in the practice of electrical and computer engineering. As the designers rely increasingly on such smart systems, the potential for improved efficiency and effectiveness in topology design becomes clear (Duffy et al., 2001). Furthermore, embracing flexibility and responsiveness in topology design is necessary to meet evolving technological requirements. The technology application environment, especially in networking and integrated circuits, is constantly evolving, necessitating designs that can match future requirements. Best practices advocate for using modular design philosophies, which facilitate simple modifications and scaling without necessitating complete revamps of existing systems. Modularity enables the scalability and longevity of the topology as well as facilitating customized-enhanced sections based on performance evaluation. Taking an approach that encourages innovation within predetermined frameworks enables engineers to proactively look ahead to impending limitations in uses. Ultimately, encouraging flexibility not only aligns with contemporary design philosophies but also future-proofs systems to manage emerging challenges in the constantly evolving topology design domain.

4.5.1. Planning and Documentation

Good documentation and planning are critical components of topology design, guiding practitioners through the complexity of system structure. In developing robust topological structures, well-established documentation practices serve as a foundation for articulating design principles and constraints. A well-structured approach to documentation not only assists teams in understanding project requirements but also bridges stakeholders through communication. For instance, on a multi-disciplinary project like the SOFIE project, requiring the development of mechatronic solutions for bicycles, agile methods can significantly minimize documentation efforts. By iterative feedback loops, these methods guarantee continued alignment with project goals and user needs, thereby resulting in comprehensive documentation capturing present as well as future considerations in design (Bonnema et al., 2012). Hence, an integration of complete documentation and a strategic planning system is the backbone of successful topology design programs. Additionally, documentation and planning are also very important in order to achieve maximum deployment and flexibility of topological designs across varied environments. Proper documentation ensures provision of detailed description of design parameters, specifications, and constraints that affect the execution of projects.

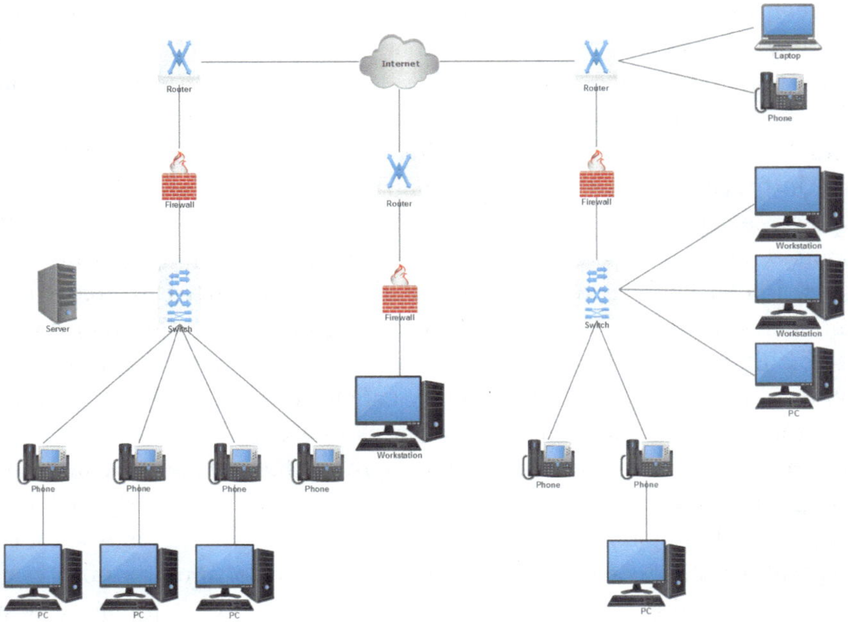

Figure 4.13. *Documentation and planning.*

Source: https://www.proprofskb.com/blog/wp-content/uploads/2024/07/Network-Topology.png.

Planning phases, together with proper documentation procedures, enable groups to identify any challenges and drawbacks beforehand, thus creating an anticipatory problem-solving approach. For instance, simulation and modeling environments like Repast enable the representation of dynamics in agent-based models in a manner where documentation of the abilities and shortcomings of the modeling environment is correctly represented. Such systems facilitate the integration of geospatial data so that groups can make not only the theoretical outlines of their designs but also how they play out in reality (Crooks et al., 2007). In turn, therefore, a good planning methodology that is based on extensive documentation can enhance the effectiveness and resilience of topological designs. Aside from that, repetitiveness in planning and documentation is essential in making way for altering project requirements and new technologies developed in topology design. Documentation and planning become a necessity to revise periodically in order to include specification or constraint variations incurred during development. Such continuous updating makes everyone conscious of the changes, which, in turn, maintains a unison of design objectives. Second, the employment of dynamic planning techniques allows teams to adjust their documentation methods in harmony with shifting methodologies and technologies. In projects in which simulation models and simulation tools are the focus, such as the employment of agent-based modeling tools, documentation flexibility and planning become highly important (Crooks et al., 2007). By establishing a culture of adaptability, teams can better prepare for the unforeseen challenges, ultimately designing more robust and responsive topological configurations that respond to the intricacies of modern engineering demands (Figure 4.13).

4.5.2. Regular Testing and Evaluation

Periodic testing and evaluation play a significant role in identifying the effectiveness of topology design rules and constraints in general. The cyclical process allows structural weaknesses and efficiency hotspots within network topologies to be identified so that they can comply with defined standards of functionality and service quality. Periodic testing makes incorporation simpler, allowing continuous optimization of topologies so that a dynamic design approach is possible for adapting to advancements in technology. With evolving techniques employed in creating network topologies, maintaining rigorous testing schedules is crucial, where designs would not only adhere to theoretical models but also perform well under practical circumstances. Furthermore, the evaluation process allows for feedback about the topological resistance and expandability, a critical factor in today's systems where demands continue to increase dynamically. Summarizing the results of regular testing considerably contributes to the knowledge base for designing topologies. By systematic documentation of the results of evaluation processes, designers can draw well-informed conclusions regarding the performance of various algorithms and configurations. Importantly, a key element of performance assessment lies in the incorporation of principles such as optimization and consistency. To these ends, TC algorithms must be subjected to scrutiny so they can be assessed on whether they fulfill operational standards without compromising efficiency. As has been discussed in previous studies, the constructive inclusion of consistency attributes in designing such algorithms enhances their reliability. It is a systematic approach that not only enhances the current state of network design but also offers directions for advancements in topology management in the future. Additionally, developments in additive manufacturing techniques and their viability within cellular materials demonstrate the efficiency of periodic testing models in transforming design paradigms. Synthesis of porous scaffolds for applications such as tissue engineering requires strict validation procedures to confirm their mechanical and biological function. (Concheri et al., 2018) discusses the importance of geometric modeling and cellular structure studies in highlighting the need for continuous evaluation in developing optimal design. Simultaneously, in communication systems, the effectiveness of TC algorithms shows how regular testing leads to increased adherence to quality service parameters, hence optimizing overall network performance. (Hollick et al., 2017) brings to the forefront how constant testing transcends the limits of theoretical models and ultimately refines the practical applications of various topological configurations and theories underlying them. All of these processes of frequent testing combined constitute a solid pillar for driving topological strategies across multiple areas.

4.5.3. Adaptation to Change

Flexibility to adapt is most important in topology design, particularly with the dynamic demand of modern applications and consumer needs. As networks evolve, topological designs must accommodate shifting data loads and operations. Digital Ecosystems bring to this challenge the concept of an innovative approach in much the same manner as biological systems function. By leveraging the properties of such ecosystems, architects can generate adaptive architectures that change dynamically over time to handle the shifting landscape of software programs. Such adaptive frameworks can result in improved performance and resilience of networks because they well adapt to the needs of real-time users and changes in application requirements as it happens in natural selection mechanisms in environmental systems. This adaptability not only enhances system performance but also facilitates resistance to interruptions, eventually satisfying user needs more effectively (Briscoe et al., 2011). In the quest to design flexible topologies, the integration of pervasive services becomes a dominating theme. These services, accessible at any time and from anywhere, call for accompanying infrastructures not only for survival but also for evolution. One of the key components in this scenario is the matching service intended to handle and screen multiple sources of diverse information, according to user needs. The challenge of having a worldwide distributed matching service lies in scaling its size and how it can be incrementally scaled as a response to evolving usage habits and technologies. Through adopting a peer-to-peer architecture model, network planners can make way for a more decentralized system that supports enhanced user activity and system responsiveness. This flexibility allows seamless transition across oscillating data forms and deployment technology, providing fertile ground for creative applications to grow (Connor et al., 2003). Ultimately, the philosophy of topological design in terms of adaptability goes beyond technological considerations; it is a matter of strategic vision in taking care of future challenges.

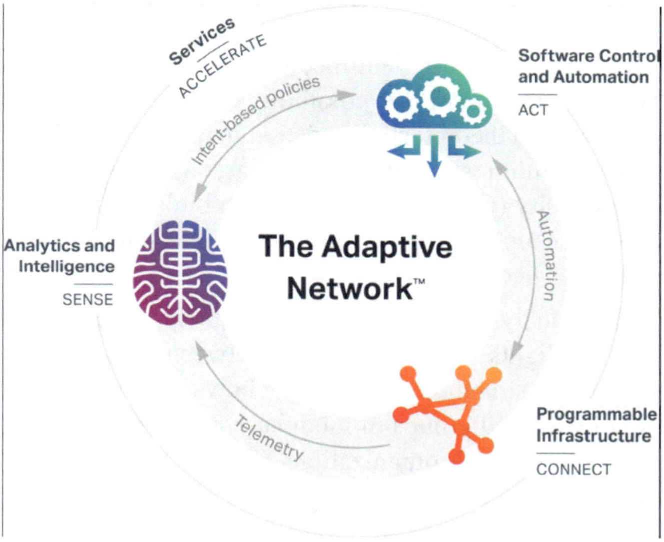

Figure 4.14. *The ability to adapt to change.*

Source: https://www.ciena.com/__data/assets/image/0026/27359/Adaptive-Diagram-2019-blog.png.

With the constantly evolving environment of digital ecosystems, a sense of the intersection of topology design and adaptive strategy is becoming increasingly vital. Designers must pay attention not only to current needs but also plan forward toward seeing future directions and potential disruption. Proactive planning can make possible more robust architectures that can sustain longer growth and evolution phases. Through continuous assessment and integration of adaptive methods, topological design can thus become a more dynamic field that serves as a blue print for addressing challenges faced by interdependent systems. With the future ahead of us, adhering to this design principles will allow networks not only to endure change but to prosper because of it, creating an environment optimally suited to innovation and resilience in a rapidly evolving digital landscape (Figure 4.14).

4.6. CASE STUDIES IN TOPOLOGY DESIGN

The study of topology design has the tendency to reveal critical findings regarding how design principles are affected by real-world constraints. A prime example of this is the study of the integration of Optimization Systems with Computer-Aided Innovation (CAI) in order to address geometrical conflicts in design procedures. The findings confirm that various topological optimizations not only present solutions to such paradoxes but also allow customized modeling features to be designed for particular special design issues. Through the modification of the density distributions that constitute the conflicting elements, designers have an efficient method of dealing with inherent design challenges. This technique shows the possibility of how the cooperation between practical application and theoretical foundation in topology design can produce creative outcomes within restricted surroundings, as is observed in the project for Cranfield University (Cascini et al., 2009). In biological systems, there are design guidelines for topology observed through mechanisms participating in function in molecular networks.

Computational analysis of the segment polarity network in Drosophila embryogenesis highlights the relationship between stable function and a particular topological structure. The study shows that robust functions are maintained only by limited groups of modular combinations, which highlights structural stability in network organizations. These topologies of modules not only allow for effective biological processes but also demonstrate a reduction in viable design options, finally leaning towards the ones fulfilling robust performance under long-term evolutionary pressures. The outcomes resulting from these biological case studies exhibit the ways in which topological constraints can contribute to the evolution of very efficient and adaptive design principles in nature and designed systems (Tang et al., 2006). Furthermore, the intersection of topology design in engineering and biology raises pertinent questions about its implementation across various domains. Examining these case studies indicates that whether in mechanical design or biological structures, the principles of modularity and functionality consistently play a pivotal role in shaping effective systems. The application of topological optimization techniques not only delivers improved performance outcomes but also triggers the adaptability required to solve various constraints provided by various contexts. As designers and scientists study these case studies in deeper detail, they sharpen their focus towards developing innovative methods that bridge theory and practice and result in advancements in both areas. This convergence of disciplines is crucial for enhancing our understanding of the principles of topology design and their implications in real life.

4.6.1. Corporate Network Implementations

In corporate network installations, selecting a sufficient topology is crucial to enable smooth movement of data and management of resources. Each topology possesses specific characteristics that could either improve or degrade corporate operations. A central hub star topology, for instance, offers management simplicity and enhanced fault tolerance, a preference of organizations seeking reliability in their network infrastructure. In contrast, however, a bus topology, as inexpensive as it is because of its low cabling needs, is highly dangerous insofar as network integrity and heavy-load performance degradation are concerned. These distinctions reflect the paramount importance of companies weighing their individual operational needs, avoiding the potential pitfalls of a poorly matched topology. Finally, the cost constraints must be balanced against the operational requirements and expandability in the future of their networks, paving the way for informed design choices within corporate settings. Also, semantic information systems (IS) standards play a critical role in corporate network development, ensuring interoperability between platforms. The standards facilitate seamless communication across heterogeneous business units, allowing for better sharing of data and collaboration. In this regard, there are several issues to be addressed by organizations, including terminological uncertainty for "business semantics" and "interoperability standards" that can detract from effective network installation. These must be resolved since ambiguity can lead to miscommunication and inconsistencies in the way things operate. Through an effective framework for semantic evaluation and comparison of Semantic IS Standards, corporations can enhance the operation of their networks and remain in accordance with best practices. Such a fundamental strategy not only completes current knowledge gaps in literature but also helps companies to optimize network infrastructures in order to grow with the rapidly transforming digital landscape (Scheer et al., 2012). Additionally, even the education industry has begun adopting cutting-edge technology to aid corporate network installations, thus bridging theoretical and practice-oriented knowledge. One such technology is Tangible User Interfaces (TUI), which facilitate interactive and interactive learning processes in sophisticated network principles. Through interactive tabletop platforms, instructors can facilitate students' grasp of complex networking topologies more effectively by allowing them to touch and see and manipulate network protocols in real time. This method of learning transcends the abstraction of networking concepts and allows them to become accessible and comprehensible for students. When universities incorporate TUIs into the curriculum, they not only enhance grades but also prepare their students to better address real problems in the corporate environment. Addition of such innovative methods is a sign of greater movement towards creative pedagogy, which will improve the skill level of the future generation of network experts (Raffaele et al., 2016) (Figure 4.15).

Figure 4.15. *The corporate network implementations.*

Source: https://www.cnet.cy/wp-content/uploads/2022/11/network1-768x576.png.

4.6.2. Educational Institution Networks

In the study of Educational Institution Networks, critical to determination is how topology design principles enhance the connectivity and functionality of such networks. Essentially, education networks require a systemic approach that interlaces diverse stakeholders like students, teachers, and administrators. The mathematical foundations provided by graph theory enable a model on which to examine the intricate interconnection of these groups, enabling education institutions to organize systemically their information exchange and communication behavior. Through the applications of graph theory models, in particular the scale-free network-based models, institutions are able to supply learning environments with environments that adapt dynamically to shifting learning needs. This adaptability allows cooperation, reinforces sharing of information, and ultimately results in improved learning performance, further emphasizing the importance of robust topology design principles for constructing learning networks efficiently (Alderson et al., 2009). Another key characteristic of learning networks in institutions is the capability to support multifunctionalities while providing operational efficiency. This challenge is typically addressed by the addition of a systemic acquis, which emphasizes the interconnectedness of systems in the academic world. While institutions struggle to create comprehensive networks integrating administrative functions and academic pursuits, they must contemplate how concepts in system theory and cybernetics may be used in their unique contexts. The principles learned from such nearby theoretical schools not only enhance the structural design but also provide the room for adaptive strategies in response to advancing educational demands. The acquis of the schooling institutions as a system, encompassing their evolutionary traits as well as cooperative processes, therefore has an impact on the network structure that is responsive to emerging pedagogical methodologies (Matei et al., 2025). In addition, with educational institutions becoming more reliant on network infrastructure, the significance of network topology extends beyond connectivity to resilience and security. The well-designed network must cover potential points of failure, be they technological malfunctions or malicious cyber-attacks. In such a scenario, the merging of topology design considerations and constraints becomes central, as institutions navigate the subtleties of protecting sensitive information while ensuring uninterrupted access for users. By employing a two-pronged approach emphasizing accessibility as well as security at the same time, educational networks can be rendered robust against outside pressures. Integrated advanced security aspects in the topology based on profound awareness of dominant limitations are required to protect the purity of education institutions in a networked world (Alderson et al., 2009; Matei et al., 2025).

4.6.3. Government and Military Applications

Government and military development rely heavily on the application of cutting-edge technology and innovative design principles. In an era characterized by accelerating capabilities, the design of tactical systems must incorporate aspects of topology to enhance operational effectiveness and responsiveness. These systems, ranging from free-flying unmanned aerial vehicles to hybrid capability weapon systems, call for a sensitive balance between versatility and dependability. Most importantly, military forces and police organizations are faced with unprecedented danger from hybrid threats that blur lines between warfare and crime. The development of effective topological frameworks carries the potential to bring revolutionary operational advantages, enabling such forces to respond effectively against complex and adaptive threats in real-time. Consequently, strategic topological design investment becomes a priority to ensure that government and military agencies attain a massive lead in tactical operations in order to finally provide national and international security. The surge of lethal autonomy technology in recent years is indicative of a commitment towards changing military and security operations through more sophisticated topological designs. For instance, the convergence of autonomous weapon systems capable of operating across various domains such as land, air, and sea hints at a strategic military paradigm change. Besides increasing operational acuteness, these systems introduce new operational and ethical dilemmas that must be addressed. Topological designs at a more advanced scale take center stage in making these autonomous systems well-skilled at driving through complex environments with minimal collateral damage and maximum mission success. This technology innovation must consider legal and ethical questions to be able to guarantee autonomous capabilities are compatible with domestic and international law. Similar to the situation in the event of incidents like the Westgate Terrorist Attack, the employment of hybrid-capability autonomous weapons can provide a legitimate means to address threats that call for military precision as well as law enforcement control, effectively bridging the gap of capability between the two (Nyagudi et al., 2013). Furthermore, the impact of topology in government and military applications extends to influence the conceptual models that guide the development and deployment of tactical technologies. The growth in hybrid threats has caused a shift in traditional strategy, with a need for a move toward designs that foster collaboration among various branches of the military and law enforcement agencies. By applying topological principles, organizations can create more holistic systems that integrate multiple functions and thus are more attuned to compound security risks. The designs must include feedback mechanisms as well, permitting ongoing assessment and adjustment through operational lessons. With the convergence of conceptual topology and strategic foresight, potent and adaptable solutions can be achieved that can better address changing threats. It is here that the ongoing controversy of the proper adoption and use of technologies, as debated in contemporary literature, becomes essential to ensuring that military and security strategies remain in sync with technological advancements and ethical concerns (Visvalingam et al., 2025).

SUMMARY

The topological concepts are the foundation upon which efficient and effective computing systems are made, particularly against the reality of existing technological advancements. From what has been discussed, we note that various topologies have specific advantages and challenges, varying in performance, scalability, and cost. The introduction of new methods, like the use of Through-Silicon Via (TSV) technology, is a good example of how bridging existing limitations aids in the development of enhanced designs. Through effective clustering of architecture without compromising the mesh structure, it is possible to strike a good balance between performance and power consumption, hence improving overall system effectiveness. The learnings resulting from such design aspects are instrumental in managing the complexities of contemporary computing environments, ultimately leading to innovation in the field. In addition, the fast-paced deployment of IoT technologies has compelled reconsideration of common topology limitations. As demonstrated by the recent advancements, development of platforms like VIoLET enables massive-scale simulations of IoT deployment on a larger scale resembling real-world conditions. Such platforms not only enhance resource efficiency and performance prediction but also eliminate the gap between the development of theory and practical implementation. With the ability to create complex interconnects to network standards, creative solutions illustrate how the design of topology can change in order to meet needs today. The study of such advancements proves the significance of dynamic design principles that are tuned based on the specific needs of modern applications. Ultimately, the fate of topology design relies on a delicate convergence between theoretical concepts and real-world constraints. As technology continues to progress, the emphasis will shift to more responsive designs that can respond to sophisticated challenges. Filling the gaps between performance, cost, and architectural correctness will be essential in the development of systems capable of withstanding increasing demands and evolving technologies. The research summarized here establishes the need for ongoing research and innovation in topology design, creating the potential for the emergence of new possibilities in high-performance computing and connected systems. With these principles adopted, future designs are not only capable of being functionally successful but can also grow sustainably within an ever-changing technological landscape.

The topology design philosophy is crucial to the optimization of network architecture, given respect for intrinsic physical and economic constraints. Topology is the framework in which nodes (e.g., routers) connect to each other, creating an annotated graph containing raw connectivity and bandwidth required for effective data transfer. The method becomes increasingly relevant in contemporary networking, where technology and infrastructure's complex interaction requires stringent analytical approaches. The combination of statistical and graph theory techniques offers improved insight by situating physical connection in a practical context, with the potential of designers to treat real constraints, such as router technology and associated link cost. This systematic examination offers evidence regarding router-level map variability, hence focusing our attention on the dynamics of the Internet as reported in the Abilene, Tier-1 ISP, and Rocketfuel project results, providing empirical evidence for the underlying design approaches (Alderson et al., 2005). In addition, topological design principles transcend classical networking usage and, in structural engineering, are applicable via means such as the Topology Optimization capability within MSC. Nastran. It is an emerging technique with the aim of identifying and locating damage in structures based on the correlation of stiffness loss and changes in modal parameters due to structural damage. The method allows us to develop models that not only represent undamaged states but also learn under evolving damage conditions, thus providing a robust analysis platform. Using a mass penalization method in conjunction with experimentally acquired modal parameters, high-resilience structures can be developed. The effective numerical and experimental verification of this technique, in particular on composite laminate test specimens, is a case of the practical application of topology principles towards conferring structural stability and toughness in the occurrence of potential damages (Gourinat et al., 2010). Finally, the integration of topology design principles in different applications highlights its supreme significance in modern engineering and networking concepts. The principles outlined emphasize the necessity for an empirical methodology, interreference theoretical foundations and empirical validation to enhance functionality and robustness. With these tenets developing further, they will continue to redefine our approach in both structural optimization and network design to ensure that systems are not only efficient but also accommodating to the needs of their relative operating conditions. The ongoing research and development in this field promises to unlock new potential, push the boundaries of what can be done in digital as well as physical infrastructures, thereby enhancing resilience and performance in order to address perpetual change.

REFERENCES

1. Alderson, D. L., & Doyle, J. C. (2010). Contrasting views of complexity and their implications for network-centric infrastructures. https://core.ac.uk/download/4885216.pdf (accessed on 9th September 2025).
2. Alderson, D., & Willinger, W. (2005). A contrasting look at self-organization in the Internet and next-generation communication networks. https://core.ac.uk/download/4869656.pdf (accessed on 9th September 2025).
3. Alderson, D., Doyle, J. C., & Willinger, W. (2009). Mathematics and the Internet: A source of enormous confusion and great potential. https://core.ac.uk/download/4882561.pdf (accessed on 9th September 2025).
4. Alderson, D., Doyle, J. C., Li, L., & Willinger, W. (2005). Understanding Internet topology: Principles, models, and validation. https://core.ac.uk/download/4870423.pdf (accessed on 9th September 2025).
5. Anabi, H. K., Imran, K., Jeong, K., Kim, J., et al. (2019). Enabling hardware green Internet of Things: A review of substantial issues. https://core.ac.uk/download/286784874.pdf (accessed on 9th September 2025).
6. Astorga Burgo, J., Higuero Aperribay, M. V., Taquet, J., Juan, E., Mendiola, et al. (2017). A survey on the contributions of software-defined networking to traffic engineering. https://core.ac.uk/download/168407472.pdf (accessed on 9th September 2025).
7. Bahrebar, P., & Stroobandt, D. (2015). Design of TSV-sharing topologies for cost-effective 3D networks-on-chip. https://core.ac.uk/download/55733751.pdf (accessed on 9th September 2025).
8. Benatallah, B., Paik, H. Y., & Toumani, F. (2005). Toward self-organizing service communities. https://core.ac.uk/download/10889990.pdf (accessed on 9th September 2025).
9. Bender, A., & Whitacre, J. M. (2009). Degeneracy: A design principle for achieving robustness and evolvability. http://arxiv.org/abs/0907.0510 (accessed on 9th September 2025).
10. Bonnema, G. M., Cooke, A. G., & Poelman, W. A. (2012). Agile development for a multi-disciplinary bicycle stability test bench. https://core.ac.uk/download/pdf/11484685.pdf (accessed on 9th September 2025).
11. Brintrup, A., Garlaschelli, D., Lafond, F., Mungo, S., et al. (2024). Reconstructing supply network. https://core.ac.uk/download/634353865.pdf (accessed on 9th September 2025).

12. Briscoe, G., De Wilde, P., & Sadedin, S. (2011). Digital ecosystems: Ecosystem-oriented architectures. http://arxiv.org/abs/1112.0204 (accessed on 9th September 2025).

13. Buysse, J., Develder, C., Dhoedt, B., Jaumard, P., et al. (2014). Joint dimensioning of server and network infrastructure for resilient optical grids/clouds. https://core.ac.uk/download/55798495.pdf (accessed on 9th September 2025).

14. Byers, J. W., & Wang, C. (2007). Generating representative ISP technologies from first-principles. https://open.bu.edu/bitstream/2144/1678/1/2007-001-ISP-topology-from-first-principles.pdf (accessed on 9th September 2025).

15. Cano, C., Dabak, A., Lampe, L., Malone, D., et al. (2016). State-of-the-art in power line communications: From the applications to the medium. https://core.ac.uk/download/297029547.pdf (accessed on 9th September 2025).

16. Cascini, G., Cugini, U., Frillici, F. S., Rotini, F., et al. (2009). Computer-aided conceptual design through TRIZ-based manipulation of topological optimizations. https://core.ac.uk/download/139012.pdf (accessed on 9th September 2025).

17. Concheri, G., Meneghello, R., Rosso, S., Savio, E., et al. (2018). Geometric modeling of cellular materials for additive manufacturing in biomedical field: A review. https://core.ac.uk/download/154326170.pdf (accessed on 9th September 2025).

18. Connor, R., Dearle, A., Dunlop, M., Kirby, G., et al. (2003). Active architecture for pervasive contextual services. https://core.ac.uk/download/9015611.pdf (accessed on 9th September 2025).

19. Crooks, A. T. (2007). The Repast simulation/modelling system for geospatial simulation. https://core.ac.uk/download/1683969.pdf (accessed on 9th September 2025).

20. De Coster, R. (2009). A business planning framework for WiMAX applications. https://core.ac.uk/download/335901.pdf (accessed on 9th September 2025).

21. De Raffaele, C., Gemikonakli, O., & Smith, S. (2016). The aptness of tangible user interfaces for explaining abstract computer network principles. https://core.ac.uk/download/76948203.pdf (accessed on 9th September 2025).

22. Duffy, A. H. B., Farrell, J., Gwyn, B., McDonald, N., et al. (2001). DEKAS–An evolutionary case-based reasoning system to support protection scheme design. https://core.ac.uk/download/9019311.pdf (accessed on 9th September 2025).

23. Dunkel, J., Ronellenfitsch, H., & Wilczek, M. (2018). Optimal noise-canceling networks. http://arxiv.org/abs/1807.08376 (accessed on 9th September 2025).

24. Feller, F., Gunreben, S., Kohn, M., Mifdaoui, A., et al. (2010). Ethernet–A survey on its fields of application. https://core.ac.uk/download/12040594.pdf (accessed on 9th September 2025).

25. Ferrer Cancho, R., Montoya, J. M., Solé Vicente, R., Valverde Castillo, S., et al. (2002). Selection, tinkering and emergence in complex networks: Crossing the land of tinkering. https://core.ac.uk/download/288625938.pdf (accessed on 9th September 2025).

26. Gourinat, Y., Morlier, J., Niemann, H., Shahdin, A., et al. (2010). Damage localization using experimental modal parameters and topology optimization. https://core.ac.uk/download/12041450.pdf (accessed on 9th September 2025).

27. Hartel, P. H., Scholten, J., & Sundramoorthy, V. (2007). A taxonomy of self-configuring service discovery systems. https://core.ac.uk/download/pdf/11468167.pdf (accessed on 9th September 2025).

28. Hollick, M., Kluge, R., Mühlhäuser, M., Schürr, A., et al. (2017). A systematic approach to constructing incremental topology control algorithms using graph transformation. http://arxiv.org/abs/1805.03386 (accessed on 9th September 2025).

29. Hollick, M., Kluge, R., Mühlhäuser, M., Schürr, A., et al. (2017). A systematic approach to constructing families of incremental topology control algorithms using graph transformation. http://arxiv.org/abs/1805.05026 (accessed on 9th September 2025).

30. Jamshidi, P., Leitner, P., van Hoorn, A., Weber, B., et al. (2017). Report from GI-Dagstuhl Seminar 16394: Software performance engineering in the DevOps world. https://core.ac.uk/download/pdf/141718346.pdf (accessed on 9th September 2025).

31. Madhavan, K., Seepersad, C. C., & Shahan, D. (2007). Multiscale design for solid freeform fabrication. https://core.ac.uk/download/287648474.pdf (accessed on 9th September 2025).

32. Manohar, R., & Moradi, S. (2018). The impact of on-chip communication on memory technologies for neuromorphic systems. http://arxiv.org/abs/1809.06016 (accessed on 9th September 2025).

33. Matei, A., & Matei, L. (2025). *The Systemic Acquis of Public Administration*. https://core.ac.uk/download/pdf/6583157.pdf (accessed on 9th September 2025).

34. Nyagudi, N. M. (2013). Post-Westgate SWAT: C4ISTAR architectural framework for autonomous network integrated multifaceted warfighting solutions version 1.0: A peer-reviewed monograph. http://arxiv.org/abs/1401.6379 (accessed on 9th September 2025).

35. Pelleau, M., Truchet, C., & Van Hentenryck, P. (2009). Sonet network design problems. http://arxiv.org/abs/0910.1255 (accessed on 9th September 2025).

36. Scheer, A. W., Tanenbaum, A. S., Hofreiter, B., Rukanova, B., Otto, B., Chang, C., Legner, C., et al. (2012). A characteristics framework for semantic information systems standards. https://core.ac.uk/download/pdf/11481917.pdf (accessed on 9th September 2025).

37. Shukla, A., Burns, B., Gupta, H., Satyanarayanan, M., & Calheiros, R. N. (2018). VIoLET: A large-scale virtual environment for Internet of Things. http://arxiv.org/abs/1806.06032 (accessed on 9th September 2025).

38. Suda, T. (1986). Issues in multi-media information networks. https://core.ac.uk/download/287623468.pdf (accessed on 9th September 2025).

39. Tang, C., Galassi, M., Kirschner, M., Lee, H. H., Lai, L., Martinez Arias, A., Ouyang, Q., et al. (2006). Robustness and modular design of the *Drosophila* segment polarity network. https://core.ac.uk/download/7511258.pdf (accessed on 9th September 2025).

40. Visvalingam, M. (2025). Standardizing basic spatial units: Problems and prospects. https://core.ac.uk/download/151162567.pdf (accessed on 9th September 2025).

CHAPTER 5

NETWORK DESIGN METHODOLOGIES

Contents

INTRODUCTION

The increasing sophistication of modern networks calls for effective design methodologies that are responsive to varied operating requirements. In network design, methodologies play a pivotal role as structures guiding designers in establishing successful, scalable networks that satisfy given performance parameters. With technology continuing to evolve, network infrastructure demands also continue to advance, prompting the use of formalized approaches that include both theoretical and empirical considerations. Effective network design is more a complicated interplay among user requirements, resource allocation, and future-proofing than it is a technical task. Consequently, a detailed introduction to network design methodologies forms the basis for exploration of many strategies and practices influencing network project success. One of the greatest problems with designing network design methodologies might be bridging the chasm between theoretical foundations and practical application. This is especially necessary for specialists who may have a strong background in their own field of practice but minimal experience with specific technological advances typical for network design. For instance, the method discussed in Bussmann et al. (2000) outlines a prescriptive method towards engineers working in production control and indicates the requirement for stipulating agent responsibilities and ascertaining role-dependent functions in a network. Such methods not only must conform to theoretical guidelines but also must be able to adapt to industry custom, so that the practitioners can implement solutions that maximize operational effectiveness. Moreover, empirical evidence and simulations being utilized in the design process play a pivotal role in influencing methodologies and practice. A critical examination of OR&S group artificial and empirical data developed demonstrates the value of using evidence-based approaches in designing networks (Vanhoucke et al., 2016). This data-based approach gives the designer insight into network structure and resource allocation, with the ultimate outcome being more informed decision-making. By using artificial and empirical data, designers are able to have a better grasp of the dynamics of how the various elements engage within a network. Such synergy of prudent design principles supported by an extensive amount of data not only contributes to academic research but also strives for practical applications in different industries that are network-dependent and efficiency-reliant.

Definition of Network Design

In the context of modern communications infrastructures, network design refers to the strategic planning and engineering of network infrastructure that meets organizational and user requirements. It is a sophisticated process intended to select proper hardware, software, and protocols in order to implement an efficient, dependable, and scalable network. A well-defined network design is the cornerstone of any IT infrastructure, providing secure information transfer and connectivity between devices and end-users. By defining bandwidth, latency, as well as security-related specifications, network design is naturally seeking to attain maximum performance with the potential to expand in the future. Moreover, service-based business models and cloud computing have more and more emphasized the requirement for flexible network solutions with the potential to host various bundled services, thus necessitating robust platforms for network implementation and design (Vasantha et al., 2010). Further, the methods employed in network designing are as varied as the networks they intend to design. Techniques range from the conventional ones that concentrate on physical and logical architecture to newer, agent-based techniques that evolve from dynamic systems. These techniques not only specify the structural components of a network but also the flow of information across the system. As industries become increasingly connected, choosing the appropriate methodology is imperative. Integration of product-oriented strategies with service-oriented approaches to network design is part of a broader trend where end-to-end solutions are desirable. As the two come together, it is easy to respond in a timely manner to shifting requirements in terms of technology in network environments, enhancing overall user experience and operational efficiency (Bond et al., 1999). Furthermore, the tension between established paradigms and emerging methodologies underscores another key aspect of network design: the necessity for continuous development and regular rethinking of strategies. With every new technology breakthrough, methodologies must adjust by incorporating new tools, processes, and considerations regarding user experience and security. The successive changes to established standard ontologies in the field are indicative of the collective efforts aimed at enhancing network design processes. This evolution not only enables more transparent communication between stakeholders but also promotes mutual comprehension of best practices in a position to fuel greater innovation. Lastly, definition of network design is anything but stable; it is an evolving construct that may only be addressed with a holistic approach to the intricacies of modern digital communication on an integrated basis (Vasantha et al., 2010).

Implication of Network Design in Modern Organizations

The importance of network design in modern-day organizations cannot be overemphasized, as it is the foundation for effective communication, data management, and operational efficacy. An effectively designed network guarantees constant connectivity among various departments, enabling easy collaboration and data sharing. With organizations increasingly relying on digital solutions, their network infrastructure decides how responsive they are to emerging technologies and attacks from the outside world. Proper network design not only addresses current business needs but also anticipates business growth in the future to help organizations grow operations seamlessly. Therefore, investing in good network design practices is of utmost significance because it actually decides the way organizations leverage technology for staying competitive and responsive in an ever-evolving marketplace. In addition, the level of sophistication of modern organizational models demands a comprehensive network design process that will take various factors into account, including security, performance, and user interface. Effective network design practices involve best practices that offset potential weaknesses while providing optimal end-user performance. For instance, using a model of layered security in the network is able to safeguard critical information from cyber threats, and this reflects an organization's commitment to safeguarding its information assets. Additionally, through user-experience-based practices, organizations can streamline workflow and enhance the productivity of employees. Last but not least, an efficiently designed network not only prioritizes performance and safety but also the overall user experience, turning the employees into more productive and more engaged people. Additionally, the interaction between network design and corporate culture is the most important concept of the modern connected age. The organization network structure can dictate the way workers collaborate, share information, and perform projects. For instance, a network that allows remote work through effective virtual working tools can change organizational dynamics, creating the type of flexibility and culture of innovation. Building a conducive network environment promotes open communication and collaboration, which is needed to propel progress and achievement of strategic plans. As indicated by certain case studies, organizations that have placed innovative network design at the forefront have not only achieved enhanced operational efficiency, but they have also directly experienced a positive impact on employee morale and engagement. This dynamic enforces the necessity of including thoughtful network design practices as part of the core management practices of modern organizations (Figure 5.1).

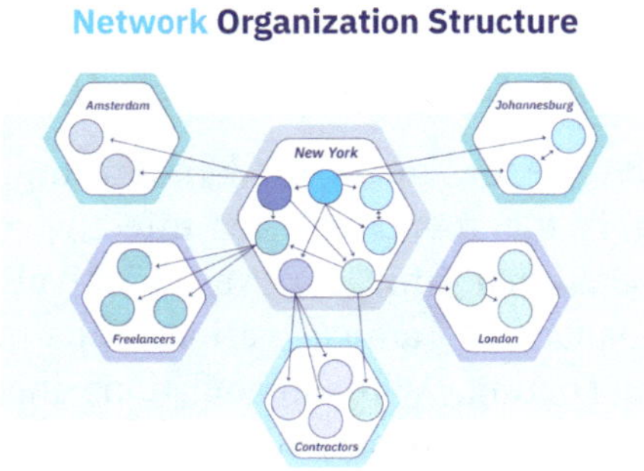

Figure 5.1. *Network design in modern organizations.*

Source: https://www.aihr.com/wp-content/uploads/Network-Organization-Structure.png.

Overview of Network Design Methodologies

The evolving technology landscape requires an integrated framework of network design strategies. Several of these strategies have been developed to enable seamless incorporation of the systems as well as maximized management of resources. Underlying these strategies is the need for systematic analysis to consider both current and future demands on network infrastructure. A sound process of network design should involve determining user needs, defining performance requirements, and policies for resource allocation. The OLnet project demonstrates a comprehensive design process by proposing tools and methodologies particularly related to evaluating and facilitating Open Educational Resources (OERs). By engaging participants in experiential experiences, this program emphasizes the importance of adaptive design that is able to dynamically respond to the needs of different groups of users (Brasher et al., 2009). The inclusion of participatory design strategies then becomes evident, guiding the creation of network infrastructures to counter future challenges. When considering network design strategies, the inclusion of stakeholder participation then becomes necessary as a crucial element. A participatory solution not only renders the design more relevant but also provides for a collaborative setting in which different views can input into decisions. The ever-evolving nature of network requirements guarantees that the methodologies employed are flexible enough to cater to technology and user expectations changes. As observed in the example of genetically modified (GM) crops, the absent comprehensive appraisals have often been the underlying cause of regulatory problems. The future European Network for systematic GMO impact assessment (ENSyGMO) is one such example, with stakeholders from different sectors being required to address environmental and socio-economic dimensions (Andersen et al., 2012). Stakeholder contribution is key to developing methodologies to the extent that they are appealing to users' multifaceted requirements and the unique characteristics of the networked landscape. Further, network design methodology needs to incorporate iterative processes to allow for continuous improvement and adaptability to emerging challenges. The process of iteration is undertaken in a series of test phases, feedback, and redesign, which become core in the development of robust networks that can sustain technological evolution. For instance, in the application of OERs, the utilization of sophisticated tools and mechanisms allows for constant testing and tuning in response to user interaction as well as feedback. These adaptive methods are equally suited for use in fields like agriculture, where the complexities of environmental impact analysis underscore the need for an iterative methodology that accommodates variation in social and environmental conditions (Andersen et al., 2012). Ideally, the integration of stakeholder engagement, participatory design, and iterative methods provides a holistic view of network design. This blended approach ensures that networks are not just innovative but also sensible and sustainable in addressing problems today.

5.1. HISTORICAL NETWORK DESIGN METHODOLOGIES

Traditional network design methods are central in the underpinnings of modern network systems' architecture. These methods tend to emphasize orderly, systematic procedures that allow network architects to create systems capable of addressing multiple organizational requirements. Traditionally, methods include the hierarchical design model, which distinguishes network components into distinct layers—core, distribution, and access—that facilitate scalability and efficient flow of traffic. By adhering to these set standards, network designers would ensure that every layer of communication efficiently interacts with other layers, thereby optimizing performance and minimizing latency. Moreover, conventional methods primarily employ standardized frameworks such as ISO/PMBOK to facilitate a better realization of project management's role in network designing. This established framework, apart from aiding resource management, also aligns the development of networks with the organizations overall business objectives, ensuring consistency and coherence in the project lifecycle. Integration of traditional methodologies in network design is also enhanced by a rigorous examination of prevalent frameworks. For example, standard tools used with conventional methodologies provide designers with the capability to handle complex networks using tried and tested project management standards and practices. These frameworks invite intense documentation and review, ensuring an open line of communication among all the stakeholders in the development of networks. As noted in current academic literature, finding balance in adherence to standard methodologies and the acceptance of fresh agile trends is imperative in preparing students and practitioners in the field ((Kaloyanova et al., 2019)). Such emphasis on maintaining entrenched practices while being open to innovativeness reflects the evolution of network design methodologies such that they are consistent with the rapidly changing needs of modern businesses. While traditional network design methodologies offer a sound foundation, consideration must be given to their failure to accommodate the fast-changing technology world of today. Adherence to set procedures in a stringent manner can stifle flexibility, especially where quick turnaround to new technologies or procedures is essential. Network design in the contemporary era is hence becoming more influenced by agile practices, which foster iterative development and continued stakeholder engagement. Synthesizing cognitive and educational science insights can also reinforce classical approaches by providing insight into how engineers and students absorb intricate technical knowledge ((Han et al., 2019)). Having an understanding that acknowledges the merits and limitations of both the classical and newer approaches will ultimately yield more robust and adaptable network structures that prepare organizations for the challenges of a digital world (Figure 5.2).

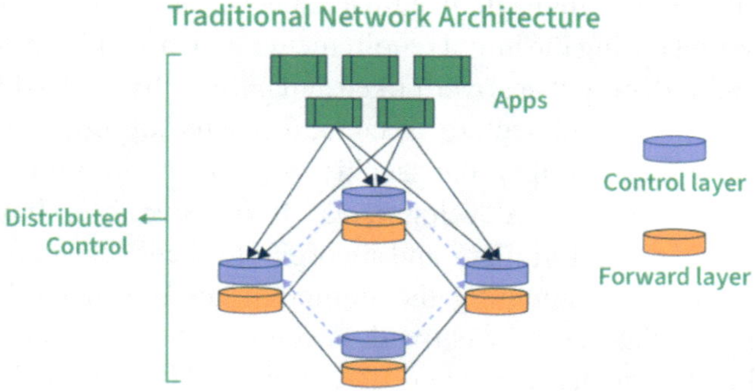

Figure 5.2. *Traditional network design methodologies.*

Source: https://media.geeksforgeeks.org/wp-content/uploads/20241014180726658038/Traditional-network-architecture.png.

5.1.1. Top-Down Approach

Top-Down Approach is a methodological paradigm that is well applied in network design, emphasizing the need to learn of top-level goals before the actual details of the network infrastructure are undertaken. The Top-Down Approach begins with general organizational requirements, establishing the top-level goals that the network will be required to achieve to facilitate business operations effectively. By ensuring that decisions about design have to adhere to these basic goals, the Top-Down Approach allows for a single network structure to be designed to satisfy the specific needs of the firm. Not only does this help with the planning of resources, but it enhances decision-making by enabling a specified environment within which technical options can be weighed against strategic needs, resulting in a more cohesive network solution. Having established the top-level network needs, the Top-Down Approach involves a sequential decomposition into lower-order, tractable components. This hierarchical decomposition enables designers to explore numerous subsystems, such as data management, security provisions, and connectivity options while remaining committed to initial business requirements. Applying this systematic decomposition, network designers are in a position to evaluate the way each subsystem corresponds with the higher-level organizational goals.

This systematic process also allows for iterative refinement, in which feedback from each design phase can inform refinement in the following phase. A focus on ongoing reevaluation is necessary because as technologies evolve, so do the strategies and designs that determine network functionalities, with the resulting long-term adaptability and operation. But while as useful as the Top-Down Approach is, it is not without its negative aspects. Of greatest concern is the danger of oversight during the initial requirements-gathering phase, in which key insights or stakeholder input are overlooked and potentially lead to blind spots in the completed network architecture. Second, a strictly top-down methodology also risks dampening flexibility and sensitivity to unanticipated organizational requirements or technology developments. It is, therefore, important that network designers remain vigilant and incorporate feedback loops within the design process, thus surmounting the limitations of the methodology. With advancements in technology for network designing, it becomes more relevant to understand and critically evaluate different methodologies, such as the Top-Down Approach, so as to be able to address complex network architectures efficiently (Fernández-López et al., 1999; Bond et al., 1999).

5.1.2. Bottom-Up Approach

The Bottom-Up Approach in network design structures emphasizes the use of bottom-up data and user-level input to define the systems architecture. The method differs from more traditional top-down approaches, which tend to rely on high-level commands and pre-established structures. Through the inclusion of end-user and operating staff input at the outset, the Bottom-Up Approach allows for a more inclusive design process that respects the actual needs and constraints of users. Such alignment generally leads to better user satisfaction and higher implementation success rates because the resulting networks turn out to be more adaptive and resilient to the dynamic issues that are inherent in actual applications of technology, particularly in complex environments. Moreover, the Bottom-Up Approach encourages innovation through a distributed decision-making process, which leverages the collective intelligence of individuals at various levels in an organization. This collaborative approach facilitates groups to quickly recognize and tackle distinct problems while operating within their environments. For example, in supply chain management, using such a Bottom-Up paradigm can result in enhanced problem-solving efficiency, enabling groups to create targeted solutions that maximize the efficiency of operations. By fostering a culture of continuous improvement and adaptation, such a strategy can also initiate superior performance across the network, with the structure evolving at the same time as its operating environment (Coudert et al., 2012). With new technologies and decentralized networks as may be the situation, the

Bottom-Up Approach is poised to be particularly useful in dealing with the uncertainties and complexities of modern network environments. Naturally occurring swarm systems exhibit the manner in which self-organization and adaptability can be exhibited in decentralized constituents, and emergent behavior produced could optimize system performance. Such characteristics are what fit design objectives in networks where response speed and flexibility in the presence of change are critical. Additionally, lessons learned from robotics can be extrapolated validly to artificial systems and aid in advancing an elucidative understanding of the functioning of decentralized control mechanisms in real environments (Albayrak et al., 2018). In the synthesis of these elements, the Bottom-Up Approach not only educates theory frameworks but also allows for the formulation of robust, collective, and adaptive network solutions (Figure 5.3).

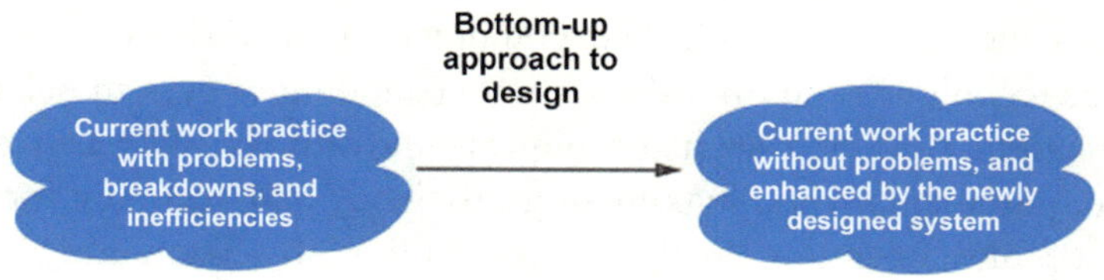

Figure 5.3. *The Bottom-up approach in network design methodologies.*

Source: https://ars.els-cdn.com/content/image/3-s2.0-B9780128053423000138-f13-02-9780128053423.jpg.

5.1.3. Hybrid Approach

In network design methodologies themselves, the hybrid approach has been an incredibly powerful strategy to leverage the strengths of several different techniques. By coupling together different methodologies—like rule-based systems and machine learning—designers are able to enhance network performance as well as address inherent complexities of modern network topologies. This paradigm not only applies the predictive power of advanced computational algorithms but also human judgment and contextual decision-making, hence it is a more powerful paradigm. For instance, financial decision-making situations, rule-based classification can simplify a lot the process of risk assessment and resource allocation, as exemplified in the approaches described in Ampazis et al. (2006). The hybrid solution thus promotes the in-depth examination of network design issues, allowing for more smart and adaptive solutions that respond dynamically to shifting operating needs. The hybrid solution is, in addition, most useful in solving the limitation felt in traditional top-down methods, namely in analog circuit design and network design. Performance trade-off fronts or Pareto fronts are used to visualize many conflicting objectives and allow design to make informed decision-making regarding design parameters. However, disadvantages of such practice tend to result from its dependency upon specific circuit environments that may not extend to the larger conditions in which networks operate. Such methods assuming no surrounding circuitry may thus be unsatisfactory for performance testing. As a response to this challenge, scholars are calling for the establishment of methods that generate trade-off fronts regardless of load conditions and present a more flexible approach based on Castro López et al. (2010). This modification expands the scope for hybrid approaches to apply universally across varying network settings. Finally, applying hybrid methods to network planning methodologies presents possibilities for innovation and performance enhancement. The combination of various computational intelligence techniques can offer deeper understanding of system behavior and user interaction. Applying such techniques innovatively, they can minimize resource requirements while maximizing efficiency and accuracy for network performance and operation analysis. In addition, by facilitating enhanced understanding of decision models, hybrid techniques allow designers to design decision-support systems that are easy to use but highly technical. This combined strategy is important in real application, with real-world applications spanning complex interdependencies and evolving performance factors. As supported by collective experience of projects employing both rule-based systems and machine learning, the hybrid approach is continuing to demonstrate immense promise for future network design methods.

5.2. STRUCTURED NETWORK DESIGN

Structured network design is an essential aspect of the wider network design methodologies context, enabling an integrated methodology for the development of efficient and effective information systems. By the concentrating of systematic organization and layout, structured network design takes into account interdependencies between various aspects of the network, so that each component works harmoniously within the overall architecture. This approach favors simplicity and accuracy, especially in intricate systems where the exchange among various nodes can heavily determine the overall performance. The significance of systematic design is emphasized by its ability to provide concise analysis and documentation, hence allowing for proper capacity planning and software performance engineering analysis, as proposed by the argument on responsive information systems and information systems analysis approaches like SSADM in Molnár et al. (1993). By incorporating structured analysis techniques into network design, the effectiveness of project management improves, particularly where complexity and dynamic change exist. As research proposed more recently, traditional project planning methods may not meet the challenges of complexities inherent in modern network requirements.

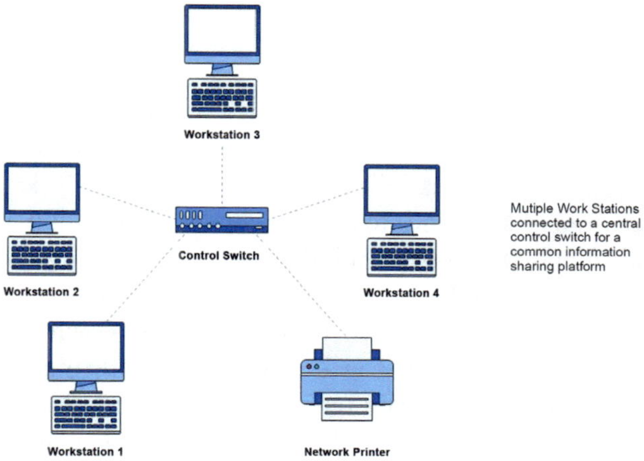

Figure 5.4. *Structured network design.*

Source: https://www.slidegeeks.com/media/catalog/product/cache/1280x720/S/t/Structured_Network_Design_Process_Ppt_PowerPoint_Presentation_Outline_Icons_PDF_Slide_1.jpg.

The lack highlights the potential of techniques such as Structured Analysis Design Techniques (SADT), and this is particularly beneficial in network infrastructure development and maintenance. SADT promotes comprehensive comprehension of production systems, rendering it easier to adopt and utilize alterations with long-lasting impacts on project outcomes. Not only does it improve the beauty and structuration of network specifications but also eradicates delays caused by poor planning, hence responding to criticism of previous planning methodologies in Agyekum-Mensah et al. (2012). Finally, the advantages of formal network design methodologies extend beyond simple technical details; they also involve strategic project delivery and stakeholder management. With the growing challenges of digital change and interconnected systems confronting companies, the imperatives of open and dynamic network infrastructures are superior. Formal design methodologies present a method of mapping network functionality against organizational goals, hence bringing about operational effectiveness and enhancing user experience. This integration is even more critical in dynamic environments where being able to quickly adapt to change can make the difference in competitiveness. Implementing formal network design approaches is therefore not only necessary for technical efficiency but also for instilling an active approach to network management and continuous improvement (Figure 5.4).

5.2.1. Layered Architecture

In the context of network design methodologies, Layered Architecture serves as a critical framework that facilitates the structured development of complex systems. By decoupling responsibilities into distinct layers, this architectural model enhances modularity and fosters a clearer delineation of functions within a network. Each layer operates independently, allowing for specialized protocol implementations and the possibility of upgrades or changes without the need to overhaul the entire system. This modular approach streamlines the troubleshooting process, as issues can be locally isolated to a specific layer, thereby simplifying maintenance and reducing downtime. As systems grow in complexity, the need for efficiency and clarity in design becomes paramount, making Layered Architecture an indispensable tool in modern network design. A significant advantage of employing Layered Architecture is its facilitation of interoperability and standardization across different network components. In ensuring that each layer adheres to a specific set of protocols and standards, diverse systems can communicate effectively without requiring extensive modifications. This is particularly relevant in today's rapidly evolving technological landscape, where the integration of various platforms and devices is commonplace. Enhanced interoperability not only mitigates compatibility issues but also supports the scalability of networks as organizations grow. By adopting Layered Architecture, organizations can better prepare for future technological advancements, allowing for seamless integration of new solutions while maintaining operational integrity within existing systems. Moreover, the concept of Layered Architecture can be instrumental in evolving towards self-managing networks, as indicated by discussions around autonomic computing. The layered approach aligns with the need for systems that exhibit self-healing, self-regulating, and self-optimizing properties, as articulated by Ganek and Corbi (2003) (Nazir et al., 2017). As networks incorporate cognitive computing and machine learning technologies, they can autonomously adapt to changing conditions and effectively predict anomalies. This adaptability becomes increasingly critical in environments where the reliability of communication capabilities is imperative for operational success, particularly in communications-critical large-scale systems (CCLSSs) (Hierons et al., 2015). By merging these advanced methodologies with Layered Architecture, network design can achieve greater resilience and efficiency, ultimately enhancing the overall reliability and functionality of complex systems (Figure 5.5).

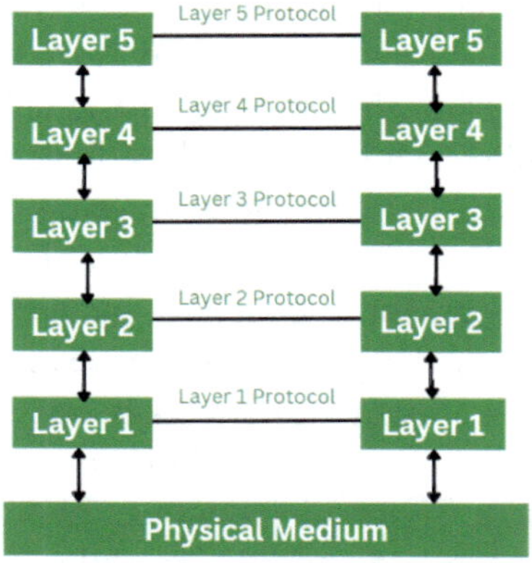

Figure 5.5. *Layered architecture.*

Source: https://media.geeksforgeeks.org/wp-content/uploads/20230831155309/2.png.

5.2.2. Modular Design Principles

The concept of modular design principles has a profound effect when addressing the development of network design methodologies, particularly addressing complexity that is inherent in current systems. Modular design makes it possible to separate a network into manageable chunks, which is easy to change and expand without disrupting the system at large. Modules enable network architects to isolate failures, deploy upgrades, and integrate technological developments with minimal disruption to routine operations. This approach, apart from enhancing flexibility, encourages innovation because teams can work on separate parts that can evolve independently. This flexibility is crucial in today's fast-moving technology age where systems must be able to keep up with ever-evolving user demands and environmental conditions without sacrificing reliability and performance. One of the greatest benefits of modular design principles is that they are amenable to self-organizing architectures, which allow for effective growth and evolution of network systems. Modular systems, as opposed to top-down designs, are capable of managing complexity in a bottom-up manner in which local modules build up towards the overall function of the network. This design promotes resilience, as the pieces can be modified to fit changing circumstances without requiring an entire overhaul of the network structure. Furthermore, as artificial intelligence is being developed, integration of modular thinking is necessary. AI systems must have a level of flexibility to learn and adapt, mirroring the modular designs inherent capability to handle different needs and functions, hence ensuring longevity and pertinence in usage (Thórisson et al., 2012). Additionally, the use of modular design principles can greatly simplify cooperation among various teams and disciplines within network architecture. By using a common interface throughout modules, teams may develop separately various parts thereof, encouraging parallel development and minimizing the overall project schedules. Parallel development encourages innovation since specialists in diverse fields may share knowledge and experience to each module, making the overall quality and functionality of the network better. Additionally, by ensuring improved documentation and comprehensibility of each module, stakeholders are better placed to make informed judgments about their investments and implementations. Lastly, the integration of module design principles not only ensures efficient solving of network design issues but also leaves room for future development akin to the principles discovered in biological patterns as outlined in existing research (Braccini et al., 2017) (Figure 5.6).

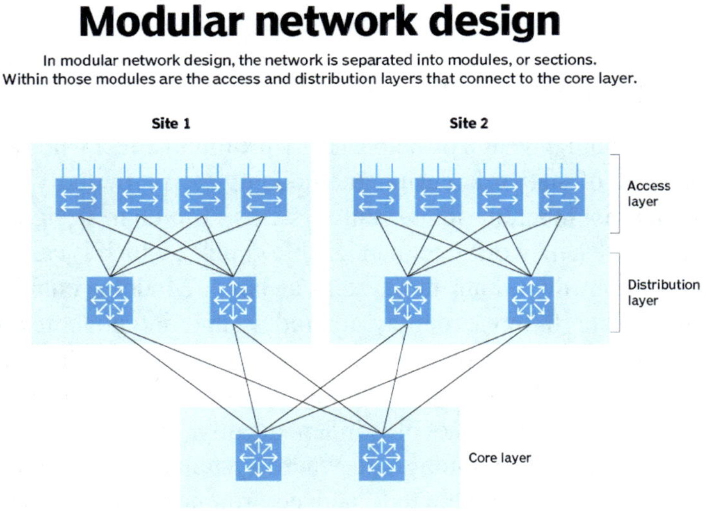

Figure 5.6. *The modular network design helps organize network devices.*

Source: https://www.techtarget.com/rms/onlineimages/modular_network_design-f.png.

5.2.3. Scalability Considerations

Scalability is the top consideration in network design practices, especially when looking ahead to future expansion and evolving needs. The properly designed network needs to support future traffic growth and growing user populations without sacrificing reliability or performance. Scalability is possible using multiple architectural solutions that improve the flexibility of a network. For instance, modular architecture offers incremental resources such as bandwidth and servers, allowing for the expanding requirements of an organization. This allows network architects to add incrementally enhancement appropriate for a specific requirement, ultimately achieving sustainable development. As identified in recent studies, scalability relies on the use of a multidisciplinary network architecture approach, which can be applied to harness all the components of the design for optimal performance and dependability, opening doors for the next generation of architectures (Casu et al., 2009). Furthermore, the application of modern programming paradigms has been at the forefront of making network architectures scalable. For example, Erlang offers a concurrency-oriented programming model that supports inherently scalable and reliable systems, especially distributed systems. With the more widespread application of massively parallel machines, there is the need to overcome limitations in existing languages and virtual machines for the promotion of scalability. Improvement of Erlang toward supporting large-scale multicore systems continuously points to a potential for programming languages to adapt to evolving computing infrastructure needs. With scalable programming infrastructure, network engineers are able to make their systems not just survive existing loads but also prepared for scalability with little refreshes of existing codebases or architectures (Chechina et al., 2012). Scalable and modular design principles are relevant in cultures of rapid technological development and unpredictable traffic patterns. As companies transition to emerging technologies such as IoT and cloud computing, their networks must be able to scale smoothly to accommodate greater loads. Scalable network design emphasizes component interaction, enabling the various technologies to be cohesively combined into one system. Moreover, issues brought by disparate technologies necessitate a malleable framework in support of such combinations. By mediating between performance and scalability, network strategies can remain valid in an increasingly dynamic digital landscape. This commitment to scale-up also enhances user experience, and positions organizations for success in the next wave of technology advancements and market requirements further justifying the necessity of scalability in network design paradigms to remain successful in the long term.

5.3. PROTOCOL-BASED NETWORK DESIGN

Among network design paradigms, protocol-based network design is a key framework that addresses the unique challenges posed by modern networked control systems (NCS). As networks advance, controlling these systems gets increasingly complex, with the need for new approaches that can cope with various types of imperfections such as random delays, packet losses, and quantization effects. The adaptive control designs offered in existing literature are a revolutionary remedy to these challenges. For example, Xu et al. (2012) introduces stochastic optimal adaptive control techniques specifically developed for linear NCS to enable the systems to effectively cope with network performance and dynamic uncertainties. Such adaptability pinpoints the importance of protocol-based frameworks as they provide tools for enhancing system reliability and efficiency under ambient network interference. Moreover, protocol-based approaches are also used to the intricate interaction between control policies and communication protocols.

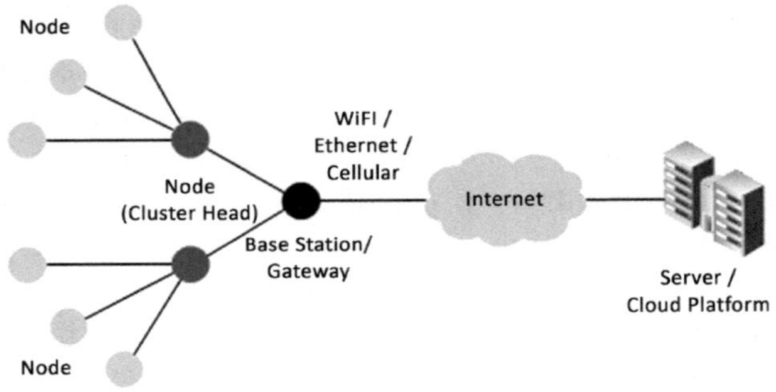

Figure 5.7. *Protocol-based network design.*

Source: https://www.mdpi.com/information/information-12-00292/article_deploy/html/images/information-12-00292-g002.png.

By understanding the behavior of protocols such as TCP and UDP, researchers can determine efficient adaptive control designs that achieve optimal performance in numerous applications. Particularly, Xu et al. (2012) points to reexamination of network protocol behaviors to ensure that linear NCS can act appropriately in response to changing conditions in a bid to enhance overall system robustness. Embedding protocol attributes into network design enables customized adjustment of control mechanisms that respond dynamically to the real-time statuses of the network in a bid to ensure that the performance and stability goals intended are achieved effectively. Moreover, the networked system's problems concerning observability further highlight the imperative demand for protocol-based design structures. State-estimate fusion, as discussed in, illustrates how high-fidelity information exchange among agents can affect the observability of a system in a networked context. Particularly in the cases where measurement fusion in isolation incurs estimation errors, the use of state-estimate fusion strategies becomes essential for enhancing system performance. This approach not only addresses the limitations posed by structured-rank (S-rank) deficiencies in system matrices but also places significance on understanding underlying protocols supporting efficient communication and information sharing. Consequently, the meeting of protocol-based thinking and adaptive control methods remains the cornerstone of robust network design approaches in contemporary applications (Figure 5.7).

5.3.1. Understanding Network Protocols

Understanding network protocols is crucial in network design methods since they are the foundation of rules for devices' communication. Protocols specify how data is exchanged, formatted, and interpreted to facilitate free communication within a network. The selection of appropriate protocols in the network design needs to be considered in order to enable data exchange to take place efficiently and securely. For instance, the Transmission Control Protocol (TCP) and User Datagram Protocol (UDP) each serve a particular purpose, with TCP providing solid communication through error-checking and UDP providing faster transmission but at the cost of reliability. Knowledge of how these protocols function and in what way they are limited allows network designers to design systems that are compatible with their requirements more easily, trading off performance with security needs. Also, the integration between security and network protocols cannot be overstated. Poor security features can create loopholes in a network, which can lead to massive financial loss on the part of organizations. As noted under web engineering discussions, security should not be considered an addon but integrated from the very beginning at the design level. This integration ensures security controls are integrated into the design of the network, safeguarding communication protocols against threat. Understanding protocols not only assists designers in having protection in place but also prepares them to respond appropriately to security breaches. This proactive planning for network design emphasizes the importance of incorporating security considerations into each protocol decision and implementation level, thus maintaining better overall network resilience and trust. Cognitive computing, as part of emerging technologies, has a disruptive potential to influence network protocol creation. As organizations adopt smart systems that mimic human cognitive processes, the protocols will have to evolve to these technologies. Autonomic computing, with its self-healing, self-tuning, and self-management capabilities, enables the capability of the network to anticipate and react to unusual situations autonomously. The incorporation of such advanced protocols in network designs enhances the robustness of the system against malicious cyberattacks and operational error mistakes. As networks become more complex, understanding and adapting network protocols to leverage cognitive computing will be essential for network designs to stay future-proofed, fix potential problems, and be capable of leveraging network management and security automation gains.

5.3.2. Protocols' Role in Design

In network design methodologies, protocols are critical frameworks that define rules for data transfer, providing the means for effective communication among different systems. The protocols specify how devices interact with each other, correct errors, and maintain connections, and this is crucial for the provision of effective and stable network operation. As the technologies such as the Internet of Things (IoT) and vehicle-to-vehicle networks evolve, the importance of protocols is increasingly relevant. For instance, the spread of V2V-V2I communication technologies is an example of how specific protocols enable enhanced traffic management systems through the real-time exchange of information between infrastructure and vehicles. This movement benefits not only operational efficiency but also contributes to achieving greater objectives, such as reducing congestion and improving safety on urban roads (Cartolano et al., 2008). Also, the design of protocols must be sensitive to the environment in which they will operate, particularly for advanced systems such as medical networks. Developing medical processor unit-specific protocols is a good example. By extrapolating basic architectural principles from successful predecessors, designers can devise protocols that allow for the special requirements of medical usage, where data can stand for important things such as patients and medical devices. This position emphasizes the necessity of protocols to cater not only to data exchange but also to the complexity of clinical environments, thereby ensuring that the operational codes provide for precise, error-free interactions which ultimately result in enhanced patient care (Ahamed et al., 2011). The ongoing evolution of network design methods also emphasizes the necessity of strict testing and verification of protocols to ensure their performance under actual circumstances. Field Operational Tests, for instance, have been necessary in order to assess the potential benefits of wireless vehicular cooperative systems. These tests provide the ability to calculate realistic protocol performance under various traffic conditions and network loads, as well as identify potential improvements. With protocol integration into network design maturing further, the reliance on end-to-end test facilities becomes unavoidable to mature these frameworks into practical platforms for advanced applications. With investment in such methods, designers not only achieve augmented network efficiency but also greater flexibility with which they can cope with forthcoming technological problems, leading to innovative traffic management and other solutions (Cartolano et al., 2008) (Figure 5.8).

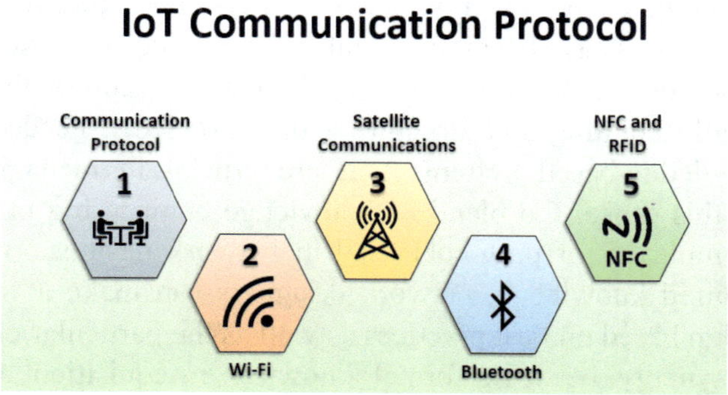

Figure 5.8. *Role of protocols in design.*

Source: https://www.designandexecute.com/designs/wp-content/uploads/2025/01/iot-communication-protocol-1-2730191704.png.

5.3.3. Examples of Protocol-Based Methodologies

Protocol-based frameworks are core in contemporary network design paradigms when it comes to enhancing the efficiency and security of operations in networks. The frameworks typically emphasize existing communication protocols, which take center stage in deciding how information is transmitted in networks. One such instance is using protocols like Transmission Control Protocol (TCP) and Internet Protocol (IP) to enable reliable and organized communication among devices. The robustness of such protocols lies at the core of their integration in various network design techniques, allowing for seamless connections and even addressing issues of data integrity and packet loss. Protocol-based approaches not only maximize performance metrics but also provide a systematic way of addressing issues of network failure, thus catering to their central position in modern networking systems. Also critical within the domain of network design is including cryptographic protocols, which are specifically designed to secure information in transit. The application of cryptography, as highlighted in the discussion of DNA-based approaches, emphasizes the need to secure the confidentiality, integrity, and availability

(CIA triad) of data within computer networks. The book DNA cryptography is inspired by the biological process of DNA molecules, establishing a new data security paradigm that merges traditional cryptographic approaches with biological principles. This is a showcase of how protocol-based techniques are bound to evolve and adopt sophisticated theories so that information remains not vulnerable to unauthorized access and cyber-attacks. These innovations present the dynamic interactive relationship between protocol deployment and emerging technologies in protecting networked systems. Moreover, knowledge elicitation procedures have become pivotal in developing sophisticated network design methodologies. According to Shadbolt et al. (2005), the techniques involve formally eliciting and structuring the knowledge needed to develop efficient knowledge-based systems that are crucial in managing complex networks. In this sense, the blend of knowledge engineering practices helps define the complexity of protocols used in network designs. By leveraging formally acquired knowledge, network designers can make a well-informed choice in design based on best practices as well as the particular organizational needs. This synergy between formal knowledge acquisition and practical network use is the finest instance of the flexibility of protocol-based approaches that demonstrate their utility not just in maintaining effective communication but also in fostering innovation and resilience in network infrastructures.

5.4. PERFORMANCE-BASED NETWORK DESIGN

Performance-Based Network Design is now a central technique in the overall domain of Network Design Methodologies, pinpointing the importance of tailored solutions that enhance system performance. The approach is premised on comprehending and streamlining network behavior by leveraging data-driven knowledge to inform design decisions. More precisely, the integration of observational data allows researchers and engineers to approximate important parameters and test network topologies effectively. Iterative refinement implies improving the network architecture based on performance criteria so that the ultimate architecture is tailored to address particular operational requirements and user needs. In this manner, a performance-driven approach not only promotes better reliability and efficiency but also helps in making networks more adaptable against changing conditions or demands. At the center of Performance-Based Network Design is the application of advanced computational tools, which are utilized to map the complexities of nonlinear systems. As a point of illustration, through applications like Bayesian inference, the designer can construct robust models that address variability and uncertainty in network performance. These models are enhanced by systematic frameworks that integrate observations into parameter estimation and structural learning, facilitating a deeper comprehension of network dynamics. As highlighted in recent research, traditional Bayesian methods typically lack scalability due to the enormous combinatorial space of potential models. But novel techniques based on improved Markov chain Monte Carlo approaches are positive strides toward mitigating these challenges, enabling practitioners to give improved network performance estimation (Galagali et al., 2019). Moreover, Performance-Based Network Design intersects with other methodologies such as network tomography with enhanced performance evaluation and diagnosis of complex networks. Statistical approaches are employed in this approach for inference of characterizations of interdependent systems from observed data in order to target key performance indicators such as traffic demand and delay. By studying one-dimensional projections of data, scientists have developed methods that yield estimators of the same effectiveness as more traditional maximum likelihood methods, in the end improving statistical efficiency in network diagnostics. These advances are not only necessary for maximizing existing networks but also for informing the design of future networks that will be required to fulfill increasingly intricate requirements. Therefore, the integration of performance-oriented methods into network design methodologies is a fundamental advancement in the quest for efficient and resilient network systems (Cao et al., 2007) (Figure 5.9).

Figure 5.9. *Performance-based network design.*

Source: https://micropro.com/wp-content/uploads/2023/07/computer-networks.jpg

5.4.1. Key Performance Indicators (KPIs)

Among network design strategies, Key Performance Indicators (KPIs) are crucial metrics that allow organizations to gauge the effectiveness and efficiency of their networks. KPIs provide the capability to quantify network performance, which facilitates stakeholders' ease of identifying areas for improvement. With the employment of a balanced scorecard (BSC) framework, organizations can group applicable KPIs under various perspectives like customer satisfaction, financial, internal processes, and learning and growth. This classification ensures that the selected KPIs support the organizational strategic objectives, ultimately leading to responsive and flexible network designs capable of reacting to changing market conditions and technology innovations (M et al., 2018).

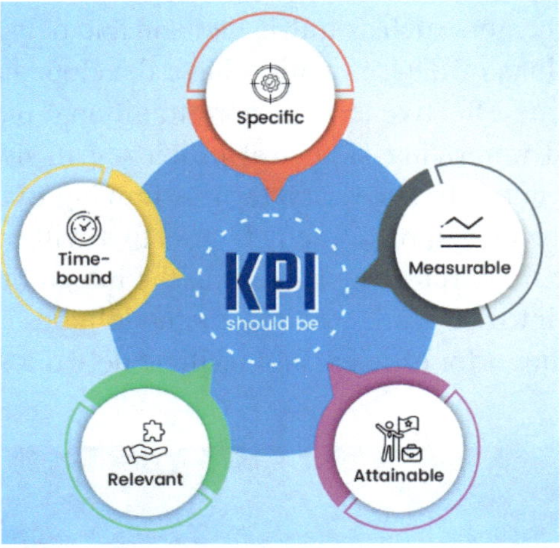

Figure 5.10. *Key performance indicators (KPIs).*

Source: https://smartreach.io/blog/wp-content/uploads/2024/01/KPI.jpg.

Moreover, the use of KPIs in the process of network design makes efficient performance management possible, which is central to organizational success. By placing stress on KPIs, firms are able to track their advancement towards established goals and therefore guarantee ongoing improvement and decision-making that is fact-driven. The strategic management system involving these KPIs enables firms to respond rapidly to changes in customer demands while having a watchful eye on delivering value. With networks increasingly sophisticated due to globalization and fast-moving advances in IT, systematic tracking and review of KPIs ever more a necessity for optimizing resource performance and responsiveness (Mehedintu et al., 2012). At the heart of this framework lies the need for organizations to grasp KPIs that reflect their individual operational targets and market environment. A structured method of choosing these KPIs can help avoid performance measure and organizational goal misalignment, as suggested in various studies. For instance, utilizing the Technique for Order of

Preference by Similarity to Ideal Solution (TOPSIS) combined with qualitative methods such as quality function deployment (QFD) enables organizations to determine critical success factors that will significantly enhance their agility. These systems approach not only assists in the identification of proper KPIs but also in making sure that they are closely linked to the company's underlying value and strategic intent, providing improved agility and performance in network design strategies (M et al., 2018) (Figure 5.10).

5.4.2. Traffic Analysis and Management

Traffic management and analysis form integral parts of network design strategies, especially in the design of urban infrastructure. Effective traffic management does not only enhance vehicle movement but also eliminates congestion, thus improving road safety. Real-time analytics of data plays a critical integration process in this area, allowing city planners to see traffic flows, identify peak hours, and implement timely interventions. By means of techniques such as modeling and simulation, traffic engineers can create better transportation networks, which cater to the changing needs of urban residents. Moreover, adopting advanced technologies such as adaptive traffic signals and intelligent transportation systems (ITS) helps in improved traffic management, ultimately leading to decreased travel times and environmental footprints. Furthermore, the coordination of traffic management and economic growth cannot be disregarded. Well-managed transport networks facilitate not only day-to-day travel, but also influence the overall economic infrastructure. For the third world, better traffic management procedures can encourage political stability and sustainable development, with research today identifying their key role in these settings. The need for a well-planned approach to studying traffic only increases as cities grow and get larger. Employing precise datasets collected over time enables planners to ascertain the maintenance needs and resource deployment. More specifically, methodologies applied in effective pavement management can demonstrate cost-saving initiatives tailored to localized conditions, which can ensure road network long-term viability (Bonin et al., 2019). Finally, although technological advances are key drivers of traffic analysis and management, do not forget the human element either. Training programs enhancing focus and performance among traffic management personnel can enhance the effectiveness of implemented strategies. Interdisciplinary coordination between researchers, public agencies, and the private sector can speed innovative solutions to pressing traffic issues. Synthesis of findings from several disciplines, as seen in treatments of cybersecurity and risk management, illustrates the merit of an interdisciplinary strategy for infrastructure resilience. As urban traffic patterns continue to change in light of shifts in demographics and technology, management strategies aligned with such evolving conditions will be critical to the formulation of effective and sustainable transport systems sensitive to the needs of the future urban way of life (Anglano et al., 2018).

5.4.3. Quality of Service (QoS) Strategies

In network planning designs, the deployment of robust Quality of Service (QoS) policies is critical in guaranteeing high reliability and high performance of network communications. QoS policies address how to prioritize specific types of traffic for guaranteed quality of service, particularly delay-sensitive applications such as video conferencing and online gaming. These methods can involve traffic shaping, bandwidth assignment, and scheduling processes that attempt to maximize the allocation of resources across the network. With increasing demand for a variety of applications with varying bandwidth and latency needs, the adaptability of QoS mechanisms becomes significant in delivering end-user satisfaction and functional performance. Also, with networks evolving to accommodate a multitude of connected devices, the scalability of QoS solutions will be crucial to ensuring the end-users' seamless experience. An advanced method of rolling out QoS solutions involves incorporating Quality of Experience (QoE) elements, an approach that emphasizes the end-users' perception of service quality. It has become more and more evident that network solutions must move beyond standard QoS factors to incorporate user-centric aspects. QoE control capabilities aim to observe individualized desired levels of application performance and dynamically select appropriate classes of service according to user needs. For instance, applying a heuristic Multi-Agent Reinforcement Learning (MARL) algorithm facilitates this dynamic choice procedure while solving the complexities involved in managing large-scale interactions among agents in the network. This new approach not only enhances users' experience but also solves real-world implementation problems, thereby enhancing the quality of service under various network scenarios and user surroundings (Priscoli et al., 2017). Furthermore, the continuous process of wireless system development points towards the necessity of advanced QoS techniques in resource allocation and scheduling. As the number of services and users increases, so too does the requirement of efficient radio resource management in creating fairness among the users. The focus on QoE as a design driver for network schedulers is key to an emerging trend in the optimization of service delivery in user satisfaction terms rather than purely technical performance. Recent scheduling techniques have shown significant advances in incorporating QoE measures into their frameworks, capturing how latency, jitter, and throughput may be traded off to optimize end-to-end service quality. Therefore, the integration of QoE-oriented techniques within wireless networks improves a more refined understanding of user experience, which directly contributes to the development of effective policies for QoS in future wireless systems (Queluz et al., 2020) (Figure 5.11).

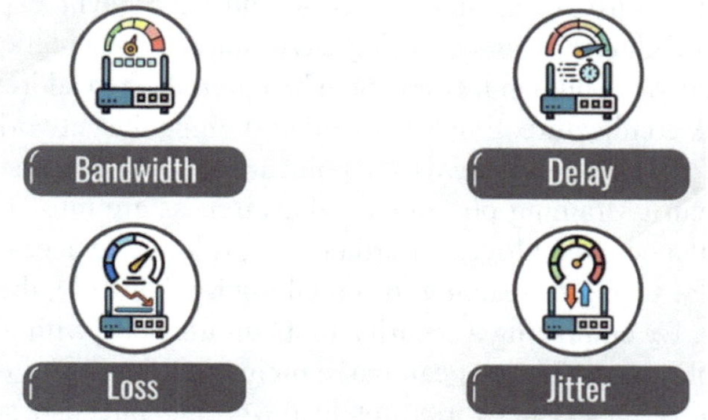

Figure 5.11. *Quality of service (QoS) strategies.*

Source: https://marvel-b1-cdn.bc0a.com/f00000000310757/www.fortinet.com/content/dam/fortinet/images/cyberglossary/qos-quality-of-service.jpg.

5.5. SECURITY CONSIDERATIONS IN NETWORK DESIGN

A comprehensive approach to network design must prioritize security considerations, as vulnerabilities can emerge from various components of the infrastructure. A fundamental aspect of securing a network involves understanding the types of threats that can exploit weaknesses in its architecture. For instance, unauthorized access, malware attacks, and data breaches are significant concerns that can compromise sensitive information and disrupt operations. Network designers need to adopt strategies that incorporate security aspects from the very beginning, which can include the installation of efficient authentication systems and configuring firewalls. Organisations can create a stronger network that can counter threats in a better way and thereby keep their information confidential and maintain its integrity by addressing these vulnerabilities beforehand. Moreover, the incorporation of virtualization technologies makes security planning all the more complex in network architecture. Virtualization provides multiple benefits, including cost-effectiveness and optimal utilization of resources; however, it presents certain weaknesses that need to be handled with care. The hypervisor layer, which is responsible for governing virtual machines, can prove to be a vulnerable point of attack, which can expose all reliant virtual environments. Therefore, the design process should strictly assess the security of virtualization technologies. Since literature acknowledges, hypervisor security has been improved, but techniques must still consider the vulnerabilities of virtual machine detection and subsequent exploitation and thus must approach testing and securing environments systematically (Coull et al., 2017). Finally, the human factor cannot be ignored when addressing security within network architecture. Employees either running the network or talking to it can inadvertently become the weakest point and thereby, cause severe security violations. Security training programs and awareness are must for instilling a culture of vigilance in employees. Furthermore, role-based access controls can limit users from seeing or reacting to something by their role, thereby limiting insider threats. By embracing a security-first culture along with good technical design principles, organizations can make their overall security posture better, which ultimately means networks not just working but also secure against emerging threats (Ahamed et al., 2011).

5.5.1. Risk Assessment and Management

Among the essential components of network design methodologies is the integration of rigorous risk assessment and management processes. Risk assessment is one part of the process of determining potential weaknesses in a network that enables organizations to scrutinize the likelihood and impact of various risks. With the proper evaluation of these risks, organizations can make an effective decision about the design and implementation of their networks. For instance, the relevance of environmental risk assessments is highlighted in the case of genetically modified organisms (GMOs) since the absence of adequate monitoring infrastructures can introduce significant uncertainties over environmental impacts (Andersen et al., 2012). Similarly, during network planning, a formal process of risk assessment ensures that technical vulnerabilities along with socio-economic factors are properly considered. It is only through such a nuanced perspective that effective network infrastructures can be developed to adapt to evolving threats. Risk management is also required to supplement risk assessment by providing an official means to mitigate discovered risks. This does not just involve installing countermeasures but also continual evaluation of the efficiency of the countermeasures. Financial constraints often complicate this, as budgetary demands need to be balanced against heightened security demands. As quoted in literature, lack of financial ability can potentially inhibit efficient selection of security countermeasures (Huang et al., 2011). It is therefore paramount that organizations adopt economic models that allow efficient prioritization of risk management strategies to enable proper allocation of resources. Strategic resource allocation, combined with proper risk assessment models, not only improves security of networks but also business as a whole sustainability. Finally, management is also interdependent with risk assessment, and it involves proactive stakeholders. In the design of a network, involving various stakeholders can facilitate more comprehension of the risks involved as a whole. Such a wide scope of comprehension facilitates developing personalized risk management plans addressing individual vulnerabilities in addition to its overall socio-economic impacts. The establishment of working frameworks like the envisaged European Network for systematic impact assessment of GMOs is indicative of the potential of multi-sector collaboration (Andersen et al., 2012). Such frameworks can facilitate knowledge exchange and foster confidence in risk management outcomes. In conclusion, this collaboration not only strengthens the network resilience but also identifies the importance of collective responsibility in securing digital infrastructures against increasingly complex forms of threats (Figure 5.12).

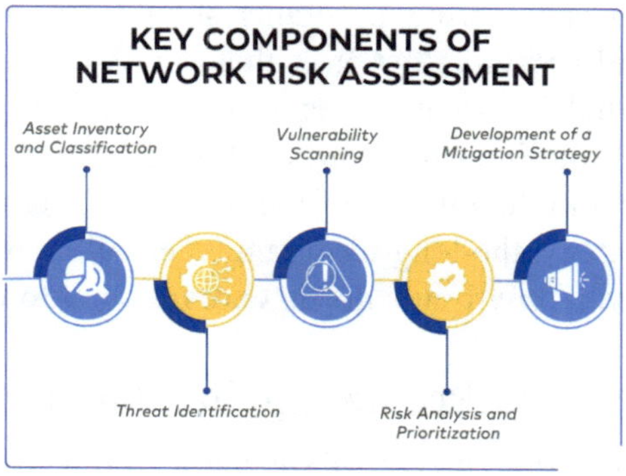

Figure 5.12. *Risk assessment and management.*

Source: https://cdn-blog.getastra.com/2025/05/10a0927f-key-components-of-network-risk-assessment.jpg.

5.5.2. Implementation of Security Protocols

The inclusion of security protocols in network design approaches is critical to protecting both infrastructure and data integrity. With more organizations becoming dependent on web applications, the need to implement security measures right from the beginning cannot be overemphasized. One of the most prevalent mistakes in web engineering is the belief that security can be an added aspect after completing a system. But Glisson et al. (2010 maintains that security must become part of the design process, implanting defense mechanisms along the way. By adopting this proactive approach, developers can ensure that programs are crafted to be able to withstand various conceivable threats, reducing exposures vulnerable to attack from malicious forces. Moreover, the dynamic character of network environments necessitates a model that is not just secure but also capable of addressing nascent threats timely. Security systems must be adaptable to the character of modern systems where individuals can react without central governance and configuration is dynamic. As taken by Priami et al. (2003), networks should be planned in such a way that they emphasis flexibility, reliability, and intense interaction between self-contained computing entities. This means that security measures need to be designed with the capability to handle system variability and the associated risks of mobility and decentralized operations characteristic of today's networks. Finally, most of the effort of installing security protocols entails having a complete knowledge of potential risks and vulnerabilities within the system architecture. Security solutions must not only guard against immediate threats but anticipate future threat problems as technologies evolve and new vulnerabilities develop. Computing and web engineering programs should thus contain courses on security forensics and proactive threat evaluation. By equipping students and professionals with vital information regarding these issues, as suggested by Glisson et al. (2010), the industry can breed a generation of developers who prioritize security as an integral part of the network design process. With this kind of informed strategy, the long-term outcome will be the creation of more secure and safer network environments that are resistant to future attacks.

5.5.3. Compliance with Regulating Standards

Compliance with the requirements of regulatory bodies is a key feature in network design policy, especially in the prevailing digital environment. Regulatory steps are taken to safeguard user data, enforce fair play, and achieve reliability in services. Ignorance of such steps can result in severe operational loss, such as legal repercussions and loss of credibility. For example, during the 1998–1999 Chilean electricity crisis, it came to light that the regulatory bodies were not able to exert their power effectively, resulting in power shortages that might otherwise have been averted with accurate knowledge of price mechanisms and regulation demands (Diaz et al., 2025). This is an illustration of the importance of not only having laws but also actually enforcing them as well as developing the regulations in step with the new world of the technology age. Network design approaches must incorporate compliance mechanisms right from the initial design concept of network design. This will ensure national as well as international regulation compliance becomes a part and parcel of system design and not an afterthought. As companies increasingly rely on web-enabled systems to manage efficiency, network architectures of such companies must support strong auditing and monitoring systems to ensure adherence to regulatory compliance standards (Glisson et al., 2007). Moreover, the systems should be flexible enough to accommodate adaptation as per evolving regulatory environments, which usually demand adjustments in compliance practices in a timely manner. Thus, using flexible methods during the design process can promote resistiveness to evolving regulatory concerns. The linkage between compliance and network design goes past mere rule-following; it is an commitment to ethical behavior that ultimately reinforces trust and reliability. Companies that prioritize compliance as a key pillar in their network design methodologies can set themselves apart from competitors by having a strong foundation of accountability in place. Regular review of compliance can identify vulnerabilities in the network, hence enable organizations to make necessary adjustments and de-activate potential threats before they expand to crisis levels. In essence, proactive compliance provides additional security to the organization as well as enabling a sustainable model of operations that benefits all stakeholders involved, including customers, regulators, and society at large. This holistic view of compliance then decides the sustainability and efficiency of network design paradigms in a more networked world (Figure 5.13).

Figure 5.13. *Compliance with regulatory standards.*

Source: https://linfordco.com/wp-content/uploads/2013/06/a-guide-to-regulatory-compliance.jpg.

5.6. EMERGING TRENDS IN NETWORK DESIGN

The rapid pace of technology advancement has triggered a revolution in network design paradigms, and changing trends reshape the landscape of data communication. The most dramatic trend is the emergence of NoC architectures, particularly in nano-electronics. The silicon-based systems that conventionally suffer from limitations due to their limits of scalability and efficiency are being counter-intuitively researched with irregular, abstract interconnect fabrics on the basis of NoC models. These new architectures provide assurance of better communication qualities, reliability over link failures, and a ease to solve complex tasks such as synchronization. By the alteration of essential parameters such as connectivity and the short- and long-distance connection pattern, these new architectures ultimately enable significant improvements over traditional network designs, thereby charting a clear course toward more flexible and efficient interconnection schemes for the newly emerging field of electronics (Teuscher et al., 2007). With the increasing importance of digital technologies, the methodologies underpinning network design more and more display convergence with ideas of morphogenesis and digital tectonics. The historic dichotomy between structural engineering and architectural design is disintegrating, as new paradigms reconfigure their symbiotic relationship. Such a shift is characterized by a trend for the integration of structure, material, and form, which results in an overall more integrated design philosophy that exploits developments in digital media and design method. Such developments make possible networks that are not only dedicated to performance but are also aesthetically compatible with their functional requirements. Through the adoption of morphogenetic models that frame processes, network designers are able to create architectures that are not only efficient but also adaptive to address evolving environmental and operational demands (Oxman et al., 2010). Among new trends in methodologies for designing networks is increased application of artificial intelligence (AI) and machine learning to enhance network management. As networks become more sophisticated, conventional methods of configuration and maintenance are becoming increasingly unsustainable. By utilizing AI-driven analytics, designers are able to forecast network behavior, identify anomalies, and respond to performance issues automatically with high efficiency. Furthermore, machine learning algorithms can browse enormous data sources to predict upcoming network demand, thereby enabling proactive adjustments in capacity and resource allocation. This shift from reactive to active management is a revolutionary step ahead in network design, allowing systems that not only address current user needs but dynamically reshape to solve upcoming problems. The integration of AI with emerging design paradigms is a key breakthrough in how networks are conceived, built, and maintained in existing technological landscapes.

5.6.1. Software-Defined Networking (SDN)

The arrival of Software-Defined Networking (SDN) is a notable shift in paradigms that guide modern network design. Unlike traditional approaches that tightly couple control and data planes, SDN disentangles these components such that they are managed centrally. This decoupling not only enables increased control flexibility in the network, but it also encourages agility in new application and service deployment. The architecture enables easier programmability, as network managers have the ability to respond rapidly to changing needs and traffic patterns. Interestingly, the present discussions in the software world contribute towards actively shaping the development of SDN as developers, systems administrators, and engineers collaborate and establish new standards and best practices for effective implementation and utilization of this new model of networking.

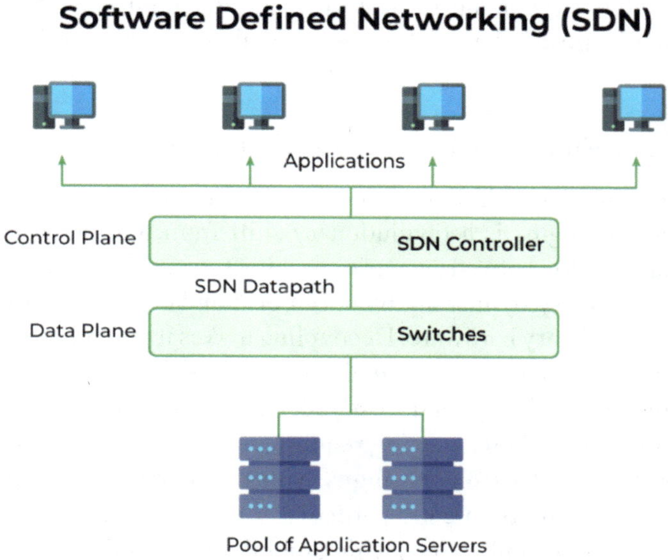

Figure 5.14. *The emergence of software-defined networking (SDN).*

Source: https://media.geeksforgeeks.org/wp-content/uploads/20230405132159/Software-Defined-Networking.png.

While SDN provides the advantages listed, it comes with difficulties that must be addressed if one is to totally reach the vision of SDN in network design concepts. The built-in centralized control in SDN design comes with threats that are vulnerable to exploitation by malicious entities. For instance, DoS and DDoS attacks can lead to considerable degradation of network performance since the controller may be a point of failure (Akowuah et al., 2023). Thus, security concerns must be met in order to render SDN deployable at scale. Advances in defense mechanisms against the attacks will not only require continuous research efforts but also ensure the establishment of effective mitigation methods that will enhance the threat resilience of SDN systems. The future of networking relies on continuous innovation of SDN approaches, which can potentially transform the design and control of the network. With organizations adopting SDN, there is a need to ensure best practices are established, particularly with security and operation reliability. Work being done on northbound interfaces, while vital, must be supported by innovation in defense technologies that can anticipate and counter emerging vulnerabilities and attack channels. Increased studies and collaboration within the sector will be essential, as the foundation for SDN is laid by collaborating in a collective way between network professionals, software developers, and hardware vendors. On this note, the innovation of SDN will definitely trigger the release of next-generation networks that not only coincidentally are efficient and scalable but also secure and robust (Figure 5.14).

5.6.2. Network Function Virtualization (NFV)

The application of Network Function Virtualization (NFV) in the current network design paradigms is a revolutionary shift from traditional hardware-centric approaches to software-centric architectures. NFV revolutionizes network service delivery by making them run on standard IT platforms, rather than relying on proprietary hardware. Decoupling makes it possible for operators to manage network functions as virtualized applications, leading to greater agility, operational efficiency, and cost reduction. With NFV, organizations can scale up rapidly based on changing requirements, generating a more robust network infrastructure. This model aligns with the increasing complexity of modern-day network environments, particularly as they expand in a manner that encompasses varied applications within mobile, edge, and cloud computing realms. Furthermore, the inclusion of NFV holds great promise for enhancing the delivery of services. Particularly, as applied to the use with Mobile Edge Computing (MEC), NFV can be applied to manage the provision of services that exploit virtualized resources distributed over several sites. SESAME EU project illustrates the application of NFV ideas in developing new paradigms for analyzing Small Cell Network security and thereby providing an extension of MEC capabilities in the expanding 5G landscape. These advancements point toward the necessity of developing network infrastructures that are not only resilient, but also able to accommodate heterogeneous and dynamically changing enterprise service needs. With this perspective on security mechanisms, network planners and operators can take a more unified approach to securing virtualized networks. But the transition to NFV is not without challenge. Security for virtualized network functions is a hot topic, and one that requires effective risk assessment and mitigation techniques. Concern for security in designs, such as that proposed in the SESAME project, emphasizes the need for robust protection against vulnerabilities introduced by virtualization. At the same time, emerging software-based communication technology requires ongoing R&D to ensure the most effective deployment of NFV. Hence, network design practices will have to evolve to incorporate such findings, creating partnership between stakeholders to create standards and best practices that address performance and security issues in virtualized environments (Nunes et al., 2016; Duan et al., 2017) (Figure 5.15).

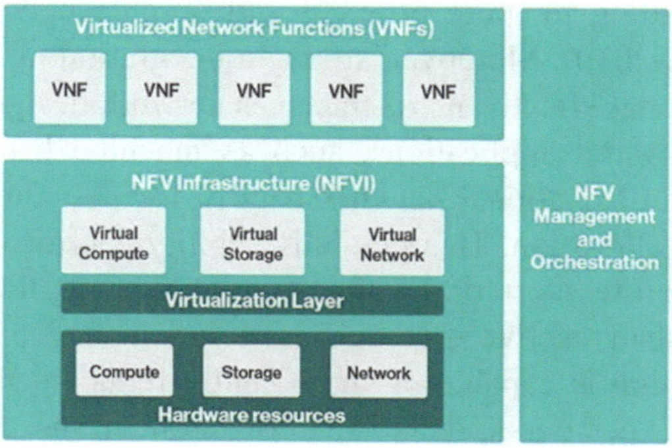

Figure 5.15. *The application of network function virtualization (NFV).*

Source: https://www.techtarget.com/rms/onlineImages/VNFs_mobile.jpg.

5.6.3. Integration of Artificial Intelligence (AI)

The incorporation of Artificial Intelligence (AI) in network design procedures is a breakthrough in the design, building, and management of network systems. With more complication in networks, traditional methods might not be effective in addressing the changing requirements of modern environments. AI-driven procedures employ cognitive computing, whereby systems are able to learn and adapt on their own in accordance with varying operation problems. This adaptability is particularly necessary because networks are faced with increasingly large volumes of data and potential security threats. By mimicking the capability of the human brain, these systems can predict abnormal situations and respond accordingly and hence enhance system reliability and network infrastructure performance. Also, the concept of autonomic computing, such that systems manage to keep themselves running, becomes increasingly relevant in a way that self-optimization and self-healing can be achieved and reduce human interaction considerably (Nazir et al., 2017). Decision support systems (DSS) are another fundamental aspect of the integration of AI into network design methodologies. DSSs have traditionally lived in silos and, often, have not been able to meet the rapid nature of today's problems faced in networks.

Evolution towards integrated decision support systems (IDSS) emphasizes systems that operate synergistically. AI powers these IDSS with analytical powers that make decision-making simpler and enable network designers to make informed decisions based on real-time data and predictive analytics. With more studies conducted on IDSS, there is an evident drive towards enhancing the integration function of these systems. By addressing integration as an overall issue, network planners can expect better decision-making and processes, leading to more efficient and durable network architectures (Kaklauskas et al., 2010). Moreover, strategic integration of AI, in addition to increasing operational effectiveness, enhances network design models through innovation. AI-powered applications, such as machine learning algorithms, aid in the analysis of historical network data to forecast future demands and optimize resource allocation. This predictive ability is critical in being able to anticipate issues before interfering with network operation, therefore exhibiting a proactive rather than reactive approach to network management. Additionally, AI-driven automation is capable of significantly reducing the administrative burden for network personnel, therefore allowing them more time to focus on strategy formulation and execution. With companies continuing to explore the benefits of incorporating AI into network design, it is probably safe to say that these advances will lead to more efficient, responsive, and resilient network designs capable of responding to the realities of an ever-connected world.

SUMMARY

The comparative analysis of various network design approaches puts in perspective the necessity for adaptive methodologies that align with evolving technology. As organizations increasingly depend on robust network architecture, it is paramount to identify how various methodologies can be implemented and realized. The employment of contemporary practices such as agile development principles indicates the necessity of adaptability in design processes. Thus, this adaptive approach enables constant improvement by performance measurement and feedback, and enables instructors and practitioners to monitor the impact of their actions on end-users. Methodologies are not only critically examined on a theoretical basis; it is essential to ascertain whether network architectures meet current and future demands. Moreover, the application of analytical tools to measure the performance of methodology and network design enables data-driven decision-making. New practices such as analyzing repositories for software reveal what drives user behavior and resistance to new systems (Hesse et al., 2019). This empirical information helps network planners and teachers to realize the extent to which methodology shifts, like transitioning from Scrum to Kanban, affect workflow effectiveness and user experience. By analyzing these factors methodically, networks can be planned to develop user efficiency and satisfaction, ultimately facilitating the objective of unfettered connectivity throughout organizational hierarchies. Lastly, stakeholder collaboration through network planning methodologies appears to be a key success factor. Engaging the experts from various sectors—academic, industry, and community—is helping in exchanging knowledge and best practices to address complex challenges (Clements et al., 2017). The learning developed through shared experiences breeds innovation, especially using low-cost solutions in approaching individual sector demands. As seen from these debates, creating partnerships not only heightens awareness but also drives practical use of methodologies in real-world applications. Finally, the awareness of the interconnectivity between methodologies, stakeholder knowledge, and data analysis will take the field of network design to greater heights and strengthen its contribution to organizational success.

In reflecting on the many methodologies essential to effective network design, it is necessary to ascertain the fundamental concepts upon which these methodologies are established. An effective network design methodology seeks to address different elements of operational efficiency, scalability, and flexibility. Among the features of effective methodologies is a systematic study of present and future network demands, thus aligning with organizational goals and user requirements. Foremost among them is that as the networks mature, the integration of new technologies is paramount. Therefore, studying multiple methodologies not only provides a template for implementation but also enables continuous evolution in keeping with the new trends in technology. Another pre-eminent consideration in the case of network design methodologies is the requirement for cooperative action among stakeholders. The design process involves inputs from end-users, management, and IT professionals so that the network infrastructure will align to operation objectives. Besides this, as organizations expand worldwide, regulatory compliance, geographical dispersal, and varied user experiences are issues to be considered in planning networks. For instance, large guidelines and recommendations are pivotal in formulating a network that accommodates different operational needs and monitors and controls the difficulties associated with large-scale deployments, as explained in Leclerc et al. (2005). Such an interactive framework significantly enhances the performance and quality of network systems. Finally, with technology advancements still accelerating, practices must also account for the integration of high-end elements, such as Phase-Locked Loops (PLLs). Within modern network designs, the roles of PLLs in coordinating data transmission and maintaining clock stability cannot be overstated. Such devices are pivotal to the operation of mixed signal and digital on chip (SOC) circuits with various architectures being employed to cater to specific applications, as illustrated in Burbidge et al. (2008). Having PLLs operate stably becomes mission-critical for the entire network infrastructure, as their synchronizing capabilities have a direct impact on data integrity and system performance. Therefore, gaining a full understanding of these methodologies directly contributes to formulating robust and efficient network architectures capable of taking on today's challenges.

REFERENCES

1. Agyekum-Mensah, G., Knight, A., & Pasquire, C. (2012). Adaption of structured analysis design techniques methodology for construction project planning. https://core.ac.uk/download/30630262.pdf (accessed on 9th September 2025).
2. Ahamed, S. V., & Rahman, S. S. M. (2011). Architecture and design of medical processor units for medical networks. http://arxiv.org/abs/1111.1768 (accessed on 9th September 2025).
3. Akowuah, E., Kommey, B., Opoku, D., Tamakloe, E., et al. (2023). Detailed review on the denial of service (DoS) and distributed denial of service (DDoS) attacks in software defined networks (SDNs) and defense strategies. https://core.ac.uk/download/593663150.pdf (accessed on 9th September 2025).
4. Albayrak, S., Hrabia, C. E., & Lützenberger, M. (2018). Towards adaptive multi-robot systems: Self-organization and self-adaptation. https://core.ac.uk/download/222444390.pdf (accessed on 9th September 2025).
5. Ampazis, N., Dounias, G., & Tsakonas, A. (2006). Towards a comprehensible and accurate credit management model: Application of four computational intelligence methodologies. https://core.ac.uk/download/4898533.pdf (accessed on 9th September 2025).
6. Andersen, E., Aslaksen, I., Bernard, J., Binimelis, R., et al. (2012). A framework for a European network for a systematic environmental impact assessment of genetically modified organisms (GMO). https://core.ac.uk/download/16386196.pdf (accessed on 9th September 2025).
7. Anglano, C., Aniello, L., Antinori, A., Armando, A., et al. (2018). The future of cybersecurity in Italy: Strategic focus area. https://core.ac.uk/download/188830442.pdf (accessed on 9th September 2025).
8. Bond, H., Harel, D., Kinny, D., Kendall, E. A., Verharen, E. M., Brazier, F. M. T., et al. (1999). A survey of agent-oriented methodologies. https://core.ac.uk/download/148663568.pdf (accessed on 9th September 2025).
9. Bonin, G., Loprencipe, G., Pantuso, A., Teltayev, B., et al. (2019). Analysis of pavement condition survey data for effective implementation of a network level pavement management program for Kazakhstan. https://core.ac.uk/download/188832523.pdf (accessed on 9th September 2025).
10. Braccini, M. (2017). Applications of biological cell models in robotics. http://arxiv.org/abs/1712.02303 (accessed on 9th September 2025).
11. Brasher, A., Conole, G., Cross, S., Culver, J., et al. (2009). New methods and approaches to the design and evaluation of open educational resources.

https://core.ac.uk/download/109232.pdf (accessed on 9th September 2025).

12. Burbidge, M., & Richardson, A. (2008). Phase locked loop test methodology. https://core.ac.uk/download/1558600.pdf (accessed on 9th September 2025).
13. Bussmann, S., Jennings, N. R., & Wooldridge, M. J. (2000). On the identification of agents in the design of production control systems.
14. Cao, J., & Chen, A. (2007). Network tomography based on 1-D projections. http://arxiv.org/abs/0705.4476 (accessed on 9th September 2025).
15. Cartolano, F., Filali, F., Gozalvez, J., Krajzewicz, D., et al. (2008). iTETRIS: An integrated wireless and traffic platform for real-time road traffic management solutions. https://core.ac.uk/download/11140413.pdf (accessed on 9th September 2025).
16. Castro López, R., Fernández Fernández, F. V., Roca Moreno, E., Velasco Jiménez, M., et al. (2010). Load-independent characterization of trade-off fronts for operational amplifiers. https://core.ac.uk/download/186617898.pdf (accessed on 9th September 2025).
17. Casu, M. R., Macchiarulo, L., Ruo Roch, M., Tota, G., et al. (2009). A case study for NoC based homogeneous MPSoC architectures. https://core.ac.uk/download/pdf/11400830.pdf (accessed on 9th September 2025).
18. Chahine, S. (2007). Building ArtsSmarts' research capacity: An interim report. https://core.ac.uk/download/71342463.pdf (accessed on 9th September 2025).
19. Chechina, N., & Trinder, P. (2012). RELEASE: A high-level paradigm for reliable large-scale server software. https://core.ac.uk/download/42370564.pdf (accessed on 9th September 2025).
20. Clements, A. L., Collier-Oxandale, A., Griswold, W. G., Hannigan, M., et al. (2017). Low-cost air quality monitoring tools: From research to practice (A workshop summary). https://core.ac.uk/download/323062776.pdf (accessed on 9th September 2025).
21. Coudert, T., De Valroger, A., Geneste, L., Romero Bejarano, M., et al. (2012). Technic and collaboration breakdown structures: Drivers of collaborative problem-solving approaches in a supply chain context. https://core.ac.uk/download/12043879.pdf (accessed on 9th September 2025).
22. Coull, N., Donaldson, S., & McLuskie, D. (2017). A methodology for testing virtualization security. https://core.ac.uk/download/141567454.pdf (accessed on 9th September 2025).

23. Delli Priscoli, F., Di Giorgio, A., Lisi, F., Monaco, A., et al. (2017). Multi-agent quality of experience control. https://core.ac.uk/download/80310148.pdf (accessed on 9th September 2025).
24. Diaz, C., & Soto, R. (2025). Open-access issues in the Chilean telecommunications and electricity sectors. https://core.ac.uk/download/pdf/6542987.pdf (accessed on 9th September 2025).
25. Doostmohammadian, M., & Khan, U. A. (2012). On the genericity properties in networked estimation: Topology design and sensor placement. http://arxiv.org/abs/1208.3691 (accessed on 9th September 2025).
26. Duan, J., Le, F., Liu, A., Peng, H., et al. (2017). Dynamic scaling of virtualized, distributed service chains: A case study of IMS. https://core.ac.uk/download/95559142.pdf (accessed on 9th September 2025).
27. Fernández-López, M. (1999). Overview of methodologies for building ontologies. https://core.ac.uk/download/148655770.pdf (accessed on 9th September 2025).
28. Galagali, N., & Marzouk, Y. M. (2019). Exploiting network topology for large-scale inference of nonlinear reaction models. http://arxiv.org/abs/1705.04678 (accessed on 9th September 2025).
29. Glisson, L. M., Glisson, W. B., & Welland, R. (2007). Secure web application development and global regulation. https://core.ac.uk/download/1393956.pdf (accessed on 9th September 2025).
30. Glisson, L. M., Glisson, W., & Welland, R. (2010). Security and computer forensics in web engineering education. https://core.ac.uk/download/10536.pdf (accessed on 9th September 2025).
31. Han, H. (2019). Connecting levels of analysis in educational neuroscience: A review of multi-level structure of educational neuroscience with concrete examples. https://core.ac.uk/download/223236302.pdf (accessed on 9th September 2025).
32. Hesse, G., Matthies, C., & Teusner, R. (2019). Beyond surveys: Analyzing software development artifacts to assess teaching efforts. http://arxiv.org/abs/1807.02400 (accessed on 9th September 2025).
33. Hierons, R. M., & Nabulsi, M. A. (2015). A new test framework for communications-critical large-scale systems. https://core.ac.uk/download/29139320.pdf (accessed on 9th September 2025).
34. Huang, W., Maple, C., & Viduto, V. (2011). Toward optimal multi-objective models of network security: Survey. https://core.ac.uk/download/30730951.pdf (accessed on 9th September 2025).

35. Jaber, X., Szeto, W. Y., & Wong, S. C. (2012). Road network equilibrium approaches to environmental sustainability. https://core.ac.uk/download/37973509.pdf (accessed on 9th September 2025).
36. Jessop, B., & Nielsen, K. (2003). Institutions and rules. https://core.ac.uk/download/371630.pdf (accessed on 9th September 2025).
37. Kaklauskas, A., Kusiak, A., Marquez, A. C., Duffy, A. H. B., Duffy, A. H. B., Chae, B., Lopez, B., et al. (2010). Integration of decision support systems to improve decision support performance. https://core.ac.uk/download/9023194.pdf (accessed on 9th September 2025).
38. Kaloyanova, K., & Kanabar, V. (2019). Addressing challenges to teach traditional and agile project management in academia. https://open.bu.edu/bitstream/2144/40819/1/984-Final-Version.pdf (accessed on 9th September 2025).
39. Kulkarni, G. (2017). Simplification of Internet ossification through software defined network approach. https://core.ac.uk/download/539894270.pdf (accessed on 9th September 2025).
40. Leclerc, G. (2005). Experimenting with the design of policies on sustainable resources management: Phase 1 final report, January 2004–February 2005. http://agritrop.cirad.fr/545377/1/document_545377.pdf (accessed on 9th September 2025).
41. Mala-Jetmarova, H., Savic, D., & Sultanova, N. (2018). Lost in optimization of water distribution systems? A literature review of system design. https://core.ac.uk/download/155789575.pdf (accessed on 9th September 2025).
42. Mehedintu, A., Pîrvu, C., & Pîrvu, C. (2012). Performance management approaches in economic organizations using information technology. https://core.ac.uk/download/pdf/26834220.pdf (accessed on 9th September 2025).
43. Molnár, B., & Simon, E. (1993). Creating responsive information systems with the help of SSADM. https://core.ac.uk/download/12355799.pdf (accessed on 9th September 2025).
44. Mondal, M., & Ray, K. S. (2019). Review on DNA cryptography. https://core.ac.uk/download/595875557.pdf (accessed on 9th September 2025).
45. Nazir, S., Nazir, S., Patel, D., Patel, A., et al. (2017). Autonomic computing architecture for SCADA cyber security. https://core.ac.uk/download/293885088.pdf (accessed on 9th September 2025).
46. Nejati, M., Nejatian, M., Zanjirchi, S., Zarei, B., et al. (2018). A hybrid approach to achieve organizational agility: An empirical study of a food

company. https://core.ac.uk/download/160050967.pdf (accessed on 9th September 2025).

47. Nunes, B. A. A., Haleplidis, E., Fetweiss, G. P., Mouratidis, H., Stojmenovic, I., Andrews, J. G., et al. (2016). Security analysis of mobile edge computing in virtualized small cell networks. https://core.ac.uk/download/46598416.pdf (accessed on 9th September 2025).
48. Oxman, R. (2010). Digital tectonics as a morphogenetic process. http://hdl.handle.net/10251/6959 (accessed on 9th September 2025).
49. Priami, C. (2003). *Proceedings of International Workshop "Global Computing: Programming Environments, Languages, Security and Analysis of Systems."* https://core.ac.uk/download/11829018.pdf (accessed on 9th September 2025).
50. Queluz, M. P., Rodrigues, A., & Sousa, I. (2020). A survey on QoE-oriented wireless resources scheduling. http://arxiv.org/abs/1705.07839 (accessed on 9th September 2025).
51. Shadbolt, N. R. (2005). Eliciting expertise.
52. Teuscher, C., Das, R., de Micheli, G., Di Caro, G., Lawniczak, A. T., Lawson, J., Levitan, S. L., et al. (2007). Nature-inspired interconnects for self-assembled large-scale network-on-chip designs. https://core.ac.uk/download/37766445.pdf (accessed on 9th September 2025).
53. Thórisson, K. R. (2012). A new constructivist AI: From manual methods to self-constructive systems. https://core.ac.uk/download/30436778.pdf (accessed on 9th September 2025).
54. Vanhoucke, M. (2016). On the use of empirical or artificial project data. https://core.ac.uk/download/84046275.pdf (accessed on 9th September 2025).
55. Vasantha, A., Cakkol, M., Evans, S., Hussain, R., et al. (2010). An ontology for product-service systems. https://core.ac.uk/download/140256.pdf (accessed on 9th September 2025).
56. Xu, H. (2012). Stochastic optimal adaptive controller and communication protocol design for networked control systems. https://core.ac.uk/download/229270214.pdf (accessed on 9th September 2025).

CHAPTER 6

TOPOLOGY AND NETWORK PERFORMANCE

Contents

INTRODUCTION

It is important to understand how topology relates to network performance within current digital systems, particularly as they grow more and more complex. Topology is the organization or architecture of a network, including nodes and the connections by which they interact with each other. In network performance, the effectiveness with which information is transmitted across these connections also often depends on the underlying topology. The ramifications of this interaction extend far beyond connectivity; they encompass efficiency, reliability, and scalability. As networks evolve further, examining how various topologies influence performance is essential to optimizing operations in industries from telecommunications to air transport. By studying these dynamics, we can determine procedures that not only enhance the usability of networks but also inform infrastructural design considerations. A good case can be seen with air transportation networks, where node connectivity and link weights are important for determining traffic flow. Airports are nodes and flight routes are the links, creating a complex network that needs to be handled by advanced modeling for effective control. Analysis indicates that such network behavior can be explored through random network topology models, illustrating the critical transitions in performance upon changing demand fluctuations. For instance, Albert et al. (2009) presents data illustrating how the appearance of a jamming transition affects the diffusion of aircraft from a high-performance to a congestion-ridden one. This shift highlights the nuanced interdependence of performance and topology, showing that topological arrangement can have an actual effect on operational efficiency and resource allocation. Additionally, the investigation into network topologies extends into the world of Internet traffic, where power law models have emerged as showing the power to reveal insights into traffic and performance. Though such models provide valuable illumination, they also reveal constraints that create a need for additional research. As exhibited in Clegg et al. (2009), existing power law models must address issues that outstandingly challenge their usability and predictive ability in relation to actual situations. These issues are paramount in the context of enhancing network performance since they are used to establish grounds for ensuring on-going improvement in modeling methods. By bridging theory and practice, researchers will have a better chance at aligning their findings more closely to the requirements of increasingly complex networked spaces, eventually leading to improved design and resource utilization techniques that optimize overall connectivity and usefulness.

Definition of Topology

Topological theory, rooted in abstract mathematics, is integral to understanding network structure and behavior. In its essential form, topology considers those properties which are invariant under continuous deformation, like bending or stretching, but not gluing or tearing. This is especially suited to application in network performance, where the structure and connectivity of nodes can have significant influence on overall system efficiency. In network theory, topologies are described generally in relation to their data transmission paths, which can be categorized into various configurations, such as star, ring, and mesh.

Choices of topology inherently influence variables like latency, bandwidth, and fault tolerance, thereby influencing system design and optimization choices for telecommunication and data transfer. Outside of its abstract foundations, topology also overlaps with practical applications involving network performance optimization. For instance, the dynamic nature of current networks requires the utilization of advanced techniques like Cell Switch-Off (CSO) to properly manage energy usage with quality of service. CSO is addressing resource allocation issues and requires knowledge of the underlying topological behavior of the network as well.

Figure 6.1. *The field of topology, rooted in abstract mathematics.*

Source: https://www.techmonitor.ai/wp-content/uploads/sites/29/2023/04/shutter-stock_1563960451.jpg.

The CSO scheme complexity shows the importance of topological analysis by exemplifying how different configurations may influence the feasibility of energy optimization methods. For instance, efficient algorithms that minimize the number of transitions and handovers are important for maximum performance under the constraint caused by the topology of networks (G et al., 2016). Another such critical domain in which topology plays a pivotal role is in virtualizing networks, wherein it makes possible the efficient allocation of resources across multiple virtual networks. Virtual network embedding then becomes a fundamental process in this case, enabling the mapping of virtual demands into the physical network substrate. The challenges related to embedding in multi-hop wireless networks have also been considered, particularly as multi-hop networks become more complex and require new solutions to guarantee service quality. Simulation-based performance assessment of embedding algorithms reveals the delicacies involved in resource management. Topology is applied in the manner in which virtual nodes are able to exist together harmoniously without compromising the integrity of the physical network, demonstrating its applicability to abstract models and concrete uses in the emerging paradigm of network performance (Ok et al., 2012) (Figure 6.1).

Importance of Network Performance

Performance analysis of the network is an essential part of understanding its pivotal role in numerous applications, most notably disaster management where connectivity means life or death. In scenarios where the extension of reachability of emergency communication by deploying auxiliary static nodes is crucial, network performance optimization is essential. Placing these nodes strategically, the rescue teams are able to reverse connectivity holes normally found in constrained and dynamic environments. Such strategies also receive a boost in efficiency through the use of advanced genetic algorithms in combination with network simulation tools like NS-2, which identify optimum point locations for the nodes. Thus, the implications of enhanced network performance exceed mere connectivity; they directly influence the effectiveness and responsiveness of emergency response interventions in severe events, and thereby highlight the critical interplay between network topology and performance in real-world scenarios (Alander et al., 2012). The recently emerged new mobile cellular technologies, namely 5G, are a revolutionary boost to network performance that can revolutionize global connectivity. With the vision of making the Internet universally accessible, especially in unserved markets, 5G functionality takes center stage to overcome the conventional limitations faced by previous architectures. Previous technologies struggled to provide economic viability in rural areas and thus ended up developing vast service coverage gaps. 5G architecture, on the other hand, encourages a topology that not only remains agile but one that addresses these limitations head-on. It further supports the possibilities of democratizing access to information and communication technologies and confirming the demand for quality network performance in progressing social justice. Thus, 5G research offers a possibility and challenge for changing the manner in which connectivity is provided for marginalized communities worldwide (Imran et al., 2016). Additionally, network performance implications impact digital economics. In an internet-based economy where economic growth relies on internet services, the performance and reliability of network topologies matter. Fast networks enable efficient business operations, enhance the end-user experience, and spur innovation across industries. Low network performance, conversely, deterrence leads to investment, stifles entrepreneurship, and increases disparities in digital divide landscapes. The multi-dimensional implication of network performance, therefore, cannot be overstated; it influences not only the experiences of individual users but also broad socioeconomic factors. In making investments in network infrastructures by public and private sectors, topology design and performance optimization choice will to no small extent determines the trajectory of technological advancement and its distribution to varying demographics. Lastly, an appreciation of network performance will be important to guiding future practice and policy in technology deployment and availability.

Overview of the Relationship between Topology and Performance

The topological complexity of interacting with performance is brought to the fore by the various types of configurations that can have a significant effect on data flow and effectiveness. Numerous topologies ranging from star and mesh to bus and ring have characteristics that affect concerns such as latency, throughput, and fault tolerance. For instance, a star topology makes it easier to manage and identify faults, enhancing performance by containing faults at a quicker rate. Conversely, a mesh topology, which interconnects numerous nodes, offers redundancy and improved fault tolerance at the cost of increased complexity that slows the network in certain circumstances. With the inclination of new applications to necessitate high-speed connectivity with minimal disruption, acknowledging these topological nuances is critical to optimizing network performance in real-time applications. One of the most important aspects of the topology-performance relationship is how it affects directly the efficiency of systems like Network Intrusion Detection Systems (NIDS). Traditionally, NIDS deployed within data centers have to monitor big streams of traffic while having to endure high availability and compliance expectations as defined within Service Level Agreements (SLAs). The deployment of high-cost middleboxes in isolated parts of the network may hinder the detection and prevention of anomalies in growing data demands. New developments point towards distributed systems utilizing event processing frameworks, for example, event-based Apache Storm. This paradigm enables a more scalable intrusion detection solution that is advantaged by the Software Defined Networking (SDN) paradigm, wherein control is centralized and distributed processing is enabled to improve overall network performance with guaranteed high throughput and low latency as seen in Jouet et al. (2017). In addition, the dynamics of traffic pattern demonstrate the chronic problems of interspersed topology and performance. In contemporary data centers, the coexistence of throughput-sensitive long flows and short delay-sensitive flows can lead to performance degradation due to congestion. Notably, long flows can hog shorter flows, particularly in shallow-buffered switches that dominate most networks. Synchronization of multiple TCP connections typically exacerbates the issue, especially in partition/aggregate traffic scenarios. Overcoming challenges of this nature includes coming up with innovative solutions, as is the case with the new link-layer design known as PABO. The design aims to mitigate transient congestion using techniques that reroute packets towards upstream switches to enhance reliability without compromising on top performance levels, according to Liu et al. (2018). Understanding such complexities is essential for network designers who desire a disruption-free performance experience.

6.1. TYPES OF NETWORK TOPOLOGIES

Among network topologies, three fundamental types emerge as pillars of performance analysis: bus, star, and ring topologies. Each of them has its peculiar features that determine data transmission efficiency, scalability, and fault tolerance. The bus topology uses a single shared cable, the bus, to which all network devices are connected. Though it is quite economical and easy to install, its performance is hampered by higher traffic when more devices are added, resulting in data collisions and transmission delays. In contrast, star topology has a central hub that has all the nodes connected individually, which enables improved management and containment of devices. This arrangement not only enhances performance through reduced collision domains but also boosts reliability, as the failure of a single link will not usually have an impact on the entire network. Ring topology offers another alternative, whereby devices are arranged in a ring configuration, each connected to two others. This form of structure can offer consistent data rates of transmission, as data travels in one direction around the ring. Its performance, however, can be severely affected when either of the connections is lost, breaking the data path and leading to network downtime. The reliance on each device to forward data contributes to the necessity to handle network health and methods for redundancy. Lastly, the topological selection typically comes at a cost versus cost, performance requirements, and anticipated network growth. Understanding these principles is crucial to network engineers that work on optimizing performance in many environments. Topology design versus performance analysis in Software Defined Networking (SDN) is becoming even more relevant. Comparatively accurate characterization of network topologies and their impact on parameters like end-to-end (E2E) delay justify the need to completely understand how data travel. Experiments demonstrate that successful SDN deployments rely on predictable topology knowledge, which informs controller data-path-programming decisions. For example, monitoring E2E delay over a group of topologies for multiple traffic conditions provides a foundation for network performance metric optimization. In addition, statistical characterization of performance—expectation and variance of delays to be measured—can facilitate more efficient routing algorithms to be designed. Such topological influence knowledge allows the enhancement of network designs and operations, creating resilient and responsive communication networks needed to deal with today's demands (Begin et al., 2016) (Figure 6.2).

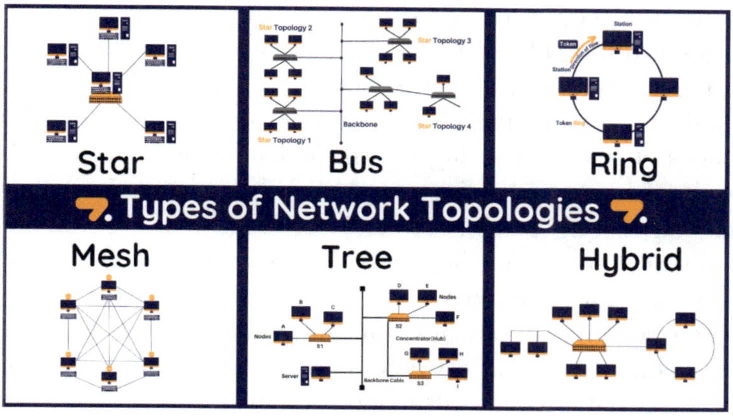

Figure 6.2. *Types of network topologies.*

Source: https://www.zenarmor.com/docs/network-topology-types.png.

6.1.1. Star Topology

In computer networking, star topology is a special architectural style that provides efficient communication among devices. The topology consists of a central switch or hub, which acts as a common point with multiple nodes. Each device is directly connected to the central point, which is efficient for data transmission and assists in systematic traffic management. This configuration is particularly beneficial in local area networks (LANs), where speedy data exchanges are paramount to network performance. Star topology's central configuration also makes troubleshooting more effective; when a device fails, the rest of the network remains unaffected, keeping total disruptions at bay. Such stability is light-years away from more decentralized topologies, highlighting the main benefits of star configurations in guaranteeing network uptime during system problems. The star topology not only simplifies network management but also supports scalability, responding to the dynamic needs of today's businesses. As companies grow, new devices are added effortlessly; the new node can be connected to the network without interfering with operations. This reactivity is best seen in environments where ongoing upgrades or expansions are anticipated. Also, its centralized form allows optimal monitoring performance since the hub can be equipped with management appliances to monitor data traffic and detect faults in real time. Also, the star topology's dependence on the single central unit allows uncomplicated maintenance procedures. Combined with excellent network management software, these capabilities ensure that organizations are able to sustain an adequate level of operation efficiency in order to leverage their network infrastructure for fast adaptation to technological advancement and evolving market demands. Although the star topology is full of numerous benefits, it is not absolutely without limitations, particularly in terms of hardware reliance and potential vulnerabilities. The hub is a single point of failure; if it stops working, the whole network is useless, showing a key risk factor in network reliability. Such dependency on central elements demands strict maintenance and monitoring practices to maintain functionality. Also, the expense of installing the required switches or hubs, especially in large implementations, is outrageous, making cost factors a pressing concern for companies. As indicated by research, the performance and resilience of network configurations, such as star topologies, are highly elevated by strategic planning and resilient systems, as shown in the evaluation of restructured systems in actual application (Allen et al., 2015). In addition, exploring the incorporation of hybrid approaches, such as marrying star topology with redundancy, can increase network reliability by minimizing hub-related failure impacts (Libarikian et al., 2002).

6.1.2. Ring Topology

Ring topology is a special type of networking that connects all devices in a circular way, forming a closed loop. This configuration enables the data to flow only in a single direction, either clockwise or counterclockwise, which can minimize packet collisions and increase data transfer speed. With this method, ring topology can deliver network performance with no variation, especially in data traffic environments with predictable data traffic. Additionally, its structural simplicity facilitates simple trouble-shooting through tracing out any failure in the ring by identifying the disruption in the data flow. However, the dependence on an active master device necessitates robust fault tolerance measures, such as redundancy protocols, to ensure service continuity. The influence of ring structure on network performance manifests particularly in its application in modern optical networks. With advancements still shaping the field of data transmission, specific uses of ring topology, particularly in the guise of Passive Optical Networks (PON), have emerged. In such situations, there is a requirement to maintain high capacity in proportion with efficient fault detection and restoration mechanisms. For instance, the requirement for component redundancy, which adds towards reliability, is balanced against running and capital expenditures. Therefore, it is necessary to study various protection schemes in the ring environment. By examining five strategies for protection, it is seen that ring topological structures with hybrid forms can minimize fiber duplication and hence enhance cost effectiveness as well as dependability to meet a larger number of subscribers (Ali et al., 2017). Ring topology implemented in contemporary network design makes it a highly desirable solution for environments which appreciate performance as well as scalability. The built-in flexibility of this structure allows systems to be capable of handling the needs of increasing bandwidth with reliability intact. As these ring deployments can provide what industry experts refer to as five nines connectivity availability, these not only address short-term performance demands but also provide a sustainable long-term strategy for network growth. Ease of adding new nodes without disrupting overall network operation further points toward its advantage. With such attributes, specifically the potential to accommodate future growth, ring topology is a milestone model in network performance optimization in most fields, demonstrating its sustained relevance in the rapidly evolving world of network technology (Colle et al., 2005).

6.1.3. Mesh Topology

Mesh topology shows its efficacy to boost network performance in various communications systems, particularly in large-scale integrated circuits. Mesh topology connects nodes in a grid with redundant multiple paths for data transmission. Such a structure not only provides redundancy but also fault tolerance since redundant paths can be utilized if there is loss of nodes or links. Under on-chip networks, communication management efficiency is a necessity at all costs, especially in the event of mounting demands on performance. Inherent in mesh is the topology that makes resource distribution even and uniform, which is a critical consideration in guaranteeing the network's optimal performance. As researchers continue to expand boundaries in this field, flexibility remains a factor in mesh's application in today's applications in networking. Technological innovations such as Through-Silicon Via (TSV) show the prevailing relevance of mesh topology in enhancing network performance in three-dimensional integrated circuits. TSV technology provides higher speed and bandwidth, and also power saving dissipation needed for inter-layer communication. However, existing TSV fabrication suffers from disadvantages such as high area footprints and loss of yield. Hence, methods such as clustering in mesh networks are proposed to optimize the utilization of resources. It allows for the sharing of a single TSV pillar by multiple routers without compromising mesh structure integrity. The tests performed show a balance in cost and performance, bringing out the innovative aspect of optimized mesh architecture towards exceeding conventional limits, thus reasserting the conventional value of mesh topology in high-performance network deployment

(Bahrebar et al., 2015). Also, the evolution of Networks on Chip (NoC) as a solution to the limitations of bus-based interconnection points to the continued relevance of mesh topology in today's computing paradigms. NoC performance is highly sensitive to the choice of topology since this influences essential parameters such as latency and throughput. In contrast to earlier models, the spidergon topology provides a static but optimized framework that meets the demands of multi-processor System on Chip (MPSoC) design. In the past, evaluations indicated that when looking for other topologies, the scalability and performance of mesh architecture have a tendency to provide improved performance outcomes under varied traffic conditions. Hence, mesh topology gives a robust platform that can support diversified needs in chip designs at the expense of cost-effectiveness and functional efficiency, placing it in the center of network design considerations in high-performance computing (Moadeli et al., 2007).

6.2. FACTORS AFFECTING NETWORK PERFORMANCE

Understanding the various factors that affect network performance is crucial for optimizing any topology. One of the primary considerations is bandwidth, which refers to the maximum data transfer rate a network can support. A topology that efficiently utilizes available bandwidth can significantly enhance performance. For instance, star and ring topologies manage data flow more effectively than bus topologies, particularly as network size increases. Additionally, network latency plays a critical role in performance, impacting the time it takes for data to travel from one point to another. High latency can lead to delays that diminish the user experience, particularly in applications requiring real-time data transfer, such as video conferencing or online gaming. Analyzing these factors underlines the importance of choosing the appropriate network topology specific to the organizational or operational needs. Another critical aspect of network performance is the role of network protocols, which dictate how data packets are transmitted and received. Protocol efficiency significantly influences speed and reliability; thus, the choice of protocol is often dictated by both the topology in use and the application requirements. For instance, protocols like Transmission Control Protocol (TCP) prioritize data integrity and order, which is vital in environments where accurate data delivery is paramount. In contrast, User Datagram Protocol (UDP) sacrifices some reliability for speed, making it suitable for applications like live streaming where timely delivery is more crucial than perfect accuracy. The interaction between protocols and topology must be careful, as mismatches can lead to bottleneck situations, slowing down the entire network and affecting overall performance, a scenario that reinforces the interconnected nature of these components. Lastly, the physical environment and hardware choices significantly influence network performance. Factors such as electromagnetic interference, physical obstructions, and network topology layout can greatly impact signal strength and data transfer rates. For instance, in wireless networks, dense urban areas may present challenges due to multipath fading and attenuation caused by buildings. Hardware capabilities, including routers, switches, and cabling, also play a decisive role in determining performance metrics. Utilizing advanced hardware paired with appropriate topology can optimize data flow, as illustrated by the findings in the development of distributed computing in wireless sensor networks, where geographical fragmentation facilitated parallel computations to enhance speed and reduce message overheads, contributing positively to performance outcomes (Kenyeres et al., 2015). Addressing these considerations holistically is essential for any network design aimed at achieving optimal performance levels (Figure 6.3).

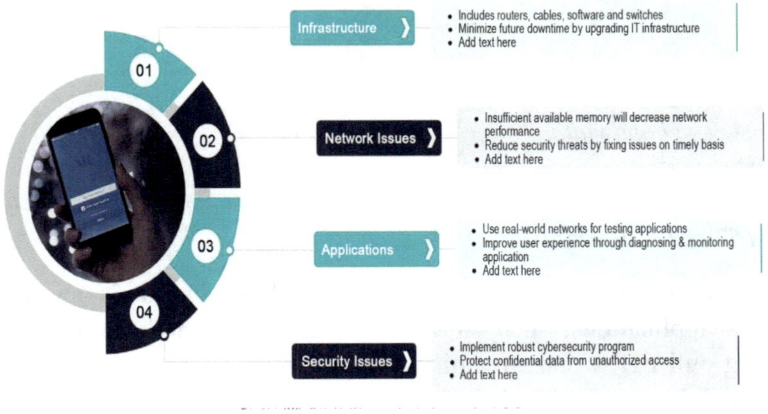

Figure 6.3. *The various factors that affect network performance.*

Source: https://www.slideteam.net/media/catalog/product/cache/1280x720/v/a/various_factors_affecting_network_performance_slide01.jpg.

6.2.1. Bandwidth

Understanding bandwidth is central to assessing network performance because it influences the efficiency of data transfer and general user experience. Bandwidth, or the maximum data transmission rate along a network path, is a critical metric for measuring the ability and capacity of networks. Topology and other environmental influences have significant effects on bandwidth consumption and effectiveness. For instance, some network architectures, such as tree or star topologies, can accommodate higher bandwidth availability with shorter hop counts data needs to make, thereby less latency. Network congestion or ineffectual network design, however, leads to bandwidth bottlenecks and performance degradation. With devices and users increasingly gravitating toward high-bandwidth applications, being cognizant of such dynamics becomes a prerequisite to ensure good network performance and acceptable Quality of Experience to end-users.

Figure 6.4. *The bandwidth.*

Source: https://files.codingninjas.in/article_images/what-is-bandwidth-0-1678550891.webp.

The interaction between network topology and bandwidth is more critical in specific applications, such as video streaming. As indicated in research contrasting pull P2P video streaming systems, overlay topology structure and chunk scheduling are critical factors in influencing bandwidth management and the functioning of a system. With improved availability of bandwidth and heterogeneity of access bandwidth considerations, network architects are able to enhance the streaming experience through effective delivery of video data without latency. This is particularly critical for real-time applications, which need timely delivery of data. Bandwidth-conscious innovations can lead to greater scalability and mitigation of transport network strain, demonstrating the feasibility of knowing bandwidth, as opposed to topology, for network development to support high-bandwidth and complex applications, for example, high-definition video streaming (Fortuna et al., 2010). Moreover, technology advances such as filtenna devices—integrating filtering capabilities in antennas—demonstrate the feasibility of bandwidth optimization using novel design approaches. Such devices' performance is typically dependent on matching filter responses with the parameters of performance of antennas. As research indicates, the implementation of an ideal filter response in a given case can significantly enhance bandwidth efficiency while retaining good signal integrity. Nonetheless, iterative design methods also result in high performance despite the lack of ideal conditions. This adaptability underscores the importance of bandwidth awareness in communication system and device design, since modest bandwidth management enhancements can yield dramatic overall network performance benefits (Collado et al., 2014). As networks increasingly evolve towards greater complexity, such bandwidth-topology synergies will play an increasing role in determining future network performance (Figure 6.4).

6.2.2. Latency

Latency is a significant factor in network performance measurement, particularly with respect to topology changes. Latency refers to the delay or lag time produced when data is being transferred from one point to another, which could potentially have a negative effect on network application performance. It is caused by a number of different sources, such as propagation delays, transmission delays, queuing delays, and processing delays. Understanding these sources is important since they can influence application performance in key areas. Latency can degrade the responsiveness of applications, impacting adversely on user experience, especially with latency-critical applications such as online gaming and real-time video conferencing. With the increased network complexity characteristic of diverse topologies, the management of latency becomes more important, with a need for a balanced approach for different data traffic types. In high-performing data centers, where concurrent processing of large datasets is ever-growing, managing latency and throughput is a significant challenge. The co-location of applications sensitive to both throughput and latency demands both peak throughput without compromising on latency levels. Recent advances in network technology have introduced techniques like Active Queue Management (AQM) and Explicit Congestion Notifications (ECN), which assume a dominant position in reducing congestion-induced latency as well as buffer bloat. Experiments have shown that the adoption of these technologies can minimize network latency significantly but still meet throughput needs of bandwidth-intensive applications, thereby optimizing overall network performance and user satisfaction. Moreover, the utilization of novel problem-specific solutions can render it more feasible to handle big data at the enormous scale in networks. Network intrusion detection systems (NIDS) are significant in modern data centers, particularly with respect to controlling latency. As data center networks grow in size and are increasingly complex, the traditional NIDS are incapable of meeting the high-throughput demands while providing reasonable latency. New approaches involving distributed intrusion detection frameworks have been created, leveraging technologies such as Apache Storm to enable rapid event processing without introducing significant latency. By splitting up the processing of the tasks across heterogeneous devices on the network, systems can maintain an end-to-end view and handle real-time information without compromising on responsiveness. Having such designs in line with the principles of Software Defined Networking (SDN) not only enhances anomaly detection but also preserves the maximum level of network performance by ensuring latency remains low, thus making the entire operational efficiency of data centers in the current compute-intensive digital era easy (Figure 6.5).

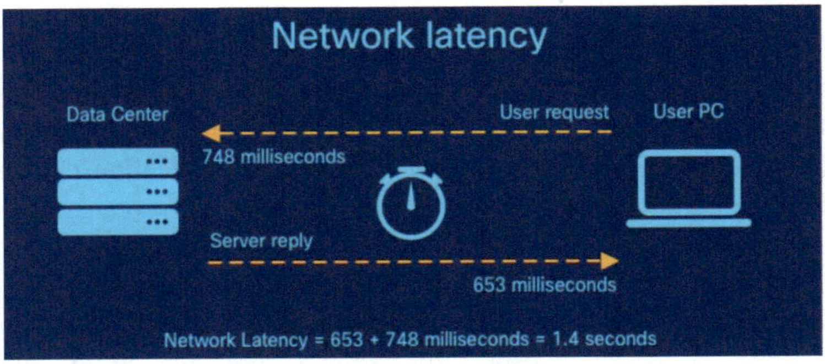

Figure 6.5. *The concept of latency.*

Source: https://www.cisco.com/content/dam/cisco-cdc/site/images/legacy/assets/swa/img/anchor-info/what-is-network-latency-628x353.jpg.

6.2.3. Packet Loss

Packet loss, defined as the failure to deliver one or more transmitted packets to their final destination, is a key indicator of network performance. Its impacts range beyond data transfer efficiency to overall user experience within networked environments. In a complex ecosystem like the Internet, where various types of traffic coexist, packet loss can be attributed to more than one reason, like network congestion, hardware malfunction, or sub-optimal routing configuration. Analysis of the causes is needed in observing the mechanisms of packet loss because such cause-and-effect chains are complicated in the overall model of network topology. Thus, this paper proves that packet loss rates are necessarily determined by network structure, so that topology becomes the core consideration deserving of study in theoretical as well as application contexts. Causality is also better established between the packet loss and network topologies in analyses of other dimensions such as redundancy and fault tolerance. Networks with redundant routes will have low packet loss as other paths can be followed if one is attacked. This redundancy allows for resilience against localized failures and allows traffic to dynamically re-route depending on network conditions. This is less so for more linear topologies, which might aggravate packet loss with increased vulnerability to single points of failure. As Albert et al. (2009) points out, the complexity involved in Internet traffic dynamics means that a careful consideration of how various network architectures work to alleviate or aggravate packet loss must be taken into account. The implications of such choices in design resonate highly throughout network performance, affecting the users' experience and applications' effectiveness in numerous areas. In addition, advances in technology through Segment Routing over IPv6 (SRv6) have introduced potential solutions to buffer packet loss and enhance network performance. SRv6 enhances Traffic Engineering and optimizes routes, and the likelihood of packet loss due to congestion or inefficient routing can decrease. By minimizing state information set up within network devices, SRv6 improves scalability and performance, thus potentially easing congestion points at which packet loss generally occurs (Filsfils et al., 2018). Such technologies being implemented within existing networks not only eliminate packet loss directly but introduce additional performance levels with which to quantify improvement. With growing reliance on data-heavy applications, learning to harness the power of topological designs and new routing protocols becomes crucial to reducing packet loss and achieving maximum network performance (Figure 6.6).

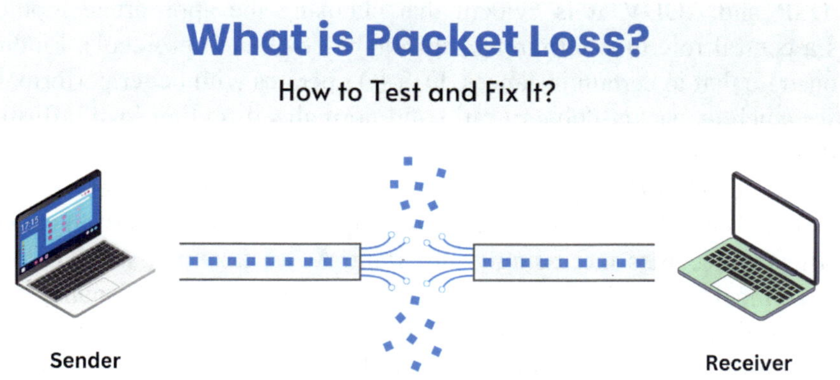

Figure 6.6. *Packet loss.*

Source: https://carnival.com.bd/uploads/images/842fb652dd1867473701f17b06d51a16.webp.

6.3. IMPACT OF TOPOLOGY ON NETWORK PERFORMANCE

Topology-performance relation is particularly crucial in the context of Software Defined Networking (SDN). The decoupling of data plane and control plane in the architectures of SDN makes central control of network resources possible, which enhances routing data efficiency. The network topology type has a direct impact on how well these controller's function; for example, a tree-based topology designed specifically can maximize performance criteria like throughput and latency. Comparative research simulations of ONOS and RYU controllers under such topologies show that the ONOS controller beats RYU, with the latter showcasing better responsiveness to traffic loads. This means that employing some topologies not only facilitates improved communication but can re-engineer the operational capabilities of network controllers in a fundamental way, impacting network performance and user experience (Milićević et al., 2022). Another important component of network topology is found in mobile ad hoc networks (MANETs), where dynamic topologies pose specific challenges to routing protocols.

With dynamic environments where nodes frequently change positions, the routing protocols must be highly adaptive in order to maintain network performance consistently. DYMO can make effective utilization under such circumstances through allowing mobile nodes to dynamically establish unicast routes as the network changes. In comparing DYMO with other protocols like DSR and AODV, it is evident that choosing the appropriate topology plays a central role in determining the suitability of such protocols. Findings demonstrate that in certain instances, DYMO operates with better performance metrics, such as packet delivery ratio and normalized routing load, affirming the idea that topology directly influences the performance of routing protocols in a network setup (Bisoyi et al., 2020). Furthermore, as networks grow in demands and complexity, knowledge of the implications of topology on network performance becomes increasingly important. As an example, star topologies or hierarchical topologies can create a balance between ease of management and scalability. Optimal data flow is usually reliant on the inherent structure and design of the network, which makes planning important in selecting the topology. As networks are grown to accommodate growing users and devices, the consequences of poorly chosen topologies become evident in latency, packet loss, and disruption of service. The coincidence of several devices and heterogeneous data loads exacerbates the requirement for effective topology evaluations in order to improve performance. Finally, understanding the intricate relationships between topology and network performance can significantly impact the design and operation of modern network infrastructures.

6.3.1. Scalability

Scalability is a key consideration in network topology design and implementation, having impacts on performance as well as future potential for growth. Scalability refers to the ability of a network to accommodate increased loads, whether in new users, devices, or applications, without sacrificing performance. So far as routing protocols go, as illustrated by RIP, EIGRP, and OSPF comparisons, scalability assumes greater significance. Although RIP is simple to deploy, its lack of speed convergence renders it slow to react as networks expand and become more complex. EIGRP, however, stays fast and efficient even as the network grows in size, demonstrating its sustainability under dynamic environments (Yousif et al., 2025). That it is adaptive ensures that business companies can expand their digital infrastructure without a complete overhaul of their existing network infrastructure. In addition to routing protocols, network topology plays a significant role in scalability.

A star topology, commonly seen at home and learning institutions, illustrates how structural designs may make a network operate more effectively. Through the centralization of connections via a hub, the star topology facilitates the addition of new devices—enhancing scalability without much disturbance to the ongoing processes. Besides, the implementation of a combination of star and extended star topologies has also been found to optimize performance in larger environments, finding a balance of speed and ease of management (Monika et al., 2025).

The combination enables institutions to increase their networks with room to accommodate growing demands while maintaining high-speed connectivity and reliability. Lastly, the implementation of correct topological designs and scalable routing protocols is required in achieving long-term network performance. The modernization of the network requires proactive scalability, particularly as schools and businesses begin to adopt new technology. The increasing trends toward cloud computing and distance education require dynamic systems that can scale quickly to meet external pressures. LAN design must consider scalability not as a technical requirement but as a strategic advantage. As indicated by the studies on various network structures, scaling emphasis enables improved security, cost-effectiveness, and simplicity in maintenance (Monika et al., 2025). Such network design vision allows enterprises to adapt to rapidly evolving environments for constant performance, as well as lowering operational downtime. As network sizes and domains continue to expand, the fundamental factors of scalability will remain crucial in shaping effective topology models.

6.3.2. Fault Tolerance

Fault tolerance is an important feature of network performance, particularly in the case of dynamic topologies of a network. As networks are becoming more complex, smooth service is the most critical concern. Fault tolerance refers to the ability of a network to perform under normal circumstances even if some of its element's malfunction or get interrupted. This capability is also particularly beneficial since the networks are to be capable of supporting a wide range of applications, many of which need a great level of dependability. Studies show that fault-tolerance-oriented networks not only enhance the dependability of service but also overall performance metrics. By the application of redundancy, dynamic rerouting algorithms, and predictive monitoring systems, network topologies are able to mitigate the impact of potential failures, hence enabling seamless operation even in the case of some parts being defective (Byers et al., 2007).

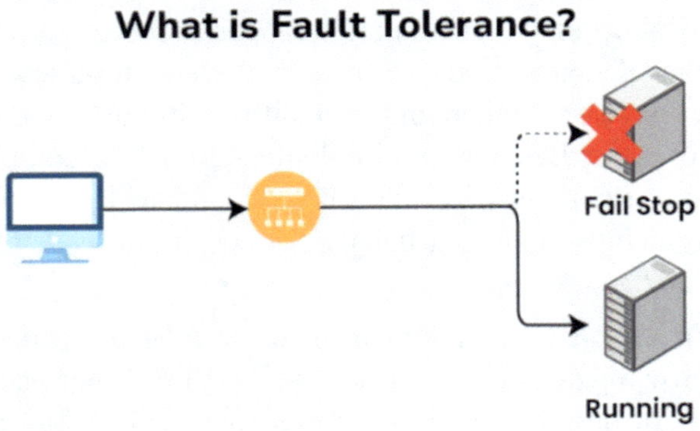

Figure 6.7. *Fault tolerance.*

Source: https://media.geeksforgeeks.org/wp-content/uploads/20240726124218/What-is-Fault-Tolerance.webp.

Creating fault tolerance mechanisms in a network topology requires proper consideration of several design issues. One such instance is where Points of Presence (PoPs) are located and how they are interconnected, which is one factor that influences the resilience of a network. By optimizing problems with a focus on fault tolerance, Internet Service Providers (ISPs) can construct more fault-tolerant networks that can withstand failures. Recent trends suggest that by annotating topologies with capacity and latency information, engineers can get more fault-tolerant network designs that meet performance constraints. Applying hill-climbing heuristics will aid in the achievement of these optimization goals, thus aligning network topology design in strong relation to the inherent complexity depicted by real-world limitations (Byers et al., 2007). Topology-fault tolerance synergy ultimately leads to improved network management and user satisfaction. Additionally, the application of emerging technologies, such as micro-synchrophasors, significantly enhances fault tolerance in power distribution systems. By using information in micro-synchrophasors, utilities can acquire up-to-date knowledge of the health and performance of the networks. With that kind of up-to-date knowledge, possible issues can be diagnosed and remedied in advance before they accumulate to be serious failures. The present ARPA-E programs aim to improve the diagnostic applications from such data, referring to the requirements of fault-tolerant systems in the electrification of modern networks. Therefore, as networks evolve, the integration of these advanced diagnostic practices and equipment will be essential to maintaining fault-tolerant capabilities in sync with growing needs and technological advancements, ultimately benefiting sustainable network performance (Figure 6.7).

6.3.3. Data Transmission Efficiency

The efficiency of data transfer becomes the core in determining the overall performance of network topologies. Various parameters, including the protocol used, network structure, and environmental conditions, play a significant role in determining how data packets get transferred over a network. For instance, in underwater sensor networks (UWSNs), the transmission of acoustic waves has lower loss rates at higher distances compared to electromagnetic waves, but energy consumption and latency persist. Advanced Medium Access Control (MAC) layers, such as the proposed ED-MAC protocol, enhance efficiency via lower packet collisions and retransmissions. This protocol employs a duty cycle mechanism that optimizes data transmission despite varying network conditions, thereby optimizing throughput and ensuring fairness among the nodes, resulting in improved overall network performance, especially under heavy traffic loads (Alfouzan et al., 2018). Another area to consider in the direction of optimizing the efficiency of data transmission is in heterogeneous cellular networks over small cells at millimeter wave frequencies. The strategic deployment of such small cells significantly enhances network capacity while providing multi-gigabit data rates for access. With a robust backhaul network, utilization of these high-frequency bands allows more data to be carried and with lower latency. The optimization is best achieved in the D2DMAC protocol, which supports device-to-device (D2D) communication. Improving path choice and parallel transmissions, D2DMAC takes advantage of spatial reuse to alleviate congestion and enhance user experience. Extensive simulations demonstrate that this ubiquitous transmission scheduling mechanism not only improves delay and throughput but is also a foundation for sophisticated network architectures in future wireless communications (Gao et al., 2015). The complement of enhanced understanding is awareness of data transmission efficiency interaction and network topologies to achieve performance optimization. For instance, the design of the topology influences directly the efficacy with which data can travel across the network. Node placement, link bandwidth, and network density are parameters that should be balanced in balanced consideration to minimize bottlenecks. Different network layouts would yield different latencies as well as error rates, necessitating the utilization of efficient protocols such as ED-MAC and D2DMAC. By addressing issues presented by heterogeneous environments and traffic patterns, these protocols make the network topology more robust and agile. A focus on the relationship between topology and transmission effectiveness ensures that the possibility of continuous innovation in the network topology ensures that systems are able to accommodate the increasing demands of modern data transmission (Figure 6.8).

Figure 6.8. *The efficiency of data transmission.*

Source: https://jetmedia-inc.com/cdn/shop/articles/10041d10b79baa11cce7b005ec7ee8a1_1024x1024.png?v=1708329894.

6.4. PERFORMANCE METRICS IN NETWORKING

The quantification of performance parameters in networking is key to the understanding of the efficiency of various topologies. Parameters such as throughput, latency, and packet loss are critical in the assessment of how effective a network topology meets users' demands. Throughput refers to the amount of data passed through a network within a time interval that is used to understand the efficiency of data flow. Similarly, latency is the duration for which data moves from source to destination and acts as a measure of response time for networked applications. A high packet loss rate can reflect congestion or defective components and will cause the performance to be substandard and ultimately impact user satisfaction. Network designers are able to design solutions that maximize the topologies of the network for a given application by analyzing such metrics and hence improve performance and user satisfaction overall. In node mobility-driven performance dynamics of mobile networks, the use of performance metrics is even more crucial. It has been proven through research that patterns of human mobility directly influence networks, particularly in intermittently connected settings like Delay Tolerant Networks (DTNs).

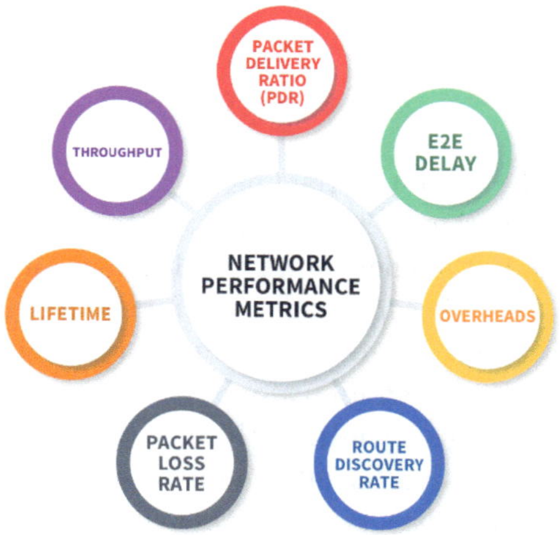

Figure 6.9. *Performance metrics in networking.*

Source: https://images.ctfassets.net/aoyx73g9h2pg/1sjQHM93CHDFQhF0hmslrj/8bb7dabd87950fbbd3d9b0182ee783e3/Performance-Metrics-Sensors-Network-Efficiency-Diagram.jpg.

By modeling behavior similarity between nodes, network protocols can be designed to utilize these patterns to facilitate better prediction of future connectivity as well as data delivery success rates. Designing a tensor-based temporal link prediction approach is one way that performance metrics can drive protocol design in mobile networks. By prioritizing node behavior and route optimization around these types of metrics, researchers are able to optimize data transport efficiency in environments with varying connectivity and unpredictable mobility patterns, highlighting the value of performance metrics in guiding existing network solutions (Gauthier et al., 2012). Performance metrics are likewise the most important measure for comparison among routing protocols in various network topologies. For example, in Mobile Ad Hoc Networks (MANETs), Dynamic Source Routing (DSR), Ad Hoc On-Demand Distance Vector (AODV), and Destination-Sequenced Distance Vector (DSDV) possess varying performance traits under varying scenarios. Analysis of these protocols on simulation platforms like NS2 shows variations in performance metrics like end-to-end delay, packet delivery ratio, and network load. Each protocol demonstrates strengths in specific conditions, leading to the suggestion of their application within real-world applications based on tailored guidelines. Detection of these differences through extensive performance analyses allows practitioners and researchers to select the most suitable protocol in diverse operational scenarios, which plays an important role in the optimization of network performance across different configurations (Iqbal et al., 2014) (Figure 6.9).

6.4.1. Throughput

Throughput is one of the most important metrics when assessing the efficiency of data transmission in various network topologies. Throughput measures data successfully transmitted over a network, typically expressed in bits per second. High throughput is vital for applications demanding high data processing volumes, such as big data analytics, streaming, and cloud computing. With advancing networks, the configuration also has to adapt to optimize throughput in the presence of increasing demands. For instance, multiplexing and switching technologies together can significantly improve throughput because several data streams can exist simultaneously without causing interference. Topology-throughput knowledge is thus highly essential in network performance guarantee, affecting both the operational efficiency and user satisfaction in a data-centric situation. Their configuration, such as Mobile Ad hoc Networks (MANETs), is an illustration of the complexity entailed in high-throughput guarantees. These networks contain dynamic node mobility and unpredictable topologies, which affect communication performance. Research verifies that the Optimized Link State Routing (OLSR) protocol can overcome some of the throughput problems but remains plagued by routing loops and self-interference. Experimental findings show that adjustments on the Media Access Control (MAC) layer, such as changing the Link Quality Window Size (LQWS), can increase throughput by improving data transmission reliability in TCP communication. This MAC and routing layer dependence highlights the need for adaptive mechanisms that are a function of the current network conditions to achieve maximum throughput in these dynamic topologies, ultimately resulting in better performance for real-time services like video streaming and online gaming. In the case of data centers, this trade-off between throughput and latency is even more drastic.

As more businesses rely on applications using big data, networks must be able to support high-throughput concurrent workloads as well as latency-critical operations. High-speed research indicates that optimizing throughput within a data center environment typically requires highly sophisticated network hardware capable of processing congestion successfully. Active Queue Management (AQM) and Explicit Congestion Notification (ECN) are important in minimizing latency while optimizing throughput. By striking a balance between these competing requirements, administrators can ensure that throughput-based and latency-sensitive applications both run optimally. This two-way consideration is particularly significant on those platforms that utilize Hadoop and the MapReduce programming model, where the analysis points out that appropriate AQM settings can realize considerable latency reductions without reducing throughput, and hence enhance overall network efficiency and customer satisfaction.

6.4.2. Jitter

In network performance, jitter has come to be seen as a key metric of the packet delivery time variation that significantly impacts data transport and communication quality. The variation is caused by a variety of factors, which can include network congestion and route changes to timing drift. As networks become more complex, particularly where there is a desire for real-time communications such as voice over IP and streaming video, jitter reduction is a very high priority. High jitter can lead to service quality deterioration through the occurrences of audio dropouts and video delay. Network designers thus must pay attention to jitter control alongside traditional measures like bandwidth and latency, embracing a holistic optimization mechanism where different application requirements are accommodated. Future automotive applications are particularly susceptible to jitter effects due to the varying demands placed on in-vehicular networks. These networks require seamless data transfer with large bandwidth and low latency to accommodate advanced driver assistance systems and autonomous driving technology. As characterized in the introduction to in-vehicular network design, the integration of Ethernet technologies points to the importance of tailored Quality of Service (QoS) features for management of various communication relationships dynamically. Not just does this complexity increase the likelihood of jitter events, but it also requires innovative solutions such as event-based simulation to meet the challenges of network planning that await us in the near future. Jitter management in these kinds of networks is crucial for the reliability and safety of operations, especially with the growing dependency on real-time data communication. The creation of applications such as telehaptics is also an indicator of the importance given to jitter management in modern networking scenarios. Telehaptic use demands stringent QoS requirements, primarily because of delay-sensitive multimedia communication across common networks. Dynamic packetization module (DPM) is one such new solution to the fight against jitter effects by adapting packetization rates based on real-time feedback of congestion. By monitoring end-to-end delay at all times, DPM not just preserves the quality of telehaptic sessions, but also performs well even in the presence of high levels of network congestion. This is the significant intersection of jitter control and network performance, showing the way that protocol innovations, such as DPM, can benefit application experience through decreased packet delivery time variability and ultimately more robust communication systems (Korf et al., 2018; Chaudhuri et al., 2017) (Figure 6.10).

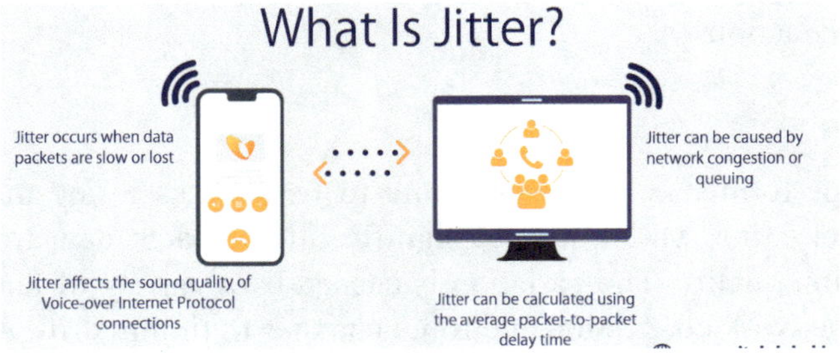

Figure 6.10. *Jitter.*

Source: https://www.vitelglobal.in/blog/wp-content/uploads/2022/10/What-Is-Jitter.webp.

6.4.3. Response Time

Response time, under network performance, is a significant parameter that describes the efficiency and efficacy of communication systems. Response time, for the majority of cases, is defined as the duration between the initiation of the request and completion of the associated action. In highly dynamic environments, that is, mobile ad hoc networks, response time is most responsive to changes in topology, which could affect how quickly nodes can communicate and relay information. Methods like those described in recent research indicate that utilizing predictive mechanisms can significantly enhance response times by anticipating network topology changes prior to their occurrence. For instance, the application of a history-based predictor (HBP) showed a massive reduction in the number of topology propagation messages used, effectively optimizing network communication and response times, thereby pointing to the intricate interrelation between network performance and topology management

(Castell et al., 2020). Another critical element for response time in network systems is its impact on the overall reliability of the systems, particularly in applications like Cyber-Physical Power Systems (CPPS). In this type of system, timely responses from operators are of prime importance as any lag will have a direct impact on system failure-related indices of reliability. Studies in this area indicate that reducing operator response time can minimize the likelihood of electrical as well as communication network failures. Through the use of models that incorporate response time in reliability indices, findings indicate that faster decision-making ability is associated with improved system performance. This interlink enhances the need to not only enhance the technicalities of communication in networks but also to create operator efficiencies, thereby proving that response time is not a standalone measure, but an important factor influencing overall system reliability (Bessani et al., 2016). In addition, the responsiveness of response time has implications on network performance in different computational environments. With the networks evolving towards more integration and complexity among various real-time monitoring systems, the ability to manage and minimize response times can be the competitive edge in performance. In industrial automation applications to smart cities, for instance, the synchronization of various network components depends largely on the efficiency of communication channels as well as the speed of decision-making. Overcoming latency and delay as a challenge is a total approach that mixes next-generation routing protocols, predictive analytics, and upgrained operator competencies. Not only do these processes enhance performance indicators like response time, but they also contribute to the robustness and responsiveness of ever-more connected networks (Castell et al., 2020; Bessani et al., 2016) (Figure 6.11).

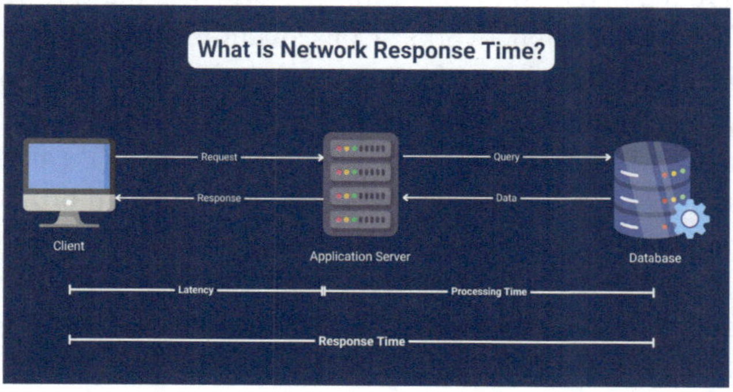

Figure 6.11. *The network-response-time.*

Source: https://obkio.com/blog/what-is-network-response-time/what-is-response-time.jpg.

6.5. CASE STUDIES OF DIFFERENT TOPOLOGIES

The study of different network topologies contributes significantly to the determination of their impact on performance outcomes, especially in complex systems such as power distribution networks. Through the use of different topological motifs, researchers have been in a position to analyze the robustness and vulnerability of such networks to extraneous attacks, that is, climate-induced perturbations and aging infrastructures. Significantly, topological analysis allows the determination of critical assets in the network and insight into how network structure contributes to overall robustness. An exhaustive exploration of the topological characteristics of power distribution networks highlighted the interdependence of asset connectivity and system vulnerability and the implication that network design improvement could result in dramatic operational reliability gains. The application of real-world data within this study further emphasizes the material significance of theoretical models, making such research vital towards more secure and efficient power grids (Koc et al., 2015). Apart from energy networks, case studies on other communication networks also exhibit the same findings related to the significance of topology on performance. Network anomalies, especially in high-dimensional settings, call for advanced analytical techniques that are attuned to the intrinsic topological configurations. Researchers have developed algorithms that seek to detect and interpret outlier behaviors in network samples through the examination of their subnetwork configurations. The capability to ascertain and interpret such subnetworks contributes not only to our understanding of network dynamics but immensely helps anomaly detection procedures. From the merging of network regression techniques with topological constraint, the techniques have the potential to maximize performance metrics, leading to the discovery of key local subnetworks. Consequently, such studies underscore that topological structure is at the heart of defining the performance and dependability of communication networks, and consequently theoretical and real-world solutions to network design and maintenance (Basu et al., 2016). Lastly, case studies from diverse topologies when combined provide a holistic perspective on network performance. Comparing outcomes from power grids and communication networks helps scientists make more universal conclusions about how structure in topology affects resilience and efficiency. Comparative research encourages network design and management breakthroughs to develop stronger infrastructures against new challenges that evolve. For instance, recognizing how different node and connection topologies influence fault tolerance can inform upgrade plans for already implemented networks. As the world becomes increasingly reliant on networked systems, one needs to employ topological insight in order to optimize performance and dependability in power and communications applications. This continued interaction between empirical data and theoretical models has the potential to advance the field significantly, serving as a point of departure for future research works in network topology (Koc et al., 2015; Basu et al., 2016).

6.5.1. Corporate Network Deployments

Implementation of corporate networks needs meticulous topological planning to realize optimized performance and efficient communication among diversified resources. Topological design impacts not just the data transfer rate but also the fault tolerance of networks. Different configurations, such as star, mesh, and tree topologies, have dissimilar benefits in terms of scalability, cost, and fault tolerance. For example, a star topology can make it easy to add devices but can isolate the hub as a single point of failure, whereas a mesh topology achieves redundancy in the form of several paths of connections and therefore helps to achieve greater performance in a distributed setting. This complexity causes organizations to take into consideration the implication of the network topology that they choose to implement, as in some business settings where the need for good interoperability and high availability results in choosing topologies that support optimal performance and scalability. Recent advancements have seen the integration of distributed computation infrastructures as a radical shift in business network deployment. The aspect of employing cloud-based resources for multi-party computation (MPC) allows companies to process data in a manner that maintains respect for privacy policies. It is argued in Bestavros et al. (2015) that this new model allows analysts to create algorithms that are privacy-agnostic and produce many different implementation versions that focus on specific needs. This innovation improves the efficiency of network resources since the architecture enables computations across various clusters without exhaustive knowledge of the underlying privacy solutions. By using a distributed approach, businesses can enhance network performance with better resource optimization and allocation, enabling them to maintain agility in a constantly evolving digital environment. Security is an equally key consideration in corporate network roll-outs, encapsulated by the analysis of threats through advanced techniques like attack graphs. The graphs offer a strategic perspective to understand potential paths of attack and how they impact corporate resources, hence informing the design of networks and security. As stressed in Cooper et al. (2016), the use of methodologies such as Bayesian inference in such systems provides organizations with an integrated overview of the security position. Scalability of inference methods' approximations, such as Loopy Belief Propagation, renders security analysis more feasible and allows corporations to assess risks in large networks in an effective manner. Thus, considering security alongside topology enables businesses not just to strengthen their defenses against potential attacks but also to provide a consistent network performance that is in synchronization with business requirements and operating stability (Figure 6.12).

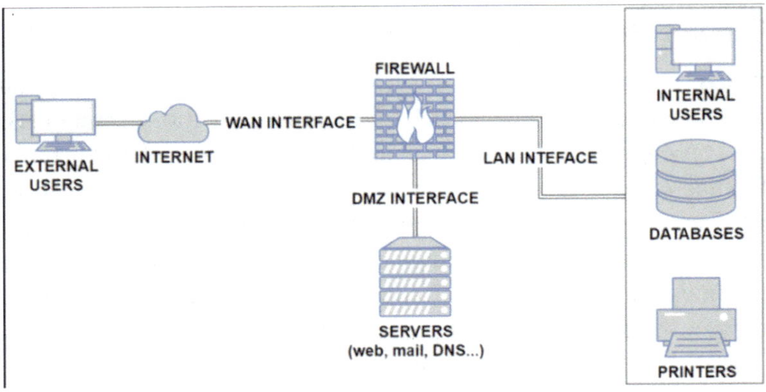

Figure 6.12. *The implementation of corporate networks.*

Source: https://www.researchgate.net/profile/Luis-Castro-Silva/publication/353368550/figure/fig1/AS:1048008447762434@1626876093465/Example-of-a-Corporate-Network-Architecture.ppm.

6.5.2. Home Network Configurations

Home network setup plays an important part in determining the overall performance and reliability of home internet connectivity. Various topological configurations, such as star, bus, and mesh designs, are implemented depending on user needs and resources available. Star topology, where every device is attached to a central hub or switch, is more fault-tolerant and more network-manageable because a faulting cable will not collapse the whole network. Bus topology is cheap and simple to install but results in a dramatic decline in performance with increasing network traffic. Also, mesh topology is highly redundant and fault-tolerant but can be costly and hard to install. Thus, the choice of topology influences not just the performance characteristics but also how far these networks can handle multiple data streams simultaneously in home networks, where several devices often compete for bandwidth. In the search for improved network performance, technologies such as Self-Organizing Networks (SON) become increasingly relevant to home network settings. As a case in point, SON functionalities bring advantages through dynamically assigning network resources for maximum performance. Deployment of SON in the home setting has particular requirements, however, particularly through potential conflictors among various independent functions. Such interactions can lead to unforeseen network behavior, thus negating the advantage of SON as desired. Knowledge of such interactions in detail can guide appropriate formulation of network management strategy. Identifying simple trade-offs among performance metrics, network engineers can create more stable home networks that settle conflicts efficiently, providing an unadulterated user experience even with integration of advanced technology (Dohler et al., 2015). The performance of a home network relies heavily on the stability and resilience of underlying infrastructure. As more devices are connected to the home network, from smart appliances to security systems, there is greater pressure on network performance. Modular approaches to network configuration, as with data centers, can be applied to home networks. Modular data centers employ variable topologies to enhance robustness and capacity for adapting to new loads and conditions. Using the same principles in home networks could enhance data management as well as dependability. Studies on the resilience of varying network topologies, for example, potential failure modes and their impact on performance, are crucial. Through an understanding of such dynamics using advanced simulation tools, such as Monte-Carlo methods, it might be achievable to understand how to improve home networks against disturbances and eventually increase user satisfaction and service continuity (Asghari et al., 2017) (Figure 6.13).

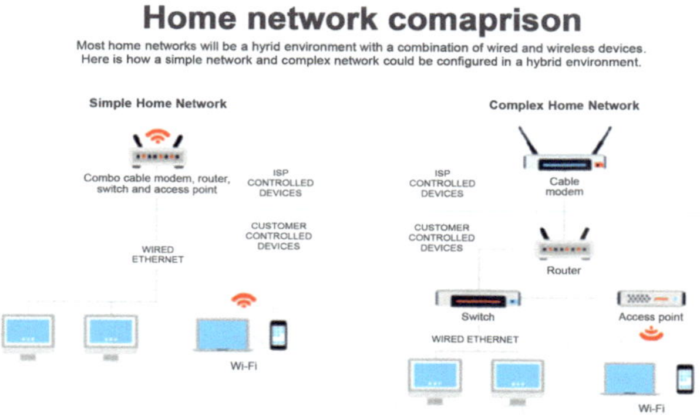

Figure 6.13. *Home network configurations.*

Source: https://www.techtarget.com/rms/onlineimages/networking-home_network_comparison-f_mobile.png.

6.5.3. Data Center Architectures

In the context of data center architectures, topology selection is a key component that influences network performance. With various architectures, for instance, modular data centers (MDCs), there is the opportunity for efficiency alongside enhanced resilience in various environments. MDCs have the additional benefit of being readily scalable, thereby an ideal choice when operating in remote sites that do not enjoy the luxury of ongoing maintenance. The core of an MDC is its network fabric, and it has the potential to be the enabling component for the entire system operation. It is essential to understand how the network topology influences such structures' performance because any failure of the network would lead to a cascading effect, de-stabilizing the efficacy of all other operational components of the data center.

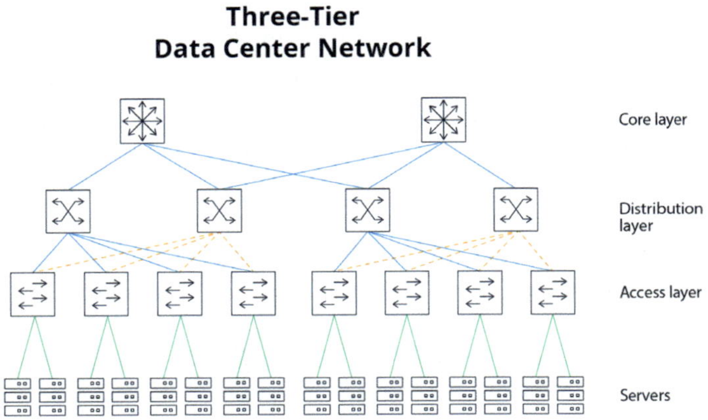

Figure 6.14. *Data center architectures.*

Source: https://d17ocfn2f5o4rl.cloudfront.net/wp-content/uploads/2024/08/BP-Data-Center-Networking-Design-infographic_3.jpg.

This insight suggests that methodical planning of network designs can reap high returns in terms of performance and reliability. Additionally, the use of many topologies, like the advanced designs of FatTree and BCube, illustrates a strategic method of dynamic response to shifting computational demands. These types of architectures are designed to optimize bandwidth utilization and reduce latency, which are significant drivers in maintaining high-quality network performance. Both topologies possess merits and demerits, most particularly when performance is viewed under stresses of failure among their components. It has been documented that a Monte-Carlo analysis technique can provide a comprehensive overview of how different architectures respond under stresses. For instance, MDCs have been shown to possess a good factor of resilience in the reduction of failure through auto-adaptation to diverse loads, thereby increasing their lifespan and functional capability. This adaptability is important since data centers themselves are becoming more and more advanced and adopting newer, more complex networking requirements. Lastly, as uses of technologies like Networks-on-Chip (NoCs) become more prevalent, the demand for innovative designs that support higher communication demands grows. Conventional NoCs are performance-bottlenecked when core numbers are increased, particularly in multicast and broadcast traffic scenarios. A hybrid approach, employing Wireless Network-on-Chip (WNoC) designs based on a common broadband channel, will endeavor to bridge these deficits. By creating low latency links for multicast traffic in addition to traditional wireline NoCs, data center implementations can achieve superior overall performance. Such multi-perspective approach not only enhances interoperability among the components but also builds a robust infrastructure that scales well with future computing demands, ensuring the continuous innovation of data center technologies for achieving ever-growing demands (Asghari et al., 2017; Cavall Aé et al., 2016) (Figure 6.14).

6.6. EMERGING TRENDS IN NETWORK TOPOLOGY

Network topology dynamics are influenced by the rapidly accelerating evolution of communications technology, pushing performance and size to be defined in ways that are unprecedented. One of the most fascinating trends to surface in network design is the integration of hybrid architecture that combines wired and wireless components to address the communications requirements of modern applications. As the networks become more complicated, particularly with the interconnection of multiple devices and platforms, the traditional wired NoC designs might not be up to par. This is further compounded by performance bottlenecks with expanding network sizes, particularly for multicast and broadcast traffic, which are necessary for dealing with diverse and simultaneous streams of data. Thus, the exploration of new topologies is a response to these heightened demands, with the emphasis being placed on having flexibility and efficiency in network topology for overall performance enhancement. In combination with the hybridization of technology, the concept of adaptive topologies has begun to gain traction. By utilizing algorithms with the ability to dynamically change the networks' structure in real-time, based on the prevailing traffic patterns, engineers are able to significantly enhance such performance factors as throughput and latency. Such flexibility is crucial, especially where user demands change rapidly. Utilization of advanced routing protocols, which are artificial intelligence and machine learning based, allows networks to maximize efficiency when situations change. These developments not only enrich users with a faster, more uniform experience but also induce energy efficiency by reduced duplicate traffic. It is against this backdrop that new trends are altering the manner in which we think about and implement network topology, paving the way for a more responsive architecture. In addition, the trend towards decentralized models of network topology mirrors generalized societal shifts towards openness and cooperation. As companies increasingly adopt decentralized networks like blockchain technology for secure transactions, the topology design must adapt to facilitate peer-to-peer interaction seamlessly. This adaptability helps data flow easily across multiple nodes with greater robustness and fault tolerance. Trends also identify the merging of network topology with edge computing concepts where data processing occurs close to the source and not centrally. Such designs reduce latency and allow real-time analysis, the building blocks of applications ranging from IoT devices to city infrastructure management. These developments ultimately reflect a topology change in networks where resilience, efficiency, and an interdependent world are priorities, which is poised to achieve the maximum benefit of technological advancements.

6.6.1. Software-Defined Networking (SDN)

In the dynamic network architecture era, Software-Defined Networking (SDN) has emerged as revolutionary in maximization of topology as well as network performance. With the separation of control plane from data plane, SDN provides centralized control of network devices to provide more efficient and flexible network traffic control. This structural transformation is facilitated by protocol like OpenFlow, which serves as the basis for the implementation of SDN through a normal means of communication between devices and the controller in a network. The potential for remote management of network resources offers a significant advantage, including quick adaptation to emerging needs and effective delivery of new services, making SDN an irresistible choice for modern companies looking to maximize their network infrastructures (Shamim, 2018). In addition, the impact of SDN on the network topology cannot be overstated. An optimal SDN deployment has the ability to lead to reduced complexity and improved visibility across the entire network infrastructure. The simplicity of managing network devices with a single central controller simplifies topology management, thereby data flow more effective. Additionally, the utilization of emulators such as Mininet provides network professionals and researchers with the ability to create and research various topologies in an efficient manner. Existing research indicates that the choice of various OpenFlow controllers such as Ryu, POX, and Pyretic can significantly affect performance metrics such as latency and throughput. By the vehicle of experimentation and analysis,

SDN facilitates organizations to design their network architectures to meet particular performance requirements (Challagundla et al., 2023). Even the application of load-balancing algorithms to SDN illustrates the latter's ability to optimize network performance in response to variable traffic volumes. With increasing reliance on cloud computing by organizations, it is essential to deal with network traffic, and SDN presents an elevated toolkit for the optimization of resource allocation. Various load-balancing methods, such as the Weighted Round Robin algorithm, have been employed in performance testing of different network setups. The ability to test such algorithms on virtualized systems allows organizations to choose the most optimal solution that best fits their needs. These advances indicate not only the more precise control offered by SDN but also the degree to which SDN can enhance network performance and reliability significantly, and thus it is an essential component of the networks in today's networks (Shamim, 2018; Challagundla et al., 2023) (Figure 6.14).

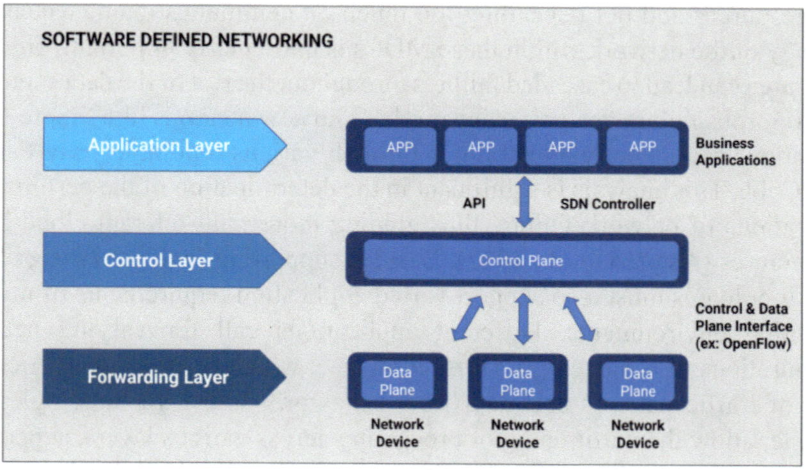

Figure 6.15. *The evolving landscape of network architecture, software-defined networking (SDN).*

Source: *https://atmecs.com/wp-content/uploads/2022/07/SDN.png.*

6.6.2. Cloud-Based Topologies

The development of cloud topologies revolutionarily affects the performance of networks, particularly in Internet of Things (IoT) implementations. The topologies facilitate seamless integration of the heterogeneous computing resources that span from the edge computing devices to core cloud servers. By developing architectures that scale dynamically based on dynamic data loads and processing needs, organizations can enhance responsiveness and efficiency. Among the most significant examples is the deployment of VIoLET, a virtual environment that supports configuration of complex topologies across multiple devices through containers. With scalability support for deployment at huge scales up to 400 devices, VIoLET assists in guaranteeing network performance aspects like bandwidth and latency are managed at optimal levels to avoid bottlenecks that negate overall system performance (Shukla et al., 2018). The flexible approach allows for the incorporation of real-time optimizations, and this ultimately results in better delivery of services in cloud platforms. The modular approach to data center planning has also emerged as another central factor in improving network performance in cloud infrastructures. Modular Data Centers (MDCs) represent a revolution away from conventional data center architecture, with an emphasis on flexibility and redundancy. These data centers are able to operate successfully in remote or adversarial areas by utilizing local resources and not depending too much on continuous maintenance. The topology of the network within these MDCs is particularly important; any flaw in this area can lead to cascaded failures throughout the rest of the data center. As such, rigorous failure analysis using models and new methods like Monte-Carlo simulations can detect vulnerabilities through various topologies, say FatTree and BCube. This analysis is significant in the determination of the performance implications of network failure, thus guiding more fault-tolerant cloud-based architectures (Asghari et al., 2017). Besides supporting fault tolerance, cloud-based topologies must also support varied application requirements of modern computing environments. Different applications call for varying network configurations to achieve optimal performance, which requires the meticulous study of traffic patterns and data flow behavior. Multi-layer topologies, for example, allow the partitioning of processing across various layers, supporting load balancing as well as aiding latency minimization. Further, cloud platforms' auto-scalability supports the fact that businesses can maintain performance levels regardless of fluctuations in demand. Therefore, use of state-of-the-art cloud-based topologies not only enhances the performance of the network but also provides businesses with the flexibility to respond quickly to fluctuating market demands. By constant evaluation and optimization of these architectures, businesses are able to retain a competitive edge within an expanding data-driven ecosystem.

6.6.3. Internet of Things (IoT) Considerations

With the quick-changing nature of the Internet of Things (IoT), topology and performance of the network are essential to enabling secure and effective communication between devices. As IoT networks usually consist of numerous nodes that are linked, the network needs to be optimized to have minimal latency and optimal bandwidth. This implies that there should be precise knowledge regarding the communication protocols that constitute the foundation of IoT deployments. Architecture deployed can play a vital role in the performance outcomes, particularly if aspects such as data flow, scalability, and fault tolerance are considered. With the application of new strategies, for instance, content-centric networking (CCN), IoT applications can presumably enhance content availability and reduce control traffic, which is often a bottle-neck in traditional architectures. Baccelli et al. (2014) emphasizes the benefits of CCN advancements to real-world IoT applications and provides useful insights toward solving energy and bandwidth constraints as well as coping with the unique challenges posed by varying topologies of networks. Another key aspect in IoT systems is energy efficiency, particularly in consideration of using sensors powered by batteries. Energy constraints will tend to lead to gigantic challenges in maintaining continuous communication that affects the overall device lifespan and performance. Experiments have revealed that deployment of strong security measures such as authentication and encryption can ironically lead to increased energy consumption, complicating design choices for the network. But neglect of security exposes IoT devices to energy depletion attacks, including denial of sleep attacks, that can severely degrade sensor performance. So, there has to be a two-pronged strategy in choosing security and energy efficiency. The application of adaptive duty cycling techniques can overcome these challenges at the cost of performance. Here, the results derived by Udoh et al. (2019) present major analyses of security mechanisms and their implications on energy consumption in wireless sensor networks, allowing for efficient topology choice with balanced performance and security. Furthermore, the integration of new protocols and strategies is essential for optimal operation of IoT networks in real-time applications. The evolution towards power-saving media access control protocols, like the proposals considered in recent research, represents promising development in balancing energy efficiency without compromising throughput. Simulation of various MAC protocols, that is, Sensor MAC and Tunable MAC, shows extensive insight into balancing energy usage and data rates. These empirical evaluations illustrate how different protocols are made to conform to the specific requirements of network size and application loads. This continuous quest for IoT design breakthroughs not only improves our insight into network performance but also bears witness to traditional paradigms on efficacious resource usage. As the research contributions have shown, further investigation into dual-faceted strategies will be essential for the fine-tuning of IoT topology and the realization of long-term sustainable network performance in dynamic settings.

SUMMARY

It is important to value the impact of topology control on communication network effectiveness. The various topology control algorithms guarantee connectivity of networks and maximize performance in dynamic environments. The more the necessity for continuous connectivity, the more the value of such algorithms is understood. By focusing on metrics such as minimizing latency and optimizing resource utilization, researchers have begun to realize the intricate interplay between network topology and performance metrics. Not only has this optimized theoretical models, but it has also been applied in the real-world deployment of networks, resulting in the general robustness and resilience of communication systems. The current advancements in caching methods, especially in the case of Information Centric Networking (ICN), further illustrate the changing dynamics of network performance. The research on various caching schemes, such as First In First Out (FIFO) and Least Recently Used (LRU), illustrates the importance of efficient content distribution mechanisms as networks progress. The comparative analysis of methods in the case of Named Data Networking (NDN) indicates that Universal Caching (UC) is a clear winner over its competitors, with potential for outstanding enhancements in both sensor networks and Internet Service Provider (ISP) domains. The study implications therefore extend beyond theoretical argument, providing practical suggestions towards network enhancement in varied operational contexts (Panigrahi et al., 2016). Moreover, the dynamic behavior of real-world networks necessitates novel solutions that account for their intrinsic variability. With more and more communication networks becoming more dynamic, the need for topology control mechanisms that are flexible and resilient increases. The development of novel approaches that incorporate visual programming and specification languages is a promising avenue under these circumstances. Through the definition of network modifications by graph transformation techniques, such methods ensure consistency and optimization characteristics required. Lastly, the incorporation of advanced topology control algorithms with current network design principles will guide toward a more efficient and reliable communications platform to satisfy the constantly increasing demands of users in a hyper-connected society (Hollick et al., 2017).

The understanding of Internet topology, specifically for Autonomous Systems (AS), plays a crucial role in network performance assessment. One observation that is significant is that the joint degree distribution of AS topologies serves as a characteristic feature describing the networks. Traceroutes and BGP exhibit different sources of data with appreciable similarities in their topological representations, whereas WHOIS data indicates significant differences. This variation highlights the value of observing data collection mechanisms, which dictate the topology views extrapolated from these sources. Through examination of these anomalies, researchers can inform themselves of how various topological models are reconcilable, and to what extent a comprehensive perception of network architectures is conceivable and beneficial. Moreover, by making input topology datasets and computation scripts available, scientists are motivated to validate their outcomes against empirical evidence, offering an open environment for network topology research development (Vahdat et al., 2005). By comparing existing AS topology generation models, one can see that the majority of them fail to effectively model the intricate local interconnection pattern in AS networks. Whereas such models may potentially perform well at reproducing degree-based characteristics, they are known to disregard the complexities of AS connectivity, particularly within the central areas of the network. A comparative analysis demonstrates that whereas local structure measures such as node centrality and clustering do vary based on the vantage points where BGP data is collected, the central degree-based measures show relatively minimal impact. This inequality represents one of the main frailties in current modeling techniques, pointing towards the need for more concrete methodologies that are responsive to localized intricacies. Thus, this study suggests that researchers should refrain from over relying on degree-based models since they tend to reduce the intricate nature of network relationships (Fay et al., 2012). As network topology advances to the cutting edge, its relationship with performance metrics becomes more transparent. It is open to researchers to adopt a multi-pronged approach that combines empirical measurement data analysis and rigorous modeling techniques for the incorporation of both local interconnectivity and degree distribution. Intermingling of knowledge extracted from several data sources not only enhances the accuracy of topology models but also supports network development in terms of maximum efficiency. The discovery that different methods of data collection affect local structure properties emphasizes that network behavior should be understood with caution. With these complexities, future research can lead to the development of improved network structures, resulting in improved performance in various applications from route efficiency to congestion control. This bird's-eye view is necessary both for researchers and practitioners who are compelled to navigate through the problems generated by increasingly complex network environments (Vahdat et al., 2005; Fay et al., 2012).

REFERENCES

1. Abadal Cavallé, S., Alarcón Cot, E. J., Cabellos Aparicio, A., González Colás, J., et al. (2016). Scalability of broadcast performance in wireless network-on-chip. https://core.ac.uk/download/81578757.pdf (accessed on 9th September 2025).
2. Alander, H., Aschenbruck, N., Aschenbruck, T., Aschenbruck, U., Aschenbruck, V., Asimakopoulou, E., Bai, Y., et al. (2012). An evolutionary computation approach for optimizing connectivity in disaster response scenarios. https://core.ac.uk/download/46170687.pdf (accessed on 9th September 2025).
3. Albert, R., Alderson, D. L., Clegg, R. G., Gibson, W., Hága, P., Kaiser, G., Kushida, T., et al. (2009). The dynamics of Internet traffic: Self-similarity, self-organization, and complex phenomena. http://arxiv.org/abs/0807.3374 (accessed on 9th September 2025).
4. Albert, R., Bagler, G., Barnhardt, S., Bollobás, B., Callaway, D., Chowdhury, A., Cohen, R., et al. (2009). Jamming transition in air transportation networks. http://arxiv.org/abs/0907.1042 (accessed on 9th September 2025).
5. Alfouzan, F., Boutaleb, T., Ghoreyshi, S. M., Shahrabi, A., et al. (2018). An efficient scalable scheduling MAC protocol for underwater sensor networks. https://core.ac.uk/download/293885609.pdf (accessed on 9th September 2025).
6. Ali, H., Idrus, S. M., Imtiaz, W. A., Iqbal, M., et al. (2017). Impact of fiber duplication on protection architectures feasibility for passive optical networks. https://core.ac.uk/download/322431005.pdf (accessed on 9th September 2025).
7. Aliagas Castell, C., Meseguer Pallarès, R., Millán Marco, P., Molina Clemente, J., et al. (2020). Predicting topology propagation messages in mobile ad hoc networks: The value of history. https://core.ac.uk/download/294829916.pdf (accessed on 9th September 2025).
8. Allen, M., Iqbal, M., Perelman, L. S., Preis, A., et al. (2015). Flexible reconfiguration of existing urban water infrastructure systems. https://core.ac.uk/download/83225252.pdf (accessed on 9th September 2025).
9. Arghandeh, R., & von Meier, A. (2014). Diagnostic applications for micro-synchrophasor measurements. https://core.ac.uk/download/288432738.pdf (accessed on 9th September 2025).
10. Asghari, V., Cheriet, M., Lemieux, Y., Moghaddam, M., et al. (2017). A Monte-Carlo approach to lifespan failure performance analysis of the

network fabric in modular data centers. http://arxiv.org/abs/1401.7528 (accessed on 9th September 2025).

11. Baccelli, E., Hahm, O., Mehlis, C., Schmidt, T. C., et al. (2014). Information centric networking in the IoT: Experiments with NDN in the wild. https://core.ac.uk/download/49601532.pdf (accessed on 9th September 2025).
12. Bahrebar, P., & Stroobandt, D. (2015). Design of TSV-sharing topologies for cost-effective 3D networks-on-chip. https://core.ac.uk/download/55733751.pdf (accessed on 9th September 2025).
13. Barolli, L., Duresi, A., Ikeda, M., Xhafa, F., et al. (2010). A testbed for MANETs: Implementation, experiences and learned lessons. https://core.ac.uk/download/157811874.pdf (accessed on 9th September 2025).
14. Bass, S. (2013). The philanthropic landscape in the United States: A topology of trends. https://core.ac.uk/download/75779050.pdf (accessed on 9th September 2025).
15. Basu, P., Dang, X. H., Silva, A., Singh, A., et al. (2016). Outlier detection from network data with subnetwork interpretation. http://arxiv.org/abs/1610.00054 (accessed on 9th September 2025).
16. Begin, T., Busson, A., Guérin-Lassous, I., Nguyen, T. M. T., et al. (2016). Evaluation of an end-to-end delay estimation in the case of multiple flows in SDN networks. https://core.ac.uk/download/52293431.pdf (accessed on 9th September 2025).
17. Bessani, M., Delbem, A. C. C., Fanucchi, R. Z., Maciel, R. H., et al. (2016). The impact of operators' performance in the reliability of cyber-physical power distribution systems. http://arxiv.org/abs/1603.07775 (accessed on 9th September 2025).
18. Bestavros, A., Lapets, A., & Volgushev, N. (2015). Scather: Programming with multi-party computation and MapReduce. https://open.bu.edu/bitstream/2144/21774/1/2015-010-scather.pdf (accessed on 9th September 2025).
19. Bisoyi, S. K., & Sahu, S. (2020). Performance analysis of dynamic MANET on-demand (DYMO) routing protocol. https://core.ac.uk/download/480906941.pdf (accessed on 9th September 2025).
20. Byers, J. W., & Wang, C. (2007). Generating representative ISP technologies from first-principles. https://open.bu.edu/bitstream/2144/1678/1/2007-001-ISP-topology-from-first-principles.pdf (accessed on 9th September 2025).
21. Carpenter, P. M., & Fischer e Silva, R. (2016). Controlling network latency in mixed Hadoop clusters: Do we need active queue management? https://core.ac.uk/download/81580303.pdf (accessed on 9th September 2025).

22. Challagundla, S. (2023). GR-343 An experimental study: Performance of load balancing algorithms in SDN-enabled cloud computing networks. https://core.ac.uk/download/572713910.pdf (accessed on 9th September 2025).
23. Chaudhuri, S., Gokhale, V., & Nair, J. (2017). Congestion control for network-aware telehaptic communication. http://arxiv.org/abs/1610.00609 (accessed on 9th September 2025).
24. Clegg, R. G., Di Cairano-Gilfedder, C., & Zhou, S. (2009). A critical look at power law modelling of the Internet. https://core.ac.uk/download/1747753.pdf (accessed on 9th September 2025).
25. Collado, C., Hueltes, A., Mateu, J., Rocas, J., et al. (2014). Filtenna integration achieving ideal Chebyshev return losses. https://core.ac.uk/download/30312133.pdf (accessed on 9th September 2025).
26. Colle, D., Demeester, P., Depré, L., Peters, J., et al. (2005). Dimensioning of a European backbone network in OPNET WDM Guru. https://core.ac.uk/download/55778812.pdf (accessed on 9th September 2025).
27. Cooper, G. F., Dechter, R., Li, W., Mooij, J. M., Murphy, K. P., Pearl, J., Schneier, B., et al. (2016). Efficient attack graph analysis through approximate inference. https://core.ac.uk/download/83926564.pdf (accessed on 9th September 2025).
28. Costes, J. P., & Lu, C. (2008). Surface profile prediction and analysis applied to turning process. https://core.ac.uk/download/29138024.pdf (accessed on 9th September 2025).
29. Dikaiakos, M. D., Loulloudes, N., & Pallis, G. (2010). The dynamics of vehicular networks in urban environments. http://arxiv.org/abs/1007.4106 (accessed on 9th September 2025).
30. Dohler, M., Giupponi, L., Imran, A., Imran, M. A., et al. (2015). LTE-advanced self-organizing network conflicts and coordination algorithms. https://core.ac.uk/download/74233072.pdf (accessed on 9th September 2025).
31. Entin, M., & Fitriah, F. (2025). PERANCANGAN JARINGAN LOCAL AREA NETWORK (LAN) DI SEKOLAH SMK 1 KEPAHIANG. *Jurnal Riset Sistem Informasi*. https://www.semanticscholar.org/paper/e4c0e4883b392bfacb8fa66c21faa559c25eb0d6 (accessed on 9th September 2025).
32. Fay, D., Haddadi, H., Jamakovic, A., Maennel, O., et al. (2012). Beyond node degree: Evaluating AS topology models. https://core.ac.uk/download/30696069.pdf (accessed on 9th September 2025).

33. Filsfils, C., Salsano, S., Tajiki, M. M., Ventre, G., et al. (2018). SDN architecture and southbound APIs for IPv6 segment routing enabled wide area networks. http://arxiv.org/abs/1810.06008 (accessed on 9th September 2025).
34. Fortuna, R., Leonardi, E., Mellia, M., Meo, M., et al. (2010). QoE in pull-based P2P-TV systems: Overlay topology design tradeoff. https://core.ac.uk/download/pdf/11416114.pdf (accessed on 9th September 2025).
35. Gao, C., Jin, D., Li, Y., Niu, Z., et al. (2015). Exploiting device-to-device communications in joint scheduling of access and backhaul for mmWave small cells. http://arxiv.org/abs/1503.02292 (accessed on 9th September 2025).
36. Gauthier, V., Slama, I., Zayani, M. H., Zeghlache, D., et al. (2012). Tracking topology dynamicity for link prediction in intermittently connected wireless networks. http://arxiv.org/abs/1205.3328 (accessed on 9th September 2025).
37. González, D. G., García-Lozano, M., Hämäläinen, J., Senarath, G., et al. (2016). A novel multiobjective cell switch-off framework for cellular networks. https://core.ac.uk/download/81578758.pdf (accessed on 9th September 2025).
38. Hollick, M., Kluge, R., Mühlhäuser, M., Schürr, A., et al. (2017). A systematic approach to constructing incremental topology control algorithms using graph transformation. http://arxiv.org/abs/1805.03386 (accessed on 9th September 2025).
39. Imran, M. A., Onireti, O., Qadir, J., Sathiaseelan, A., et al. (2016). Will 5G see its blind side? Evolving 5G for universal Internet access. https://core.ac.uk/download/42552730.pdf (accessed on 9th September 2025).
40. Iqbal, M., Mehmood, Z., & Wang, X. (2014). Comprehensive experimental performance analysis of DSR, AODV and DSDV routing protocol for different metrics values with predefined constraints. https://core.ac.uk/download/146489522.pdf (accessed on 9th September 2025).
41. Jouet, S., Pamukchiev, A., & Pezaros, D. P. (2017). Distributed network anomaly detection on an event processing framework. https://core.ac.uk/download/46664260.pdf (accessed on 9th September 2025).
42. Kenyeres, J., Kenyeres, M., & Skorpil, V. (2015). Split distributed computing in wireless sensor networks. https://core.ac.uk/download/30312868.pdf (accessed on 9th September 2025).
43. Koc, Y., Kumar, T., Raman, A., Warnier, M., et al. (2015). Structural vulnerability analysis of electric power distribution grids. http://arxiv.org/abs/1506.08641 (accessed on 9th September 2025).

44. Libarikian, A. L. (2002). Robustness of bus overlays in optical networks. https://core.ac.uk/download/4384822.pdf (accessed on 9th September 2025).
45. Liu, Z., Mühlhäuser, M., Shi, X., Wang, H., et al. (2018). PABO: Mitigating congestion via packet bounce in data center networks. https://core.ac.uk/download/303692001.pdf (accessed on 9th September 2025).
46. Milićević, M., Pavlović, P., Rančić, D., Čabarkapa, S., et al. (2022). Investigating the impact of tree-based network topology on the SDN controller performance. https://core.ac.uk/download/542478798.pdf (accessed on 9th September 2025).
47. Moadeli, M., Ould-Khaoua, M., Sharabi, A., Vanderbauwhede, W., et al. (2007). An analytical performance model for the Spidergon NoC. https://core.ac.uk/download/1393976.pdf (accessed on 9th September 2025).
48. Ok, J., Park, S., Shin, B., Yi, Y., et al. (2012). Embedding of virtual network requests over static wireless multihop networks. http://arxiv.org/abs/1207.1878 (accessed on 9th September 2025).
49. Panigrahi, B., Rath, H. K., Sengottuvelan, S., Shailendra, S., et al. (2016). Performance evaluation of caching policies in NDN–an ICN architecture. http://arxiv.org/abs/1612.00352 (accessed on 9th September 2025).
50. Shamim, S. M. (2018). Performance analysis of different OpenFlow based controller over software defined networking. https://core.ac.uk/download/539593423.pdf (accessed on 9th September 2025).
51. Shukla, A., Burns, B., Gupta, H., Satyanarayanan, M., & Calheiros, R. N. (2018). VIoLET: A large-scale virtual environment for Internet of Things. http://arxiv.org/abs/1806.06032 (accessed on 9th September 2025).
52. Udoh, E., & Udoh, E. (2019). An energy aware and secure MAC protocol for tackling denial of sleep attacks in wireless sensor networks. https://core.ac.uk/download/305119264.pdf (accessed on 9th September 2025).
53. Vahdat, A., Krioukov, D., Dorogovtsev, S. N., claffy, k. c., Fomenkov, M., Mahadevan, P., Rekhter, Y., et al. (2005). The Internet AS-level topology: Three data sources and one definitive metric. http://arxiv.org/abs/cs/0512095 (accessed on 9th September 2025).
54. Yousif, Y. E., & Elnageeb, O. A. O. (2025). Performance evaluation and comparison of RIP, EIGRP and OSPF routing protocols. *European Journal of Applied Science, Engineering and Technology*. https://www.semanticscholar.org/paper/7be6161179116e2795899e79fa07c8ea8906aac6 (accessed on 9th September 2025).

CHAPTER 7

SECURITY IMPLICATIONS OF TOPOLOGY DESIGN

Contents

INTRODUCTION

The topological design of networks is critically analyzed to show an ever-evolving and dynamic landscape, particularly regarding security issues. As the reliance on interconnected networks by organizations continues to rise, the physical structure of network elements—referred to as topology—has a pivotal function to determine the way security mechanisms are implemented and maintained. The traditional network designs were prone to emphasizing operational efficiency over security protection, which is now deemed not sufficient in an era where sophisticated cyber-attacks are the norm. Consequently, engineers and designers who are undertaking planning topologies are required to tackle security protection simultaneously so that they can create strong structures that can withstand imminent intrusions and attacks, leading to the merging of design and defense strategies. The advent of technologies such as Software-Defined Networking (SDN) has increased topology design complexity, introducing new challenges for the conventional security models. Although SDN promises better control over network resources, it simultaneously introduces risks inherent in its very nature of reliance on centralized control systems. Current implementations of SDN, presented in Gehrmann et al. (2018), reflect an ecosystem still grappling with the formalization of access control structures, the basis for protection against adversarial attacks. The absence of standardized protocols underscores the need for an end-to-end solution toward security integration into the design phase to facilitate more resilient architectures with the ability to evolve according to shifting threats. Without such a focus, topological models can inadvertently turn into points of failure rather than defenses against intrusions. In addition, decentralized systems exploration offers insightful learning on how security may be fostered through varied design philosophies. As mentioned in Danezis et al. (2017), decentralized designs distribute control, in essence managing the threats of one point of failure while enhancing privacy and integrity. But this will have its own difficulties; the added complexity and necessity of coordination across multiple authorities create new exposures. For designers of topology frameworks, an understanding of these trade-offs is essential to balancing value against risk. By integrating decentralization knowledge with traditional security strategies, network designers will be able to formulate strategies that not only concentrate on making data movements more optimal, but also construct secure defenses and, ultimately, design secure network environments that are capable of addressing the needs of today's digital environment.

Definition of Topology Design in Network Architecture

Topology design of network structure is the arrangement of various elements of a network, including nodes, links, and connecting relationships. It exists in various types, including star, ring, bus, and mesh topologies, which impose varying effects on performance, reliability, and security. When designing the topology of a network, designers consider scalability, fault tolerance, and ease of exploitation by malicious actors. A well-designed topology can enhance network robustness against attacks, thereby enhancing overall security posture. Conversely, poorly designed topologies can offer vulnerabilities, making critical systems open to unauthorized access and data corruption. It emphasizes the need to understand how architectural choices affect security, which makes it a significant aspect of the overall examination of network integrity. Decentralized network designs have introduced complexity and new issues into topology design. In decentralized systems, the components are independent, demanding careful balance between independence and dependence. Decentralization can offer better privacy and integrity along with opposing potential adversarial behavior of components. Decentralization also introduces advanced security vulnerabilities that must be identified and managed proactively. Designers must contend with complexity-tradeoffs, performance-tradeoffs, and decentralization-tradeoffs. The knowledge gained across multidisciplinary fields such as cryptography and distributed systems becomes very helpful in overcoming such challenges because it provides the basic knowledge necessary for building safe and efficient networks. Specifically, the way the insights will mix and shape the creation of future systems will determine their resistance to future threats (Danezis et al., 2017). Besides, topology details also play a significant consideration for specialized networks such as wireless sensor networks (WSNs). WSN structure often employs unique topologies specifically designed for data-centric applications, which can lead to significant performance enhancement. For instance, proper topology design allows efficient routing and data dissemination, which are primary contributors to the operation efficacy of these networks. But designers must be conscious of the security impact of the communication structures that they design. As explained in recent research, the manner in which the architecture is selected can determine the extent to which inter-task communication and dynamic reconfigurations are managed optimally. Secure structures within these architectures become imperative as the threat in the cyberspace continues to advance and permeate various levels of technology (Dulman et al., 2005). This integration of functionality and security highlights the importance of intentional topology creation.

Importance of Network Security in Design

The importance of security during the design of networks cannot be exaggerated, considering that organizations are increasingly relying on interlinked networks to facilitate operations. Proper security measures play an imperative role in safeguarding sensitive information from malicious use and cyber-attacks whose effects can be financially and reputational disastrous. By including security measures during network design topology, organizations can minimize vulnerabilities and develop a sound infrastructure. Security design-oriented networks build layers of defense, thus strengthening their defenses against intrusions and disruptions. In addition, the integration of security considerations in the process of network design not only boosts reliability in information exchange but also enhances trust among users within an environment required to ensure safety in digital space. The evolving nature of cybersecurity threats means that network design needs to be anticipatory, where security concepts are built into the structure itself. Special operating requirements of critical infrastructure, for instance, have their own security requirements. Current research undertaken on behalf of the UK government put forward the necessity of high-level tools designed to evaluate and improve security dynamics within such critical infrastructures. The findings emphasize that interdependency analysis must itself be economically viable for it to actually safeguard interdependent network components effectively. It is through the incorporation of these end-to-end security mechanisms during the design phase that organizations are in a position to provide a solid basis for resistance to increasingly advanced cyber-attacks and hence realize long-term operational continuity and security integrity (Bloomfield et al., 2009). In addition to securing information, the embedding of security into network design ensures effective content distribution across the network and decreases attack surfaces. The information-centric networking research is a typical case study of the shift from traditional legacy host-to-host models to data-driven ones, which are inherently optimized to reduce exposures. However, data-driven protocols expose the network to new forms of security threats, which have to be thoroughly understood and solved. An analysis of these novel attack vectors confirms the need to design networks securely as well as for performance. Strategically weaving security mechanisms into the topology design will enhance the systems overall robustness and ensure that likely threats do not compromise the stability and operation of the network (Schmidt et al., 2012) (Figure 7.1).

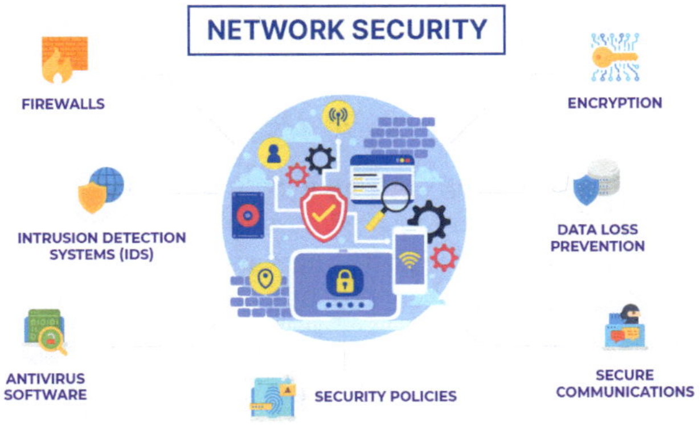

Figure 7.1. *The importance of security in network design.*

Overview of the Essay's Focus on Security Implications

The implications of topology design in network systems for security are becoming a priority of utmost importance as technology advances keep changing the way communication infrastructures are defined. As we venture into this, it is evident that network architecture dictates its vulnerability to attacks in a number of ways. Topology design not only defines the communication between devices but also determines the preparedness of the whole network for attacks. Paradigm design changes, in particular the trend towards more decentralized architectures, have changed the way data flows and security is enforced. Future networks, like the 5G and its future version the 6G, will need robust security measures in place because of the extensive variety of applications these will facilitate as well as the highly sensitive data these will transmit, as explained in Tataria et al. (2021). This topological-security interaction thus lays the basis for our conversation. Furthermore, emerging trends such as edge computing and artificial intelligence are redefining the network security gamebook. The integration of these technologies means that security solutions must rethink the way they must change to address new challenges. Edge computing locates computation resources near the data source, improving efficiency but also presenting new avenues of attack which need to be lessened for the sake of data integrity and privacy. At the same time, the use of AI for network management improves responsive security functions but adds complexity as well. For instance, the decision making by means of AI may produce unanticipated vulnerabilities that could be used by the attackers if the systems are not tightly controlled. Based on this, as explained in Zhou et al. (2019), the present essay puts its emphasis on possessing complete strategies incorporating properly designed topologies coupled with advanced security measures to secure the next-generation networks. Ultimately, the combination of topology design and security features is a reaction to a continuing debate over how networks must grow and develop responsibly. The danger posed by increasing complexity of cyber-attacks calls for preemptive action in structuring network designs that build security into every layer inherently. This preemptive action involves identifying not only potential vulnerabilities but implementing sweeping protocols that counter them. With increasing network complexity and the ubiquitousness of IoT devices spewing out humongous amounts of data, there is a need for a topology that can hold strong against not just present threats, but also future ones. By so doing, we lay the groundwork for secure systems that are able to protect user data and be reliable in an increasingly interconnected world, thereby highlighting the interdependent relationship between topology design and implications of security.

7.1. TYPES OF NETWORK TOPOLOGIES

It is important to have an understanding of the numerous network topologies in assessing their implications on security. Star, bus, ring, mesh, and hybrid topologies each have distinct structural advantages and disadvantages. The star topology, which involves a hub connecting all nodes in the center, favors effective data management but raises significant security concerns. Compromising the central node will lead to total network failure, and therefore the necessity for robust access controls and redundancy provisions. Mesh structure, where each node talks to many others, makes a network more robust and functioning even if there is node loss. However, added operational complexity and extra cost can introduce additional vulnerabilities, and extreme caution needs to be exercised in the design process. The distributed topology of some topologies imposes unique challenges and opportunities regarding security. Control in distributed systems resides in numerous nodes, so there is less likelihood of single-point failure, yet such a design imposes potential adversary moves from individual nodes. Decentralized architectures are able to enhance privacy, integrity, and availability but must strike trade-offs among levels of decentralization and system complexity, as the recent work demonstrates (Danezis et al., 2017). Besides, as the architecture of network topologies increases, there is a need for designers to incorporate aspects of distributed systems and cryptography in designing new solutions to suit privacy-sustaining agendas. The intricacies suggest that one solution may be inadequate, and instead, there is a need for bespoke measures to suit particular security demands in different topological designs. From the research on real-world applications, it is evident that security measures in different topologies are relevant. Distributed hash tables (DHTs), an omnipresent aspect of decentralized networks, are typically under attack by threats such as Sybil attacks, whereby malicious nodes hyper-inflate their presence so that they can disrupt network operations. Aspects such as X-Vine, which piggyback on social network connections for messaging, offer a new mechanism for reduction of these threats while maintaining user anonymity and privacy (Borisov et al., 2011). With proof-of-concept through real-world simulations and deployment, X-Vine provides an example for building robust, scalable systems that take advantage of unique topological properties to provide enhanced security. As network topology choices have direct correlations to exposure to attack as well as overall robust operation, understanding those implications becomes critical as technology evolves and networks grow more complex.

7.1.1. Star Topology and Its Security Features

Star topology has gained popularity as a network configuration since it is centralized and comprises all the devices being connected to one switch or hub.

The layout offers several security advantages. Specifically, the centralization allows for efficient traffic monitoring and the implementation of strong security, which significantly enhances the integrity of the network. Positioning security appliances such as firewalls and intrusion detection systems inside the hub makes it easy for administrators to monitor traffic trends effectively and instantly detect potential threats. Not only is this method effective in detecting malicious activity, but also in minimizing risks through fast response to impending security threats. Thus, the simplicity of the architectural design of the star topology enhances understanding of network behavior, crucial to enforce security protocols and protect against sensitive information. However, the star topology is not immune to security attacks. The central hub is a potential vulnerability point; if compromised, it is capable of causing general disruption of network services.

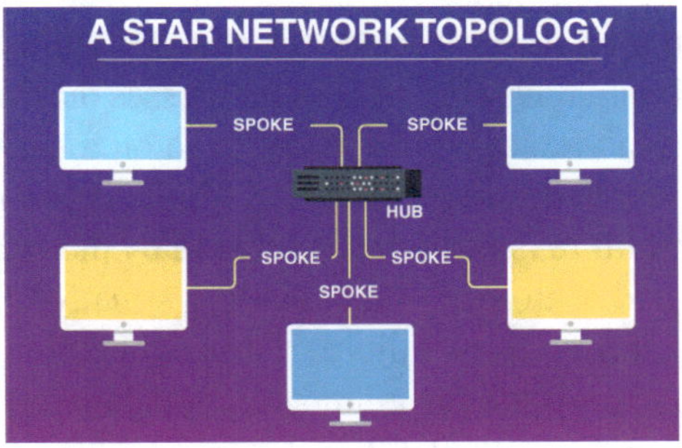

Figure 7.2. *Star topology and its security features.*

Source: https://cdn1.byjus.com/wp-content/uploads/2022/07/star-topology.png.

The attackers can target this hub node to intercept or manipulate communications, and therefore stringent security practice is to be implemented on the hub itself. Additionally, having a single point of failure implies that firms need to incur the costs of redundancy systems and provide the central node with failover functionality. Such investments also increase the reliability of the network as well as the resilience of security, such that although one part might be attacked, the network can still perform optimally. Such vigilance is important in upholding the integrity of the system to avoid cascading failures, which may be targeted during a cyber-attack. Besides, the use of star topology does not just confine itself to traditional networking applications to sophisticated fields such as Industrial Wireless Sensor Networks (IWSNs). Such networks, which are prevalently utilized in industries ranging from automation to monitoring, experience peculiar problems in light of their ubiquitous and dynamic environments. As has been stressed in Aslam et al. (2018), even though IWSNs owe much flexibility and scalability, it is their susceptibility to environmental factors that create critical security threats. Integrating star topology with IWSNs can enhance security by centralizing communication nodes that monitor data integrity between sensors. Conversely, as awareness of challenges surrounding such industrial environments, in the form of interference and vulnerability to data tampering, exists, then a need to be in an effective position to design responsive security solutions arises. Eventually, a combination of the optimum practices of star topology with tailored security solutions can help reinforce IWSNs against developing threats within a more interconnected world (Figure 7.2).

7.1.2. Ring Topology and Potential Vulnerabilities

In network structure, ring topology has a unique shape in which all the devices are linked in a circular structure. Despite its ability to encourage data transmission speed, it inherently has some weaknesses that must be studied. One of the fundamental weaknesses lies in its reliance on a single route to transfer data; if any of the nodes is destroyed or attacked, the entire network falls apart. This susceptibility to failure is further exacerbated by the fact that any attacking attempt against one node can lead to a cascading situation, impacting multiple devices in the topology. In reality, failure of one connection not only halts data transmission but also poses issues in redundancy and fault tolerance mechanisms, significantly impacting the overall network security environment of networks applying ring topology. The relevance of these flaws resonates heavily within the big picture of security technologies and technological progress. In line with the emergence of the Industrial Internet of Things (IIoT), where all sorts of systems interface with the physical world, the vulnerabilities of ring topology become increasingly difficult. For example, the idea of interconnectivity is a two-sided sword when multilayered security arrangements have to be taken to offset risks from node failure or malicious attack. Given that the IIoT environment can involve data streams from a multitude of intermediaries, it is increasingly complex and difficult to achieve a coherent and safe network infrastructure. This means that as networks evolve, particularly with the shift towards more and more interconnected devices, reevaluating ring topologies' security provisions is core to fighting inherent vulnerabilities and adapting to the ever-evolving threat landscape (Κωνσταντίνος et al., 2021). Moreover, the dynamism of technological advancement, particularly in fields such as quantum computing, only adds to ring topology vulnerabilities. As quantum processing brings with it the potential for novel forms of attack, traditional forms of encryption can be rendered obsolete in an environment of continuously increasing computer power. With faster processing being achieved in quantum devices to make increasingly advanced calculations, they can render traditional encryption useless, thereby compromising networks, including ring topology networks, to unprecedented levels. Constant vigilance and current security framework patches are necessary, which stresses the importance of developing solutions that are flexible and resilient enough to withstand contemporary and future threats. As such, the relationship between topology design, technological advancement, and its associated vulnerabilities remains central to ensuring network architectures with security in today's fast-changing digital landscape (Gill et al., 2021) (Figure 7.3).

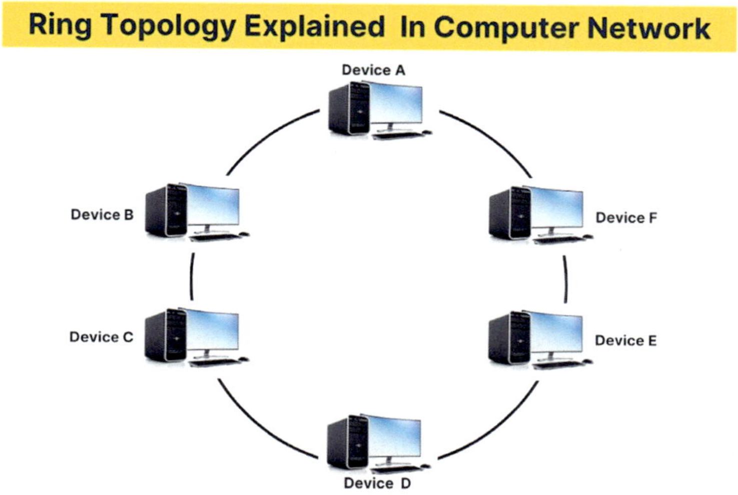

Figure 7.3. *Ring topology and potential vulnerabilities.*

Source: https://d8it4huxumps7.cloudfront.net/bites/wp-content/banners/2024/2/65c9cac6bd67d_ring_topology_infographic.jpg?d=700x400.

7.1.3. Mesh Topology and Its Resilience Against Attacks

It is the mesh topology architecture that makes mesh topology especially resistant to any form of network attack than any other network architecture. In mesh topology, every node is connected with multiple paths to other nodes so that if one node is compromised or fails, it will not damage the network function. This redundancy offers duplicate avenues for data transmission, enhancing reliability in offensive attacks when enemy activity is directed against individual nodes or links. Therefore, even in systematic interferences, such networks remain operational, providing critical services with minimum disruption. In addition, the decentralized attribute of mesh networks complements prevailing security paradigms, promoting systemic address of privacy and integrity, becoming increasingly vital in shaping digital communications. However, while mesh topologies are more resilient, they are also vulnerable to certain attacks and must implement strict security measures. The various layers of the communications protocol stack in Wireless Mesh Networks (WMNs) can themselves be vulnerable to a range of threats that range from unauthorized access to data tapping.

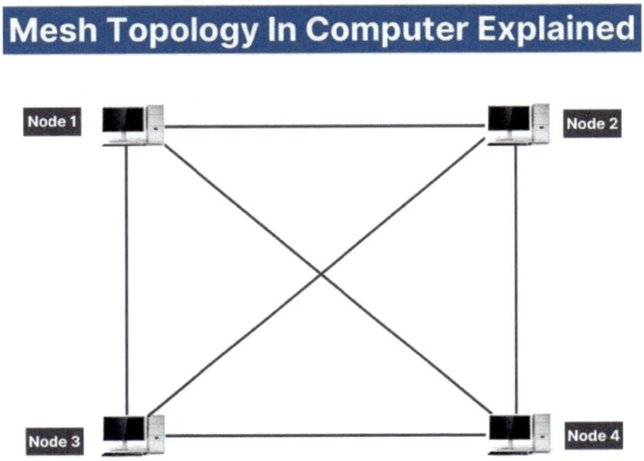

Figure 7.4. *Mesh topology and its resilience against attacks.*

Source: https://d8it4huxumps7.cloudfront.net/bites/wp-content/banners/2024/2/65c60970b6714_feature_image_of_mesh_topology_in_computer_networking.jpg.

Addressing vulnerabilities at these layers, designers are in a better position to resist malicious intrusions targeting both the physical layer as well as the application layer. For instance, adequate user authentication and access control mechanisms are critical towards preventing attacks by malicious agents attempting to breach the network. Moreover, an examination of existing security systems illustrates the importance of employing layered security solutions that address every vulnerability in its entirety based on the principles in various studies on WMN security (Gupta et al., 2013). Furthermore, decentralization system evolution has an impact on mesh topology security profiles. Not only can decentralization be a significant enhancement to resilience, but privacy and integrity through the network as well. By dynamic reallocation of trust throughout nodes, the impact of a single point compromise is diminished, providing a field in which adversarial attempts are effectively neutralized. This approach necessitates careful analysis of compromises, for example, potential increases in system complexity and adequate provision of incentive for cooperation among nodes. As mesh topology continues to evolve, it will be essential to borrow concepts from cryptography and mechanism design in developing scalable, privacy-preserving protocols that meet the future needs for secure communication systems (Danezis et al., 2017) (Figure 7.4).

7.2. SECURITY RISKS ASSOCIATED WITH DIFFERENT TOPOLOGIES

The architecture of the network topology fundamentally decides the security posture of the system it comprises. Each topology, whether hierarchical, bus, or ring, has certain properties which will enhance or disrupt security mechanisms. For instance, a star topology, although it offers centralized control that makes monitoring easier, has a single point of failure; if the central node gets attacked, the entire network gets compromised. While decentralized structures such as mesh networks provide resistance to attacks with data traveling along several paths, these come with the unforeseen effect of increasing complexity and introducing more vulnerabilities through the heterogeneous node-to-node linkages. Identification of these features is critical to organizations seeking to prevent security breaches while guaranteeing their network maximum performance and reliability, particularly when sensitive data exchanges are involved and breaches would be catastrophic to their processes. Moreover, topology design implications also reach into the realm of upcoming technologies, where the use of new systems can introduce unforeseen weaknesses. With companies adopting advanced technologies like hydrogen energy systems, the topological complexity of their network is critical. The study of hydrogen technologies illustrated in contemporary literature more accurately than ever conveys the notion of the central significance of securing communication channels between different components to be utilized in hydrogen production and supply. In such systems, simultaneous interaction among several topologies can establish safe channels for data transmission or, alternatively, generate overall system weakness if properly planned. Thus, continual development and sophistication of threats necessitate organizations to proactively change their topological structures to negate increasingly dynamic security issues, evincing the need for careful planning based on the specific architecture of a topology. Lastly, the advent of data-centric technologies—like machine learning—adds an additional layer of complexity to topology-centric security. These technologies create a requirement to access vast datasets typically found in siloed environments, which creates inherent privacy and security concerns. Federated learning, which allows machine learning to train on decentralized data without centralization, offers a promising means of overcoming these challenges; nonetheless, its implementation introduces new security issues. Specifically, various topologies can affect the effectiveness of federated learning approaches, as each systems arrangement impacts data exchange and training operations on the model. The balance between the application of data to add predictive ability and ensuring robust security control is delicate; thus, addressing such issues needs careful commitment to both technical innovation and comprehensive policymaking. The engagement of the forces emphasizes the strategic imperative necessity of organizations understanding and planning their network topology to defend against any future security attacks, particularly as they navigate the complexities of contemporary data usage (Yue et al., 2021; Rieke et al., 2020) (Figure 7.5).

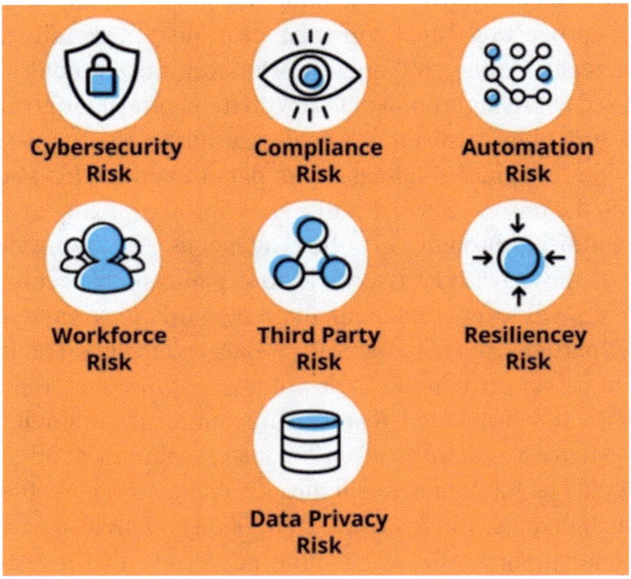

Figure 7.5. *Security risks associated with different topologies.*

Source: https://zindagitech.com/storage/2022/06/Picture3.2-Shweta.jpg.

7.2.1. Single Point of Failure in Star Topology

When talking about the star topology, a key issue to note is the inherent vulnerability brought about by the existence of one point of failure. With this configuration, every node is connected to a central switch or hub, which will be the principal go-between for data interchange. In case the central hub fails, the entire network would be made useless, leading to serious disruptions. This design flaw has critical security consequences, as it hampers data transfer reliability and responsiveness of connected devices. Centralization of network functions not only affects the operation continuity but also makes organizations more vulnerable to being attacked at this point. Organizations must have a firm security system to protect the hub since it is considered to be a critical asset that requires redundancy levels to absorb potential failure. The exposure of the star topology to single point failures points to a larger problem regarding network resilience and security. Redundancy techniques such as the utilization of redundant hubs or alternate paths can help mitigate the impact of a failure. But solutions like this also create complexity and expense, which can make network resource management harder. Organizations need to weigh the expense of implementing such redundancies against possible data integrity and productivity loss if one network goes down. Besides, where data integrity is essential in real-time, like in Industrial Wireless Sensor Networks (IWSNs), the effect of hub failure is a high one. IWSNs, so beneficial for their cost-effectiveness and flexibility, still have to counter these weaknesses in their structure so that critical industrial processes remain functional in the event of potential disruptions (Aslam et al., 2018). For countering the threat of the single point of failure in star topology, cutting-edge technologies such as Quantum Key Distribution (QKD) can provide revolutionary solutions to enhance network security. QKD enables theoretically secure key generation between hosts, a requirement in the integrity of data shared over an insecure network topology. Although enterprise application of QKD is not without its limitations, application thereof could potentially eliminate interception risks and unauthorized access to data. When firms consider ways of solidifying their network security frameworks, the addition of expandable key management services with the utilization of quantum technology is among the possibilities. This multi-layered adoption not only introduces security but also ensures that nodes within the network can be autonomous, thereby reducing reliance on a single point of failure (Ling et al., 2017). By implementing such measures, organizations are more able to manage the security aspects associated with their network topology designs.

7.2.2. Risk of Data Interception in Ring Topology

The ring topology design method to network architecture brings with it strange data interception dangers that are worthy of close attention within the overall context of security implications. In ring topology, data packets move in a circular manner, forwarded from node to node during transit until they finally arrive at the destination. This structure, however, has attendant opportunities for vulnerability; an intercepted packet could be captured by any node in the perimeter. Thus, after gaining access to any single node, a malicious user can intercept and manipulate information as it flows through the network, exposing sensitive information. This type of risk is particularly profound in systems with minimal security controls, like in consumer applications with the Internet of Things (IoT) where deployment speed generally takes precedence over good security design, as established in Jiménez et al. (2018). In addition, the limitations of traditional security controls in ring structure are a significant cause for alarm regarding data integrity and confidentiality.

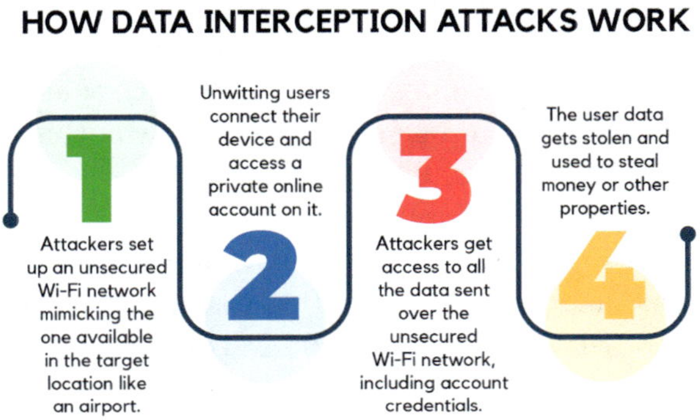

Figure 7.6. *Data interception risks in ring topology.*

Source: https://lh7-us.googleusercontent.com/ayVYffOYNtCKDFBvnmEWLkuT-ZI7cRsMZ7oEKbLX5yVRbYTrAiQ4Ag5nUx7rxElLDxBFk8W7yJDEnUkZ-rusoU-vM4idNMK0FSBcvsUcLJEQ5TJi7IEKCEbGVk27PBr4bqI4afoJ7yI2H94URsk-mRUNLA.

The circular path necessarily means that every packet goes through every node, and an interception at any point can potentially lead to malware injection or data manipulation. Consequently, when one node is compromised, it provides an opportunity window for bad actors to disrupt communication or steal confidential data. Lack of effective encryption methods in most IoT devices adds to this issue further, thus negatively impacting the potential for securing data communication in such environments (Jiménez et al., 2018). The design needs to therefore implement robust security measures specifically for safeguarding against interception attacks, which have become increasingly prevalent as more devices get connected. In addition to that, regulatory control has also been regarded as crucial because organizations attempt to restrict such interception threats associated with ring topology. Governments and regulators are now realizing the importance of having effective policies that govern applying security standards in network infrastructure. These measures not only protect users but also ensure an equal playground for players in which security is prioritized over speed and cost. The regulatory model debate, for instance, the ones being formulated by the government of Indonesia for Internet services in the context of over-the-top (OTT) services, reflects more sensitivity towards the impact of network topology on privacy and security of data. Ultimately, adopting substantive regulatory policies that entail stringent requirements for security can actually reduce the danger from data intercepting in ring topology and foster a more secure cyberspace (Figure 7.6).

7.2.3. Complexity and Management Challenges in Mesh Topology

The intricate mesh topology where each node is linked to every other node puts a unique set of complexity and administration challenges. Mesh networks establish robust connectivity and redundancy, and this makes the network more resilient to single points of failure. This interconnectedness complicates network administration by sheer quantity and complexity of connections. Administration becomes difficult for administrators in terms of monitoring and establishing multiple nodes since an individual node can be utilized for a variety of functionalities within the system. The bigger the network, the harder it is to offer equal performance and reliability. Even the concerns find their way into security management; mesh complexity of configuration can also lead to neglect and make it easy for vulnerabilities to be overlooked. Thus, even though the advantages of flexibility and resilience are appealing to most organizations, the complexities of management issues for mesh topology cannot be overstated. The other fundamental aspect of mesh topology complexity is data traffic and utilization. In a scenario with high connectivity, there is a high probability of data congestion, not only compromising network efficiency but also the security posture of the network. Simultaneous data transmission via redundant paths can lead to bandwidth contention, ultimately causing latency and impacting applications sensitive to timing. Also, the role of resource management is augmented, as optimum use of network resources is required to meet performance standards. The inherent complexity of routing algorithms—required to determine the most efficient route in sending data—is another level of complexity. As companies roll out mesh networks, the balance between improving performance and keeping robust security frameworks is a pressing management concern that needs special treatment in order to counter threats while leveraging the topology's strength. In addition, the transient nature of mesh networks creates unprecedented hurdles for security management. The relentless exercise of adding or removing nodes introduces variability into the game that can make it challenging to sustain a secure environment. Every new relationship has potential paths for unauthorized access, and therefore ongoing network monitoring and threat analysis are essential but increasingly challenging.

The security controls and appliances must be agile enough to respond to these ongoing changes efficaciously. Moreover, effective incident response plans require extensive knowledge and mapping of the network topology that is often obscured by the complexity of native relationships. Overcoming these challenges necessitates a multi-headed approach that combines continuous monitoring, predictive threat analysis, and reactive security solutions so that the specific benefits of mesh topology are not liabilities in the security framework of modern network design (Figure 7.7).

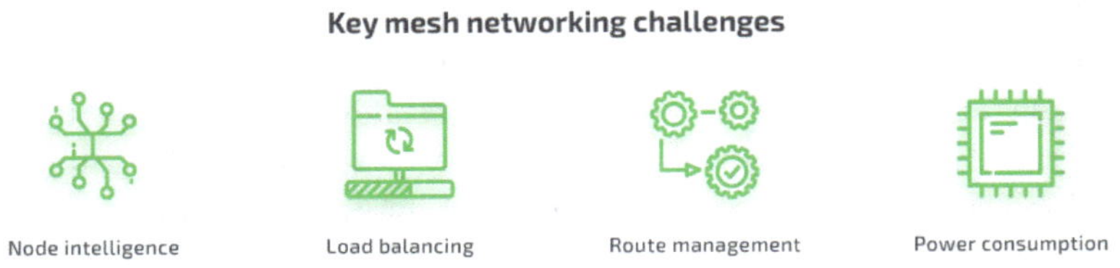

Figure 7.7. *Complexity and management challenges in mesh topology***.**

Source: https://www.apriorit.com/wp-content/uploads/2020/04/figure-7-1.jpg.

7.3. IMPACT OF TOPOLOGY ON NETWORK PERFORMANCE

Network topology design plays a crucial role in determining network performance as well as the reliability of communication networks. In essence, node organization and how they are interconnected determine the effectiveness of data transmission within the network. For instance, star, bus, and mesh topologies possess their respective strengths and weaknesses in terms of speed, latency, and fault tolerance. In vehicular ad hoc networks (VANETs), the topological structure is critical in determining routing performance, particularly at intersection areas, which are crucial towards maintaining seamless communication among vehicles. A study illustrated in Mansoor et al. (2018) provides evidence that conventional routing protocols are ineffective in addressing the challenges brought about by the variety of intersection geometries, where topography-oriented solutions are required to enhance communication reliability and reduce end-to-end delay. The topological implications extend beyond simple data transfer efficiency; they also have a determinative effect on security design. Different topological designs may produce different attack surfaces, thereby affecting the vulnerability of the network to security breaches. A completely meshed topology, for example, might provide multiple routes for data, which would possibly make the network more able to withstand node loss but which would complicate security management methods. Conversely, simpler topologies like star networks might be safer due to centralization but present a single point of failure that could be targeted by intruders. Studies of inter-vehicle communication in VANETs identify that topology not only affects the efficacy of communications but also the security protocols' resilience, and it is therefore crucial that security-focused topology design be taken into consideration, as presented in Mansoor et al. (2018). While city infrastructure is becoming smart cities, the network topology must also evolve by accepting the utilization of smart technologies to push performance as well as safety. The smart grid revolution illustrates how multiples of diverse sources of energy generation and active demand participation reinvent the traditional model for analyzing network architecture. A flexible topology is capable of supporting the management of renewable resources better but introduces extra security issues, particularly with respect to dealing with decentralized systems. As, power grid modernization must address the interplay among topology, performance reliability, and cybersecurity. Thus, it is essential to construct robust, topology-aware platforms for communication and energy distribution networks to enhance operational effectiveness while securing against inherent vulnerabilities of distributed, complex networks.

7.3.1. Latency Issues Related to Topology Design

Designing network topology significantly affects the latency of devices and users in a system. Latency refers to the time it takes for data to travel through a system, something that can heavily affect performance, especially in real-time applications such as video conferencing and online gaming. A poorly designed topology might translate to increased hop counts—each new node a data packet must travel through can introduce potential delays. Also, the distance of servers from end-users is critical; where servers are distant, latency must be increased. Proper topology design therefore must consider not only the minimum physical distance but also overall network architecture to optimize data transmission so as to mitigate latency problems that can compromise security measures that rely on rapid response. One of the most prominent aspects of topology design latency is the edge computing and latency reduction relationship. As it has been demonstrated by the rise in popularity of distributed architecture, it can actually reduce the time taken for data packets to reach their destination. With the use of edge computing, latency issues can be minimized by organizations, thereby optimizing the responsiveness of applications that are real-time data processing based. This shift of edge intelligence not only reduces latency but also introduces new security models; however, this calls for robust security mechanisms for protecting data while it is transmitted through numerous nodes closer to the end-user. The topology design with delicacy along with edge resources can thus lead to improved latency values even while it raises new security concerns that must be addressed carefully. In general, topological latency problems must be solved within the framework of topology planning if user experiences are to be enhanced and good security standards maintained. The outcome of topology choice extends beyond performance levels, significantly influencing the ability to adopt good security measures that involve the need for quick data exchange. For instance, involving federated learning as a new approach can utilize reduced latency to execute data locally with privacy protection and, hence, gain a balance between security and performance. While companies race to keep up with increased amounts of information and demands for speed, network topology design will be a key focus area where latency solutions will have to support more abstract security objectives to deliver a secure and effective digital environment (Figure 7.8).

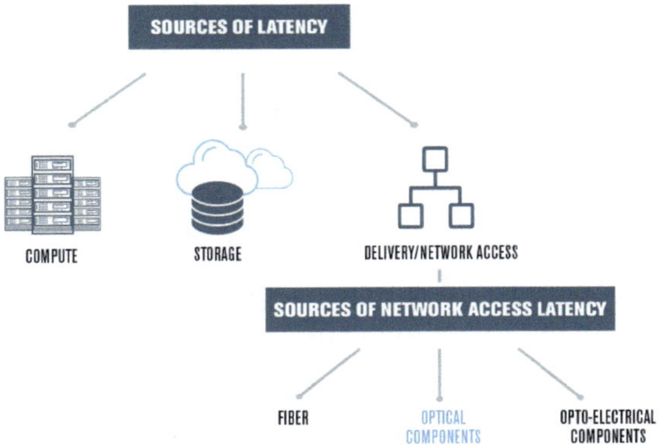

Figure 7.8. *Latency issues related to topology design.*

Source: https://integraoptics.com/wp-content/uploads/2019/09/INF-IO_Latency_Diagram2-01.png.

7.3.2. Bandwidth Allocation and Its Security Implications

The bandwidth allocation principle is the core of network topology design since it directly affects performance and security. As the complexity of the network increases, effective allocation of bandwidth can help prevent bottlenecks and ensure that commitments of Quality of Service (QoS) are met. The threat of improper bandwidth allocation can come in many different forms and introduce a number of vulnerabilities. For example, in the case of poor bandwidth use, it gives an opportunity to attackers to exploit network vulnerabilities, such as through Denial of Service (DoS) attacks, by flooding resources and disrupting valid traffic. An anticipatory approach, drawing from Software-Defined Cloud Computing (SDC) methodologies, is required to reshape bandwidth allocation according to real-time demands while maintaining network security. The automation provided by SDC not only enhances the operational efficiency but also enhances the security position of the network by enabling quick adaptation to respond to detected threats (Buyya et al., 2014). Moreover, the interdependency between network security and bandwidth allocation becomes even more significant in cloud computing environments. The need for effective resource discovery and signal routing is critical in such cases, as worst-case effects can be triggered by mismanagement, including data leaks and system downtime. Guaranteeing bandwidth allocation is properly managed, particularly in federated networks, can help limit unauthorized access and resource exhaustion-related risks. As outlined in new proposals concerning the FEDERICA network, a synchronized effort on the control plane architecture can offer an environment that is secure and well-equipped with proper resource allocation mechanisms, thus reducing exposure to potential weaknesses (Cervelló et al., 2009). The architecture of such mechanisms needs to factor in the intricacies of user needs and potential threat avenues, thereby offering a holistic approach to designing the network topology. Finally, efficient bandwidth allocation management must also include round-the-clock monitoring and analysis of data movement to forestall the occurrence of potential security threats. By keeping track of bandwidth consumption, administrators can determine unusual activity that may indicate exploitation attempts or service interruption. Methods like real-time tracking and adaptive resource management can act as a first line of defense, with a capability for real-time adjustment of responses against shifts in traffic profiles and malicious attacks. Incorporating new algorithms into the control systems that manage resource allocation ensures security components are thoroughly tested in topology design innovations. These integration procedures can ultimately serve to create a more resilient network structure, one with the capability to adapt to shifting security threats while meeting performance requirements (Buyya et al., 2014; Cervelló et al., 2009).

7.3.3. Scalability Concerns and Their Effect on Security

Scalability is a natural aspect of network topology planning and has a direct influence on security mechanisms. As systems expand—whether through deployments of new devices, applications, or services—the complexity of handling security protocols increases exponentially. Scalability problems tend to create holes in securing elements, which inadvertently introduce weaknesses. For instance, in rapidly expanding Internet of Things (IoT) setups, scalability must be addressed without compromising security. Application of cloud-focused architectures can hinder implementation of the need-spurring edge-based activities, especially in cases of AI technologies and UAVs. These types of technologies depend on low latency and robust security measures; where scalability is overlooked when these come into play, it can create tremendous security loopholes that undermine the system's overall integrity (McEnroe et al., 2022).

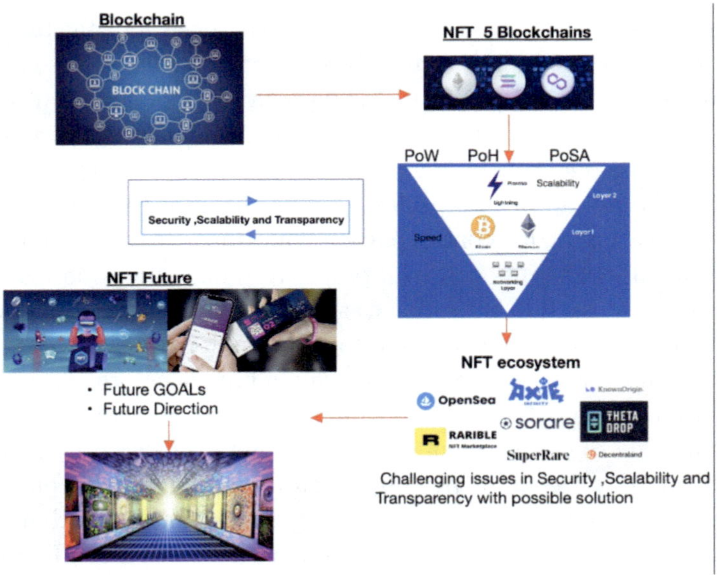

Figure 7.9. *Scalability concerns and their effect on security.*

Source: https://pub.mdpi-res.com/sensors/sensors-22-08833/article_deploy/html/images/sensors-22-08833-ag.png?1669095845.

Moreover, the dynamic nature of modern-day networks amplifies the security consequences because of the problem of scalability. When infrastructures expand in scale, organizations adopt a patchwork approach to security by implementing incompatible solutions that can lead to inconsistency and protection loopholes. It is a fragmented setup that can be exploited by malicious components to gain access to the system. For example, where various components of a network do not adhere to a shared security standard, they may inadvertently open doors for unauthorized entry. The requirement for a unified and extensible security framework consequently comes into the limelight, particularly in complex configurations such as financial networks where threat management and monitoring are essential in upholding system integrity (Ando et al., 2022). Furthermore, scalability emphasis has to cover proactive measures against upcoming threats as well. Cybersecurity attacks evolve and develop more rapidly than security measures, especially for large and complicated systems. Topology designs that not only aid growth but also have adaptive security solutions that adapt to upcoming threats become inevitable. This proactive approach is critical in ensuring that as organizations increase their operations, they also improve defenses against potential vulnerabilities that arise from increasing system complexity. Through failure to include scalability in the security plan, organizations risk creating a foundation that will become increasingly susceptible to attacks, thereby undermining their operational reliability and credibility within an even more competitive market (McEnroe et al., 2022) (Figure 7.9).

7.4. BEST PRACTICES FOR SECURE TOPOLOGY DESIGN

In secure topology design, the common practice is the definition of the boundaries of networks. Each zone or segment must be well planned to thwart threats of illegal entry as well as data attack. Organisations can break their networks into smaller parts by a concept named segmentation so that tight access control and surveillance within each zone is a must. This strategy not only segments sensitive data but enhances overall network resiliency to attack as well. With the boundaries established, organizations can more effectively implement security policy tailored to the particular requirements of each segment, allowing for the assurance that threats are being addressed in a focused manner, significantly reducing the attack surface exposed to the adversary. One crucial element of safe topology design is the integration of advanced encryption methods and key management. Key emphasis in new technology such as Quantum Key Distribution (QKD) is the securing of communications as a basis for organizational integrity. QKD provides a secure mechanism for key generation, theoretically resistant to all forms of cryptographic attacks, including those applicable under quantum computing. Notwithstanding this, the use of such technologies in enterprise infrastructure is still difficult, particularly in metropolitan network expansion and key management (Ling et al., 2017). The organizations must adopt best practices using layered architectural models that are compatible with a heterogeneous set of encryption methods, thereby creating a flexible security infrastructure which is aligned with enterprise objectives and operational requirements. Furthermore, Software-Defined Networking (SDN) introduces new solutions for secure topology design to make networks adapt to new security threats. Although existing SDN provides sophisticated abstractions for the control plane and forwarding plane, efforts towards standardizing network management applications persist, leaving large access control mechanism gaps (Gehrmann et al., 2018). Best practices in this case involve allowing access control functionality to include bundled frameworks that partition resource access effectively. With augmented protocols governing access on behalf of network providers, operators, and application developers, organizations can strengthen the security of their topology's. This facilitates a structured means of resource distribution leading ultimately to a better secured, flexible, and expandable network environment that can resist threats from internal as well as external threats.

7.4.1. Implementing Redundancy to Enhance Security

Redundancy implementation is the central process in making networks secure in network topology development. Redundant systems by definition have backup paths for data delivery and operation that can drastically limit the impact of security breach. For instance, in a redundant network topology, if one link or system is breached or down, traffic can be rerouted through a spare channel and normal service is maintained. This trait is especially critical to infrastructures based on the Internet of Things (IoT) and wireless sensor networks (WSN), where network robustness becomes the central factor in real-time data processing and monitoring. As outlined in earlier literature, application of redundancy within such frameworks not only functions as a preventive measure but also directly contributes to a risk management approach in the new Industry 4.0 framework, where the operational integrity stakes are comparatively high (Majid et al., 2022). Furthermore, the establishment of redundant paths also serves to boost defenses against malicious attacks that are increasingly sophisticated in today's digital environment. The replication of data among nodes serves to successfully mitigate risks presented by data tampering or unauthorized access. This decentralization of information both enhances the integrity of information and allows for better detection of anomalies, since out-of-normal patterns can more readily be observed when streams of information are coming from various directions. The challenge of maintaining coherent network security increases with the maturity of distributed systems. Redundant infrastructure will function as a backup and provide the infrastructure required to maintain the monitoring and logging of network activity on a continued basis, essential for threat detection and mitigation prior to its more severe manifestation (Verbraeken et al., 2020). Redundancy, ultimately, is not simply a fail-safe but an active security solution. Redundancy is also optimal best practice in incident response and disaster recovery design for network topological design. Whenever there is a security violation, the ability to restore services quickly with no long-term downtime is critical. Redundant systems provide this by giving duplicate processes and data structures that assist in providing minimal potential for service interruption. Moreover, redundant designs' efficiency can also be achieved with data recovery techniques, which enable organizations to maintain updated copies within various geographic locations. This topological variety not only protects against localized attacks but also meets data protection needs for the majority of industries, which insist on strong data protection measures. As organizations navigate the complexities of topology design, sheer redundancy becomes a cornerstone of security tactics, ultimately leading to a firm and responsive network configuration that will be able to adapt to shifting threats and vulnerabilities (Figure 7.10).

Figure 7.10. *Implementing redundancy to enhance security.*

Source: https://www.givainc.com/images/it_redundancy.png.

7.4.2. Utilizing Segmentation to Limit Attack Surfaces

Segmentation is a very key concept in cybersecurity, especially when it comes to network topology and design. When a network is segmented into smaller, manageable parts, organizations are able to reduce their attack surfaces, thereby reducing the risks posed by possible breaches. Every segment can have specific security protocols without exposing sensitive information. For instance, a bank can segment its transaction networks from the rest of employee access networks to limit the opportunity for an outsider to exploit a vulnerable area and breach a relatively secure zone. Such segmentation, as has been emphasized in recent research, not only provides security but also compliance with legislation and total system resilience in extensive network environments (Ahmed et al., 2023). Also, using segmentation makes it easier to monitor and manage vulnerabilities. Slicing networks into distinct segments helps security operations apply custom threat-detection measures that are applicable to the specific needs and functionality of individual segments. For example, real-time monitoring and rapid response incident plans can be tailored specifically for segments with mission-critical systems. This segmented approach allows anomalies or possible intrusions to be identified early. Moreover, segmenting with this capability can contain an incident so that it is unable to cascade across the network and affect more comprehensive operations. Segmentation becomes most obviously critical in regards to projecting the security impacts inherent in topologies that leverage next-generation technologies like Machine Learning or AI systems, which, as valuable as they are, bring new threats into play in the environment (Chamola et al., 2023). But as with any promise, there must be discretion applied by practitioners in its use. Over-segmentation can result in operational inefficiencies, causing system architecture to become too complicated and impeding the data-sharing velocity needed by business processes. There could also be vulnerabilities at the segmentation boundaries if poorly handled, creating unwanted weak points that an attacker could leverage. To this end, an integrated approach is required; organizations have to consider the necessity and extent of segmentation in their specific operating environment. As the topography of cyber threats continues to shift, addressing these challenges through the meticulous design of topology can substantially enhance the resilience of security systems. Employing a well-designed segmentation strategy facilitates advancing organizational goals alongside safeguarding important assets against growing cyber-attacks and sophisticated attack surfaces (Ahmed et al., 2023).

7.4.3. Regularly Updating and Patching Network Devices

The protection of network appliances is most dependent on the regular updating and patching of firmware and software. It is a key process in evading the loopholes that cyber-attacks aim for, hence shielding sensitive data in network frameworks. Network appliances, like routers, switches, and firewalls, are the major forms of defense against external attacks. Failing to update these devices can lead to critical vulnerabilities as an attacker would likely attack known vulnerabilities in dated software. Keeping these devices up to date not only complies with industry regulations but also enhances the overall network posture of security. Adding timely updates keeps organizations better prepared to remain secure from growing threats and reduces the chances of a data breach and consequential financial or reputational damage. In multifaceted topologies of network architecture, the effects of missed updates could be especially severe. Under a star or mesh network, for instance, the interconnecting aspects of devices result in the failure of one device having the potential to jeopardize the entire system. With more sophisticated cyber threats out there, they often rely on automated software to probe networks and determine devices that are not updated, so proactive patch management becomes more appealing. Additionally, introducing new devices or technologies, such as those applied in Healthcare 4.0, calls for a strict update regimen to maintain legacy systems secure while linking to next-generation technologies such as AI and IoT. Hence, a systematic updating and patching procedure not just optimizes the lifespan of networked devices but also enhances the robustness of security designs, a critical design factor in topology security. Besides, following best practices in patching and updating is more than mere compliance; it fosters security sensitivity among network administrators and users. Having standard operating procedures for updates, with scheduled days and processes for emergency patching, foster an environment where security is the priority. It involves proactive as opposed to remedial action, which encourages a more vigilant organizational culture. In addition, organizations must look into automation tools that handle patch rollouts, reducing the potential for human errors and efficient updates on all devices in the network. The commingling of autonomous systems and sophisticated devices, such as the one observed in autonomous vehicles (Αναστάσιος et al., 2023) and the Internet of Medical Things Osama et al. (2023), confirms the necessity for meticulous patch management procedures that account for the complexity of modern-day network architecture while ensuring ongoing protection against likely cyber-attacks (Figure 7.11).

Figure 7.11. *Regularly updating and patching network devices.*

Source: https://cdn.prod.website-files.com/642bc0503c186417b1329fbc/6526ca31b57fc4fdb9a86abb_SecOps%20Solution%20(55).jpg.

7.5. CASE STUDIES OF SECURITY BREACHES

Case study analysis of security breaches reveals deep implications for planning network topology. One striking aspect is the interconnection between organizational size and the likelihood of experiencing a data breach. Larger organizations have a higher chance of being breached, as statistical modeling indicates that breach sizes should relate to the size of the involved entity. For example, the aggregate amplification of compromised personal data presents an extreme threat since millions of records can be in jeopardy at a time.

This fact makes it imperative to have network topologies that include strong segmentation and isolation methods to reduce the effect of a single breach on the entire system. A good topology design could serve as a deterrent, enabling organizations to better safeguard sensitive data and reduce the attack surface, thereby reducing the frequency and severity of incidents that could lead to large-scale identity fraud (Maillart et al., 2016). In addition to studying size relations, there is a requirement to consider the evolution of cyber threats and how they impact security controls.

Current malware patterns and techniques in creating command and control (C2) channels have placed great emphasis on the need for dynamic and responsive topology designs. In turn, attackers have become increasingly more advanced with their methods, employing detection-avoiding techniques against conventional security tools. Organisations are therefore compelled to adopt topological designs centered on the integration of sophisticated security controls that can detect anomalies and disrupt potentially malicious C2 channels. Through network design harmonization with contemporary threat scenarios, companies may encourage resilience against emerging threats while preserving business integrity (Cova et al., 2014).

Additionally, the implications of compromised data go beyond direct financial implications and organizational reputation. Loss of user privacy is an important concern to be addressed by network topology design. With projections describing an astronomical increase in the total amount of compromised data—two to four billion items over the next five years—companies are challenged to rethink their data protection strategies. A topology that emphasizes data locality, access controls, and encryption can go a long way toward reducing risks of breaches significantly. When organizations design their infrastructure, they must factor in privacy-oriented principles in the designs of their topology to safeguard sensitive data and uphold the confidence of the users. This end-to-end approach can ultimately lead to more secure postures that are breach-resistant in a world where breach is the omnipresent threat (Maillart et al., 2016).

7.5.1. Analysis of a Breach in a Star Topology Network

Inspecting a breach in a star topology network reveals sensitive information about the security implications of this network structure. A star topology, characterized by its central hub connecting all peripheral nodes, has many benefits, such as simpler maintenance and ease in fault detection. However, this centralized structure also has serious vulnerabilities. In the event of a compromise, an attacker is able to seize control of the central hub and gain access to all data and devices linked to it.

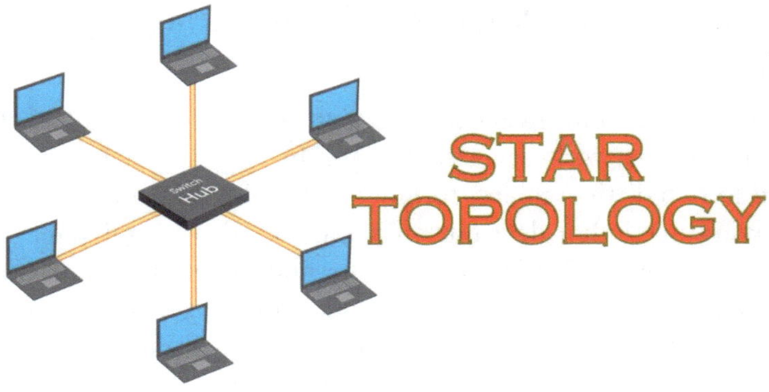

Figure 7.12. *Analyzing a breach in a star topology network.*

Source: https://images.shiksha.com/mediadata/images/articles/1708935748phpjFZsqg.jpeg.

This vulnerability is exacerbated in those systems where security measures are weak or outdated, allowing malicious users to exploit the single point of failure effectively. Moreover, each device's dependence on the hub increases the likelihood of cascading failures if proper precautions are not taken. One of the major determinants of the efficacy of security within star topology networks is the type of communication protocols that they deploy. The central hub tends to employ different communication technologies, which could differ in terms of resilience against security breaches. The breach is possible in the event that the hub is not securely well-protected from such threats, as seen in various case studies where poorly secured devices were compromised. As underscored by recent research, the possession of effective security requirements on all devices that are linked is crucial towards mitigating risks of network intrusion. Connectivity, communication, and management protocol issues need to be handled in creating an effective security plan to defend the network effectively against misuse (Tariq et al., 2023). Apart from this, the use of emerging technologies such as IoT increases the security concerns of star topology networks. IoT devices typically consist of limited security and processing capabilities that are a desired target for hackers. Several devices form complex management, which demands rigorous risk analysis and planning to make the infrastructure secure. Developing a comprehensive security strategy needs collaboration between stakeholders like network designers and security experts to devise solutions for both known and unknown vulnerabilities. The reliance of the devices in a star topology amplifies the effect of a security breach, emphasizing the very real need for qualified topology design to ensure the integrity and safety of components as well as the entire network (Eshrat et al., 2023) (Figure 7.12).

7.5.2. Examination of Vulnerabilities in a Ring Topology Incident

The study of vulnerabilities inherent to ring topology attacks has significant implications for network security design. In ring topology, each node is connected to two distinct nodes, forming a closed-loop pattern. The structure, though giving maximum data transmission, can also magnify the impact of certain vulnerabilities. For instance, if one node fails or becomes hacked, it can lead to the failure of the entire network, in turn causing potential denial-of-service attacks. The dependency on the operational integrity of each node points out a primary weakness: a disruption in one node has knock-on effects on nearby nodes and eventually destabilizes the network as a whole. It is vital to comprehend these dynamics in creating sound security protocols that protect against both actual and perceived threats while acknowledging the topology's limitations to enable resilience and redundancy. Besides, ring topology's data flow direction is part of its risk profile. The linear flow of data, where packets travel in one direction, can be exploited by attackers to block or alter network data. The application of methods such as packet sniffing or replay attacks using this linear flow, with assistance from the linear direction, enables attackers to disrupt data integrity or confidentiality. Also, the absence of inherent fault tolerance protocols makes ring topologies highly susceptible to such attacks. This is in stark contrast to other topologies like mesh or star configurations, which usually involve redundant paths for data exchange. For this reason, it is a requirement for network designers to set up efficient encryption mechanisms and traffic monitoring systems that can provide countermeasures for these vulnerabilities and are also compliant with the special operating characteristics of ring topologies. Also, the effects of these vulnerabilities extend beyond individual network functionality to touch security strategies as a whole. In thinking about the grand security paradigm, it is necessary to integrate defense systems targeting technical, social, and behavioral vulnerabilities that extend to network security. For instance, the trust relationships within a network play a critical function to mitigate threats from user-created vulnerabilities like unintentional exposure of threats through defective security protocols. Deployment of advanced security measures like intrusion detection systems and real-time traffic inspection can do wonders in generalizing the security of a ring topology network. As indicated by the literature, social network-based solutions facilitate the attainment of maximum user privacy and defense against all forms of attack vectors, including those provided by distributed hash tables ((Borisov et al., 2011; Gupta et al., 2013)). Thus, proper consideration to design elements and user behavior is of vital importance in the enhancement of the security implications emanating from ring topology architecture.

7.5.3. Lessons Derived from a Mesh Topology Security Failure

The complexity of mesh topology, while providing greater connectivity and dependability, may also reveal critical vulnerabilities when security controls are poorly established. A case study of a security breach in a mesh topology indicates that the same design meant to offer fault tolerance may easily enable large-scale attack surfaces. With lots of interconnected devices, every device presents itself as a threat point for intruders. When such points remain inadequately secured, they can lead to extensive compromises, with an attacker focusing on vulnerable areas in a bid to establish entrance into the entire network. This highlights the extreme importance of adopting uniform and robust security measures across every node in a mesh topology, in support of the adoption of vigilance in the operation and design of networks. In addition, lessons that should be drawn from such security vulnerabilities highlight the necessity of integrating cyber resilience assessment techniques into mesh topology planning. With businesses relying on the mesh network as the foundation of their operations, assessment of cyber resilience becomes imperative.

Figure 7.13. *Lessons learned from a mesh topology security failure.*

Source: https://howtofunda.com/wp-content/uploads/2023/07/mesh-topology-computer-networking-working-model-for-science-project-exhibition-diy-howtofunda-1024x576.jpg.

By evaluating the security controls implemented and testing against probable threats, organizations are better positioned to detect vulnerabilities inherent in their topology. Traditional evaluation methods may prove inadequate; therefore, the application of dynamic and simulation-based methods can ensure more accurate conclusions about network resilience. Specifically, it is necessary to stress some details, that is, pre-configuration resilience and flexibility of network topology, as expressed through comparative studies indicating effective approaches to reinforcing defenses, as discussed in research on resilience frameworks (AlHidaifi et al., 2024). Additionally, the impact of a mesh topology breach is not only limited to short-term technical issues. The incident can cause dire reputational damage and financial sanctions on organizations, indicating the business-technology interdependency. Such has been exemplified in current research where measuring the impact on organizational processes subsequent to the breach indicates the necessity of having integrated incident response procedures. Firms ought to focus not just on repairing the weaknesses but also on maintaining core operations during the recovery phases since faulty recovery procedures may aggravate the initial failure. This overall strategy demands robust planning, in which the organizations need to deal proactively not only with the structuring of their network organization but also with the protocols governing incident recovery and response to ensure long-term security and stability, which underscores the need for end-to-end enhancement in all phases (Fayad et al., 2024) (Figure 7.13).

7.6. FUTURE TRENDS IN TOPOLOGY DESIGN AND SECURITY

As the topology design field keeps evolving, future trends reflect a significant shift towards resilient and adaptive network topologies that can adapt dynamically to threats and changing conditions. Integrations of flexible sensor networks in various applications like industrial automation and environmental monitoring capture best this trend. Such networks, boosted by advanced technology, promise enhanced situational awareness and operating effectiveness. However, commercialization of flexible sensors is confronted with obstacles to be resolved in order to enable its successful implementation. Mitigation of obstacles is paramount because they not only involve technological barriers but also nontechnical aspects such as regulatory and ethical concerns, which could hinder adoption progress (Luo et al., 2023). Therefore, providing a comprehensive guide for development emerges as the hour of need to overcome these hurdles and achieve the complete potential of flexible topology designs in security applications. The integration of the Internet of Things (IoT) with topology design is another rapidly growing trend, particularly in line with the fourth industrial revolution (Industry 4.0). Intrusions and security attacks on wireless sensor networks (WSNs) are an utmost concern with the greater interconnectivity of devices, thus increasing the attack surface for possible intrusions. IoT device advancements to make data processing and transmission easier only lead to further complicated security challenges that need to be addressed by powerful countermeasures to ensure malicious access does not occur. Future research must not only enhance IoT and WSN technology capabilities but also design sophisticated security measures that can anticipatorily identify and neutralize threats (Majid et al., 2022). This dual focus on function and safety necessitates the transformation of the landscape of topology design such that systems are not only effective but also resilient. Though innovative advances in topology design are critical, the effect of these advances on security must not be ignored. The networks of the future will demand end-to-end security models that can match the whirlwind pace of technology development and the ever-increasing complexity of interconnected devices. What the future could be like, going by trends, is a move towards a holistic model, where security is a natural aspect of network topology rather than an afterthought. The emphasis on proactive security solutions such as predictive analysis and machine learning code allows for a more anticipatory protection of prospective vulnerabilities. Therefore, as topology design continues to progress, the intersection of new architectural paradigms and security frameworks will be paramount in safeguarding critical data and infrastructure. This combined method of design and security will ensure that future networks are not merely efficient but naturally safe against emerging threats.

7.6.1. The Role of Artificial Intelligence in Topology Security

The use of artificial intelligence (AI) in enhancing topology security is increasingly being recognized as one of the mainstays of contemporary cybersecurity systems. In topology design, AI can scan enormous volumes of data gathered from network systems to perform instant review of vulnerabilities and attacks. This capability is vital given the sophistication and dynamic nature of contemporary networks that respond poorly to traditional security protocols. Through machine learning algorithms, AI can identify strange patterns and behavior typical of security violations, hence being capable of acting in response ahead of time prior to extensive damage being caused. As has been discussed by scholarly literature on sensor uptake and its impacts on the environment, the necessity for advanced security is highlighted by increasing reliance on technologies that subtly become part of our lives (Luo et al., 2023). This coupling of network security and AI is a future-oriented method of guarding topology design. It also raises network designs' level of responsiveness to future threats with the integration of artificial intelligence into security. The traditional security methods tend to lack the adaptability required in order to match the velocity of cyberattacks, especially in Industry 4.0 environments involving the Internet of Things (IoT) and wireless sensor networks (WSN) as primary drivers of architecture (Majid et al., 2022). AI systems can learn from the ever-newly erupting threats by monitoring real-time streams of information and, consequently, refine their detection algorithms. This cycle of continuous learning not only makes security mechanisms more resilient but also enables the networks to defend themselves against sophisticated intrusions. Organizations, therefore, can create more resilient topology designs that consider current vulnerabilities as well as those potential vulnerabilities that may occur in the future. The application of AI in topology security also contributes significantly in making response plans for incidents simpler. When a threat has been suspected, AI-based systems can self-automate alarm to administrators and initiate pre-determined actions to quarantine breaches. Automation decreases detection-to-response time significantly, restricting the potential impact of security breaches. Moreover, in the analysis of flexible sensor technologies, commercialization challenges and effectiveness in operation are created by inadequate security implementations in network deployment (Luo et al., 2023). By incorporating AI into not only security but also into design, companies can make systems whose primary priority is security. This harmonious integration streamlines the development of topology designs that are not only creative but also able to effectively resist the intricacies of today's cyber-attacks (Figure 7.14).

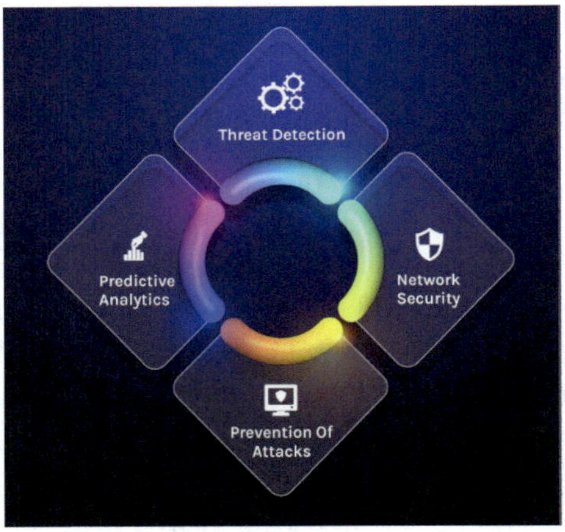

Figure 7.14. *The role of artificial intelligence in topology security.*

Source: https://codestoresolutions.com/wp-content/uploads/2022/02/1-3.png.

7.6.2. Emerging Technologies and Their Impact on Network Design

The rapid emergence of new technologies, particularly distributed systems and cloud computing, has dramatically changed the topology scenario of network planning. With increasing use of decentralized models in organizations, the security implications of topology emerge as the primary concern. In decentralized networks, where the control is distributed among multiple nodes, each node may be adversary in mindset, necessitating robust security measures at all layers. This complexity is a unique challenge for designers to navigate with a series of trade-offs between system integrity, availability, and user privacy. Empirical research on decentralization illustrates the ability of such systems to enhance data security—providing resilience against single points of failure—but open to careful design to prevent unintended weaknesses due to added complexity (Danezis et al., 2017). As such, it is significant to understand the nuances of decentralized technology so that a strong network architecture can be maintained in present applications. Through incorporating technologies such as high-speed optical links and high-performance computing capabilities, the platform-based infrastructure of FABRIC illustrates the manner in which present-day network architecture can leverage new technologies. Through connecting various testbeds for cloud research and high-performance computing, FABRIC provides a setting for shared experimentation across a range of fields. This combined but expert approach makes it possible to examine advanced networking solutions that have the potential to improve security mechanisms and data management procedures. However, there is a necessity to pay attention to security loopholes that arise when these different systems are interplaying. The convergence of the technologies necessitates critical examination of physical and cyber security concerns, compelling network designers to implementations that reinforce robustness in topology and consequently provide main data from emerging vulnerabilities (Baldin et al., 2019). Ramifications for emerging technologies also include the application of artificial intelligence and machine learning to security processes. As the systems become more advanced, the integration of AI-based tools can potentially improve the processes of threat detection and response, enriching the overall security framework. Such sophisticated systems can analyze vast datasets and search for patterns typical of security violations, enabling preemptive measures against attacks. The flip side is the increased complexity involved in depending on AI; it is necessary to protect these systems from being targeted by the adversary. Against this backdrop, network architects are called upon to balance the need to harness leading-edge technologies such as AI for improved security with their need to avoid creating new vulnerabilities. Therefore, a comprehensive knowledge of technological innovation and its security implications become paramount as organizations learn to navigate the changing digital environment.

7.6.3. Projections for the Future of Secure Network Topologies

With the increasing demand for effective and dependable communication networks, network topology projections all the more emphasize resilience and flexibility. The future wireless systems generation, that is, transitioning from fifth generation (5G) to sixth generation (6G) technology, emphasizes the need for creating innovative topology designs. 6G networks are anticipated to provide enormous coverage and record-breaking bandwidth, utilizing frequency bands from frequencies below 6 GHz to as high as 1 THz. This revolutionary shift requires the redesign of traditional hierarchical network architectures, which typically introduce gigantic delays and vulnerabilities. With adaptability and real-time capability as highest priorities, the future network topologies will likely consist of decentralized structures that strengthen security functions with the heterogeneous demands of next-gen applications. Thus, evolution of network design should hence address both the technological intricacies of 6G systems and the implications in security caused by increased interaction among nodes in a network (Tataria et al., 2021). Principles of a viable supply chain (VSC) model can also lead the formation of secure network topologies. The VSC model addresses the requirement for agility, resilience, and sustainability, which are necessities when networks are to endure uncertain challenges. When environments become increasingly complex and involve adaptive mechanisms that will be able to support rapid network design change, it will be essential. Flexibility can be observed as dynamic path reconfiguring to quarantine and mitigate threats in a timely manner, enhancing overall security. The capacity to absorb and recover from perturbations is equally well-suited to the systemic design for networks of the future. The incorporation of these traits in topology evolution not only enhances long-term functionality but also stabilizes networks against prospective interruptions. Thus, the interaction between VSC ideas and secure network topology designs would significantly enhance network resilience against prospective threats (Ivanov, 2020). In the future, the future of secure network topology design is toward increased interaction with artificial intelligence (AI) and machine learning (ML) technologies. These advanced computational techniques will allow for anomaly detection and real-time threat analysis, which are both essential to the security of centralized and decentralized networks. Smart system deployment will allow for automatic network configuration adjustments, thereby neutralizing potential vulnerabilities before they can be exploited by harmful individuals. Besides, with more and more devices being networked, the necessity for end-to-end, adaptive security solutions that can maintain pace with network complexity becomes apparent. Topologies in this case need to support collaboration between AI-driven security solutions and legacy protocols to offer comprehensive protection against diverse threats. This advancement will ultimately shape a connected future in which secure network frameworks are not just pillars of technological progress but also imperative to safeguard digital ecosystems from unfolding threats (Tataria et al., 2021).

SUMMARY

It becomes apparent that security and network architecture become increasingly interdependent. Technological advancements have brought an exigent appreciation wherein traditional security schemes must evolve to accommodate complex, dynamic networking systems. Highlighted by research recently undertaken on behalf of the UK government is the imperative to close existing gaps in capabilities and requirements in relation to Critical Infrastructure. This project aims to nurture interdependency analysis as a commercially valuable service that will ultimately create the security framework from network topology. This transcends the reinforcement of resilience in infrastructure to the extent that it indicates the course of development towards an increasingly proactive trend in network design and security alignment that targets very crucial interlinks supportive of system integrity and reliability (Bloomfield et al., 2009). Besides, the introduction of Software-Defined Networking (SDN) has ushered in an age of transformation in the management and security of networks. SDN, while providing increased flexibility, programmability, and manageability, also introduces inherent security challenges. Since research indicates, the absence of tools enforcing policy compliance and monitoring network activity leaves systems open to abuse. In addition, the distributed nature of state updates in reconfigurations increases the possibility of inconsistent network operations. Meeting these challenges requires new technologies, for example, SDNsec, to focus on forwarding accountability and secure communication in the SDN context. Being able to deploy such solutions underscores the need to hard-wire security measures into topology design, strengthening the argument that a well-architected topology must make security a fundamental aspect (Hoefler et al., 2016). Thus, the conclusion from this analysis is that there exists a compelling imperative to appreciate topology designs security implications holistically. As networks become more complex, the need to have holistic solutions that integrate topology design and security mechanisms is exigent. In the future, it is important for industry stakeholders to continually engage in discussions concerning emerging threats and the security controls required to neutralize them. Developing a comprehensive plan that not only realizes demands in the present but also anticipates future demand will be crucial in achieving network integrity. Ultimately, investment in research and innovation, as extrapolated by government-sponsored projects, will prove crucial in enabling security to be the priority in topology design, leading to more secure and stable infrastructures in the long run.

The revelation of security aspects in topology design highlights significant issues in the context of decentralization and anonymity. As technology advances, adopting decentralized designs comes with the advantages and disadvantages that need to be cautiously navigated by designers. The research identifies the fact that decentralized systems, free from central control, can foster privacy and integrity improvements in addition to avert risks from central collapses. However, these benefits come at a cost; increased complexity and the need for explicit knowledge of the trade-offs are fundamental aspects of effective design. Designers must draw upon knowledge from distributed systems, cryptography, and mechanism design to devise scalable, privacy-sensitive solutions, thereby emphasizing the need to strike a balance between system resilience and performance and decentralization (Danezis et al., 2017). Shifting to energy systems, the topological design implications strike starkly in the functioning of the electricity networks. The convergence of intelligent technologies and renewable sources necessitates reconsideration of inherent network vulnerabilities. Such developments, being beneficial for sustainability, also introduce new threats stemming from an interconnected grid's complexity. Interferences within this network can have extensive economic and social repercussions, demanding the expectation of vulnerability analysis. Thorough research of the dynamics of the electric grids in use—for example, storage solutions—can facilitate the decision-making process by identifying key areas to be improved. Such a study shows that the effective utilization of storage technologies can improve network resilience, particularly in cases characterized by overproduction. Thus, security-oriented designing is imperative to incorporate the complexities introduced by modern energy requirements (Millis et al., 2019). Moreover, the topology design discussion points towards the necessity for an overall approach in dealing with security concerns in various systems. With the inclusion of various knowledge domains—such as decentralized systems and energy security—designers can improve understanding and mitigate vulnerability inherent in their networks. Balancing decentralization benefits and security trade-offs calls for careful study and innovative problem-solving. For both online and physical infrastructures, there is a pressing need to put security foremost from the outset of the design process, such that systems are resilient to potential adversarial behavior. Ultimately, the ongoing advancement of technology must reinforce the commitment to security-driven design principles, guiding the creation of robust systems in an increasingly interconnected world.

REFERENCES

1. Ahmed, S. F., Alam, M. S. B., Hassan, M., Rozbu, M. R. R., Ishtiak, T., Rafa, N., Mofijur, M., et al. (2023). Deep learning modelling techniques: Current progress, applications, advantages, and challenges. *Artificial Intelligence Review, 56*, 13521–13617. https://doi.org/10.1007/s10462-023-10466-8 (accessed on 9th September 2025).
2. Alahi, M. E. E., Sukkuea, A., Tina, F. W., Nag, A., Kurdthongmee, W., Suwannarat, K., & Mukhopadhyay, S. C. (2023). Integration of IoT-enabled technologies and artificial intelligence (AI) for smart city scenario: Recent advancements and future trends. *Sensors, 23*, 5206–5206. https://doi.org/10.3390/s23115206 (accessed on 9th September 2025).
3. AlHidaifi, S. M., Asghar, M. R., & Ansari, I. S. (2024). Towards a cyber resilience quantification framework (CRQF) for IT infrastructure. *Computer Networks, 247*, 110446–110446. https://doi.org/10.1016/j.comnet.2024.110446 (accessed on 9th September 2025).
4. Ando, T., Greenwood-Nimmo, M., & Shin, Y. (2022). Quantile connectedness: Modeling tail behavior in the topology of financial networks. *Management Science, 68*, 2401–2431. https://doi.org/10.1287/mnsc.2021.3984 (accessed on 9th September 2025).
5. Aslam, N., Cao, Y., Hussain, S., Khan, W., et al. (2018). A critical analysis of research potential, challenges and future directives in industrial wireless sensor networks. https://core.ac.uk/download/96885354.pdf (accessed on 9th September 2025).
6. Baldin, I., Deelman, E., Griffioen, J., Lehman, T., et al. (2019). FABRIC: A national-scale programmable experimental network infrastructure. https://core.ac.uk/download/322493913.pdf (accessed on 9th September 2025).
7. Bloomfield, R. E., Chozos, N., & Salako, K. (2009). Current capabilities, requirements and a proposed strategy for interdependency analysis in the UK. https://core.ac.uk/download/9559636.pdf (accessed on 9th September 2025).
8. Borisov, N., Caesar, M., & Mittal, P. (2011). X-Vine: Secure and pseudonymous routing using social networks. http://arxiv.org/abs/1109.0971 (accessed on 9th September 2025).
9. Borm, P. E. M., Hamers, H. J. M., & Lindelauf, R. (2025). Understanding terrorist network topologies and their resilience against disruption. https://core.ac.uk/download/pdf/6651508.pdf (accessed on 9th September 2025).
10. Buyya, R., Calheiros, R. N., Dastjerdi, A. V., Son, J., et al. (2014). Software-defined cloud computing: Architectural elements and open challenges. http://arxiv.org/abs/1408.6891 (accessed on 9th September 2025).

11. Cervelló Pastor, C., Machado, R., Monje Hernández, Á., Óskarsson, H., et al. (2009). Deliverable DJRA1.2. Solutions and protocols proposal for the network control, management and monitoring in a virtualized network context. https://core.ac.uk/download/187264912.pdf (accessed on 9th September 2025).
12. Chamola, V., Hassija, V., Sulthana, A. R., Ghosh, D., Dhingra, D., & Sikdar, B. (2023). A review of trustworthy and explainable artificial intelligence (XAI). *IEEE Access, 11*, 78994–79015. https://doi.org/10.1109/access.2023.3294569 (accessed on 9th September 2025).
13. Cova, M., Gardiner, J., & Nagaraja, S. (2014). Command & control: Understanding, denying and detecting–A review of malware C2 techniques, detection and defenses. http://arxiv.org/abs/1408.1136 (accessed on 9th September 2025).
14. Danezis, G., Halpin, H., Isaakidis, M., Troncoso, C., et al. (2017). Systematizing decentralization and privacy: Lessons from 15 years of research and deployments. https://core.ac.uk/download/141515178.pdf (accessed on 9th September 2025).
15. Dulman, S., & Havinga, P. (2005). Architectures for wireless sensor networks. https://core.ac.uk/download/pdf/11463575.pdf (accessed on 9th September 2025).
16. Fayad, A., Cinkler, T., & Rak, J. (2024). Toward 6G optical fronthaul: A survey on enabling technologies and research perspectives. *IEEE Communications Surveys & Tutorials, 27*, 629–666. https://doi.org/10.1109/comst.2024.3408090 (accessed on 9th September 2025).
17. Gehrmann, C., & Paladi, N. (2018). SDN access control for the masses. http://arxiv.org/abs/1811.08094 (accessed on 9th September 2025).
18. Gill, S. S., Kumar, A., Singh, H., Singh, M., Kaur, K., Usman, M., & Buyya, R. (2021). Quantum computing: A taxonomy, systematic review and future directions. *Software Practice and Experience, 52*, 66–114. https://doi.org/10.1002/spe.3039 (accessed on 9th September 2025).
19. Hoefler, T., Lee, T., Pappas, C., Perrig, A., et al. (2016). SDNsec: Forwarding accountability for the SDN data plane. http://arxiv.org/abs/1605.01944 (accessed on 9th September 2025).
20. Hutabarat, L. R. (2019). Regulatory policy of over-the-top industry. Case: Ministry of Communication and Information Technology of Republic of Indonesia regulatory policy. https://core.ac.uk/download/650082234.pdf (accessed on 9th September 2025).
21. Ivanov, D. (2020). Viable supply chain model: Integrating agility, resilience and sustainability perspectives—Lessons from and thinking beyond the

COVID-19 pandemic. *Annals of Operations Research, 319*, 1411–1431. https://doi.org/10.1007/s10479-020-03640-6 (accessed on 9th September 2025).

22. Jiménez, V. J. E., Marksteiner, S., Vallant, H., Zeiner, H., et al. (2018). An overview of wireless IoT protocol security in the smart home domain. http://arxiv.org/abs/1801.07090 (accessed on 9th September 2025).
23. Ling, X., Lütkenhaus, N., Mosca, M., Tysowski, P., et al. (2017). The engineering of a scalable multi-site communications system utilizing quantum key distribution (QKD). http://arxiv.org/abs/1712.02617 (accessed on 9th September 2025).
24. Liu, A. L., Chen, Y., & Oren, S. (2015). Special issue on smart grid and emerging technology integration. *Journal of Energy Engineering-ASCE, 141*. https://www.semanticscholar.org/paper/207f333ac463891d98445c763985cd64f1b856ca (accessed on 9th September 2025).
25. Luo, Y., Abidian, M. R., Ahn, J. H., Akinwande, D., Andrews, A. M., Antonietti, M., Bao, Z., et al. (2023). Technology roadmap for flexible sensors. *ACS Nano, 17*, 5211–5295. https://doi.org/10.1021/acsnano.2c12606 (accessed on 9th September 2025).
26. Maillart, T., Sornette, D., & Wheatley, S. (2016). The extreme risk of personal data breaches & the erosion of privacy. http://arxiv.org/abs/1505.07684 (accessed on 9th September 2025).
27. Majid, M., Habib, S., Javed, A. R., Rizwan, M., Srivastava, G., Gadekallu, T. R., & Lin, J. C. W. (2022). Applications of wireless sensor networks and Internet of Things frameworks in the Industry Revolution 4.0: A systematic literature review. *Sensors, 22*, 2087–2087. https://doi.org/10.3390/s22062087 (accessed on 9th September 2025).
28. Mansoor, A. M., Sarea, A., & Md. Sabri, A. Q. (2018). Influence of intersections on the performance of position-based routing protocols for VANETs: A case study–smart cities. *World Journal of Entrepreneurship, Management and Sustainable Development, 14*, 168–177. https://www.semanticscholar.org/paper/e6d9d7824a4e9aece321b511d715bfcafa824cbe (accessed on 9th September 2025).
29. McEnroe, P., Wang, S., & Liyanage, M. (2022). A survey on the convergence of edge computing and AI for UAVs: Opportunities and challenges. *IEEE Internet of Things Journal, 9*, 15435–15459. https://doi.org/10.1109/jiot.2022.3176400 (accessed on 9th September 2025).
30. Millis, M. (2019). Vulnerability analysis of modern electric grids: A mathematical optimization approach. https://core.ac.uk/download/215464251.pdf (accessed on 9th September 2025).

31. Osama, M., Ateya, A. A., Sayed, M. S., Hammad, M., Pławiak, P., Abd El-Latif, A. A., & Elsayed, R. A. (2023). Internet of Medical Things and Healthcare 4.0: Trends, requirements, challenges, and research directions. *Sensors, 23*, 7435–7435. https://doi.org/10.3390/s23177435 (accessed on 9th September 2025).

32. Rieke, N., Hancox, J., Li, W., Milletarì, F., Roth, H. R., Albarqouni, S., Bakas, S., et al. (2020). The future of digital health with federated learning. *npj Digital Medicine, 3*. https://doi.org/10.1038/s41746-020-00323-1 (accessed on 9th September 2025).

33. Schmidt, T. C., Vahlenkamp, M., & Wählisch, M. (2012). Backscatter from the data plane–Threats to stability and security in information-centric networking. http://arxiv.org/abs/1205.4778 (accessed on 9th September 2025).

34. Tariq, U., Ahmed, I., Bashir, A. K., & Shaukat, K. (2023). A critical cybersecurity analysis and future research directions for the Internet of Things: A comprehensive review. *Sensors, 23*, 4117–4117. https://doi.org/10.3390/s23084117 (accessed on 9th September 2025).

35. Tataria, H., Shafi, M., Molisch, A. F., Döhler, M., Sjöland, H., & Tufvesson, F. (2021). 6G wireless systems: Vision, requirements, challenges, insights, and opportunities. *Proceedings of the IEEE, 109*, 1166–1199. https://doi.org/10.1109/jproc.2021.3061701 (accessed on 9th September 2025).

36. Verbraeken, J., Wolting, M., Katzy, J., Kloppenburg, J., Verbelen, T., & Rellermeyer, J. S. (2020). A survey on distributed machine learning. *ACM Computing Surveys, 53*, 1–33. https://doi.org/10.1145/3377454 (accessed on 9th September 2025).

37. Yue, M., Lambert, H., Pahon, E., Roche, R., Jemeï, S., & Hissel, D. (2021). Hydrogen energy systems: A critical review of technologies, applications, trends and challenges. *Renewable and Sustainable Energy Reviews, 146*, 111180–111180. https://doi.org/10.1016/j.rser.2021.111180 (accessed on 9th September 2025).

38. Zhou, Z., Chen, X., Li, E., Zeng, L., Luo, K., & Zhang, J. (2019). Edge intelligence: Paving the last mile of artificial intelligence with edge computing. *Proceedings of the IEEE, 107*, 1738–1762. https://doi.org/10.1109/jproc.2019.2918951 (accessed on 9th September 2025).

39. Γιάνναρος, A., Karras, A., Theodorakopoulos, L., Karras, C., Kranias, P., Schizas, N., Kalogeratos, G., et al. (2023). Autonomous vehicles: Sophisticated attacks, safety issues, challenges, open topics, blockchain, and future directions. *Journal of Cybersecurity and Privacy, 3*, 493–543. https://doi.org/10.3390/jcp3030025 (accessed on 9th September 2025).

40. Τσίκνας, K., Taketzis, D., Demertzis, K., & Skianis, C. (2021). Cyber threats to industrial IoT: A survey on attacks and countermeasures. *IoT, 2*, 163–186. https://doi.org/10.3390/iot2010009 (accessed on 9th September 2025).

CHAPTER 8

CASE STUDIES IN TOPOLOGY DESIGN

Contents

INTRODUCTION

Topology design is a basic underlying concept in much of engineering, in particular, the knowledge of how structural element topology impacts performance and functionality. Essentially, topology design is placing components in positions to optimize some performance measure under physical constraints. This concept is particularly prevalent in mechanical engineering, civil engineering, and systems engineering, where interactions among varying elements can significantly impact global system behavior. Upon designers' exposure to topology design, they engage in a debate between optimizing geometrical parameters and meeting functional requirements. The integration of optimization systems will be capable of bridging the gaps between the conceptual design and actual implementation, also reemphasizing the importance of topology in engineering design approaches (Cascini et al., 2009). At the core of topology design is the principle of optimization, which can impart robustness and efficiency to systems. Applying optimization algorithms to topology design makes it possible for engineers to resolve difficult problems with constraints and conflicting objectives. For example, for power grid networks, it has been shown to influence the transient response as well as the stability of the grid under external disturbances. Using a unified framework based on the H2 norm enables researchers to compare various performance measures like loss reduction and agreement of phase angle deviations. Besides, radial and loopy grid topological design presents challenges which are computationally solvable using combinatorial tools, providing not just implementable solutions but also theoretical studies for their graph-theoretic properties (Kameshwar et al., 2017). As the field matures, its integration with computational technology has become increasingly prevalent. Utilizing advanced computational tools enables designers to see and shape geometric arrangements in real-time. This complementarity can lead to the detection and resolution of design contradictions, that is, geometrical conflicts that arise inevitably in the design process. Techniques involving the manipulation of density distributions can lead to new solutions particularly suited to specific design tasks, showing flexibility of topology design principles. In addition, the continued research into combinatorial and optimization techniques points to the need for a multidisciplinary approach, with the integration of concepts in mathematics, engineering, and computer science to provide new avenues for design and engineering problems (Cascini et al., 2009).

Definition and Importance of Topology Design

Topology design can be described as the structure of network elements to achieve maximum performance, reliability, and efficiency. This structure forms the basis for data communication systems, allowing information to be exchanged across various nodes and links. Topology design has a number of reasons why it is so critical, as it directly impacts operational capacity as well as scalability. Well-designed topology makes it possible for data centers to absorb increased loads of traffic without compromising performance, leading to improved user experience. Topology is also important in the context of resilience, making it possible for networks to maintain functionality even during failure or during maintenance processes. With understanding of the design concepts of topology, organizations are able to construct resilient infrastructures that adapt based on shifting technology requirements and environmental conditions. The use of robust topology design is particularly critical within the context of modular data centers (MDCs), which are an innovative approach to ICT infrastructure. MDCs are particularly designed in such a manner that they can operate in suboptimal environments, that is, remote areas away from metropolitan cities and in aggressive climatic conditions. In this regard, the network fabric is an issue of great concern as issues there have the ability to jeopardize the whole operation of data centers. A thorough analysis of various topology structures with techniques such as Monte-Carlo simulations presents the potential performance and longevity of architectures like FatTree, BCube, and MDCube. These evaluations enable designers to anticipate component failure and make the best topology choices, providing service continuity and functional efficiency within the data center environment (Asghari et al., 2017). The evolving nature of data networks calls for the adoption of clean-slate architectures to drive control and management mechanisms to the next level. This is particularly evident in the research on 4D architecture that incorporates the addition of a logically centralized Decision plane for improved network resource management. With the use of a dynamically scalable algorithm, network managers are able to dynamically assign data plane devices in a better manner without excessive manual configuration overhead. This is especially useful for Internet Service Providers (ISPs) and large enterprises with geographically dispersed networks, where traditional methods are not scalable and fault-tolerant. Being able to automatically respond to network failures and optimize configurations in real-time completely changes the art of network management and highlights the importance of effective topology design. The thorough examination conducted under this system highlights the process by which such sophisticated methodologies can lead to improved operational outcomes, demonstrating the importance of new strategies in topology design in contemporary network infrastructures (Iqbal et al., 2009).

Historical Context and Evolution

The historical context of topology design illustrates an ongoing dynamics between architectural innovation and structural engineering. Early in the 20th century, modernist trends set architects the challenge of reinventing their approach to spatial composition and material with a stronger focus on form-function unity. It was this essential shift that laid the groundwork for contemporary approaches in topology design, as various fashions emerged blending aesthetics with structural efficiency. The tectonic history of building structures and materials, that is, the symbiosis between them, increased in importance. As critical theorists have argued, the change in this symbiosis can be tracked through milestone periods throughout history and with each new concept that now influences current design. The use of computer technologies has further fueled this development, enabling never-before-possible experimentation and creativity in architecture (Oxman et al., 2010). From the mid-20th century, computational design methods progressed to a turning point in the evolution of topology. The evolution of computer-aided design (CAD) technology enabled architects and engineers to analyze complex geometrical forms and material relationships to an unprecedented depth. These technologies facilitated a superior understanding of structural performance, leading to more economic structural systems that both responded to and shaped architectural expression. Secondly, digital morphogenesis turned into a central idea where design processes are emulating nature's growth patterns, leading to adaptive and individual shapes. In addition to how this paradigm shift transformed architecture's design, it also ushered in a new paradigm where topology was understood and dealt with by advanced digital practices (Oxman et al., 2010). Such strategies allowed for a future in which topology design transcends the limitations of traditional constraints to facilitate innovative solutions to spatial issues. Contemporary network topology design also demarcates the evolution of utilizing complex relations between function and structure. Initially typified by mental models like simple graphs, topological analysis now has demonstrated that such oversimplifications fail to represent the intricacy of real networks like the Internet. Dramatic enhancements in network annotation and correlation profiling are now essential to comprehend the underlying geometry that differentiates classes of nodes and links. This new appreciation for the complexity of network topology places a premium on tailored modeling frameworks, which enhance the accuracy of simulations and guide the development of subsequent network architectures. Through embracing such sophisticated tools, topology design continues to progress, yielding strong ideas that challenge traditional paradigms and advance new forms of addressing technological challenges

Overview of Applications in Various Fields

The applications of topology design are varied across different fields, from materials science to environmental modeling and drug delivery systems. In materials science, researchers use topological principles in designing materials with specific properties, making it possible to manufacture light but strong components that are essential in the aerospace and automotive industries. The mentioned materials are typically explored in the context of complex structures like dendrimers that are used as sophisticated platforms for developing novel drug delivery systems. Rational design and synthesis of dendrimers are faced with scalable synthesis challenges, where topological modeling and simulation become critical to structural assignment. Using automated assembly approaches and bespoke toolkits, researchers can streamline the building of these intricate structures, ultimately enhancing their functionality in healthcare applications, as demonstrated in the evidence of Kwok et al. (2017).

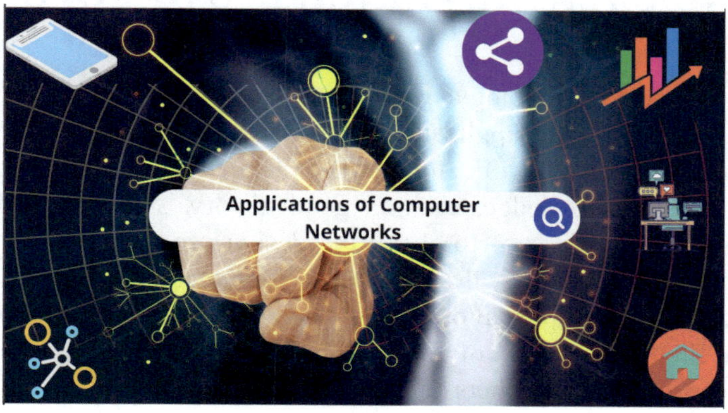

Figure 8.1. *An overview of applications in various fields.*

Source: https://i0.wp.com/conceptsall.com/wp-content/uploads/2022/08/Applications-of-Computer-Networks-in-Various-Fields.png.

Environmental modeling also strongly benefits from topological design methods, particularly within the field of surface representation and analysis. Through the study of Surface Networks, the character of two-dimensional surfaces can be successfully modeled by focusing on critical points and lines. The approach supplants outdated models like Digital Elevation Models (DEM) and Triangulated Irregular Networks (TIN) that are redundant and inefficient in surface data storage. Surface Networks' flexibility enables researchers from a host of disciplines—geography and meteorology being examples—to construct intelligent models of terrains, population patterns, and air pressures. Such topological models not only facilitate data visualization, but also improve decision-making systems for city planning and environmental control, as highlighted by Morley et al. (2002). In addition, topological thinking is applied to computer graphics and virtual reality, as the construction of realistic surfaces can lead to breakthroughs in animation and game technology. Topology provides the ability to manipulate and distort geometrical shapes while preserving both the aesthetic and functional integrity of computer-created objects. Using techniques of topological optimization, programmers are able to create more realistic simulations at lower computational expense. This capability is of extreme relevance as the demand for quality graphics and natural interactions in virtual worlds grows. Though industries continue to research the potential of topology in design, its applications to industries such as entertainment, education, and virtual training spaces are great and are worth focusing on further (Figure 8.1).

8.1. FUNDAMENTAL PRINCIPLES OF TOPOLOGY DESIGN

The core concepts of topology design include a wide range of theoretical constructs and real-world applications that are essential in the development of high-performance network topologies. These concepts are based on diverse bodies of knowledge, such as graph theory, statistics, and systems engineering, which all serve to shape the design process. One of the most important aspects of topology design is the representation of network elements and links as labeled graphs, allowing for structured study of connectivity and bandwidth. Empirical studies of networks such as Abilene and the Rocket fuel project can provide researchers with a better understanding of the physical infrastructures of networks and design them accordingly. This method, apart from enhancing our knowledge about routing dynamics, takes into account factors of practical importance such as router technology and economic constraints, thereby making the designs theoretically sound but also practical enough for implementation in real life (Alderson et al., 2005). Topology design is also closely associated with the principles of resilience and adaptability in network systems. As the network size and complexity grow, the networks will have to remain robust against failures and fluctuations in demand. Designing topologies that are redundant—through extra connections or redundant routing paths—can play a significant role in making the system more reliable. This means having other objectives for creating the network, for example, rendering congestion improbable and throughput optimal. Topological design principles can be underpinned by the integration of empirically supported resilience, which verifies the way greater physical connectivity understanding equips users with readiness to respond to unexpected router system breakdowns. The achievement of this entails not only minimizing danger but also promoting a collaborative effort among network professionals that is critical in finding solutions to contemporary internet infrastructure issues (Alderson et al., 2005). Furthermore, the history of mathematical biophysics itself is a compelling model for exploring topology design evolution. Just as Nicolas Rashevskys early efforts in mathematical biophysics have set the stage for the resolution of intricate biological interactions, preliminary theoretical frameworks in topology design have created a blueprint for subsequent strategies. His efforts, including the establishment of special journals, are a model of how specialized outlets are able to provoke multidisciplinary strategies and validate innovative ideas. In topology design, an understanding of the importance of relational structures—similar to Rashevsky's vision—is able to give a greater understanding of how various elements interact within a network. Therefore, as topology design evolves further, incorporating historical awareness can help increase the understanding of interdependence between elements and, ultimately, lead to more advanced and effective network solutions.

8.1.1. Key Concepts of Topology

The finding of the key topology principles is the background component of modern topology design, particularly in the context of network infrastructures. Topology is defined as the study of which spatial properties will be invariant under continuous deformation. Such an outlook becomes especially relevant when designing systems like power distribution networks, which must operate despite many stresses, such as severe weather or aging infrastructure. Through topological analysis, scientists can quantify the resilience and vulnerability of such networks and thereby fortify their security standards. With increasing complexities of demands on electric networks, the intersection of real-world applications and topology becomes increasingly pertinent, with much yet to be researched in terms of how such paradigms can render power delivery systems more efficient and reliable (Koc et al., 2015). Furthermore, the implications of topological ideas extend to areas such as architectural design, where the relationship between structural forms and their inherent qualities can be reconsidered. The history of tectonics' evolution—where it is particularly understood as the relationship of interdependency between structure and form—is a good example of that relationship. Recent advancements in computer-aided design technologies have brought new means of uniting the thinking on structure and materiality into novel architectural expressions. This morphogenetic process provides one unique opportunity to redefine traditional design concepts by close association with emergent behavior and adaptive structure. With the help of topology's principles, active frameworks can be designed by architects that not only respond to environmental conditions, but also have aesthetic and functional cohesion, thereby pushing the boundaries of architectural possibility (Oxman et al., 2010). Finally, the application of topology across various design fields demonstrates the interdisciplinary nature of this discipline, bridging theory and practice. This understanding of the complexity of topological spaces allows designers and engineers to exercise good judgments regarding the control of assets in complex systems. For example, during distribution grid analysis, topological measures can determine critical nodes and channels to upgrade and strengthen more intelligently. By placing emphasis on the topology of such networks, decision-makers are able to identify areas of vulnerability and target interventions to limit potential disruption. Therefore, the investigation of salient topics within topology not only informs theoretical discussions but also provides tangible benefits in the planning and management of essential infrastructure systems, promoting sustainability and resilience across sectors (Figure 8.2).

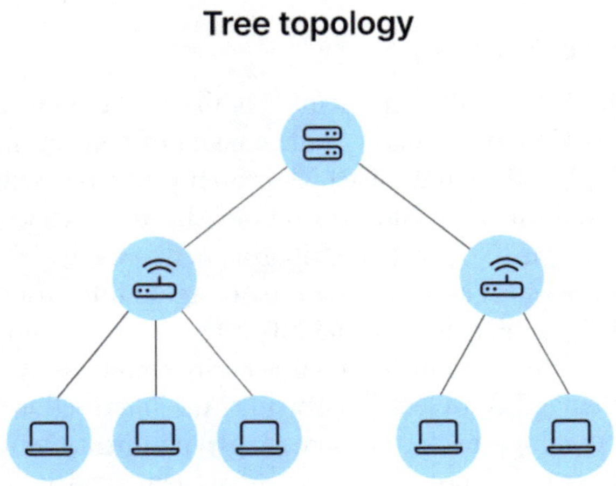

Figure 8.2. *The exploration of key concepts in topology.*

Source: https://ic.nordcdn.com/v1/https://sb.nordcdn.com/m/6dd951748ccebe07/original/infographic-tree-topology.svg.

8.1.2. Design Methodologies and Approaches

Topology design methods are increasingly concerned with systematic procedures for attempting to comprehend complex networks. One milestone in this research area is the development of the dK-series of probability distributions, which offers researchers a tool for the investigation of degree correlations within d-sized subgraphs. This procedure encodes much information inherent in a graph G and allows for a rich representation in accordance with varying complexity. With the dK-series for different values of d, researchers are able to quantify graph distances and create random graphs that capture essential statistics of real networks, particularly topologies of the Internet. Such methodological techniques not only enrich network topology researchers' analytical tools but also facilitate improved understanding of the underlying structural dynamics characterizing modern communications networks (Vahdat et al., 2006). In addition to systematic approaches, the use of advanced mathematical tools, such as Machine Learning (ML), also greatly enhances the design methodology in topological design nowadays. Because telecommunication networks generate large quantities of heterogeneous data, ML becomes a crucial tool for making useful information from network traffic, alarms, and user behavior. Through the application of ML techniques, network analysts can automate self-configuration and fault management processes that are key to maintaining operational efficiency under increasing complexity. The growth of optical communications networks, spurred by new technologies, requires the application of such ML techniques in adjusting various adjustable network parameters. While its usage in this field is yet to be explored, it is also a fruitful area of future practical innovation and study in network topology design (Macaluso et al., 2018). Furthermore, the combination of systematic analysis and machine learning paradigms offers possibilities for adaptive, dynamic network designs that are capable of more effective responding to evolving challenges. The combination of traditional design practice and the high-performance computing capabilities is a rich ground for innovation, and it allows scientists to not only model today's topologies but predict and construct tomorrows' networks that are resilient and robust. The capability of the dK-series to reproduce the fine characteristics of graph properties facilitates the capability of ML to predict and expands the arsenal of tools for topology design. Such synergy not only enhances theoretic development but is also subject to use in the optimization of network operation, enhancing security measures, and scaling problems. Lastly, integration of such diverse methodologies marks a paradigm in topology design procedure both academically and practically (Vahdat et al., 2006; Macaluso et al., 2018).

8.1.3. Role of Mathematical Models in Topology

Mathematical models are a central part of topology discovery and design as they serve as an interface for the theoretical and practical manifestations. In the process of topology design, the models assist scientists in simulating and optimizing networks under varying conditions. By application of sophisticated equations and algorithms, mathematicians can predict how changes in one aspect of the network will affect overall functionality. For instance, the application of optimization techniques in network resource management allows for efficient provisioning, particularly regarding failure or varying traffic demands. Such adaptability is exhibited in new designs of networks where mathematical models govern the construction of resilient, responsive structures with the aim of maintaining performance under disturbances. A case in point concerning the impact of mathematical modeling's on topology design is the automatic switched optical networks (ASON). These networks illustrate how mathematical theory enables dynamic network path reconfiguration. As discussed in Colle et al. (2011), generalized MPLS usage for circuit provision enhances IP layer topologies' survivability during failures. Mathematical models facilitate determining the optimal resource allocation—interfaces, wavelengths, and amplifiers—through various states of the network. By reducing costs pertaining to such resources, mathematical models gain huge economic benefits while maintaining good communication potential. This synergy between topology and mathematics is essential for creating networks that can respond to real-time issues. Mathematical modeling also broadens its application area beyond classical network topology, as illustrated by applications in pharmaceutical processes like freeze-drying. In this case, a black-box model of neural-network construction presented in Barresi et al. (2012) applies mathematical principles to solve for optimal operation. It forecasts temperature and residual ice content over time and aids in recipe development and real-time monitoring. This intersection of topology, optimization, and mathematical modeling illustrates the versatility of these approaches. With professionals evolving continually, the role of mathematical models in topology design remains vital, driving evolution in most fields where optimal performance and reliability are the ultimate aim (Figure 8.3).

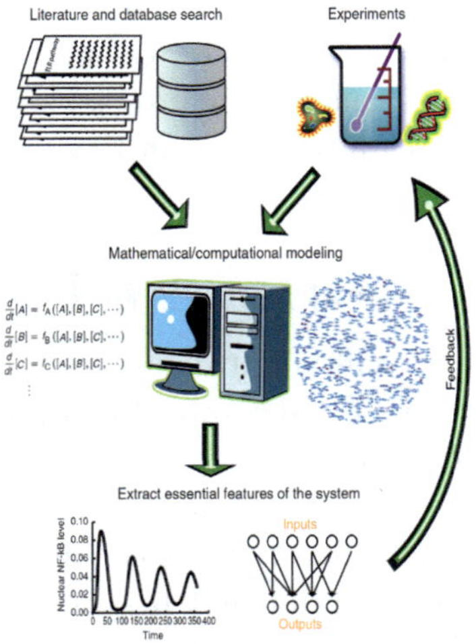

Figure 8.3. *Role of mathematical models in topology.*

Source: https://www.researchgate.net/profile/Alexis-Vandenbon-2/publication/227400547/figure/fig2/AS:268249245941770@1440967012432/Schematic-picture-of-mathematical-modeling-approaches-to-toll-like-receptor-TLR-signal.png.

8.2. CASE STUDY: TOPOLOGY IN NETWORK DESIGN

In network topology, application comes into play in establishing the manner in which nodes communicate and interact within a network. Placement of such nodes, spanning from computers, routers, and servers, affects the efficiency, reliability, as well as scalability of a network. An example case study is the optimization of a freeze-drying process application in the pharmaceutical industry that employs a black-box model for structural and parametric optimization. This model utilizes neural networks to monitor key parameters such as temperature and residual ice content in real time, enhancing both process as well as products quality. Through the design of the network structure that links the various sensors and processors in this architecture, the implications of topology on processing time and data transmission are achieved, illustrating how better network design can lead to drastic increases in operational efficiency and product consistency (Barresi et al., 2012). Applying the concepts of topology in network design to consumer services, its applicability can be observed in high-definition television broadcasting. With demands for bandwidth increasing on platforms that offer services such as HDTV and Ultra HDTV, the need for new means of content delivery that not only meet quality but also remain affordable arises. An example par excellence is the WiLiTV framework presented that integrates different wireless access technologies to construct an effective distribution network for live TV. With the minimization of injection points for satellites and the maximization of Quality of Experience (QoE), this topology facilitates effective data streams via different nodes of the network. As can be observed from the study, the topology consumes significantly fewer resources compared to traditional designs, demonstrating how prudent network topology can effectively reconcile performance and cost in a competitive environment (Jana et al., 2017). aside from infrastructure, topology study in network designing is also associated with performance measures that are determinant to strategic decision-making. From the broadcast and pharmaceutical case studies, it is clear that the network topology not only determines the quality of the output but also has an impact on how fast and reliably that output is delivered to the end user. Topology choice directly influences latency, fault tolerance, and scalability, which are indispensable for applications these days where the user expectations are more than ever. As companies strive towards operational excellence, it is imperative to understand the intricate relationships between topology and network performance. These case studies illuminate the profound effects that well-thought-out network designs can make, and they are the foundation for future exploration of optimized topology practices across different industries.

8.2.1. Overview of Network Topologies

Network topologies are basic in computer networking study and essential in topologically efficient design. Network topology determines the structure of different components, such as nodes and links, that constitute a network. Various topologies—such as star, ring, mesh, and tree—are dissimilar in nature and efficiency of operation and have an effect on performance and scalability.

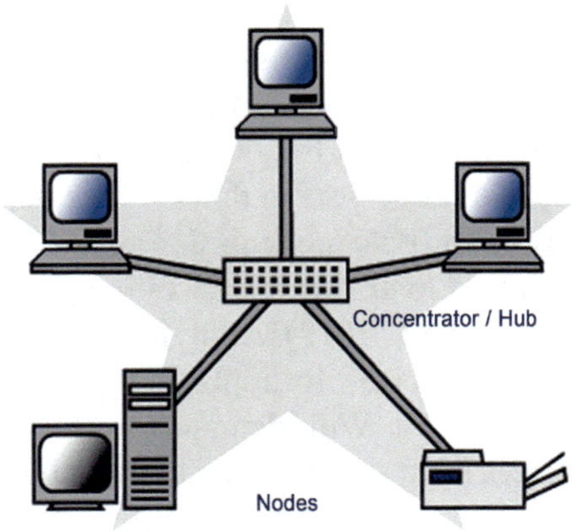

Figure 8.4. *Understand network topologies.*

Source: https://fcit.usf.edu/network/chap5/pics/star.gif.

The topology design used influences not only network installation complexity but also failure resiliency and maintenance costs. An example is the mesh topology, which has fault tolerance and redundancy, but a star topology simplifies configuration at the cost of a point of failure. Hence, the implications of topology selection echo in every stage of network planning, and it is a principal consideration at the network network's design phase. Network needs also demand advanced modeling of network topologies due to their dynamic character. Common methods utilize basic graphs to model complicated networks, but this often does not capture the intrinsic richness of real relationships. To escape this limitation, new models have been built that incorporate additional metadata, or annotations, that define relationships and properties of nodes and links in the topology. One example is the use of a rescaling algorithm that allows researchers to create networks of varying sizes but preserve key structural properties. This technique, as presented in Vahdat et al. (2009), offers good insights for simulating network behavior and helps in the development of future Internet architecture. An accurate representation of network topologies enhances our knowledge of connectivity, scalability, and overall functionality of extensive networks. In addition, the effectiveness of network topology design is also put into context in terms of resource constraints and reliability issues, as strongly demonstrated in sensor networks. These networks have some limitations, including energy spendings, communication expenses, and potential link failures that degrade the performance. The issue is to design a topology which, in addition to maximizing communication reliability under such limitations, adheres to budgetary limitations. A work in José et al. (2007) highlights the necessity of a strong mathematical formalism for addressing these matters, applying convex optimization techniques to determine the optimal topologies. By analyzing network graph algebraic connectivity, the paper delivers a step toward enhancing consensus algorithms in different applications, thereby proving the multidisciplinary impact of topology design on network operations and resource management (Figure 8.4).

8.2.2. Analysis of Performance Metrics

Investigation of performance indicators in topology design is core to the evaluation of the effectiveness and viability of engineering solutions. With the use of hybrid approaches that integrate quantum computation and classic optimization procedures, researchers are pushing the boundaries of conventional performance assessment. These procedures, particularly for structural design of ultra-high-performance concrete (UHPC) bridge structures, enable engineers to navigate more effectively in complex spaces of design. The integration of the Quantum Approximate Optimization Algorithm (QAOA) and Variational Quantum Eigensolver (VQE) plays a critical role in elevating computational methods. With the application of these newer algorithms, performance parameters extend to structural stability in addition to sustainability parameters like reduced material utilization and embodied carbon. This paradigm shift emphasizes the importance of continuous innovation in monitoring and keeping track of performance metrics on topology design platforms (Azanaw, 2025). A comprehensive performance measure framework must consider the reliability of the distribution network, especially in the case of today's energy systems. The double Q approach presents a new mechanism for reconciling economic feasibility with system reliability while including key assessment metrics in the design. By utilizing a linearized power flow method within a mixed-integer linear programming solution, the approach easily overcomes computational-expensive issues based on varying network configurations. Involvement of the adaptive ε-constraint approach subsequently further enhances the research with the inclusion of an examination of the global Pareto frontier based on reliability and cost. This two-objective approach allows planners to make decisions confidently that achieve the optimal network performance while delivering a more reliable and cost-effective distribution network. Consequently, the integration of such knowledge is a pioneering achievement towards boosting topological design operational efficiency as a whole (Jiang et al., 2025). Moreover, the coupling between new computational models and field applications underscores the importance of sustaining performance metrics observability. As case studies indicate, sophisticated models culminate in the mitigation of construction and operating costs at levels that are practically acceptable with respect to system reliability. But achieving this balance usually means sacrifices, and thus necessitates a holistic appreciation of the points of intersection between design choices and performance indicators. Such aggregated learnings must feed into driving subsequent development activity aimed at optimizing both sustainability and resilience. There is an analogous need for collaborative ventures across academia and industry that ensure emerging technologies can be tested and scaled-up for real-world application. By resolving these challenges through performance metrics discovery, topology design can move towards more innovative and more sustainable engineering solutions (Azanaw, 2025; Jiang et al., 2025).

8.2.3. Real-World Applications and Examples

Applications of topology design are applied in the real world in a wide variety of fields as a foundation for controlling and optimizing complicated networks. Structural controllability is crucial when dealing with complicated networks since it determines how well a system can be controlled from one state to another. It is useful in fields such as transport, where routing at its best can avoid congestion. A recent study exemplifies the use of graph theory and control theory to cope with the challenges posed by large networks, showing that local topology information can significantly be used to enhance system manageability. Using a distributed local-game matching strategy, systems are able to reach a suboptimal solution with reduced computational complexity, hence supporting more adaptable and responsive control schemes in dynamic situations (Deng et al., 2018). Thus, effective topology design has a direct reflection on the reliability and performance of complex networks in real-time systems. Process management in industry is another good example of topology design, with process tomography representing one of the revolutionary technologies that have found their way in it. The method permits one to see intricate internal processes so that engineers are able to achieve comprehensive knowledge about system dynamics. Through the establishment of a reality visualization model (RVM), professionals can merge multidimensional sensor data, both for design model verification and real-time monitoring of plant processes. The application of RVM is especially worthwhile for its ability to represent process contents and behaviors graphically, which is key to effective decision-making and control in manufacturing plants. The schema established in existing literature facilitates the integration of RVM as an important tool for achieving process subtlety, hence validating the position of topology design as a means of obtaining improved operational performance in complex industrial systems (Hoyle et al., 2005). Furthermore, integration of topology design into ecological systems provides another avenue for viable application. In ecological networks, understanding species interactions and habitat structures is fundamental in the conservation of biodiversity and natural resource management. Advanced topology analysis provides information on network stability and resilience and educates scientists about crucial species and habitats behind ecosystem functioning. This is particularly vital in the context of climate change, where shifting environmental conditions can interrupt established interactions. Through employing topological approaches in ecological modeling, scientists can develop strategies that provide resilience of an ecosystem to disturbance. Such applications illustrate the significance of topology design methodologies with potential for breakthrough to fit changing ecological parameters for sustainable practices in line with conservation. Topology application to real ecological models reveals its flexibility and significance in multiple fields, further placing it in real-world applications (Figure 8.5).

Figure 8.5. *The real-world applications of topology.*

Source: https://files.codingninjas.in/article_images/real-time-applications-0-1681709516.webp.

8.3. CASE STUDY: TOPOLOGY IN STRUCTURAL ENGINEERING

In structural engineering, topology optimization is utilized to achieve the highest performance and efficiency of materials and designs. A prime example is the application of the Bi-directional Evolutionary Structural Optimization (BESO) method, which is notable for simplicity in algorithms and adaptability in various types of engineering problems. This method has been embraced in industrial and research applications with particular emphasis in addressing the deficits presented by traditional finite element software. The integration of an ABAQUS–MATLAB cooperative platform is quintessential innovation as it facilitates real-time sensitivity and optimization through direct communication between platforms. These advancements have necessitated crucial optimizations, as seen in one case where a hydraulic transmission test bench adapter minimized volume by as much as 31% while not reducing required strength and stiffness requirements. This also underscores the revolutionary capability of topology optimization in achieving cost-effective, efficient engineering applications (Sun et al., 2025). Besides, with technology advancement, quantum computing holds promising potential for topology optimization in structural engineering. The arrival of methods such as QCHGEA-TOF that employ a quantum-classical hybrid approach is a leap in the right direction. With the power of quantum computing—such as parallel processing and efficient handling of complex computation—designers can navigate structural configurations more effectively than previously possible using traditional means. Structural components mapping to qubits allows probing of optimized structures using quantum superposition, and classical algorithms guarantee structural integrity of the designs. Case studies demonstrating this framework have indicated less structural compliance compared to established optimization techniques, underscoring quantum computing's capacity to address complex global design challenges. As research advances, the study of such early frameworks potentially has the capability to redefine the geometry of topology optimization in structural engineering (Wang et al., 2025). As a complement to optimization techniques, real application shows the interface of theoretical design and real implementation. Structural engineers are increasingly being challenged with the need to produce lightweight structures that remain strong and capable of tolerating high stress and environmental loads. The result gained from the application of advanced topology optimization techniques indicates a significant reduction in material usage without compromising structural strength. For instance, efficient use of the ABAQUS–MATLAB framework not only accelerated computation but also facilitated the design of complex structures that meet stringent performance requirements. This capability highlights the blend of functionality and creativity in engineering design in which structures that are not only stunning but also economical are facilitated. As the case studies progress, one can easily see that the addition of topology optimization methods will further influence the structural engineering of the future, encouraging innovation and optimality (Sun et al., 2025; Wang et al., 2025).

8.3.1. Importance of Topology to Structural Integrity

Topology finds relevance in structural optimization, particularly where engineering designs require optimum strength and weight distribution. By application of advanced topology optimization techniques, engineers can create structures with less material wastage while realizing maximum mechanical performance. Not only does this lead to the generation of strong components, but it also leads to the significant minimization of the weight of structures, which is critical in applications such as aerospace and automobile. Also, topology optimization allows for the optimization of material location based on load paths such that the stress concentrations are managed appropriately. This is important in the scenario of fluid-structure interaction problems, where structural behavior of components must align with dynamic aerodynamic conditions. The constraints of working with traditional manufacturing processes have already restricted the use of innovative designs, but accelerating development in additive manufacturing has opened up new directions towards realizing complex topological geometries and hence proving their worth in maintaining structural integrity in modern applications. Topology is more valuable than even reducing weight; it is essential to optimizing performance for various loading conditions. A great case study comes from the aeronautical engineering field, where wing structural aerodynamic efficiency is of paramount importance. As outlined in research that is part of the EU RIBES project, the half-wing model was designed and tested with meticulous care to observe structural dynamics in a real-life context. It highlighted the need to perform true aerodynamic forces over strict theoretical models. Data obtained from such experimental setups enables better understanding of the dependency between topology and structural response, making weaknesses and failure areas distinguishable. In this case, topology serves not only as a design principle but also as a predictive tool that informs engineers of how structures behave in dynamic loads and conditions and thus the cause of enhanced reliability and safety in sensitive applications like aerospace ((Biancolini et al., 2018)). In addition, the intersection of topology with advances in technology has had a significant impact on the evolution of new materials and structures. The incorporation of structural integrity into the design from the outset enables the utilization of multiple approaches, merging physical testing with computational models to replicate performance accurately. Techniques such as isothermal titration calorimetry and NMR spectroscopy, although initially developed for biochemistry, can be metaphorically extended to structural integrity testing of structure, emphasizing material stress metabolism. Engineers can draw lessons from the varied disciplines by promoting inter-disciplinary approaches, thus enhancing the role of topology in the analysis of complex structural interactions and failure. The continuous evolution of topology design methods will be crucial in advancing the boundaries of what is possible under structural integrity, paving the way for innovations within fields where performance and reliability are non-negotiable alternatives ((Wright et al., 2010)) (Figure 8.6).

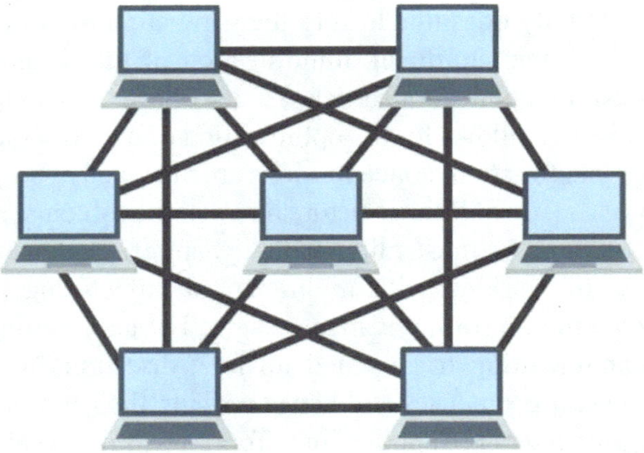

Figure 8.6. *Importance of topology in structural integrity.*

Source: *https://virima.com/wp-content/uploads/2024/07/Mesh-topology-1024x512.png.webp.*

8.3.2. Innovative Design Techniques

New design processes are, both in topology design, a source of innovation and a means of addressing complex problems. One of the newer processes is algorithmic design, where computer systems are used to explore and design complex geometrical shapes. This process enables designers to reduce shapes and amounts of material while achieving minimum standards of performance. Aside from this, through emulation of various environments, designers are able to make systems responsive to users' demands and environmental needs. The flexibility of algorithmic design inspires creativity, making it possible to create previously unattainable forms and shapes. By integrating such techniques into design work, practitioners are able to push the boundaries of conventional topology, resulting in new discoveries and applications in architecture and engineering (Poorter et al., 2016). Another vital innovative design technique is the use of cartograms, which alters geographical displays to highlight statistical data. As a visual means to display complicated data sets, cartograms re-scales areas within a geography in proportion to quantitative factors, such as population or economic data. The method brings out patterns and contrasts hidden on traditional maps, providing new insights into data analysis. Cartogram efficacy relies on their ability to balance statistical, geographical, and topological accuracy with spatial relation understanding and statistical significance. The increasing application of cartograms in data visualization is a reflection of their potential as a form of efficient communication, allowing designers to narrate compelling stories appealing to various individuals (Alam et al., 2016). Lastly, parametric design as applied to topology has changed the way in which designers think and carry out projects. The process allows for manipulation of various parameters, which might have a decisive role in determining the final outcome. By establishing relationships between variables and objects, designers are able to create adaptive and sustainable systems that respond to transforming environments. This level of customization enhances the efficiency and effectiveness of designs, particularly in complex projects wherein context plays a central role. With the growing demand for innovative solutions, parametric design at the forefront of architectural and engineering innovations enables creators to counteract the complexity of the world today with flexibility and sophistication (Poorter et al., 2016).

8.3.3. Case Examples of Successful Structural Designs

The study of efficient structural shapes has a tendency to highlight the innovative use of tensile membrane structures (TMS) that have gained increased popularity in contemporary architecture due to their unique functionalities. Famous world landmarks such as the Eden Project in Cornwall and the Sydney Opera House are proof that TMS can create both useful and aesthetically pleasing areas. These buildings incorporate light materials which can span distances as huge as they are without massive support, allowing room for free-flowing forms and dynamic shapes that provoke the visual senses. In Elnokaly et al. (2006) proposal, the shift towards utilizing such materials addresses the growing requirement for sustainable architecture that does not compromise on performance or aesthetics. When engineers and architects prototype TMS, they begin laying the foundations for responsible and attractive designs, a testament to the current values of sustainable use while satisfying occupant comfort and design needs. In addition, the ability of TMS to be adaptable to various climates plays a pivotal part in its successful adoption. For instance, tensile membrane structures can be extremely helpful in hot desert climates since the material can be designed to improve natural ventilation and realize maximum thermal performance. TMS's capability to use in a variety of climates, especially where considerable energy consumption is the most significant concern, indicates how they have the ability to revolutionize traditional architectural procedures. As Chilton et al.

(2002) explains, the use of such structures not only makes them more beautiful but also demands that one be aware of their behavior in the environment, including their thermal dynamics. Evolution of computer form-finding software aids in developing more reliable structural designs, contributing to the wider field of how architects can apply these materials to construct responsive and sustainable buildings. Last but not least, while there are numerous advantages to accrue to TMS, challenges remain inherent in their implementation, namely in comparison to their environmental performance. While the integrity of the structures has been increased by improvements in materials technology and structural analysis, knowledge of how to deal with their environments is still developing. The low mass and thermal insulation properties of TMS make them climate-sensitive, and therefore, they are a limitation to their extensive application within the building industry. As Chilton et al. (2002) identifies, additional research is important in making full realization and utilization of such buildings. Through solving thermal performance problems and pioneering novel methods of improving air flow and occupant comfort, the discipline of topology design can certainly gain from effective case studies utilizing TMS, eventually creating a sustainable architectural design future (Figure 8.7).

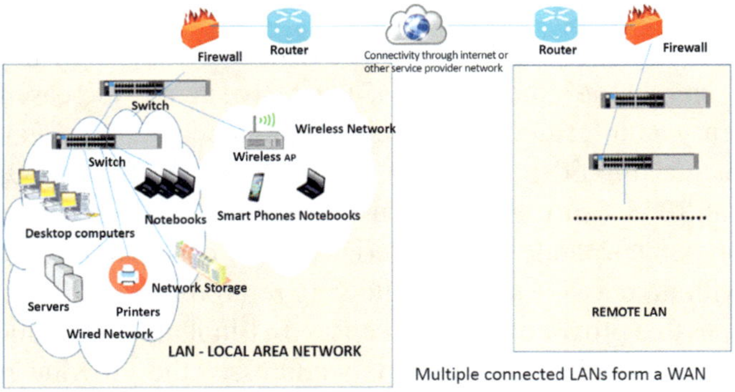

Figure 8.7. *The exploration of successful structural designs often highlights the innovative use of tensile membrane structures (TMS).*

Source: https://study.com/cimages/multimages/16/canva-photo-editor_2.png.

8.4. CASE STUDY: TOPOLOGY IN ROBOTICS

The application of topology optimization to the design of robots is a significant move towards achieving maximum function and performance across various applications. In robotics, particularly in soft robotic grippers, it is hard to achieve flexibility while maintaining enough load-carrying capacity. New studies demonstrate how the topology optimization method has been utilized to come up with more efficient designs for soft grippers, which are crucial for handling delicate objects. For instance, design for a gripper from the fin-ray finger triangular structure shows the capability to integrate biological principles and computational methods in order to obtain high-level functional specifications for robotics. The design principle focuses on minimizing deflection while maximizing wrapping capacity as necessary for delicate grasping in dynamic environments, which illustrates the concordance of natural and engineered form (Srinivas et al., 2024). Also, application of cutting-edge tools such as additive manufacturing improves topology optimization, granting untold design liberty. Traditional design platforms usually impose limitations that hamper performance optimization; however, the combination of generative design and topology optimization offers a solution to avoid these limitations. For instance, case studies of gripper arms used for specific operations—like handling meteors—illustrate the impact of such advanced tools on component performance as well as structural integrity. Through the use of software such as Autodesk's generative design, designers can sift through many potential answers to structural issues, significantly enhancing overall performance at minimal material cost and with regard to manufacturability constraints (Lkadi et al., 2024). Not only design innovation, but the implications of topology optimization are also transforming the entire realm of manufacture in robotics. By optimizing component function and enabling intricate geometries, designers can create solutions that are not only lighter and more durable but are also better suited to the nuances of robotic engagement with the world. These advancements reveal the potential for robots that can successfully grasp, manipulate, and interact with objects directly addressing the intricacies of their working worlds. Lastly, the current case study of robotic gripper topology design optimization illustrates how certain engineering combined with innovative production methods can impact robotics in a revolutionary way, leading to future research and applications within the field.

8.4.1. Topological Problems in Robot Design

With the emergence of robotics, topological considerations have emerged as paramount in the performance and adaptability of robot systems. The design process now extensively employs concepts of topology to create adaptable, efficient, and robust robots that can navigate complex environments. Neuro-evolution of augmenting topology (NEAT) is one of the significant approaches where network topology and weight of connections can be optimized together. This method addresses the inherent issue with traditional artificial neural network implementations that they have a tendency to apply pre-defined topologies that may not be optimal for performing in adaptive environments. By integrating a multi-objective neuro-evolution algorithm, engineers can design networks that not only function optimally but can also search, ultimately creating higher generalization across a variety of operating environments (Behjat et al., 2018). The development of testbeds, such as the Robotarium, highlights the importance of topological thinking in robotics engineering. The lab eliminates the logistics constraints of multi-robot research by providing a remotely accessible environment, with enhanced collaboration among researchers and mitigated resource constraints. Usability and safety come first when designing such infrastructure; safety features must be added without compromising control program flexibility to be made available for use by users.

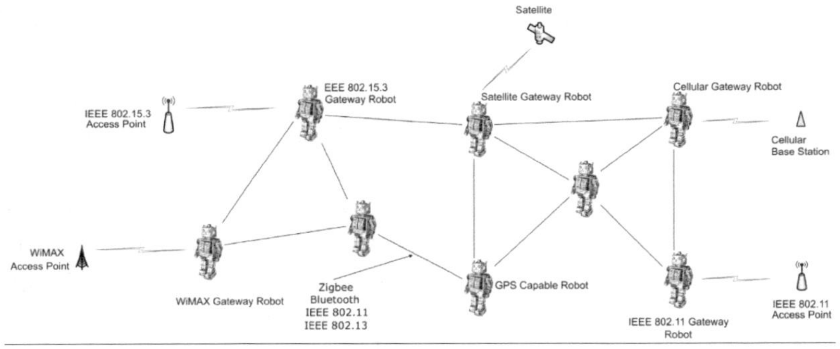

Figure 8.8. *Topological considerations in robot design.*

Source: https://www.mdpi.com/jsan/jsan-07-00052/article_deploy/html/images/jsan-07-00052-g001.png.

Topological considerations underlie the design and cooperation of many robots in these environments such that the system can autonomously deal with diverse scenarios without direct human intervention but is versatile enough to open up pathways for new exploration of coordinated control strategies. Safety measures that correlate with ease of use ultimately enhance the research environment, opening up avenues for epiphanies in multi-agent systems (Ames et al., 2016). Besides, an understanding of the topological behavior of robotic systems can inform paths to designing more sophisticated behaviors in robots. The topological space that a robot explores has a significant impact on its navigability and performance in the completion of tasks. For instance, with responsive topological characteristics, robots are capable of reconstructing their locomotion based on the geometrical constraints and changes in their environment, leading to enhanced exploration and interaction strategies. As topological design emerges, integrating principles of modularity and redundancy can potentially allow for more efficient performance over a variety of mission parameters. By focusing on topological dynamics, researchers can potentially enhance not only individual robots but overall multi-agent system effectiveness, leading eventually to innovation in autonomous robotics where adaptability and efficiency are the design drivers (Figure 8.8).

8.4.2. Impact on Mobility and Functionality

The intricate relationship between topology design and mobility is fundamental to modern logistics, particularly military. With the shifting fleets of vehicles becoming less focused on traditional, fixed transport assets and more on modular arrangements, the effect on mobility and functionality is obvious. The conversion enables the use of tailored transportation logistics in which vehicles can be optimized to address specific mission requirements. The evaluation of such systems points not just to the efficiency of resource allocation but also to the enhancement of operational responsiveness. Based on strategic planning simulations, researchers conduct study on scheduling and routing problems, ultimately demonstrating how modular vehicles can significantly increase mobility under various operation conditions. This vehicle design innovation, enabled by high-level topology, mirrors the imperative of adaptable logistics within dynamic environments in accordance with broader moves toward innovative transportation solutions in military applications (Abbass et al., 2008). Relative to use within the military, topology design application extends into conditions of disaster relief where mobility and communication are critical. The use of Unmanned Aerial Vehicles (UAVs) as emergency communication infrastructures during the occurrence of crises illustrates this phenomenon. When there are emergency occurrences, such as severe flooding, traditional communication networks may fail, and other options are required. Having the deployment of UAVs makes it possible to deploy the coverage of cellular networks rapidly, and communications are kept open when most crucial. This capacity not only facilitates rescue coordination but also facilitates efficient mobilization of the displaced towards shelter. With cities grappling with the effects of climate change and disasters, incorporating agile UAV-assisted communication in topology design models contributes significantly to mobility and functionality, ultimately leading to more resilient community support systems (Casetti et al., 2019). Moreover, the interdependence of mobility and functionality in topology planning is brought out by advances in communication and transport technology, which reinforce one another in complex scenarios. As observed in the discussion on modular vehicle fleets and UAV deployments, the optimization of transport and information traffic is essential in achieving productive operational outcomes. The ability to quickly adapt vehicles and communications infrastructure in response to shifting environmental and logistical requirements characterizes the very essence of topology design innovation. By reviewing these case studies, one can recognize deeper trends of success premised upon better mobility solutions as well as functional responsiveness. Finally, these integrations not only enhance operational effectiveness but also create a more responsive and resilient infrastructure capable of meeting various challenges in both military and civilian spheres.

8.4.3. Notable Robotic Systems Utilizing Topology Design

The use of topology design in robotic platforms has significantly enhanced their performance efficacy and versatility. One good example is the application of the neuro-evolution of augmenting topology (NEAT) framework in small-robot path-planning applications. Through this operation, robots are endowed with artificial neural networks (ANNs) that adaptively evolve their network topologies as well as connection weights through an evolutionary process. By offering multi-objective optimization based on performance and experience-gain, the NEAT system reverses the drawbacks of static architectures that have been common before, leading to enhanced generalization in divergent operating conditions. Experiments indicate that robots employing multi-objective neuro-evolution are superior to robots that optimize performance alone, particularly in unseen environments, with the former exhibiting an enormous improvement in their adaptability and robustness. The other realization of topology design innovation in robotic systems is the use of communication networks based on observability. These networks, having a foundation in graph theory concepts, are most applicable in situations that require very high security. The resulting algorithm best selects the optimal communication weights in order to maximize node secrecy against intrusion attacks and create a robust synthesis among network design and control theory. In application, the adaptive characteristic of such communication topologies facilitates robotic systems to automatically alter their configurations online, effectively limiting the information accessible to hostile parties. This aspect not only increases the privacy of the network but also allows robotic systems to keep functioning and remaining robust in such hostile or uncertain settings, further demonstrating the pivotal role well-designed topologies play in maintaining operational integrity. The consequences of employing optimal topology design are multiplied by its ability to facilitate cooperation between plural robotic agents. In swarm robotics, for instance, decentralized communication topologies may provide for efficient communication and task allocation among a free-roaming fleet of robots. By controlling the interconnectivity among robots through strategic means, topology design not only improves performance but also ensures energy efficiency and failure tolerance. Through adaptive measures such as adaptive weight allocation and dynamic reconfiguration according to changes in the environment, cooperative robotic systems are defined by higher cooperative levels and problem-solving capacities. Such cooperation demonstrates the groundbreaking power of topology design in making robots work together toward complex tasks, thus addressing the ever-dynamic demands of robotics through innovative design paradigms such as those in Behjat et al. (2018) and Alaeddini et al. (2017) (Figure 8.9).

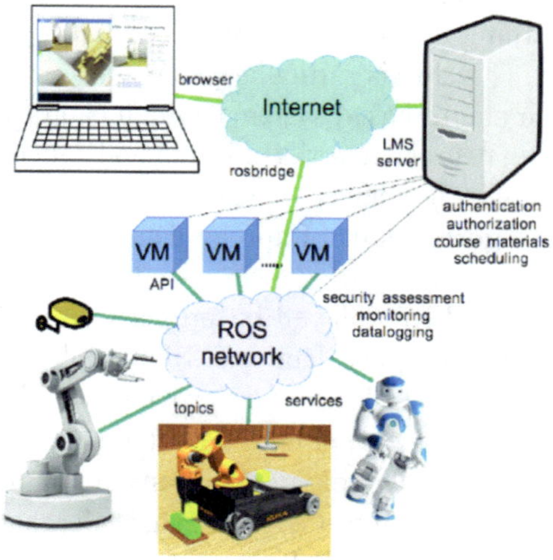

Figure 8.9. *Notable robotic systems utilizing topology design.*

Source: https://www.researchgate.net/publication/325638468/figure/fig1/AS:1086425852325908@1636035516208/Overall-architecture-of-the-Robot-Programming-Network-the-user-is-connected-to-Internet.jpg.

8.5. CASE STUDY: TOPOLOGY IN DATA SCIENCE

Entering into the marriage of data science and topology displays a groundbreaking way of how data is structured and operated upon. Behind the union is the concept of Surface Networks, a new data structure that generalizes two-dimensional surfaces based on highlighting intrinsic points and lines of the surface. These networks break from previous methods, such as Digital Elevation Models (DEM) and Triangulated Irregular Networks (TIN), which are rigid and wasteful in executing complex analysis. Focusing on basic surface properties,

Surface Networks enable a more intuitive means of data presentation, enabling researchers across any discipline—meteorology and population studies, to name a couple—to extract insights previously buried in more classic models (Morley et al., 2002). This evolving world illustrates how topology prescribes the structure of data structures that enable our navigation and comprehension of complex datasets. Topology also comes to the forefront with the creation of learning techniques in data science. An example is the progression of Self-Organizing Maps (SOM), which have traditionally utilized Kohonen learning. But this is limited since it incorporates an epoch-based training mechanism that diminishes the learning rate and radius slowly. This differs from contemporary methods such as diffusive learning that poses a new alternative by allowing improved learning in one epoch. This shift is particularly relevant as it is closer to biological processes observed in nature-based systems, which can provide more accurate models when modeling neural networks or biological data (Hřebík et al., 2019). From observing these developments, we can observe how the incorporation of topology in learning algorithms can improve data representation and analysis more effectively. Lastly, the topology case study in data science serves to demonstrate the influential role played by properly formulated mathematical models in understanding complex data sets. Methodological innovations like Surface Networks and diffusive learning improve processing efficacy and also our understanding of the underpinning data relationships. They showcase a bigger trend where high-order topological notions are applied to solve actual-world scientific challenges. With further research, such practices will inevitably evolve, growing with every new challenge the volume and intricacy of data pose in our ever-more data-drenched world. The topic of topology becomes a necessity here, no longer as an esoteric mathematical science but as an essential tool for effective applications in data science.

8.5.1. Topological Data Analysis (TDA) Overview

Topological Data Analysis (TDA) has emerged as a generic toolset in understanding complex data structures recently. Essentially, TDA leverages the principles of topology, a branch of mathematics that deals with properties invariant to continuous deformations. Through projections of high-dimensional data sets into topological representations, TDA enables the discovery of latent patterns which are masked by traditional analytical approaches. For instance, persistent homology, a central TDA technique, computes topological features such as loops and connected components at varying spatial scales, providing a full description of the data's shape. This ability to express data structure in terms of topology makes TDA particularly valuable across a range of fields, from biology to sensor networks, where the data shape and connectivity is critical to analysis and decision-making. The application of TDA has had a major impact in machine learning, where conventional methodology would not work in handling non-Euclidean data representations. The majority of datasets contain complex relationships, which are most conveniently illustrated in graph structures, hence the application of approaches such as Graph Neural Networks (GNNs) is of great importance. Evidence from recent studies indicates that GNNs are effective in handling data of such a type, as they incorporate the graph topology upon which the data is inscribed into the machine learning process and maintain the intricate inter-data point relationships (Wu et al., 2020). When combined with GNNs, scholars can make machine learning models interpretable and robust, especially with the case of high-dimensional data or data of irregular structure. This intermixture not only broadens the horizon of TDA applicability but also brings vigor to the significance of topological techniques in frontier data analysis methods. Furthermore, TDAs concepts find relevance outside standard data analysis, illuminating physical phenomena explained by topological invariants. Integer quantum Hall effect's immunity to disorder, for example, exemplifies how topological features can be behind governing the quantum system's behavior. Study of these phenomena has been enriched by the study of photonic systems like waveguide arrays and metamaterials that exhibit topological effects in novel physical regimes (Ozawa et al., 2019). This marriage of topology with physically measurable attributes indicates the multidimensional usability of TDA, which suggests its use in both theoretical frameworks as well as applied technologies. As the topological science is examined with increasing specificity, the hope for applying TDA to direct the design of systems from material science to data-driven implementations comes into sharper relief, illustrating a significant frontier for topology design as a discipline (Figure 8.10).

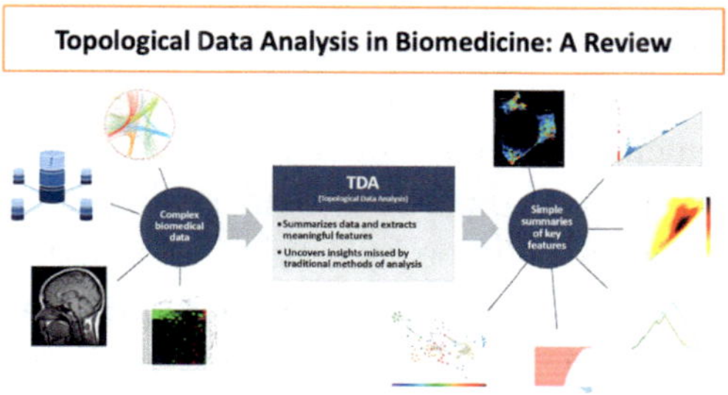

Figure 8.10. *Topological data analysis (TDA) overview.*

Source: https://ars.els-cdn.com/content/image/1-s2.0-S1532046422000983-ga1_lrg.jpg.

Topological considerations underlie the design and cooperation of many robots in these environments such that the system can autonomously deal with diverse scenarios without direct human intervention but is versatile enough to open up pathways for new exploration of coordinated control strategies. Safety measures that correlate with ease of use ultimately enhance the research environment, opening up avenues for epiphanies in multi-agent systems (Ames et al., 2016). Besides, an understanding of the topological behavior of robotic systems can inform paths to designing more sophisticated behaviors in robots. The topological space that a robot explores has a significant impact on its navigability and performance in the completion of tasks. For instance, with responsive topological characteristics, robots are capable of reconstructing their locomotion based on the geometrical constraints and changes in their environment, leading to enhanced exploration and interaction strategies. As topological design emerges, integrating principles of modularity and redundancy can potentially allow for more efficient performance over a variety of mission parameters. By focusing on topological dynamics, researchers can potentially enhance not only individual robots but overall multi-agent system effectiveness, leading eventually to innovation in autonomous robotics where adaptability and efficiency are the design drivers (Figure 8.8).

8.5.2. Applications in Machine Learning

The application of machine learning in various domains is also revolutionizing methods and outcomes, and its integration into topology design is no exception. Techniques such as Bayesian optimization leverage the strength of machine learning to enhance vaccine formulation processes, evident in viral vaccine case studies where critical factors influencing quality were monitored. With the application of advanced algorithms, researchers made revolutionary improvements in model accuracy, showing that the prediction of outcomes is not only feasible but also scalable within complex biological systems. The application of such advanced frameworks points to a wider application of machine learning in scientific studies, underlining its contribution toward achieving an optimal health solution by making informed, data-driven choices about formulation parameters and manufacturing operations (Li et al., 2025). Furthermore, the creation of deep symbolic regression (DSR) provides another exciting line of research into the application of machine learning in engineering disciplines, specifically the control systems for permanent magnet synchronous machines (SPMSM) surface-mounted. The proposed scheme based on DSR is superior to traditional linear proportional–integral (PI) controllers because it generates reflective analytical models with an intensive understanding of complicated dynamics. The use of machine learning not only enhances performance indicators in control designs but also offers the potential for generalizing and extrapolating outcomes to novel datasets. Such the ability to develop prediction models from intricate system behavior warrants the groundbreaking contribution of machine learning towards enhancing control strategy in various applications (Usama et al., 2022). From these examples, it is evident that machine learning is a powerful method in topology design that allows innovations that would not be possible otherwise. The combination of data science and engineering facilitates improved decision-making and optimization of designs, something that is crucial considering that these fields are dynamic. By leveraging the most advanced analytical methods, researchers are able to gain more insight into system performance and interactions between influencing factors. This has important consequences for sectors like health and energy; whereby enhanced models can lead to enhanced solutions that address the concerns of the present. The continued research into machine learning applications serves as proof of its potential to guide future areas of research and technological development (Li et al., 2025; Usama et al., 2022).

8.5.3. Examples of TDA Cases in Practice

In recent applications of topology design analysis (TDA), significant bounds have been highlighted in research that involved merging optimization systems within the framework of computer-aided innovation (CAI). The focus of this effort, specifically, was on rectifying geometrical inconsistencies that arise throughout the design process. By varying density distributions, researchers were able to generate solutions that effectively addressed these inconsistencies while enhancing design efficiency. This approach not only demonstrates the use of TDA but also confirms the capability of topology optimization in providing customized modeling features to a specific engineering problem. These developments emphasize the importance of bringing TDA together with robust methodologies in order to push design innovation within engineering fields (Cascini et al., 2009). Another major example in topology design is the application of surface networks as advanced data structures for the understanding of intricate surfaces. Surface networks have been used by researchers to describe critical points and lines for enhanced manipulation of continuous surfaces in a broad range of applications, from geography to materials science. Surface networks are unlike traditional methods such as Triangulated Irregular Networks (TIN) or Digital Elevation Models (DEM), as they offer a superior abstraction of surfaces. With improved representation, geometric details are easier to discern, which makes it easier for designers to handle and optimize surfaces in their projects. The flexibility of surface networks places the importance of TDA on streamlining intricate data correlations to bring about meaningful applications across various industries (Morley et al., 2002). In addition, case studies in investigating the meaningful applications of TDA have also made importance placed on the multidisciplinary nature of topology design, connecting engineering, computer science, and environmental study. With the help of topology optimization techniques, researchers have been able to effectively streamline design procedures with the ultimate goal of improved performance and sustainability. Such cross-disciplinary research not only leads to innovation but also encourages solution tailoring to address specific operation requirements. TDA facilitates the dynamic reconfiguration of designs and therefore allows engineers to perform problem-solving activities more effectively, as evidenced in examples from these papers. Therefore, the procedures and results based on such examples of cases point significantly towards the prevailing debate in topology design and its significant application in addressing engineering problems today (Figure 8.11).

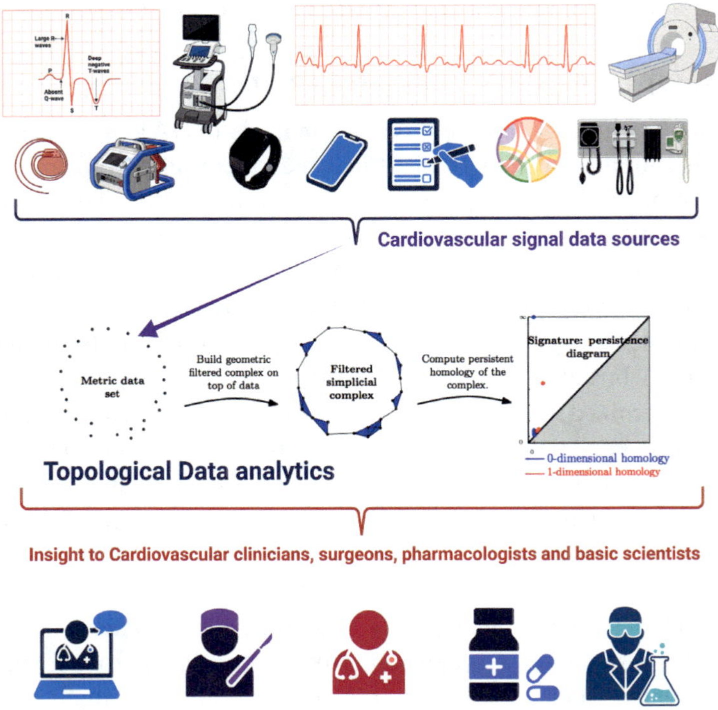

Figure 8.11. *Case examples of TDA in practice.*

Source: https://www.mdpi.com/entropy/entropy-26-00067/article_deploy/html/images/entropy-26-00067-g001.png.

8.6. CHALLENGES AND LIMITATIONS IN TOPOLOGY DESIGN

The field of topology design is faced with many challenges and restrictions, particularly with technology accelerating system complexity growth. A key challenge is integration of dissimilar components that have distinct failure modes and operational characteristics. Perhaps the complexity results in the inability to model system performance accurately because simple models do not account for interdependencies that occur among the components. For instance, in safety-critical systems, an understanding of how to configure and interact various components is essential for safe usage. New approaches, such as model-based dependability analysis, try to overcome these limitations by constructing predictive models of failures but are also faced with applicability and effectiveness challenges in various contexts (Kabir et al., 2015). The restrictions inherent in such methods underscore the need for ongoing research and development, particularly in creating combined models which accommodate high-order topologies. The second main challenge to topology design occurs in combining renewable sources with the system. While the move to sustainable and clean energy producers is imperative, this necessarily injects variability and uncertainty into power generation. Renewable energy sources (RES) operate intermittently, giving examples of low supply that traditionally run systems are not designed to match effectively. The intermittent nature complicates the ability to ensure provision of continuous power supply and thus the need to create advanced power electronics interfaces with the ability to cater to multiple energy sources. The application of multiport converter topologies aims at tackling such challenges and offers a way to integrate many RES with a capability to achieve maximum efficiency and reliability. However, research has revealed that there are inherent limitations to component efficiency and size, and that there is always the need for innovative designs that can work around such inefficiencies (Rehman et al., 2017). Lastly, the iterative process of topology design solutions generally has resource and cost constraints. Optimizing topology to an ideal point demands reconciling performance parameters against practical considerations such as manufacturing cost and material limitations. There are compromises in high-performance designs at the cost of either cost or complexity. Furthermore, testing and verification of new topologies take lots of time and money, thus making the design process more complicated. With emerging technologies that emerge to counteract existing limitations, effective implementation is not only dependent on sound understanding of theoretical principles but also on efficient management of resources. This multidisciplinary tack to topology design, taking into account economic as well as practical considerations, is key to developing solutions that suit the changing needs of contemporary systems.

8.6.1. Technical Challenges in Implementation

Implementing new topology architectures is fraught with many technical problems that significantly impair the efficiency and reliability of systems. Scalability is one of the main issues. As the number of devices in a network increases, particularly with the proliferation of the Internet of Things (IoT), existing routing architectures struggle to maintain performance.

This stress manifests in terms of increased routing table sizes and issues with packet delivery reliability, causing congestion as well as potential data loss. Various schemes like Location-Based Forwarding and ID-based routing have been suggested in an attempt to counter these effects; however, they tend to fall short of offering comprehensive solutions. Efficiently solving scalability is not merely a matter of applying advanced routing techniques but also requires redesigning the networks underlying structure to accommodate development by doubling in size without compromising operational integrity (Williams et al., 2017). The second serious problem lies in the dynamic nature of topology design in smart grids. Compared to traditional electric power systems, where generation and supply are the primary issue, smart grids introduce advanced interactions between a vast number of controllable devices, incorporating complexity layers. Physical infrastructure and information network co-evolution necessitates topology implementation by a dynamic approach, in which electrical and data flows are managed simultaneously.

This sophistication is the origin of emergent behavior such as synchronization failure and cascade effects that can greatly degrade the grids performance. Research indicates that incorporating models that are cognizant of the multilayered nature of these systems are the essential ingredients to understanding and controlling their dynamics in the right manner.

Thus, the use of effective topology for smart grids is not only based on sophisticated computational models but also on inter-disciplinary views encompassing both engineering and systems theory (Baptista et al., 2014). Finally, operational dependability is a priority in the practical implementation of innovative topology models. After being implemented, unforeseen fault may happen due to environmental change, software defects, or hardware defects. These are issues that demand the creation of robust testing frameworks that can simulate diverse operating environments before they are even deployed. System ability to respond to cybersecurity attacks is also of crucial importance, especially with topology designs becoming more intertwined with digital networks. The fast evolution of threats and weaknesses in systems under connectivity necessitates a good system design flexibility with the capability to adapt with changing risks. As a result, the route to successful deployment is not simply a technical issue but a means of building proactive measures to avoid inevitable interruptions and achieve long-term dependability in actual practice (Williams et al., 2017; Baptista et al., 2014) (Figure 8.12).

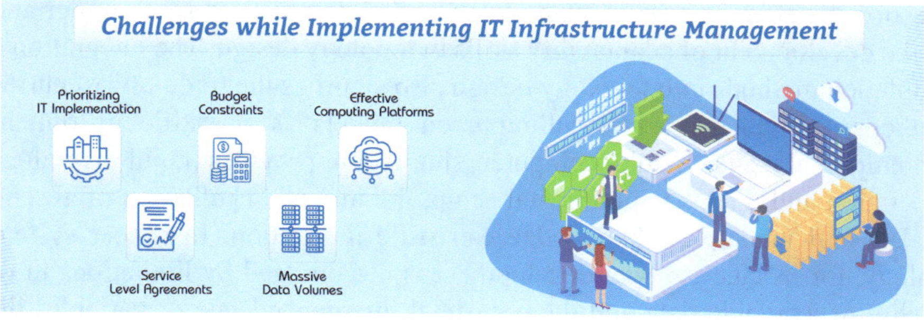

Figure 8.12. *Technical challenges in implementation.*

Source: https://www.fidelsoftech.com/news-and-blogs/wp-content/uploads/2023/01/challenges-implementing-IT-infrastructure-management.jpg.

8.6.2. Limitations of Current Methodologies

The topology design approaches analysis reveals significant limitations inbuilt in available designs, particularly in their ability to respond to dynamic and complex systems. The traditional methods prefer fixed schemas that fail to include the dynamism of environments in reality, where change is incessant and drastic. A system's scientific guide, as outlined in research focused on in the IST/ FET forward-looking initiative on GLOBAL COMPUTING, necessitates a move away from conventional data manipulation and towards coordination and interaction among independent components in a networked system. These kinds of methodologies frequently disregard the unique behaviors of computational objects varying in time and space, and therefore their application in the modern flexible systems where responsiveness and responsiveness are of the utmost importance is limited (Priami et al., 2003). As a result, existing models are likely to provide rigid designs unsuitable for adaptation to unforeseen variations and adaptive problems. Moreover, the application of incomplete information poses additional limitations for modern topology design methodologies. The rapid progression of information technology leads to data relevance degradation, a particular challenge for system designers wishing to capitalize on dependability in their systems. Based on current research on computing paradigms, these limitations can impede the construction of systems that require updates and revisions according to shifting environmental conditions in a timely and effective way. The majority of methodologies overlook the necessity for sound mechanisms for processing and acquiring real-time data, which is vital for achieving resilience in system performance (Priami et al., 2003). Consequently, designs may fail under the pressure of unexpected variables, which calls into question the effectiveness of methodologies that do not place much importance on the development of adaptability skills in topology design. The integration of simulation methods into topology design also signifies the trade-offs of current methods, particularly when calling upon models as scientific instruments for empirical tests. While computer simulation provides rapid hypothesis generation and directs experimental setup, the intrinsic challenges of absence of data and incomplete knowledge can stifle innovation. In cancer systems biology, for instance, model development is discouraged by limitations in the fidelity of available data and the nontrivial interdependence of variables that cannot be disregarded. These are more generic problems within current models that fall short in bridging the gap between theoretical constructs and practical uses. Responding to the challenge of demanding simulation requirements over interactive, dynamic visualization requires advanced methodologies that can facilitate multi-scale interactions and ensure models not only to be biologically plausible but also maintain their applicability to real situations. All these innovations are critical in overcoming the limitations of existing topology design approaches.

8.6.3. Future Research and Development Directions

As the field of topology design progresses, the need for innovative approaches to optimization grows increasingly apparent. Through research in the future, Computer-Aided Innovation (CAI) can be combined with Product Lifecycle Management (PLM) through sophisticated Optimization Systems. When resolving geometrical conflicts—advanced problems which fall under the TRIZ methodology—scientists would find it possible to enhance design efficiency and adaptability. The recent developments suggest that solutions obtained from topological optimizations can be adapted into personalized modeling features specifically designed for specific design tasks. Such innovations have the promise to not only settle issues of geometry clashes but also rationalize the design process to make it easier to use and more intuitive. The finding of effective density combination methods gives ground knowledge for creating varied structures in architecture and engineering, indicating a promising avenue for topology design and optimization techniques to be further researched (Cascini et al., 2009). Future research may utilize the synergy of robotics and computational approaches as another research area in topology design. The new discipline of robotic extrusion of space has already shown powerful means of extruding intricate 3D truss forms. However, there are ongoing challenges faced in planning robot motions and extrusion sequences in automation, especially for unconstrained topologies of structures. Future research must be ready to challenge these obstacles stringently by way of hierarchical planning frameworks. This new methodology would attempt to decouple sequence and motion planning to facilitate efficient solving of complex spatial truss configurations. Through the investigation of these more advanced computational techniques, researchers can assist in pushing fabrication techniques forward, paving the way for new structures that are both stable and aesthetically pleasing (Garrett et al., 2019). In addition to breaking through current barriers, promoting interdisciplinarity will be essential to forging topology design's future. Collaboration between material scientists, engineers, and computational designers across disciplines can facilitate fundamental knowledge of material behavior and performance under a range of conditions. Integrating these aspects can enhance the understanding of how various materials can be caused to interact with intricate topologies, enabling the design of more efficient and resilient structures. Interdisciplinary research will also guide the creation of novel algorithms and computational tools that are more appropriate to address the particular demands of contemporary design challenges. By shared experience, academia and industry can join together to push the frontiers of topology design, exploring new vistas that are born out of inter-disciplinary fusion, permitting an integrated path to design and construction.

SUMMARY

As one synthesizes the array of case studies represented throughout this essay, it is apparent that topology design is a vital lens through which to understand the dynamic interaction between technology and society. The analysis of these cases is oriented towards the emergent properties of relations developed through socio-technical interactions, wherein one observes theory and practice merge as they act within real-world environments. This convergence is further emphasized by initiatives like the Game of ANT, which indicates the interactive potential of technologies as a means of interacting with theoretical ideas more vigorously (Paoli et al., 2018). Such initiatives not only enrichen the learning experience but also affirm that topology is no longer merely a theory but a crucial instrument for dissecting the multilateral relations present in human and non-human relations in the contemporary world. Furthermore, the analysis of topological conceptions within technology reveals the necessity of adopting a discerning lens through which to view the implications of technological advancements. As digital technologies proliferate, they enable both innovative and reductive interpretations of socio-technical relations. For instance, while some applications of topology have spurred a more engaged conceptualization of technology as a plural construction, others persist in supporting outdated understandings of technological determinism (Marres et al., 2025). Such critical consideration of topology requires scholars to challenge simplistic thoughts of technological impact, enabling more evolved analyses that consider the richness of contemporary social arrangements. Thus, the call for more involvement with topological ideas is not merely speculative; it is required for a proper answer to the social impact of emerging technologies. In short, the case studies in topology design overall is a sound argument for employing interdisciplinarity wherein mathematical rigor is integrated with pragmatic engagement. The multiple meanings of topology in these studies suggest that it can function both as a critique tool as well as a method for developing new design practice. By employing the tools and concepts of topology, researchers, practitioners, and educators have the ability to understand the intricate relationship between technological advancements and social processes. Lastly, the ongoing development of topological strategies will play a significant role in shaping our understanding of future socio-technical environments. To the future, the development of critical conversation will be central to leveraging topology as a means of analysis as well as design, shaping adaptive and accountable technologies that resonate with the complexity of our globalizing world.

In investigating the intricate relationship between topology and biochemical signal cascades, new research results offer pivotal information as to how structural features influence physiological responses. To that effect, research into four-layered phosphorelays has indicated that the type of signal-response relationship is not haphazard; rather, it is strongly determined by the kinetic rates of phosphorylation and hydrolysis reactions. This groundbreaking paper delineates a set of mathematical requirements that can accurately predict how these interactions take place, and suggest that altering certain parameters, for example, total protein concentration, in the relay dynamically alters the response features. These discoveries emphasize the inherent significance of topology for explaining and potentially designing intricate biological phenomena, opening the door to advances in synthetic biology and therapeutic goals (Cardelli et al., 2013). Moreover, graph theory approaches applied to biology have also opened new avenues of inquiry to explore the complexity of biomolecular networks. Centrality measures and network motif analysis by researchers have offered greater understanding of the structural as well as functional dynamics of cell interactions. These approaches not only show the hierarchical nature of biological systems but also emergent properties developed through such complex association. This methodological strategy enables researchers to establish correlations between structural properties and dynamic behaviors, as evidenced in reports regarding synchronization phenomena and disease transmission in networks. As graph theory continues to increase its presence in the biological sciences, it is a badge of honor for the vital role topology plays in interpreting the underlying biological processes (Mason et al., 2006). The convergence of evidence from both graph theoretical analysis and phosphorelays is noteworthy for emphasizing the pivotal role of topology in biological systems. Not only does this improve our understanding of signal transduction, but also the model that can be created to simulate biological interactions and forecast outcomes through structural changes. Notably, the ability to predict response dynamics from known outcomes validates the relevance of topological properties in evolutionary biology. Such predictive approaches could revolutionize network design in the synthetic systems, where topology is being engineered for desired phenotypic results. Overall, these advances are reflective of profound conclusions in topology design with applicability for broad use in theoretical insight into biological systems as well as practical application in biotechnology and medicine, reflecting the potential for innovation in the discipline (Cardelli et al., 2013; Mason et al., 2006).

REFERENCES

1. Abbass, H. A., Baker, S., Bender, A., Fan, Z., et al. (2008). Network topology and time criticality effects in the modularized fleet mix problem. https://core.ac.uk/download/pdf/87230.pdf (accessed on 9th September 2025).
2. Alaeddini, A., Mesbahi, M., & Morgansen, K. (2017). Adaptive communication networks with privacy guarantees. http://arxiv.org/abs/1704.01188 (accessed on 9th September 2025).
3. Alam, A., Beck, B., Bhatt, A., Biedl, T., Borkin, M., et al. (2016). The state of the art in cartograms. http://arxiv.org/abs/1605.08485 (accessed on 9th September 2025).
4. Alderson, D., Doyle, J. C., Li, L., & Willinger, W. (2005). Understanding Internet topology: Principles, models, and validation. https://core.ac.uk/download/4870423.pdf (accessed on 9th September 2025).
5. Ames, A., Diaz-Mercado, Y., Egerstedt, M., Feron, E., et al. (2016). Safe, remote-access swarm robotics research on the Robotarium. https://core.ac.uk/download/211387956.pdf (accessed on 9th September 2025).
6. Andrews, P. S., Bown, J. L., Deeni, Y. Y., Goltsov, A., et al. (2012). Engineering simulations for cancer systems biology. https://core.ac.uk/download/228177087.pdf (accessed on 9th September 2025).
7. Asghari, V., Cheriet, M., Lemieux, Y., Moghaddam, M., et al. (2017). A Monte-Carlo approach to lifespan failure performance analysis of the network fabric in modular data centers. http://arxiv.org/abs/1401.7528 (accessed on 9th September 2025).
8. Azanaw, G. (2025). Quantum–classical synergies in topology optimization for 3D-printed UHPC bridge structures: A critical review of computational paradigms, sustainability metrics, and scalability barriers. *International Journal of Emerging Science and Engineering*. https://www.semanticscholar.org/paper/3a448ecb12b85bc7afc78a75287ae6ac77f8f5bf (accessed on 9th September 2025).
9. Baptista, M. S., Cardieri, P., Latva-aho, M., Nardelli, P. H. J., et al. (2014). Models for the modern power grid. http://arxiv.org/abs/1401.0260 (accessed on 9th September 2025).
10. Barresi, L., Ozer, B., Bosca, A., Brest, J., Chouvenc, D., Curteanu, S., et al. (2012). Freeze-drying modeling and monitoring using a new neuro-evolutive technique. https://core.ac.uk/download/pdf/11426544.pdf (accessed on 9th September 2025).

11. Behjat, A., Chidambaran, S., & Chowdhury, S. (2018). Multi-criteria evolution of neural network topologies: Balancing experience and performance in autonomous systems. http://arxiv.org/abs/1807.07979 (accessed on 9th September 2025).

12. Biancolini, M. E., Cella, U., Chiappa, A., Coppotelli, G., Della Vecchia, P., Giorgetti, F., Groth, C., et al. (2018). Structural validation of a realistic wing structure: The RIBES test article. https://core.ac.uk/download/196295678.pdf (accessed on 9th September 2025).

13. Bowers, J., Desmarais, B. A., Frederickson, M., Ichino, N., et al. (2018). Models, methods and network topology: Experimental design for the study of interference. http://arxiv.org/abs/1601.00992 (accessed on 9th September 2025).

14. Cardelli, L., Feliu, E., Kothamachu, V. B., Soyer, O. S., et al. (2013). Phosphorelays provide tunable signal processing capabilities for the cell. https://core.ac.uk/download/18327729.pdf (accessed on 9th September 2025).

15. Cascini, G., Cugini, U., Frillici, F. S., Rotini, F., et al. (2009). Computer-aided conceptual design through TRIZ-based manipulation of topological optimizations. https://core.ac.uk/download/139012.pdf (accessed on 9th September 2025).

16. Casetti, C., Chiaraviglio, L., Chiasserini, C. F., Malandrino, F., et al. (2019). Planning UAV activities for efficient user coverage in disaster areas. https://core.ac.uk/download/234928144.pdf (accessed on 9th September 2025).

17. Chilton, J., Elnokaly, A., & Wilson, R. (2002). Environmental aspects of tensile membrane enclosed spaces. https://core.ac.uk/download/17353406.pdf (accessed on 9th September 2025).

18. Colle, D., De Maesschalck, A. S., Demeester, P., Groebbens, K., et al. (2011). Logical topology design for IP rerouting: ASONs versus static OTNs. https://core.ac.uk/download/55843534.pdf (accessed on 9th September 2025).

19. De Paoli, S., & Minniti, S. (2018). Learning by gaming: ANT and critical making. https://core.ac.uk/download/228178464.pdf (accessed on 9th September 2025).

20. De Poorter, E., Fortuna, C., Moerman, I., Skraba, A., et al. (2016). Data driven wireless network design: A multi-level modeling approach. https://core.ac.uk/download/84042270.pdf (accessed on 9th September 2025).

21. Deng, L., Hu, W., Li, G., Pei, J., et al. (2018). Enabling controlling complex networks with local topological information. https://core.ac.uk/download/289166503.pdf (accessed on 9th September 2025).

22. Elnokaly, A., & Elseragy, A. (2006). 'Appropriateness' of the use of tensile membrane structures in hot arid regions. https://core.ac.uk/download/17353400.pdf (accessed on 9th September 2025).
23. Garrett, C. R., Huang, Y., & Mueller, C. T. (2019). Automated sequence and motion planning for robotic spatial extrusion of 3D trusses. http://arxiv.org/abs/1810.00998 (accessed on 9th September 2025).
24. Hoffmann, D. S. (2015). The dawn of mathematical biology. https://core.ac.uk/download/228911655.pdf (accessed on 9th September 2025).
25. Hoyle, B. S. (2005). A schema for generic process tomography sensors. https://core.ac.uk/download/58768.pdf (accessed on 9th September 2025).
26. Hřebík, R., & Kukal, J. (2019). Anomalous and traditional diffusion modelling in SOM learning. https://core.ac.uk/download/287889404.pdf (accessed on 9th September 2025).
27. Iqbal, H., & Znati, T. (2009). On the design of clean-slate network control and management plane. https://core.ac.uk/download/12214624.pdf (accessed on 9th September 2025).
28. Jana, R., Kumar, R., Liu, Y., Margolies, R., et al. (2017). WiLiTV: A low-cost wireless framework for live TV services. http://arxiv.org/abs/1701.02669 (accessed on 9th September 2025).
29. Jiang, J., Luo, Q., Xu, Z., Li, H., & Gao, C. (2025). Enhanced reliability assessment in distribution network planning via optimal double Q strategy with explicit topology-variable consideration. *Radio Engineering*. https://www.semanticscholar.org/paper/d39d01832dfcbbfc2c7111cb1972a88b4f693386 (accessed on 9th September 2025).
30. Kabir, S., Papadopoulos, Y., Sharvia, S., Walker, M., et al. (2015). Model-based dependability analysis: State-of-the-art, challenges and future outlook. https://core.ac.uk/download/151160986.pdf (accessed on 9th September 2025).
31. Kameshwar, K., Kundur, D., No, J., Olshevsky, A., Pai, M., & Ulbig, A. (2017). Optimal topology design for disturbance minimization in power grids. http://arxiv.org/abs/1703.00558 (accessed on 9th September 2025).
32. Koc, Y., Kumar, T., Raman, A., Warnier, M., et al. (2015). Structural vulnerability analysis of electric power distribution grids. http://arxiv.org/abs/1506.08641 (accessed on 9th September 2025).
33. Kwok, A., Quintana, A., Naylor, A. M., Roberts, B. P., Yu, C., Schwieters, C. D., Brown, C. W., et al. (2017). Practical computational toolkits for dendrimers and dendrons structure design. https://core.ac.uk/download/287581216.pdf (accessed on 9th September 2025).

34. Li, L., Back, S. I., Ma, J., Guo, Y., Galeandro-Diamant, T., & Clénet, D. (2025). Bayesian optimization and machine learning for vaccine formulation development. *PLOS One, 20*. https://www.semanticscholar.org/paper/07d81cbf4f3bd44d6d056ac85e97b136d34a8f3b (accessed on 9th September 2025).
35. Lkadi, O., Nassraoui, M., & Bouksour, O. (2024). The effect of generative design and topology optimization on the design and manufacturing of components in additive manufacturing. *Incertitudes et Fiabilité des Systèmes Multiphysiques*. https://www.semanticscholar.org/paper/188d35a774b3a309167d7b1d0d914f0f95c16f3d (accessed on 9th September 2025).
36. Macaluso, I., Musumeci, F., Nag, A., Rottondi, C., et al. (2018). An overview on application of machine learning techniques in optical networks. https://core.ac.uk/download/224788320.pdf (accessed on 9th September 2025).
37. Marres, N. (2025). On some uses and abuses of topology in the social analysis of technology (Or the problem with smart meters). https://core.ac.uk/download/9656943.pdf (accessed on 9th September 2025).
38. Mason, O., & Verwoerd, M. (2006). Graph theory and networks in biology. https://core.ac.uk/download/297011475.pdf (accessed on 9th September 2025).
39. Morley, J., & Rana, S. (2002). Surface networks. https://core.ac.uk/download/1668899.pdf (accessed on 9th September 2025).
40. Moura, J. M. F., & Kar, S. (2007). Sensor networks with random links: Topology design for distributed consensus. http://arxiv.org/abs/0704.0954 (accessed on 9th September 2025).
41. Oxman, R. (2010). Digital tectonics as a morphogenetic process. http://hdl.handle.net/10251/6959 (accessed on 9th September 2025).
42. Ozawa, T., Price, H. M., Amo, A., Goldman, N., Hafezi, M., Lü, L., Rechtsman, M. C., et al. (2019). Topological photonics. *Reviews of Modern Physics, 91*. https://doi.org/10.1103/revmodphys.91.015006 (accessed on 9th September 2025).
43. Priami, C. (2003). *Proceedings of International Workshop "Global Computing: Programming Environments, Languages, Security and Analysis of Systems."* https://core.ac.uk/download/11829018.pdf (accessed on 9th September 2025).
44. Rehman, Z. (2017). Multiport power electronics circuitry for integration of renewable energy sources in low power applications: A thesis presented in partial fulfilment of the requirements for the degree of Doctor of

Philosophy in Electrical Engineering at Massey University, Palmerston North, New Zealand. https://core.ac.uk/download/148645579.pdf (accessed on 9th September 2025).

45. Sobester, A., Stanescu, C., & Tudose, L. (2011). Improving machine dynamics via geometry optimization.
46. Srinivas, G. L., Alshawabkeh, M., & Brandstötter, M. (2024). Design and development of Fin-Ray finger using topology optimization with multiple load cases. *2024 International Conference on Cognitive Robotics and Intelligent Systems (ICC - ROBINS)*. https://www.semanticscholar.org/paper/c758d61111f0d709f6e3ebe7805cfd48c15e14a8 (accessed on 9th September 2025).
47. Sun, D., Yang, X., Liu, H., & Yang, H. (2025). BESO topology optimization driven by an ABAQUS-MATLAB cooperative framework with engineering applications. *Applied Sciences*. https://www.semanticscholar.org/paper/6f36981385309188cfa85722df37d314dd2fcdbe (accessed on 9th September 2025).
48. Usama, M., & Lee, I. Y. (2022). Data-driven non-linear current controller based on deep symbolic regression for SPMSM. *Sensors (Basel, Switzerland), 22*. https://www.semanticscholar.org/paper/5b39e310a7b4c2f491b43aff18907ae2dfe68519 (accessed on 9th September 2025).
49. Vahdat, A., Bu, T., Krioukov, D., Dorogovtsev, S. N., Erdős, P., Fraigniaud, P., Gkantsidis, C., et al. (2006). Systematic topology analysis and generation using degree correlations. http://arxiv.org/abs/cs/0605007 (accessed on 9th September 2025).
50. Vahdat, A., Chang, H., Dimitropoulos, X., Krioukov, D., Erdős, P., Gao, L., et al. (2009). Graph annotations in modeling complex network topologies. http://arxiv.org/abs/0708.3879 (accessed on 9th September 2025).
51. Wang, Z., & Wang, X. (2025). Quantum-classical hybrid genetic evolutionary algorithm for topology optimization of continuum structures. *International Journal for Numerical Methods in Engineering*. https://www.semanticscholar.org/paper/6bcb2b7903f384d5c853b137a6277fa3ef7c0bc2 (accessed on 9th September 2025).
52. Williams, A. C. (2017). The design and implementation of a PCIe-based LESS label switch. https://core.ac.uk/download/213463241.pdf (accessed on 9th September 2025).
53. Wright, A. J., Bunschoten, A., Postma, B., Gerber, B. O., de Haas, C. J. C., Stotz, C. E., et al. (2010). A peptide mimic of the chemotaxis inhibitory protein of *Staphylococcus aureus*: Towards the development of novel anti-inflammatory compounds. https://core.ac.uk/download/16458595.pdf (accessed on 9th September 2025).

CHAPTER 9

TOOLS AND TECHNIQUES FOR TOPOLOGY SIMULATION

Contents

INTRODUCTION

Topological simulation has witnessed remarkable velocity in recent years as it has been at the core of numerous scientific and engineering disciplines. The demand has been fueled by the need to simulate complicated systems with accuracy, be it communications, materials science, or social networks. The innovative instruments and techniques applied in topology simulation enable scientists to examine and control the intricate interactions between such systems; thus, gaining a more advanced comprehension of their workings and behaviors. By integrating traditional computational methodologies with leading-edge analytical systems, researchers can model topological designs to unprecedented levels of complexity and accuracy, as evident from the changing dynamics in artificial intelligence and machine learning technologies enhancing simulation processes. Further, the convergence of diverse technologies also presents specific challenges and opportunities for topology simulation. For instance, technological advancements in communication technology and materials and things (IoT) have equipped researchers with a method of linking distinct objects physically, hence enabling more sophisticated and interactive simulated environments. This linking not only facilitates real-time data analysis but also smartens decision-making processes as it presents actionable insights from intricate data. The ability to model and analyze topological information of interrelated systems also emphasizes the importance of effective protocols and designs that enable software and hardware elements to interoperate. The capability to understand these systems further enhances the potential for the manufacture of more precise simulations with broader usage in various disciplines, making topology simulation an essential field of study today. As the area of topology simulation also advances, it is worth mentioning the part played by techniques that are more advanced when it comes to streamlining such simulations for better performance. Tools like Squeeze-and-Excitation Networks are leading in such innovations, emphasizing the part hierarchical encodings play in significantly enhancing representational capacity when it comes to simulations. Through adjusting feature responses as well as mapping interdependencies, these techniques ensure that the worlds simulated have a better representation of real-world interactions and events. The synergy of these new approaches and the traditional ones is the basis for a comprehensive toolbox that scientists can rely on in creating robust, scalable, and efficient topology simulations. Through collaboration with these new tools, not only is innovation sparked but also scientists are empowered with the capacity to tackle the intricacies that accompany current scientific inquiry.

Definition of Topology Simulation

A detailed understanding of topology simulation is required in simulating complex systems in all areas of science. Essentially, topology simulation revolves around the modeling of objects of interest and their interactions via graph-like models. It is through this process that scientists are able to view the interaction and dynamics within a network, a very critical aspect in fields like biology, where interaction among genes, proteins, and metabolites is studied in detail. The ability to influence and analyze such topological representations enables the identification of key elements that determine system behavior. According to relevant literature, the topology provides the schema that represents the biology taking place beneath the networks accurately, enabling the simulations with the ability to predict experimental results (Karperien et al., 2014). Such simulations not only facilitate the understanding of existing systems but also in creating new interactions, and thus the importance of topology simulation in the methods of contemporary research. In addition to representing relations, topology simulation is also core in model-refinement iterative process. Whenever discrepancies are faced between simulated predictions and actual observations, researchers are often left at a crossroads.

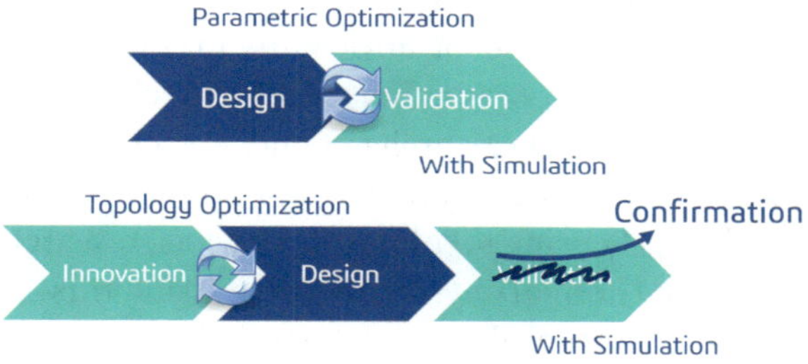

Figure 9.1. *Understand of topology simulation.*

Source: https://blog-assets.solidworks.com/uploads/sites/2/2019/10/image1-1.png.

On the one hand, modifications to its parameter models might make it a more accurate predictor. On the other hand, updating the topology to account for new interactions and components is usually an appealing option. The challenge lies in finding a balance, since too many updates can sabotage the model's simplicity and ease of use. Specifically for biological modeling, as commented in the ANIMO setting, inserting hypothetical nodes and edges can create a burdensome structure harder to manage analytically (Karperien et al., 2014). This point makes researchers seek improved parameter tuning prior to turning to radical topology adjustments, stressing the intricate interplay among theory, practice, and computational demands. Moreover, the use of nature's teachings has emerged as a key field in topology simulation methodology development. Nature, with its intricate but often failure-resistant patterns, offers plenty of design concepts to draw from for model development. For instance, studies on self-organizing patterns in trees and biological forms reveal a principle by which structure shapes minimize material use to the utmost and maximize strength, a principle suited to simulation approaches. By computing such natural philosophies, scientists can apply better algorithms for simulating growth and adaptation in engineered systems. These bio-inspired methods not only accelerate the efficiency of topology simulations but also promote sustainability by reducing resource utilization in designs. As the subject develops, ongoing study of natural phenomena also offers creative new means to further topology simulation practices and methodologies (Figure 9.1).

Importance of Topology in Various Fields

Topology is an overarching structure to numerous various areas of science, and it provides profound understanding of structure and behavior in complex systems. In physics, for example, topology finds application when studying various phases of material, how materials can possess various properties based on only their geometry. This is evident sufficiently in condensed matter physics, where topological insulators possess unique electronic characteristics which are immune to disorder. This kind of research not only extends our understanding of material science but also paves the way for quantum computation and information technology applications. By using topological concepts, researchers can explore phenomena that transcend normal physics, building an interdisciplinary dialogue that enhances both fundamental theory and applied utilization. In cosmology, topology helps to shed light on the structure of the universe at a large scale, significantly contributing to our knowledge of galaxy formation and evolution. By applying advanced topological structures like the Morse-Smale complex, researchers have been able to visualize and characterize cosmic filaments that cover this enormous distance. These filaments are pivotal in understanding the distribution of matter in the universe, where dense regions and voids are determined. Tools such as the Felix framework allow simple querying and visualization of these filaments, which allow further advanced examination of the cosmic web. Since the filaments are seen to extend over a very varying density range, novel means of good visualization and analysis are needed (Bos et al., 2015). The use of topology in cosmology not only enhances data interpretation but also reveals inherent patterns that were previously concealed. Furthermore, topology becomes of enormous significance in molecular modeling, particularly in the design and optimization of complex macromolecules such as dendrimers. These hyperbranched topologies possess unique topological characteristics that influence how they engage with biological systems. Computational methods employed in molecular simulation provide scientists the possibility of predicting patterns of interaction at a molecular level, which is crucial while designing effective drug delivery systems. It has been reported that parameter adjustment such as dendrimer size and surface topography can enhance their efficacy as drug carriers, capable of targeted and effective therapy (Buhleier et al., 2014). Furthermore, the application of topological concepts in the description of molecular interaction increases our knowledge of biophysical phenomena with useful implications for experimental design as well as therapeutic application. This confluence of topology and molecular biology illustrates the universality and fundamental character of topological analysis across the fields.

Overview of Tools and Techniques

In understanding the methods and tools employed in topology simulation, it is important to value the fundamental role that topology control algorithms play in communication networks. Topology control algorithms optimize network topologies to ensure both efficiency and connectivity, reacting to the ever-changing nature of real-world environments. Because nodes of a network are frequently joining, leaving, or moving, these algorithms must operate incrementally and evolve with changes as they occur. Graphical programming languages and specification tools are essential tools applied in modeling such adaptations, through which researchers are able to specify certain constraints for consistency and optimization. Using a visual graph transformation methodology, as described in Hollick et al. (2017), developers are able to create stable topology control algorithms that guarantee required performance as well as satisfying specified requirements, and thereby facilitate topological breakthroughs in network simulation. Furthermore, automation and synthesis of physical geometry in topology simulation is attractive to other distinct analog circuit layout challenges. Analog layouts have fewer standardized methods and automation compared to digital layouts owing to the subtle handling of continuous variables and signal behavior. Recent research identifies methodologies developed to address specific challenges in analog circuit topology and how these can be applied to guide best practices in topology simulation. By examining what has already been written, it is clear that many general techniques, as outlined in Rentmeesters et al. (1990), can be applied to tackle topological problems even though full levels of automation are not achieved. This indicates that considerable progress has been made, yet the intricacies of analog systems mean that further investigation and development of tools and methods is essential. Finally, the convergence of programming environments such as simulation software and design automation systems is crucial to ensuring the highest level of effectiveness for topology simulation. These software systems enable detailed modeling and experimentation, providing insight into what the various topologies can perform in a variety of situations. Visual graph transformation and constraint programming-based software enables researchers not only to model topologies but also to optimize them based on outlined specifications. By employing such advanced modeling techniques, network designers are able to evaluate performance on their topologies in real-time, supporting incremental optimization that is critically important in dynamic environments. Ensuring balance between responsiveness and efficiency at design and simulation steps is crucial, wherefore, as hinted in Hollick et al. (2017), a comprehensive methodology to topology design in computer networks is warranted (Figure 9.2).

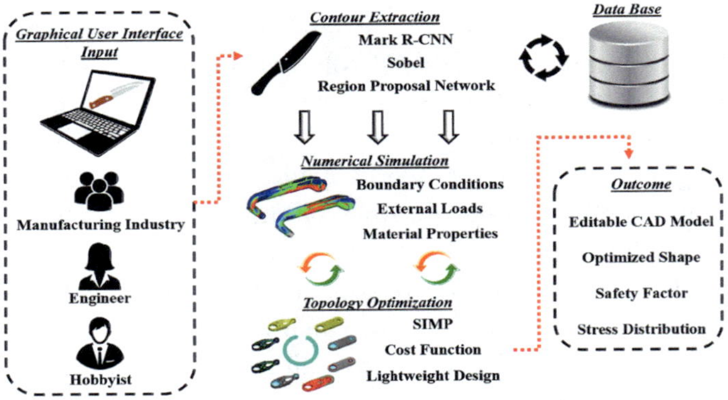

Figure 9.2. *The tools and techniques employed in topology simulation.*

Source: https://www.mdpi.com/jmmp/jmmp-08-00285/article_deploy/html/images/jmmp-08-00285-g001-550.jpg.

9.1. HISTORICAL BACKGROUND OF TOPOLOGY SIMULATION

The background to topology simulation goes way back into the initial history of system analysis and computational modeling when scientists wanted to describe complex network behaviors using various simulation methods. Initially, discrete-event simulations were prevalent owing to their relative achievement in modeling systems with sporadic state change, such as telecommunications networks. These early methods provide the basis for more refined understanding of network dynamics, and system dynamics methods were added in as a natural extension. With the development of the discipline, stress came to be placed on combining methodologies with hybrid model techniques that combine the advantages of discrete-event simulation with continuous system dynamics. These developments are part of a broader long-term pattern of syncretic syntheses of diverse methodologies in the expectation of enhancing analytical capability in special fields, including business and defense, where experience-based evidence suggested a growing preference for such sophisticated methodologies in practical applications, thus illuminating the historical evolution of topology simulation (Eldabi et al., 2008). As the complexity and size of networks increased, particularly with the internet and mobile communications revolution, the need for strong simulation tools increased increasingly vital. The second half of the 20th century and beginning of the 21st century witnessed substantial advances in simulation methods driven by high-level technological advances and the demand for better performance measures. It is characterized by the emergence of various simulation frameworks that offered assistance for modeling of intricate topological structures and real-time performance metrics. In particular, service-oriented traffic flow analysis was an essential part of assessing key performance indicators (KPIs) such as throughput and delay. Researchers discovered flaws in traditional discrete-event simulators, and this resulted in the development of more agile and accurate models such as the fluid flow queuing model CURSA-SQ that demonstrated near real-time performance prediction capabilities on converged networks (Escribano et al., 2019). The coupling of data science methods with simulation techniques also changed the topological simulation environment in recent times. The integration of machine learning models into simulation platforms enhances predictive modeling and enhanced decision-making capability, enabling practitioners to simulate various scenarios with greater precision. This change not only reflects the call for increasingly sophisticated analytical tools but also towards a shifting focus towards more adaptive, hybrid approaches that continually adapt to evolving network states. The ongoing progress in simulation techniques identifies a common understanding that hybrid M&S methods are essential for performance evaluations at the optimum level within newly integrated mobile-fix networks and traditional infrastructures. As we remain witnesses to improvements in computational algorithms, the historic background of topology simulation illustrates an elastic reaction towards the ever-evolving world of technology (Eldabi et al., 2008; Escribano et al., 2019).

9.1.1. Early Progress in Topology

Initial topological work laid the foundation for significant advances in mathematical modeling and simulation techniques. In the late 19th century, mathematicians such as Georg Cantor and Henri Poincaré began exploring space's properties independent of continuous transformations. To focus on qualitative properties of space instead of merely distances and angles topology defined as a distinct area of mathematics. The creation of concepts like open and closed sets, compactness, and connectedness brought about basic tools to address complex systems. These ideas were also very useful in other fields, as they provided the means to comprehend continuity and convergence. Such an early work in topology not only contributed to mathematics as such but also provided a basis for procedures later used in topology simulation, where systems needed to be analyzed through various transformations without losing their inherent characteristics. With topology's continued growth into the 20th century, the applications began to take root in several scientific disciplines, notably engineering and computer science. The use of topological concepts for applied purposes was especially induced by increasing system complexity in these fields. In particular, the need for sound engineering solutions provoked renewed attention for model-based solutions capable of predicting system behavior. From recent surveys, two paradigms of dependability analysis were considered—one for the creation of predictive failure models from system topology and the other based on design models like state automata for fault injection studies (Kabir et al., 2015). These advances bridged the gap among theoretical topology abstractions and usages, creating sophisticated simulation methods allowing for greater precision in modeling complex systems. Besides, the continuous advancements in topology have made room for automated techniques, particularly in situations where the spatial reasoning is highly intricate, such as in structural engineering and circuit design. The automation of layout methods, especially in analog integrated circuits, demonstrates how topological concepts that were developed a long time ago have been influencing technology design. The challenges associated with analog layouts, which significantly differ from digital layouts, identify the need for professional topological tools capable of efficiently addressing issues in circuit designs which are unique (Rentmeesters et al., 1990). These developments are imperative in enhancing the level of automation in topology simulation so that researchers and engineers can explore different design paradigms more conveniently. Thus, topological advancements in the initial eras not only contributed to the development of mathematical theories but also gave a boost to advanced simulation tools pivotal in contemporary technological infrastructure.

9.1.2. Evolution of Simulation Techniques

Advancements in simulation techniques have significantly transformed the topology simulation field and enabled researchers and engineers to simulate complex systems more precisely and efficiently. Early techniques made use of conventional particle or continuum models that operated irrespective of the multiscale structure that was occurring in these systems. Nevertheless, augmented computational capability along with more advanced mathematical frameworks has driven the development of advanced techniques. Network science tools are also being integrated into simulation techniques to offer deeper analysis of heterogeneous structures and to facilitate improved understanding of complex material behavior. With the growing significance of multi-dimensional data sets, these novel simulation methods are not merely transforming existing models but also leading to revolutionary leaps in materials science, especially in areas such as granular materials and their reaction to applied forces (Bassett et al., 2017). Also, the application of simulation approaches, particularly in the fields of materials science and electronics, has brought considerable improvement to design and optimization processes.

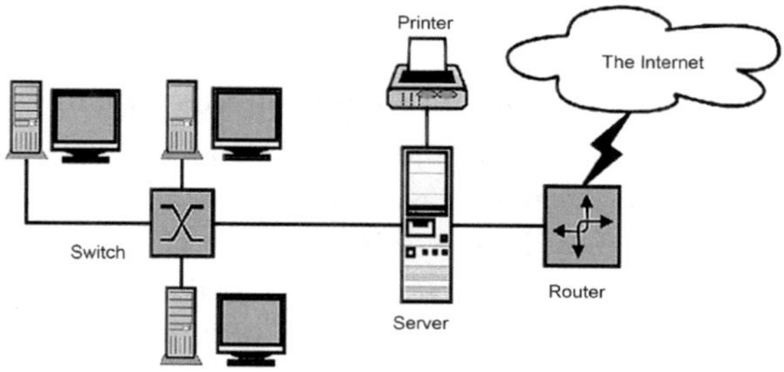

Figure 9.3. *The evolution of simulation techniques.*

Source: https://www.elprocus.com/wp-content/uploads/network.jpg.

One such instance is that the introduction of simulators based on high-level synthesis for Digital-to-Analog (D/A) and Analog-to-Digital (A/D) converters has proved the feasibility of applying simulation along with optimization techniques. MATLAB®, together with SIMULINK®, has facilitated immediate modeling of electronic equipment while enhancing the accuracy of their simulations with S-functions. This integration not only hastens the simulation process—losing valuable CPU time—but also enhances model granularity, allowing designers to estimate various subcircuits and error mechanisms with ease. Hence, the creation of simulation techniques aims at the condition that computational efficiency and model complexity coexist, signifying an important improvement in topology simulation techniques (Restituto et al., 2005). Additionally, as the simulation techniques continue to evolve, the emphasis on interdisciplinary endeavor becomes more pronounced. The intersection of various disciplines—computer science, physics, and materials engineering—has created a platform on which innovative simulation tools can flourish. The study of new paradigms not only makes it easier to understand materials at different scales, but also prompts researchers to answer open questions and construct novel methodologies. When the systems being studied are increasingly complex, demands for robust and adaptable simulation tools become unavoidable. The future studies in this direction may include the merging of machine learning and artificial intelligence algorithms, whose high potential for enhancing the performance of simulations and designing optimum variables can be utilized. The eventual future evolution of simulation techniques will transform our approaches to topology simulation, enabling us to handle the challenges inherent in more complicated systems (Bassett et al., 2017; Restituto et al., 2005) (Figure 9.3).

9.1.3. Key Milestones in Topology Simulation

Within the field of topology simulation, certain milestones can be observed that highlight the progress of tools and techniques in this dynamic sector. Perhaps the most important of these developments is the emergence of advanced computational algorithms that enable researchers to simulate complex topological entities with greater precision than ever before. These algorithms facilitate the simulation of various topological objects, which enables researchers to analyze their properties and behavior under simulated conditions. This has turned out to be particularly helpful for space exploration where topological data simulation can be useful in dealing with difficult environments, as seen in NASAs activity in the Artemis program. These projects show the extent to which potent simulation software can enhance our understanding of topological phenomena, ultimately leading to the advent of future missions that require accurate navigation and decision-making abilities within unmapped areas, thus marking a milestone in the topo simulation process (Dankanich et al., 2025). In addition, the use of machine learning techniques in topology simulation marks a milestone. It is only with the development of convolutional neural networks (CNNs) that researchers can now make predictions on a per-pixel basis for objects in simulated topological spaces. These networks, specially designed to work with data from liquid argon time projection chambers (LArTPC), demonstrate the deep learning ability of reconstructing complex topological information. For instance, the MicroBooNE experiment has already demonstrated successfully how to use CNNs in real LArTPC data, highlighting the potential of deep neural networks to make data processing easier and simulate more precise topologies. This advancement not only enhances the accuracy of simulations but also demonstrates a shift towards data-oriented research in topology study, thus solidifying the place of machine learning as a core tool in modern scientific work (Adams et al., 2018). Lastly, the establishment of multidisciplinary teams has greatly enhanced the research of topology simulation, promoting innovation and broadening research scope. Collaborations between institutions, such as the collaborations within the Marshall Space Flight Center, have led to resource, know-how, and technology consolidation, and have made possible the revolutionary development of simulation methods. By integrating knowledge across different fields of science, interdisciplinary teams have developed overall solutions that solve complex problems in topology simulation. Such partnerships not only maximize the technical ability of simulation tools but also provide a window into integrating these technologies into active applications, such as human exploration of Mars. In this way, the breakthrough highlights the importance of partnership in solidifying the tools and methods of successful topology simulation, taking the discipline towards new horizons and innovations (Dankanich et al., 2025).

9.2. SOFTWARE PACKAGES USED TO SIMULATE TOPOLOGY

The topology simulation field is highly enhanced by an array of specialized computer programs that are aimed at supporting elaborate modeling and analysis. Amongst these programs, software like OptFlux offers a structured platform for metabolic flux analysis (MFA), which plays a paramount role in deciphering cellular metabolic networks. The program plays its most important role in strain optimization, as it allows scientists to unravel key metabolic engineering targets through phenotype simulation. The capacity to simulate engagements with stoichiometric metabolism models makes OptFlux invaluable since it employs approaches such as Flux Balance Analysis (FBA) in modeling wild-type and mutant strains. The graphical user interfaces provided also enhance usability by allowing users to see simulation output, as well as the network topology that gives rise to the simulations, hence providing intuitive ability to visualize complex metabolic interactions, as outlined in Carreira et al. (2014). Yet another fundamental software to do with MetabolIc Network Ratio Analysis (MiNeRAl), which operates efficiently within OptFlux. MiNeRAl is specifically designed for assessing labeling experiments to obtain flux constraints from perturbed metabolic networks. From mass isotopomer distribution vectors of 13C-labeling experiments, the software calculates flux ratios that are fundamental in understanding metabolic pathways and interactions. MiNeRAls freedom from calculations of flux distributions renders it a viable complement to other MFA approaches. Moreover, its user-friendly interface and its ability to accommodate a broad range of metabolite fragmentation strategies, particularly those originating from GC-MS experiments, render it a useful instrument in various experimental contexts, and one that offers greater insight into the topology and function of metabolic networks, as indicated in Carreira et al. (2014). As a complement to metabolic modeling, LUNES is a gargantuan leap towards simulating huge networks within its agent-based design. The tool tries to address the issues faced in simulating large unstructured networks with numerous nodes. Compartmentalizing the tasks of topology generation, protocol simulation, and performance analysis, LUNES ensures that it can be made flexible in integrating outside tools into its design. The middleware supports sequence and parallel simulation approaches, and it demonstrates excellent performance and scalability based on its communication overhead reduction. The efficiency of LUNES has been empirically proven by simulating gossip protocols on various peer-to-peer network topologies, which exhibits its capability to process and analyze highly complex network interactions efficiently. These resources are essential for furthering the study of topology simulation, with researchers able to model and predict the behavior of complex systems as described in (Figure 9.4).

Figure 9.4. *Software tools for topology simulation.*

Source: https://networksimulationtools.com/wp-content/uploads/2020/12/Network-Simulation-Tools.png.

9.2.1. Overview of Popular Software Packages

In topology simulation, there exist various software packages that have evolved as fundamental utilities complementing both test and design phases of network planning. They are crucial for simulating complex systems where scalability and performance are determined by node-to-node interaction. For instance, Ethernet technology is applied increasingly in automotive solutions for purposes of offering high-bandwidth communication among multiple electronic control units (ECUs). As vehicular network requirements based on data rise with the future, simulation platforms can actually model situations in a real-life context and establish how target systems will respond to varied communication demands and quality of service (QoS) needs. It is of specific importance in the development of reliable in-vehicle networks to enable advanced driver assistance and autonomous vehicle systems, where they rely heavily on ensuring proper topology design for smooth integration (Korf et al., 2018). Cloud computing has also been at the forefront of constructing and running the infrastructure needed for effective topology simulation. Open-source platforms like OpenStack provide a general-purpose infrastructure for institutions to construct secure cloud infrastructures that allow distributed computing applications. The cloud deployments are vital as they allow for testing and iterative experimentation of various network configurations within a scalable and controlled environment. Organizations also benefit from the flexibility of such software packages to automate the simulation process in an attempt to facilitate faster deployment of technology necessary for modern network systems. OpenStack's compatibility with legacy systems as well as third-party solutions adds a wide-range applicability, in that it can be used for diverse academic and industrial projects that aim to enhance network performance and resilience (Al-Shaidy et al., 2017). As simulation topography's topography evolves, it is evident that the convergence of the power of software and emerging technologies will drive next-gen advancements. The integration of sophisticated simulation technologies enables experts to visualize how topology change affects overall network behavior, particularly in complex environments such as smart cities and IoT systems. In addition, the requirement for high-performance, secure simulations demonstrates a growing acknowledgement of the importance of the inclusion of security protocols in topology designs. Familiarity with these popular packages is being identified as essential for researchers as well as engineers, enabling improved understanding of not only how networks work, but how they could be designed to support future needs in an increasingly interconnected world (Korf et al., 2018; Al-Shaidy et al., 2017) (Figure 9.5).

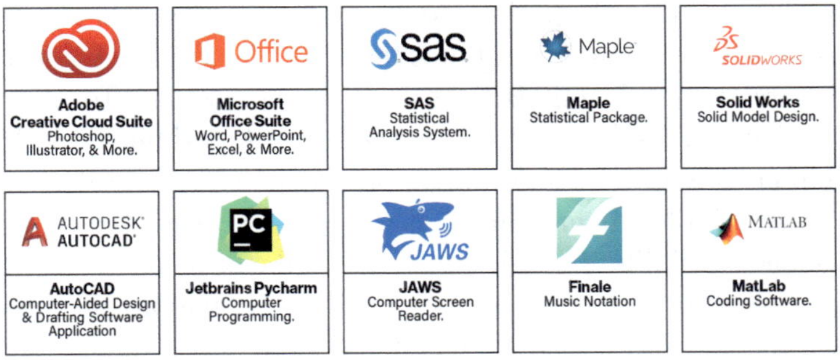

Figure 9.5. *Overview of popular software packages.*

Source: https://it.usu.edu/labs/connections/images/PopularComputerPrograms_NoLocations.png.

9.2.2. Comparison of Features and Usability

Comparison in topology simulation with regard to features and usability of alternative tools is necessary to guide researchers and practitioners to the optimal choice. Some simulators have unique functionalities such as levels of scalability, user interfaces, and inherent computational algorithms. These inconsistencies may have a significant impact on the user experience, impacting both the learning process of new users and the degree to which experienced researchers are able to conduct experiments. A thorough examination of usability will typically reveal a tradeoff between feature-rich set and accessibility, since features-rich applications may contain steep learning curves, which may deter the adoption by non-specialist users. These compromises involve precise concern with a user's research objectives, technical expertise, in the decision of a tool that will be used so that the tool is correctly matched with their project needs. Furthermore, research needs for reproducibility place closer inspection of simulation tool's ability to test results. Where many pieces of software can be used, Agosti et al. (2013) observes that researchers then end up relying on proprietary, closed-source simulators, despite open options that offer greater transparency and shared utilization among users. This is a sign of one of the large usability gaps in most popular tools, since replicability does not appear to be feasible where researchers are not able to gain access to or modify the original code. Absence of a standard procedure for confirmation of simulation results can lead to inconsistency in research findings, underscoring the greatest need for simulators to facilitate easy sharing of methods and results. The equilibrium between the vast amount of simulation power and accessibility remains one of the driving factors for guaranteeing widespread use of confirmed tools in topology simulation. Also, as topological characteristics are increasingly sophisticated, programs that provide advanced algorithms for geometry extraction and optimization are gaining traction. To this end, the Ordered Statistics Vertex Extraction and Tracing Algorithm (OSVETA) has considerable potential through providing precise judgments of the importance of vertices based on local curvature, for example, in Vasic et al. (2012). Such features enhance usability through the ability of the user to focus on the most significant aspects of geometric shapes in their simulations. Vertex ranking based on geometric significance translates to more efficient processing, allowing researchers to streamline their simulation processes without sacrificing top-notch results. Such unison of advanced technical proficiency and practical usability continues to facilitate greater innovation in the field, demonstrating that complicated algorithms may be supplemented with simple interfaces, eventually leading to a vast array of applications in topology simulation.

9.2.3. Case Studies of Software Applications

The exploration by software packages within topology simulation uncovers significant advancements with support from case studies that exhibit new design approaches. One prime instance is the development of toolkits that are specifically focused on molecular modeling, including for complex structures like dendrimers. Dendrimers are highly branched molecules with extremely complex architectures that become challenging in their synthesis as well as structural characterization.

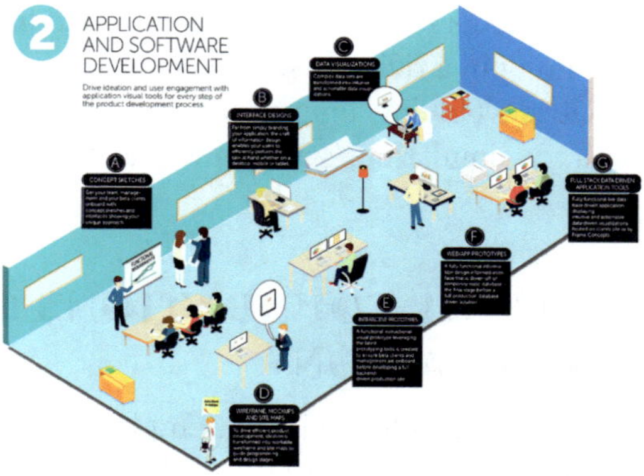

Figure 9.6. *The exploration of software applications in topology simulation.*

Source: https://home.frameconcepts.com/wp-content/uploads/2014/10/2.jpg.

The integration of molecular modeling and simulation platforms has been found to overcome these challenges. For example, novel GUI toolkits, which are written in Python, automate the building of dendrimers and produce both 2D and 3D structures efficiently. This automation streamlines the time-consuming exercise of generating complex dendrimer structures, thus to underscore the critical role of software programs in addressing topology simulation's urgent challenges, according to the recent literature (Kwok et al., 2017). This effort, at a broader level, is a manifestation of the practical use of software solutions in several hardware platforms to make computing operations more energy efficient. Through the application of task-based programming models in a heterogeneous computing system, LEGaTO aims to establish a robust software ecosystem integrated by CPUs, GPUs, FPGAs, and dataflow engines. Not only does this project establish the capability of increasing energy savings by an order of magnitude, but also uses the implementation of software tools adaptation as a case study for supporting different hardware needs. By optimizing across platforms, the project is a case study in topology simulation of the importance of flexible computer programs in computationally demanding calculations where energy is of great value (Alvarez et al., 2018). In addition, constant innovation in software programs specifically created for topology simulation marks a broader trend toward more interactive and user-focused design. As seen in the above case studies, the creation of automated programming models and toolkits is a big leap towards facilitating research and development on complex molecular structures. These advancements are not only facilitating the ease of simulation of complex topologies for researchers but also to perceive and handle the resulting data in meaningful ways. The focus on enhancing usability in such software tools facilitates increased adoption and collaboration across disciplines, resulting in a richer research environment. Eventually, these case studies emphasize developing innovative software tools to address the complexities of topology simulation, setting the stage for future innovations (Figure 9.6).

9.3. MATHEMATICAL FOUNDATIONS OF TOPOLOGY SIMULATION

Mathematical foundations of topology simulation play a significant role in the study of intricate systems in a wide range of fields like computer science, physics, and engineering. Lying at the base of these foundations is the mathematics of topological spaces that provides formal abstraction for terms like continuity, convergence, and compactness. Mathematical definition of these terms facilitates easy modeling and simulation of intricate networks and systems. For instance, the mathematics of homology and homotopy provide understanding into the mapping and classification of spaces, and these can be translated into algorithms for enhancing the simulation of topology. The development of such mathematical tools provides a sound basis upon which further research and application can be conducted so that the methods of simulation continue to be grounded in sound theoretical constructs. The integration of advanced computational techniques is in harmony with rigorous mathematical principles underpinning topology simulation. Recent works have shown the advantage of blending neural network modeling with the study of topological spaces, particularly for the decomposition of big data and the detection of patterns. The utilization of software tools such as CoCalc brings top-shelf mathematical tools into actual-world learning settings in order to shed light on intrinsic principles in mathematics and informatics. As explained in the study, the elements of neural networks are applicable in approximating complex functions, thus bridging the theoretical mathematics and computational practice. Integrative approaches, through such application, not only enhance education course curricula but also advance innovation in topology simulation, suggesting novel directions for exploration and utilization in a wide range of technical fields (Markova et al., 2018). In addition, formal verification techniques applied to ensuring integrity of the results of simulation are of most significance. Formal verification techniques provide a structured way of verifying performance of various algorithms, particularly for gossiping protocols—a demonstration of closely relevant instances of distributed computing and network interaction. Through the verification that simulated models actually describe real-world behaviors, scientists can enhance confidence of conclusions drawn on the basis of topology simulation. The process of formal verification constructs a bridge between empirical findings and theoretical abstractions, and thus establishes the mathematical foundation for such simulations. Such empirical rigor is required to establish confidence in computer simulations relying on complex mathematical framework, and thus ensuring the general acceptability of simulation techniques across various disciplines (Bakhshi et al., 2007) (Figure 9.7).

Figure 9.7. *The mathematical foundations of topology simulation.*

Source: https://media.geeksforgeeks.org/wp-content/uploads/20240402190354/Applications-of-Topology.webp.

9.3.1. Key Theorems and Concepts

The foundation under which topology simulation is based has been immensely reliant on a set of basic theorems and concepts that guide researchers in the exploration of complex space. One of the critical theorems is the homeomorphism principle, which provides a measure of determining whether two topological spaces are homeomorphic. Equivalence is pivotal to topology because it allows for the exploration of invariant properties under continuous deformations. Understanding homeomorphic spaces enables topology simulation to focus on pertinent properties independently of the exact geometry of objects. The significance of this theorem transcends several fields, including physics and computer science, where the classification of shapes and spaces forms the crux of theoretical models as well as practical applications. Apart from homeomorphism, compactness is another significant theorem in topology simulation. It is stated that a space is compact if it can be covered by a finite number of open sets, a feature highly applicable in numerous analyses. Compactness brings with it essential benefits including the simplification of sequences that converge and the assurance of continuity properties during simulations. This theorem is essential to assure stability of numerical algorithms employed in topology simulation. Additionally, compactness has the effect of minimizing computational complexity so that complex systems can be modeled successfully without full representation of all possible configurations. Consequently, the employment of compact spaces maximizes the accuracy and efficiency of topology simulation techniques automatically. The other critical concept of topology simulation is connectedness, which describes whether a space is in one piece or may be partitioned into disjoint subsets. This idea is crucial in a range of applications, including network planning and geographic information systems. Connected space enables smooth paths within simulations whereas disconnected space can be used to model fragmented systems where interactions change substantially. Successful integration of connectedness into simulations can result in a closer representation of real-world phenomena, where connectivity impacts behavior and processes. Further, understanding the relations of interlinked and non-linked regions is critical because it dictates how agents or processes evolve over time in simulations. Thus, theorems emphasize the fundamental principles that enhance the applicability and complexity of topology simulation, guiding researchers into new ways of modeling.

9.3.2. Role of Algebraic Topology

Algebraic topology is central to topology simulation because it provides mathematical constructs that allow the exploration of topological spaces. Through the application of concepts such as homology and homotopy, algebraic topology allows detection of intrinsic properties of spaces that remain constant under continuous deformations. These invariants are powerful tools employed for distinguishing among different topological structures so that scientists may classify and analyze complex geometries in a rigorous way. Additionally, the ability to investigate the global properties of spaces by algebraic methods makes it an important tool in simulations, particularly in applications where conventional geometric techniques are ineffective. With the use of these algebraic structures, scientists are capable of gaining significant information used for simulating various phenomena in theoretical and also practical contexts, thus enhancing the overall robustness and richness of topology simulation techniques. The use of algebraic topology in topology simulations has brought with it new avenues for studying complex networked systems. Recent advancements show how topological methods can be used to analyze the concealed structure of networks in order to understand dynamics of different systems, such as social networks, biological organisms, and grain materials. Scientists, through the use of algebraic topological techniques, are able to efficiently search and manage the intricate relations among nodes, yielding improved methods of distributed learning and adaptive signal modeling, as elaborated in Banelli et al. (2017). Therefore, the study of such interactions gives scientists and engineers the tools to address challenges in the modeling of high-dimensional data sets and systems that have significant variability and uncertainty. Besides, the richness of algebraic topology extends beyond theoretical study but has seen tangible applications in many scientific disciplines, including physics and computer science. Techniques borrowed from algebraic topology have been found valuable in the study of multiscale structure and material phenomena, as evidenced by research on granular materials and their inherent properties ((Bassett et al., 2017)). Such interdisciplinarity speaks to the strength and value of algebraic topology as a foundation methodology in topology simulation. As new computational techniques become accessible, the collaboration between algebraic topology and simulation processes will improve as well, with the potential to offer increasingly powerful methodologies for comprehending and communicating with complex topological structures. Such advances have the potential to do more than enhance the accuracy of simulation, but also reveal the underlying rules governing networked systems in various scientific contexts (Figure 9.8).

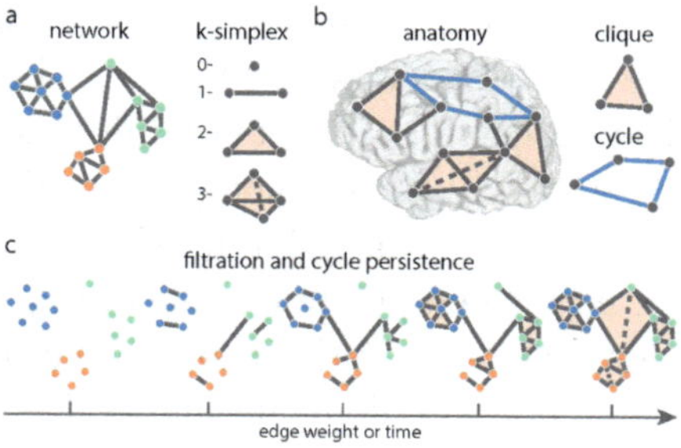

Figure 9.8. *Role of algebraic topology.*

Source: https://www.researchgate.net/profile/Ankit-Khambhati/publication/311900931/figure/fig2/AS:443380174987268@1482721479898/Tools-for-Higher-Order-Interactions-from-Algebraic-Topology-a-The-human-connectome-is.png.

9.3.3. Computational Methods in Topology

The very subtle interplay between topological science and computation has revolutionized the study of complex systems, particularly in biological networks. ANIMO is one such program that showcases the vast potential of these computer algorithms through the simulation of biological interactions with simply understood topologies. The program fills the gap between the concept of network topology and the dynamics of biological processes wherein a node represents important biological entities and edges stand for their interactions. Thus, ANIMO not only characterizes the structural properties of biological networks but also includes interaction parameters that specify the rate of such processes. When model predictions diverge from experimental findings, researchers are faced with the task of refining such models, which underscores the give-and-take nature of computational topology in which parameters are adjusted before refining the topology itself in an attempt to find balance between function and complexity within biological models (Karperien et al., 2014). Also, the field of computational topology has undergone advancement in various geometric analyses, particularly that of analog integrated circuit design. The complexities facing this discipline, including component interconnection complexity and various functionalities, are a disadvantage in traditional automated design methods. As researchers move into the realm of creating methodologies for automatic synthesis of physical geometries, they move into the realm of algorithms and techniques that assist in making the design process easier. Here, the goal is to design stable and efficient layouts that closely follow the unique needs presented by analog systems, compared to digital systems. This distinction emphasizes the complexity that goes into analog designs, with the awareness that even as advancements keep unfolding, the level of automation similar to that which has been achieved in digital design still remains elusive (Rentmeesters et al., 1990). Finally, using computational methods in topology does not just extend beyond theoretical exploration but has tangible implications in other scientific areas. As the computational landscape keeps on developing, so does the potential for future simulations to be able to model and predict behavior in intricate networks. Topological data analysis and computational geometry are two of the tools that play a key role in allowing researchers to draw valuable insights from complex data sets, leading to innovation in biological as well as technological realms. This cycle of model enhancement and tool augmentation used in topology simulation is a continuing process of feedback that stimulates innovation. In this way, the use of computational methods in the study of topology not only enhances knowledge of existing systems but also propels future research programs that may uncover new paradigms of complex system dynamics and interaction.

9.4. DATA VISUALIZATION METHODS IN TOPOLOGY

Visualization of complex topological data is critical in understanding the intricate interconnections encoded in mathematical objects. Techniques such as network visualization are of critical significance in rendering high-dimension data in a readable format. Scientists can de-sophisticate the underlying trends and patterns that would otherwise be masked in traditional forms of data by means of various visualizations. For instance, workflows created in collaboration with leading research institutions demonstrate how interactive visual analysis significantly enhances understanding in industrial automation and telecommunications. Interactive probing of the various components of the topology is facilitated by users, as they modify the choice of methods and parameters, leading to greater insights and more informed decision making in real-world scenarios (Holmgren et al., 2008). Thus, effective utilization of these visualization tools is key to researchers being able to untangle complex topological spaces. Other notable contributions in topology visualization include the utilization of advanced imaging technologies within biological science.

Figure 9.9. *Techniques for data visualization in topology.*

Source: https://www.analyticssteps.com/backend/media/thumbnail/3723983/9803950_1614245939_Data%20visualization%20(2).jpg.

As electron microscopy continues to advance, it enables researchers to observe cellular structures in three dimensions at resolutions never previously achieved. This capability not only allows for accuracy in biological simulation but also necessitates the processing of high-level image data into computational simulation representations. As an example, the conversion of segmented micrographs into watertight meshes is needed for numerical simulations that examine cellular processes utilizing methods like the Finite Element Method. The process using software packages such as GAMer 2 is a prime example of the need for merging visual data with simulation-ready formats, thus creating an improved understanding of the geometric nature behind cellular function (Amaro et al., 2019). These methods detail the integration of topology and visualization technology in the development of scientific research. Furthermore, the data visualization process interacts with topology and extends beyond representation; it is a critical tool used for hypothesis generation and testing. Visualization allows scientists to pose new questions by revealing emergent structures or patterns in the data that warrant further investigation. Visualization techniques' capacity to represent sophisticated topological interactions in terms of graphs or contour plots maximizes interpretability and thus leads to theoretical and applied sciences advances. With the advancement of data in various disciplines, the power of using robust visualization techniques assumes an ever more crucial role. As a result, incorporating new data visualization techniques not only aids in the explanation of topological data but also enables new discoveries, thereby consolidating the position of this field in the overall context of science and technology (Figure 9.9).

9.4.1. Importance of Visualization in Simulation

Accurate visualization plays a critical role in the simulation field to a very large extent improve the understanding of complex data engaged in topology simulations. Dealing with complicated structures such as the cosmic web, visualization techniques interpret computational information into graphical representations that are more understandable, facilitating perceptive analysis of intrinsic patterns and relationships. For instance, programs like Felix utilize the Morse-Smale complex to visualize filamentary structures in cosmic filaments in massive-scale cosmic simulations so that scientists may view and analyze the density and connectivity of these filaments interactively. Such visualization not only explains cosmic structure hierarchy but also allows for a complex evaluation of phenomena that could remain invisible to traditional numerical analysis, thereby highlighting the crucial role played by visualization in topology simulation studies (Bos et al., 2015). In addition, the interactive nature of visualization tools facilitates enhanced hypothesis testing and scenario analysis. In telecommunications and industrial automation, dynamic visual workflows enable users to dynamically alter parameters and views, enabling richer interaction with accessible data. Interactive design not only helps in selecting proper data sets but also allows for real-time change without knowledge of exploratory outcomes. The ability to easily traverse different levels of information enhances cognitive comprehension, particularly in networked environments where relationships are potentially multi-faceted and complex. With interactive visualization, researchers and practitioners are able to describe trends and outliers that would otherwise be obscured, lending weight to the perspective that beneficial visualization is paramount in providing valuable insights through simulation (Holmgren et al., 2008). In reality, the function of visualization in simulation is more than just the graphical rendering of data; it is an intrinsic method of interpreting and understanding data, and in the specific case of topology simulation, this is truer than ever. As the intricacy of spatial relationships and network configurations becomes greater, the mechanisms of visualization employed must also be more sophisticated if they are to remain accurate representations of the underlying data. Development and application of advanced visualization software, such as that applied in the study of cosmic filaments, provide an important platform for scientific investigation. Utilizing the visual aids makes scientists better equipped to comprehend interdependencies of elements in virtual worlds, which in turn fuels the development of theoretical comprehension as well as practical applications in various fields of scholarship (Bos et al., 2015).

9.4.2. Topological Data Visualization Tools

Visualization of topological data is a critical component of modern computational analysis, providing insight into the behavior and structure of complex systems. Various tools have been developed to assist with the process, allowing researchers to examine data sets that are high-dimensional and often abstract in character. Methods such as topological data analysis (TDA) are employed nowadays as a means to capture dense relationships in data by constructing simplicial complexes. These representations can facilitate the explanation of connectivity and spatial relationships among data points, and thus provide a better understanding of underlying patterns. For instance, a visualization system based on TDA can quantify uncertainties in network coverage, especially in sensor networks where sensor positions are not necessarily known precisely. By sufficient visualization of such uncertainties in the form of simplicial complex representations, researchers can gain insightful judgments concerning operational effectiveness as well as potential coverage faults in network scenarios (Hair et al., 2017). Apart from TDA, various other methods have been developed to enhance visualization of topological data, particularly that of alignment tensor fields. One of the significant methods involves seeding hyper streamlines for visualization of complex dynamics, such as those occurring in nematic liquid crystals. This technique derives its efficiency from the incorporation of topological ideas and practical visualization methods that avoid common failures associated with mixing hyper streamlines near orientational defects. Through the allotment within domain boundaries following a systematical manner, the hyper streamlines can project significant features of the tensor fields without incorporating iterative failures and hence offer effective visualization. This method significantly improves alignment tensor field understanding, vital in fields such as material science and physics, where information about particle orientation within a medium can make a difference in the material's properties in question (Abukhdeir et al.,

2014). Interactive visualization systems have also revolutionized the field of topological data analysis. These systems not only allow static visualizations but also provide interactive exploration of the data. By changing various parameters of the data set, say sensor positions or parameter values, researchers can gain better understanding of the topology involved. Visualization software for sensor networks in uncertainty demonstrates this application by enabling users to interact with the underlying data, exploring how coverage varies as sensor configurations differ. Interactive investigation results in an improved understanding of the topological properties in play and therefore helps real-world application from robotics to environmental monitoring. Lastly, the creation of visualization methods and tools in topology simulation can attest to the importance of effective data representation in underpinning well-informed decision-making and scientific understanding in complex systems (Hair et al., 2017) (Figure 9.10).

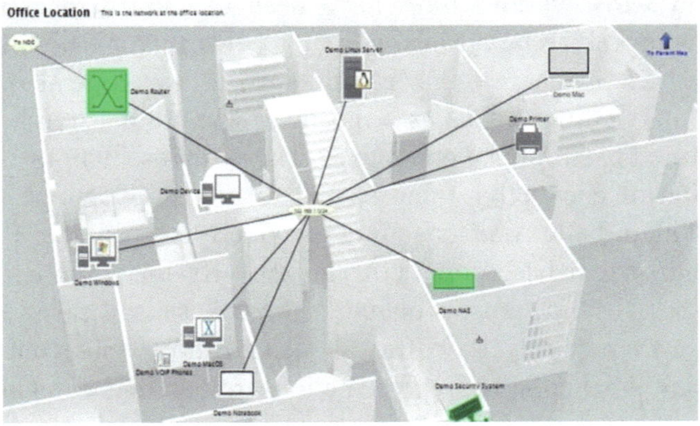

Figure 9.10. *The visualization of topological data is a critical component of modern computational analysis.*

Source: https://cdn.networkmanagementsoftware.com/wp-content/uploads/Inter-Mapper-Network-Visualization_643x400.jpg.

9.4.3. Challenges in Data Representation

In topology simulation, one of the biggest challenges is how to model complex data structures that cross many dimensions and interactions in systems. With increasingly complicated networks, particularly in applications like automotive communication systems, the ability to represent and manage data well becomes crucial. An evolving topography of data streams demands not only large bandwidth capacity but also efficient management of low-latency demands, which turns simulation in such environments even more demanding. The sophisticated interaction between sensors, actuators, and electronic control units (ECUs) turns these demands even greater in the sense that they need sophisticated simulation models that can encapsulate the systemic relationships and operating thresholds in real-time environments (Korf et al., 2018). Without such data representation breakthroughs, the efficiency of topology simulation would take a big hit, thereby diminishing the accuracy of ensuing analyses. Moreover, the heterogeneity of data from diverse application domains often leads to conflicting quality of service (QoS) demands, further complicating data representation. In vehicular networks, for instance, the need for real-time transmit protocols adds another dimension to data representation complexity. This is further complicated by the three-dimensional nature of the interactions now to be represented, making the task of representation one of quality and operational fidelity rather than quantity. The simulation models must meet these evolving needs, necessitating a unification of domain-specific languages capable of describing both the networking and computational facets effectively. As has been outlined in recent research into in-vehicular networks, there is a compelling need for novel frameworks that can handle these complicated data sets without sacrificing a promise of accuracy and dependability in the derived simulations (Korf et al., 2018). Furthermore, these data representation challenges are not specific to automotive applications but rather extend to overall paradigms for safety-critical systems. As highlighted in contemporary studies in model-based dependability analysis, systems with complex topologies require robust predictive models of component interactions and systemic behavior under fault occurrence. The two predominant paradigms—component-level failure models and state automata designs—demonstrate how various methodologies lead to the comprehension of system vulnerabilities and resilience. Nevertheless, the inherent problems of precise representations of fault modes and coupling in these models necessitate further research and development. Overcoming these issues is extremely critical to the reliability of topology simulations because inadequate or inaccurate representations of data would have undesirable impacts on system safety and reliability. As a consequence, the creation of procedures that strengthen the functionality of data representation will play a leading role in the topological simulation tool and method development.

9.5. APPLICATIONS OF TOPOLOGY SIMULATION

Applications of topology simulation penetrated a variety of domains, affecting network planning and system evaluation in particular. Recent research allows one to simulate topologies in networks and gain better understanding of systems like the Internet. Applying a model framework for network topology, researchers can incorporate varying aspects of network annotation while maintaining the delicate details that would otherwise not be visible in graph form. This methodology will permit the scrutiny of network attributes like those that are important for genuine application simulations. For instance, through the use of synthetic graphs derived from real data, the information can be utilized to inform next-generation Internet designs, essentially facilitating better network protocol designs and applications, as the research findings stipulate that it is necessary to replicate basic characteristics of network annotations in simulations (Vahdat et al., 2009). In addition, topology simulation holds particular significance in Internet protocol testing, since it provides a systematic basis for testing an enormous number of various network conditions. Previous methodologies often consist of random or intuitive cases, which tend to lack edge conditions and could result in suboptimal designs. To address these limitations, researchers have introduced algorithms to synthesize worst-case and best-case scenarios automatically to allow more comprehensive boundary-point analysis of protocols. Utilizing fault-oriented algorithms for test generation, the state space of protocol systems might be explored systematically. This is of significant value in assessing protocols under stressful conditions, identifying performance disparities that go unnoticed in average-case studies. Thus, with such introduction of systematic tools of topology simulation, network protocols' reliability and efficiency can significantly be enhanced (Estrin et al., 2002). Finally, topology simulation has more new uses in augmenting traditional network deployment than in classical uses, since it becomes a fundamental part in addressing next-generation communication paradigms issues like Internet of Things (IoT) and vehicular networks. The above systems are heterogeneous in nature and therefore require advanced simulation techniques to deal with their heterogeneity and dynamicity. The ability of topology simulation software to accommodate a flexible simulation of operational environments allows for simulations of different operating environments, and this is highly important in evaluating the strength and effectiveness of IoT networks. Because these networks often have varying connectivity levels and data traffic patterns, simulation of these by precision is very important. With the use of advanced simulation techniques, researchers can predict potential bottlenecks and optimize resource allocation efficiently. Hence, topology simulation is a necessary instrument which works greatly towards the progressive development and optimization of modern communication networks.

9.5.1. Use in Network Analysis

Systematic generation of scenarios is now a critical tool in network analysis for performance comparison of several protocols. Standard techniques rely on designers intuition or on random values, which are good for average-case analysis but are not capable of capturing boundary conditions. Synthesizing worst-case and best-case scenarios is of utmost concern for establishing what protocols do in worst- and best-case scenarios. A viable solution lies in the use of fault-oriented test generation (FOTG) algorithms that walk through the state space of a protocol in order to generate these mission-critical situations. With the help of an enhanced finite state machine model incorporating timing semantics, researchers are able to conveniently simulate and analyze performance metrics such as response time and overhead, and hence have a complete picture of protocol capability. This systematic methodology not only maximizes the strength of network evaluation but also sets the bar for systematic practice within relevant analysis, as highlighted in Estrin et al. (2002). The compounded sophistication of in-vehicular networks demands the application of advanced simulation techniques geared towards individual requirements. As automotive use trends towards increased data demands and real-time communication, challenges of in-car communication system design increase significantly. Use of event-driven simulation facilitates designers to address such complexities by employing domain-specific models, which simplify understanding how different network setups can influence performance. By adhering to high quality of service (QoS) requirements, for example, those offered by Time-Sensitive Networking (TSN) extensions to Ethernet, engineers can make communication between heterogenous modules consistent and hence ensure that they will be efficient and reliable. The iterative design process, made possible through simulation models, allows for testing various configurations and ensuring that in-vehicle network deployment occurs within harmony with increasing demands for speed and bandwidth, as illustrated (Korf et al., 2018). Ultimately, the integration of systematic analysis and tailored simulation strategy is central in further enhancing our understanding of network performance. This approach not only offers insight into the viability of specific protocols under varying conditions but also stimulates innovation in network design by highlighting shortcomings of existing methods. With growing demand for high-quality networking solutions in a broad spectrum of applications, particularly in automotive, the implications of improved network analysis are more and more compelling. Methods like FOTG and event-based simulation offer an environment in which it is possible to test new technology while also meeting the performance requirements and complexity of modern-day systems. By the emphasis on empirical validation and systematical scenario building, follow-up studies will render network simulations more credible and base innovations in technology on sound analytical underpinnings further developing the network analysis and topology simulation literature, as exemplified by the results encapsulated in Estrin et al. (2002) and Korf et al. (2018) (Figure 9.11).

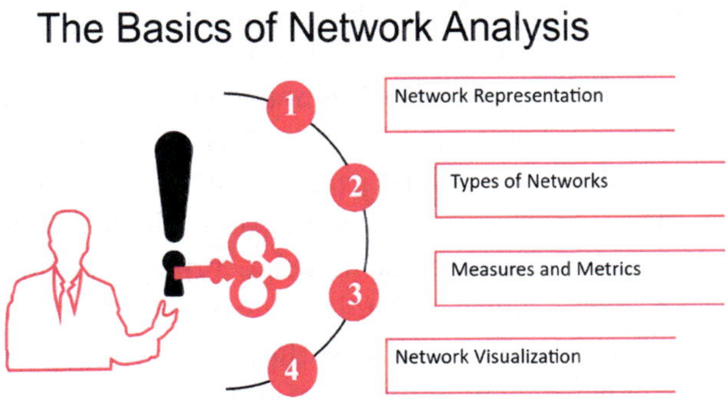

Figure 9.11. *Use in network analysis.*

Source: https://fastercapital.co/i/Network-Analysis-and-Mosaic-Theory--Mapping-Interconnections--The-Basics-of-Network-Analysis.webp.

9.5.2. Applications in Biological Systems

The applications of topology simulation in biological systems have been a major area of emphasis in recent research, particularly in drug delivery and molecular interaction. Topological models allow scientists to analyze complex molecular structures such as dendrimers, which possess certain branching architectures that greatly enhance their functional capacity. These macromolecules can be optimized with the aid of computers to predict how their size and surface properties change influence their interaction with biological targets, that is, proteins and nucleic acids. The potential for modeling these interactions makes possible a clearer understanding of their biological behavior *in vivo*, such as more effective therapeutic agents and delivery systems. Dendrimers, for instance, demonstrate how topology is the dominant factor in determining biological efficacy. Computational studies are especially beneficial to guide experimental designs in a way that the researchers can optimize dendrimer properties iteratively towards biomedical uses (Buhleier et al., 2014). The added advantage of the coupling of topology and additive manufacturing (AM) technologies further enhances the application scope within biological systems. Topology-based design frameworks make it possible for scientists to create and construct intricate geometrical structures that are optimized for certain biological functions. The paradigm of Design for Additive Manufacturing (DFAM) makes it possible to seek out design spaces, from which, new biomaterials and devices that can mimic natural biological behavior are derived. For example, utilizing cellular structures based on specific mechanical properties is capable of enhancing tissue engineering applications in the sense that it provides scaffolding that can induce cell development and differentiation. The integration of AM with topology simulation supports the design of complex biomedical solutions by addressing the restraints of traditional methods of fabrication (Rosen et al., 2007). In biomolecular engineering, advanced topology simulation tools offer unhemmed insight into the dynamic functioning of biological macromolecules. The simulation can interpret how molecular conformations affect enzymatic activity and signal transduction processes. By accurately mimicking the protein and nucleic acid interactions and reorganizations, scientists are able to better design potential drug targets and inhibitors. In addition, topology simulation enables us to understand how molecular machines work in cell environments, and this information results in the establishment of new therapeutic methods against diseases. As the region develops, continuing refinement of simulation techniques will fuel ever-more advanced breakthroughs in our understanding of biological systems, enhancing biomolecule design and utilization for therapeutic and biotechnological applications (Buhleier et al., 2014).

9.5.3. Role in Materials Science and Engineering

In material science and engineering, the application of advanced tools and techniques like topology simulation is fundamental to designing materials with specific functions. Simulation of material behavior under multiple conditions allows for the creation of new design spaces that would otherwise be inaccessible. Additive Manufacturing (AM) technologies, for instance, transform the manufacturing world by enabling the production of complex geometries and customized material compositions. This capability for the intricacies of design requires a strategy that facilitates designers to effectively venture into these complex design spaces. As recognized by the Design for Additive Manufacturing (DFAM) strategy, an understanding of the process-structure-property-behavior model can significantly enhance design outcomes, providing engineers with important frameworks for the creation of optimized materials relative to specific standards of performance (Rosen et al., 2007). Topology optimization methods also further enhance the proficiency of engineers in material science. For example, the Proportional Topology Optimization (PTO) approach, as presented in existing research, offers a non-gradient solution which is straightforward and efficient. Through its provision for the precise optimization of stress constraints as well as minimum compliance, PTO allows the design of structures with maximum performance at minimum material usage. The concurrent application of PTO algorithms offers insights regarding stress and compliance trade-offs, enhancing the design process through iterative optimization of material properties (Biyikli et al., 2014). Iterativeness is one of the advantages of topology simulation in material science, whereby it can be possible to explore and obtain cutting-edge materials that are designed specifically to meet specific engineering needs. Ultimately, the integration of topology simulation tools within material science and engineering not only enhances the design process but promotes innovation in numerous disciplines. With reduced time and cost being spent on experimental testing, these approaches allow engineers to focus on enhancing material performance and functionality with unparalleled precision. The improvement of techniques such as DFAM and PTO is indicative of how simulation strategies are able to make a valuable contribution towards product design and development. The continuous advancement of these techniques marks the start of a new era in material science that drives the expansion of modern engineering methods while driving Eco compatibility through optimization of materials (Rosen et al., 2007; Biyikli et al., 2014). Thus, the role of topology simulation surpasses theoretical appreciation since it serves as a motivational force for real-world application that dictates the future of engineering design (Figure 9.12).

Figure 9.12. *Role in material science and engineering.*

Source: https://omdayal.com/wp-content/uploads/2023/06/the-importance-of-networking-header-1024x307.jpg.

9.6. CHALLENGES AND LIMITATIONS OF TOPOLOGY SIMULATION

The search for advanced topology simulations often comes with serious challenges that hamper their effectiveness and usability. The primary challenge is the inherent complexity of representing and modeling real systems with accuracy. These systems often involve intricate interdependencies between numerous components, which prove to be challenging to simulate within an environment. As allusions, the lack of complete knowledge and insufficiency of data highly complicate modeling. Without full and high-fidelity data, the validity of simulations decreases, which could result in prediction and outcome errors. Researchers are therefore faced with the formidable challenge of not only developing sophisticated models but ensuring that they are also based on accurate, empirical data that can confirm the inferences drawn. Another significant shortcoming in topology simulation is the computer capacity required to run large or high-fidelity models. Since simulations become increasingly more realistic and advanced, they need exponentially greater amounts of computing power, which is beyond the reach of most research institutions or groups. In the picture described by D'Angelo et al. (2011), overcoming the scale disparity between models and biological systems requires a significant amount of computer power to realistically simulate cellular interactions and behavior. This need can create resource allocation or more advanced computational technology needs, for example, concurrent programming, to break through limitations in extent and detail. These needs complicate not just the development of the simulation but also limit how high-quality topological simulations become available for broad application. There is also the concern about integrating appropriately different technologies and methodologies into the simulation process. As identified in the digital ecosystems paper, a unified interoperability framework across various tools and protocols is required for the facilitation of innovation and robustness in simulation approaches (D'Angelo et al., 2011). In its absence, there could be inconsistencies, inefficiencies, and difficulties in disseminating the results among researchers. Together with the expansion in the area of topology simulation, there is an urgent need to create methodologies for improving seamless integration and collaboration. This will improve the reproducibility of results and allow more sophisticated models to be designed. Lastly, going beyond the restrictions and limitations to which topology simulation is relegated is crucial in advancing the reliability and practicality of these tools in the majority of scientific disciplines.

9.6.1. Computational Complexity

In topology simulation, computational complexity plays a central role in determining the efficacy and feasibility of various modeling techniques. With the simulations trying to replicate complex biological processes, for example, cell signaling in cancer, an estimate of the computational resources required becomes essential. High-dimensional models tend to require enormous processing, which becomes a hinderances to real-time examination and accessibility. With the help of concurrent programming, the size gap between intricate cellular models and larger-sized tissue structures can be bridged. This technique ensures that the essential information is gained and not oversimplified to an unreasonable extent, thereby making it a closer representation of dynamic biological functions. Mitigating computational complexity through innovative programming methods ultimately enhances the validity and usability of simulations in experimental environments, as observed in cancer systems biology and related fields (Andrews et al., 2012). Agent-Based Modeling (ABM) is a vital component of the topological simulation platforms, particularly when dealing with computational complexity. ABM can model the individual agents within a system, that can be applied to model various biological entities and interactions. Individual-based modeling results in highly dynamic models that simulate localized behavior and systemic outputs, which are crucial in simulating complex biological processes.

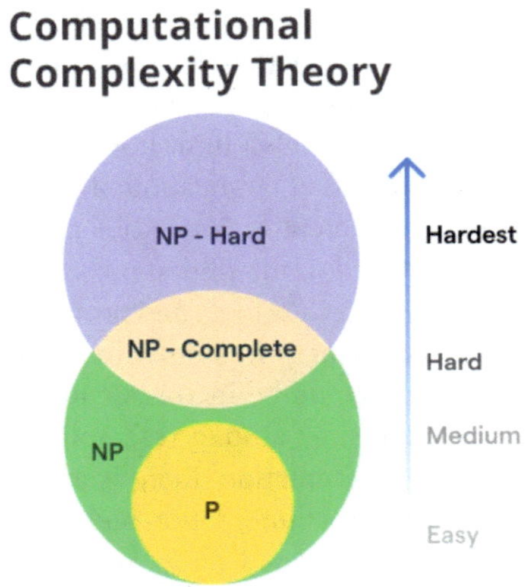

Figure 9.13. *Computational complexity.*

Source: https://cdn.botpenguin.com/assets/website/Computational_Complexity_Theory_cb0b0bf408.webp.

ABM calls for vigilance on the need for computation, however, especially when the population of agents becomes large. Coupling ABM and advanced visualization can alleviate these problems using intuitive interfaces that support exploration and interaction with the models. Combining ABM and visualization is particularly essential for biologists wishing to experiment with hypotheses and improve experimental design, and demonstrating the applied importance of addressing computational complexity in simulation (Castle et al., 2006). Lastly, computational complexity is not merely a technical issue; it is a matter of scientific rigor and reproducibility for topological simulation. With models developed under a partial comprehension of computational demands, results will become inconsistent or unintelligible and lead to seismic discrepancies in scientific findings. There cannot be enough emphasis placed on the significance of a well-organized framework for building simulations, particularly one that compartmentalizes scientific and engineering problems. Through ensuring clear documentation, calibration, and verification, scientists can ensure that their simulations are quality scientific instruments. This approach not only helps manage computational complexity but also enhances the reproducibility of simulations from study to study or application to application. In essence, a concerted effort to enhance computational methods within the context of topology simulation will lead to increased comprehension of sophisticated biological systems, from the level of requirements supported by modern scientific research (Andrews et al., 2012) (Figure 9.13).

9.6.2. Limitations of Current Tools

Limitations in current tools for simulating topology impact the efficiency and accuracy of design activities within the field. The majority of contemporary simulation tools, as sophisticated as they are, are usually marred by scalability issues when handling complicated topological designs. As designs grow in size and complexity, traditional tools cannot maintain efficiency, and the simulation process becomes too time-consuming, thereby impacting the overall design process. This shortage not only results in dissatisfaction with the engineers but may also lead to suboptimal design decisions being made as practitioners must employ less accurate simulations due to time pressures. The fact that such tools are unable to handle the intricate nuances of large circuits presents a huge limitation to achieving favorable design outcomes, thus calls for further development in simulation tools that can handle larger and more complex frameworks. Moreover, existing topology simulation software tend to lack the ability to combine multi-aspect components of various domains, which has the effect of producing inaccurate results. The difference between analog and digital implementations creates challenges in simulating hybrid systems in a holistic way; therefore, designers may need to go back to various tools, rendering it inconvenient to design. For instance, the limitations on automating physical geometry synthesis within analog integrated circuits indicate this intricacy. As noted in the literature, inherent differences between analog and digital designs have precluded the achievement of a comparable level of automation across disciplines (Rentmeesters et al., 1990). In addition to making project scheduling more difficult, this incompatibility also increases error potential as a transfer is being made from one simulation environment into another, emphasizing the vital need for even more integrated and flexible tools to facilitate bridging the gap. In addition, accuracy of results remains a problem in the face of current topology simulation software. While improvements in behavioral modeling have improved simulation fidelity, errors can still occur when simulating output against real performance. Individual approaches, such as those presented in the example of A/D and D/A converters, demonstrate that even sophisticated hardware is not always capable of approximating the intricacies of circuits within real operating conditions (Restituto et al., 2005). These discrepancies can typically be attributed to the inadequate modeling of circuit parameters, non-ideal characteristics, and environmental conditions. Thus, improving modeling technique accuracy and simulation fidelity is crucial to bringing simulated outcomes into line with actual performance, thereby lessening one of the greatest weaknesses inherent in modern tools within the topology simulation field.

9.6.3. Future Directions for Improvement

With topological simulation improvement, the chances of furthering it by integrating complex computational techniques are immense. This is attainable through venturing and implementing task-based programming models. Employing hardware that facilitates parallel processing, as in initiatives such as LEGaTO, simulations can be more efficient and accurate. These models allow researchers to allocate resources effectively in heterogeneous hardware platforms, lightening the computation burden. Not only would this improve the performance of topology simulation, but it also has the potential to significantly reduce energy consumption. With energy efficiency becoming more and more the determining factor to work with in computational research, further research should aim to close these high-level programming paradigms and topology simulation, hence making sustainability and performance in the field even improved (Alvarez et al., 2018). Aside from computational developments, the need to enhance knowledge-sharing processes between topology simulation stakeholders is crucial. As the richness of network structures grows, so does the need for effective collaboration between academic and industry researchers. The use of network theory, as expounded in the study of tourist destinations, offers an effective model on how knowledge can be shared between entities. Through picturing research networks as networked nodes, the initiatives of stakeholders are brought to converge more efficiently and share useful information, with the possibility of topological innovations in simulation approaches. Future improvements in this area can be spurred through policy measures that promote collaborative work, ultimately driving a more competitive and innovative research landscape (Baggio et al., 2009). Lastly, the incorporation of numerical modeling and simulations has tremendous potential to enhance the accuracy of topology simulations. By applying sophisticated algorithms that take advantage of data-driven models, scientists can create more accurate models that are close to reality. This transition to more sophisticated simulation techniques not only makes the results more credible but also allows for a better understanding of the underlying topological complexities. The future directions must emphasize developing and testing the models in a manner that makes them adaptable to all types of applications across disciplines. By encouraging developments in theoretical models as well as applications, the field of topology simulation will be adequately prepared to contend with the evolving threats and take advantage of new scientific opportunities (Alvarez et al., 2018; Baggio et al., 2009) (Figure 9.14).

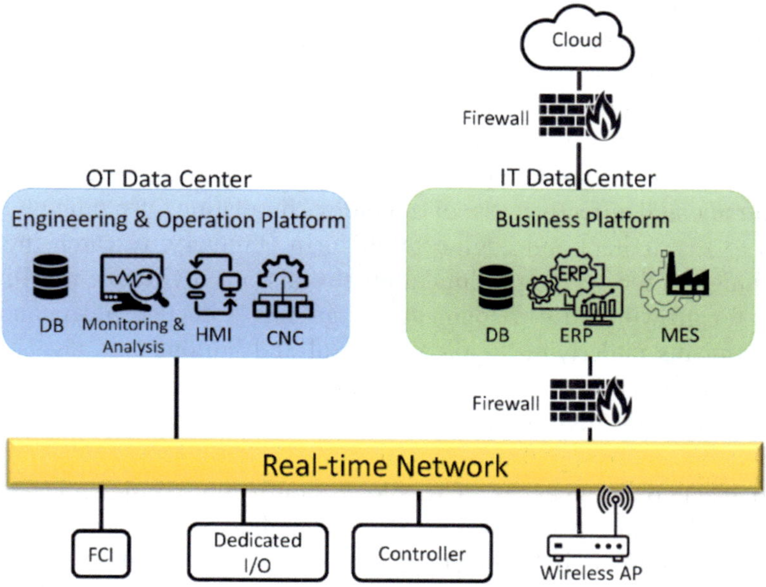

Figure 9.14. *Future directions for improvement.*

Source: https://www.mdpi.com/applsci/applsci-11-03345/article_deploy/html/images/applsci-11-03345-g002.png.

SUMMARY

It is crucial to understand the fine balance between the requirements for consistency properties and sought-after optimization results. As observed in the literature, a topology control algorithm that is efficient should lead to connectivity given the dynamic nature of real-world networks. This flexibility is an issue of visual programming and specification languages as specifications and models to address both structural and optimization features of topologies. The approach explained reveals the way graph transformation and graph constraint languages can be used to define incremental modifications required in topology control algorithms so as to prioritize in-depth strategies adhering to pre-defined constraints (Hollick et al., 2017). Such innovations not just enhance the theoretical aspect of topology simulation but also find practical applicability in real-world use, hence proving the significance of such research. Careful examination of the existing topological simulation tools shows that the majority of methods rely upon analog techniques that have not achieved automation to the same extent that their digital-based equivalents have. The recent development emphasizes the discussion that though a lot of progress is made in automatic synthesis, analog system intrinsic challenges pose unique challenges (Rentmeesters et al., 1990). Thus, this gap implies a requirement for continuous research and development specific to furthering the automation of topology work. As these analogous layout problems are solved in a methodical way, adding new methodologies can achieve a significant advancement in the accuracy and effectiveness of topology simulation, providing valuable insights to researchers and engineers alike. In summary, research into tools and techniques for topology simulation reveals an environment with great promise for growth and development. By gaining a deeper understanding of the mechanisms underlying topology control and building on advancements in visual programming, researchers can better control the complexity of dynamic communication networks. Further, recognition of the distinction between analog and digital methods allows tailored solutions specifically in order to react to the nuances of topology simulation. As the science keeps developing, the combination of these diverse methods is responsible for future breakthroughs, ultimately leading to more robust and powerful systems that can cater to the demands of an increasingly interconnected globe (Hollick et al., 2017; Rentmeesters et al., 1990).

During the above exploration of topology simulation landscape, a number of tools and methods seem to be central in reconciling complexity of network design. Among these, simulation software is a critical component in facilitating effective model building and checking. For instance, through the application of more advanced models and simulation tools, assessments can be made far more precise, as seen in a review of power amplifiers at 144 MHz. Here, the presence of high-Q inductors within the simulation environment facilitated low-loss output networks, thereby achieving maximum output power and efficiency. This paper illustrates how the employment of precise simulation environments is able to alter results to make theoretical expectations closely resemble practice results, something which can ultimately lead to technological innovation across various technological areas. Moreover, the necessity for sophisticated communication systems necessitates a type of simulation, most particularly in the instance of in-vehicular networks. As automobiles assume increasingly sophisticated driver assistance and autonomous driving capabilities, the complexity of in-car communication systems increases as well. Next-generation vehicle networks will be anticipated to depend on Ethernet technology, which facilitates high bandwidth and low latency sophistication of communication needed to transmit data in real-time. The significance of consideration of tailored attributes in network services becomes critical to combat heterogeneous application domains in car scenarios. With event-based simulation techniques, designers are required to come up with mechanisms around these challenges to design very resilient and efficient in-car communication systems, which strongly foretells the necessity of methodology that is well-coordinating with future automobile technologies, as recent research has stressed. Lastly, the intricacy of developing effective communication backbones in automobiles necessitates a deep understanding of simulation processes and models. Academic discourse reveals the truth that apart from their role in specifying the requirements of in-vehicular networks, domain-specific description languages are applied to produce models effectively in simulating sensor and actuator interactions with electronic control units (ECUs). These modeling procedures must take into account future quality of service (QoS) restrictions as this will have a defining influence on both design decisions and operational characteristics. The findings from the application of these simulation techniques to premium car network case studies only serve to reinforce the significance of tailored simulation methods in driving automobile technology. Collectively, these points reflect a topological simulation paradigm shift that is characterized by greater accuracy, efficiency, and flexibility to meet the needs of future car innovations.

REFERENCES

1. Abukhdeir, N. M., & Fu, F. (2014). A topologically-informed hyperstreamline seeding method for alignment tensor fields. http://arxiv.org/abs/1312.7034 (accessed on 9th September 2025).
2. Adams, C., Alrashed, M., An, R., Anthony, J., et al. (2018). A deep neural network for pixel-level electromagnetic particle identification in the MicroBooNE liquid argon time projection chamber. http://arxiv.org/abs/1808.07269 (accessed on 9th September 2025).
3. Agosti, M., Basu, A., Annapureddy, S., Barcellos, M., Baumgart, I., Boufkhad, Y., Cheng, B., et al. (2013). The state of peer-to-peer network simulators. https://core.ac.uk/download/9836534.pdf (accessed on 9th September 2025).
4. Aksoylu, B., Bernstein, D., Bond, S., Holst, M., Alvi, K., Andersson, L., Mars, M., Simon, W., et al. (2008). From geometry to numerics: Interdisciplinary aspects in mathematical and numerical relativity. http://arxiv.org/abs/0712.2332 (accessed on 9th September 2025).
5. Al-Fuqaha, A., Guizani, M., Mohammadi, M., Aledhari, M., & Ayyash, M. (2015). Internet of things: A survey on enabling technologies, protocols, and applications. *IEEE Communications Surveys & Tutorials, 17*, 2347–2376. https://doi.org/10.1109/comst.2015.2444095 (accessed on 9th September 2025).
6. Al-Shaidy, A. N. M. K., Kamala, M. A., Kinteh, S., Kiran, R., et al. (2017). Technical report on deploying a highly secured OpenStack cloud infrastructure using BradStack as a case study. http://arxiv.org/abs/1712.09152 (accessed on 9th September 2025).
7. Alvarez, C., Bautista, L., Becker, T., Billung-Meyer, M., et al. (2018). LEGaTO: First steps towards energy-efficient toolset for heterogeneous computing. https://core.ac.uk/download/224976296.pdf (accessed on 9th September 2025).
8. Amaro, R. E., de La Beaumelle, N. A., Holst, M. J., Laughlin, J. G., et al. (2019). 3D mesh processing using GAMer 2 to enable reaction-diffusion simulations in realistic cellular geometries. http://arxiv.org/abs/1901.11008 (accessed on 9th September 2025).
9. Andrews, P. S., Bown, J. L., Deeni, Y. Y., Goltsov, A., et al. (2012). Engineering simulations for cancer systems biology. https://core.ac.uk/download/228177087.pdf (accessed on 9th September 2025).
10. Baggio, R., & Cooper, C. (2009). Knowledge transfer in a tourism destination: The effects of a network structure. http://arxiv.org/abs/0905.2734 (accessed on 9th September 2025).

11. Bakhshi, R., Bonnet, F., Fokkink, W., Haverkort, B., et al. (2007). Formal analysis techniques for gossiping protocols. https://core.ac.uk/download/pdf/11479580.pdf (accessed on 9th September 2025).
12. Banelli, P., Barbarossa, S., Di Lorenzo, P., Sardellitti, S., et al. (2017). Distributed adaptive learning of graph signals. http://arxiv.org/abs/1609.06100 (accessed on 9th September 2025).
13. Bassett, D. S., Daniels, K. E., Papadopoulos, L., Porter, M. A., et al. (2017). Network analysis of particles and grains. http://arxiv.org/abs/1708.08080 (accessed on 9th September 2025).
14. Bernal Escribano, Á. (2019). Fluid flow queue models for fixed-mobile network evaluation. https://core.ac.uk/download/224975922.pdf (accessed on 9th September 2025).
15. Biyikli, E., & To, A. C. (2014). Proportional topology optimization: A new non-gradient method for solving stress constrained and minimum compliance problems and its implementation in MATLAB. https://core.ac.uk/download/78481904.pdf (accessed on 9th September 2025).
16. Bos, E. G. P., Natarajan, V., Pranav, P., Rieder, S., et al. (2015). Felix: A topology-based framework for visual exploration of cosmic filaments. https://core.ac.uk/download/597499417.pdf (accessed on 9th September 2025).
17. Buhleier, C., Carbone, F., Florindo, H., Hess, K., Klajnert, B., Silva, L., et al. (2014). Molecular modeling to study dendrimers for biomedical applications. https://core.ac.uk/download/29849184.pdf (accessed on 9th September 2025).
18. Carreira, R., Pont, M., Rocha, I., Rocha, M., et al. (2014). Flexible and user-friendly tools for the incorporation of fluxomic data into metabolic models. https://core.ac.uk/download/55631789.pdf (accessed on 9th September 2025).
19. Castle, C. J. E., & Crooks, A. T. (2006). Principles and concepts of agent-based modelling for developing geospatial simulations. https://core.ac.uk/download/1671867.pdf (accessed on 9th September 2025).
20. D'Angelo, G., & Ferretti, S. (2011). LUNES: Agent-based simulation of P2P systems (extended version). http://arxiv.org/abs/1105.2447 (accessed on 9th September 2025).
21. D'Angelo, G., Ferretti, S., Ghini, V., Panzieri, F., et al. (2011). Mobile computing in digital ecosystems: Design issues and challenges. http://arxiv.org/abs/1105.2458 (accessed on 9th September 2025).
22. Dankanich, J. W., & Morris, H. C. (2025). Marshall Space Flight Center research and technology report 2019. https://core.ac.uk/download/pdf/288485478.pdf (accessed on 9th September 2025).

23. Delgado Restituto, M., Rodríguez Vázquez, Á. B., de la Rosa Utrera, J. M., Ruiz Amaya, J., et al. (2005). Simulation-based high-level synthesis of Nyquist-rate data converters using MATLAB/SIMULINK. https://core.ac.uk/download/286565261.pdf (accessed on 9th September 2025).
24. Eldabi, T., Jahangirian, M., Mustafee, N., Naseer, A., et al. (2008). A survey of simulation techniques in commerce and defense. https://core.ac.uk/download/8035.pdf (accessed on 9th September 2025).
25. Estrin, D., Gupta, S., & Helmy, A. (2002). The STRESS method for boundary-point performance analysis of end-to-end multicast timer-suppression mechanisms. http://arxiv.org/abs/cs/0208023 (accessed on 9th September 2025).
26. Hair, J., Phillips, J. M., Sodergren, T., Wang, H., et al. (2017). Visualizing sensor network coverage with location uncertainty. http://arxiv.org/abs/1710.06925 (accessed on 9th September 2025).
27. Hollick, M., Kluge, R., Mühlhäuser, M., Schürr, A., et al. (2017). A systematic approach to constructing incremental topology control algorithms using graph transformation. http://arxiv.org/abs/1805.03386 (accessed on 9th September 2025).
28. Holmgren, F., & Janson, S. (2008). Interactive visual analysis of networked systems: Workflows for two industrial domains. https://core.ac.uk/download/11434682.pdf (accessed on 9th September 2025).
29. Hu, J., Shen, L., Albanie, S., Sun, G., & Wu, E. (2019). Squeeze-and-excitation networks. *IEEE Transactions on Pattern Analysis and Machine Intelligence, 42*, 2011–2023. https://doi.org/10.1109/tpami.2019.2913372 (accessed on 9th September 2025).
30. Jaworski, P. L. (2006). Using simulations and artificial life algorithms to grow elements of construction. https://core.ac.uk/download/1671441.pdf (accessed on 9th September 2025).
31. Kabir, S., Papadopoulos, Y., Sharvia, S., Walker, M., et al. (2015). Model-based dependability analysis: State-of-the-art, challenges and future outlook. https://core.ac.uk/download/151160986.pdf (accessed on 9th September 2025).
32. Karperien, M., Langerak, R., Post, J. N., Schivo, S., et al. (2014). Setting parameters for biological models with ANIMO. https://core.ac.uk/download/pdf/31146505.pdf (accessed on 9th September 2025).
33. Korf, F., Meyer, P., Schmidt, T. C., Steinbach, J., et al. (2018). Simulation of mixed critical in-vehicular networks. http://arxiv.org/abs/1808.03081 (accessed on 9th September 2025).

34. Kwok, A., Quintana, A., Naylor, A. M., Roberts, B. P., Yu, C., Schwieters, C. D., Brown, C. W., et al. (2017). Practical computational toolkits for dendrimers and dendrons structure design. https://core.ac.uk/download/287581216.pdf (accessed on 9th September 2025).
35. Markova, O., Popel, M., & Semerikov, S. (2018). CoCalc as a learning tool for neural network simulation in the special course "Foundations of Mathematic Informatics." http://arxiv.org/abs/1807.00795 (accessed on 9th September 2025).
36. Rentmeesters, M. J. (1990). Automatic synthesis of analog layout: A survey. https://core.ac.uk/download/287623298.pdf (accessed on 9th September 2025).
37. Rosen, D. W. (2007). Design for additive manufacturing: A method to explore unexplored regions of the design space. https://core.ac.uk/download/287648539.pdf (accessed on 9th September 2025).
38. Rutledge, D. B., & Zirath, H. (1999). An LDMOS VHF class-E power amplifier using a high-Q novel variable inductor. https://core.ac.uk/download/4870796.pdf (accessed on 9th September 2025).
39. Vahdat, A., Chang, H., Dimitropoulos, X., Krioukov, D., Erdős, P., Gao, L., et al. (2009). Graph annotations in modeling complex network topologies. http://arxiv.org/abs/0708.3879 (accessed on 9th September 2025).
40. Vasic, B. (2012). Ordered statistics vertex extraction and tracing algorithm (OSVETA). http://arxiv.org/abs/1211.1345 (accessed on 9th September 2025).

CHAPTER 10

FUTURE TRENDS IN NETWORK TOPOLOGY

Contents

INTRODUCTION

Network topology is at a juncture where it has to evolve with rising technology innovations and changing demands of world communications. As more and more organizations and users rely on quick, reliable internet connectivity, there is an added necessity for new network topologies. New technology trends, such as Low Earth Orbit (LEO) satellite networks, are revolutionizing traditional communication paradigms with round-the-clock high-bandwidth data transfer over extended distances. This transformation in operation not only improves access but also ensures to bridge the digital divide, thus facilitating inclusive growth and balanced access to information technology. An accurate understanding of these new architectures is critical to anticipating their influence on connectivity and communication patterns globally, representing a key milestone in the evolution of network topology's toward more global interaction and responsiveness. With the satellite communications innovations comes the integration of Software-Defined Networking (SDN), emphasizing even more the radicality in modern network topologies. Separating the data plane from the control plane, SDN introduces more flexibility and programmability, which are critical in disrupting the inefficiencies prevalent in traditional networks. The architecture enables applications of advanced routing procedures, backed by machine learning algorithms to actively optimize network performance. The shift towards intelligence-based routing presents new horizons for research and development as networks become increasingly responsive to altered conditions and user demand. Not only do such advances deliver enhanced efficiency on the whole, but they also force us to consider basic questions about security, scalability, and operational complexity involved in constructing such dynamic networked environments. As network topology keeps evolving, it is important to research the implications of these trends on future communication infrastructures. The convergence of LEO networks together with the power of SDN is a paradigm shift in which traditional limitations may be overcome through smart design and architecture. But while the potential of enhanced connectivity and performance is gigantic, problems like spectrum management and space debris are huge deterrents that must be addressed in order to make growth sustainable. The evolution of network topologies to the future therefore must focus on designing resilience against such threats, quantifying how emerging technologies can be balanced to form holistic, inclusive, and sustainable networked infrastructures serving an evolving global society.

Definition of Network Topology

The term network topology is the arrangement or organization of different elements (links, nodes, etc.) within a computer network. It determines how different devices, such as computers, switches, and routers, are interconnected and share data. There are numerous fundamental types of topologies, that is, star, ring, bus, and mesh topologies, each with advantages and disadvantages. For example, in star topology installation and management are easy, whereas in mesh topology redundancy and reliability are boosted because there are various paths between the nodes. It is essential to know these simple structures in network design and analysis, especially as organizations become increasingly dependent on scalable and trustworthy networks to meet growing demands and facilitate sophisticated communication. Network topology evolution is still a major component of addressing problems today and staying ahead of tomorrow's technology curve. Future network planning is based on moving towards more robust, more responsive network topologies. As the Internet of Things (IoT) and dynamic resource allocation create greater demands for the way network's function, the best of both world model's hybrid topologies is destined to be tomorrow's norm. Such networks can optimize performance and resource utilization through clever reaction to varying loads and equipment needs. Furthermore, using the concepts of quantum computing to develop network architecture has the potential to create a technological revolution in data-handling capability, with optimized data processing and transfer. As revealed in recent research, the behavior of quantum arithmetic algorithms in distributed systems is evidence of the contribution of network structure to optimizing operations. Network node organization and the application of efficient quantum operations can potentially re-engineer how we structure computational tasks, subsequently influencing the future network design (ACM. et al., 2007). Moreover, the integration of emerging technologies requires us to re-engineer existing topologies and constraints within networks. Since networks become increasingly complicated, fault-tolerant and adaptable structures are needed. A captivating area of research is the representation of biomolecular interactions as networks, mentioned in frontier areas such as quantum interactomics. This novel imagery reflects the manner in which structures in cells function similar to network topologies, emphasizing the use of networking ideas across a variety of disciplines, from biology to information technology (Baianu et al., 2010). As the difference between fields erodes, understanding of network topology in a broader context will allow researchers and practitioners to design increasingly sophisticated, adaptable networks that are pivotal to the future technology environment. The relationship between these evolving paradigms illustrates that the principles of network topology will continue to direct our knowledge and innovations in computing and other aspects of life.

Importance of Network Topology in Modern Communication

The significance of network topology in modern communication cannot be overstated, as it is the foundation on which data transmission and connectivity are based. Organization of network components—that is, nodes and links—defines not only the efficiency of data transfer but also system resilience to failure. For instance, star, mesh, and ring topologies all possess inherent features that impact parameters like speed, reliability, and maintenance ease. The implications of such topological decisions become increasingly important as organizations become more and more dependent on continuous communication and data exchange facilities. Moreover, as bandwidth and low-latency connections become more in demand, network topology knowledge will be indispensable in ensuring performance optimization and making today's communication infrastructures scalable and sustainable. While technology keeps redefining communication paradigms, the networks must also evolve to keep up with ever-growing demands.

Figure 10.1. *The significance of network topology in modern communication.*

Source: https://media.licdn.com/dms/image/v2/D4D12AQGQt_uYVLlI0w/article-cover_image-shrink_600_2000/article-cover_image-shrink_600_2000/0/1659011887161?e=2147483647&v=beta&t=sMikTVD7w-9yEySdXJmkC3XmQechuY-wkl26Eu1toVPc.

Power over Ethernet (PoE) and direct current (DC) networks are a prime example of how this evolution is taking place, as it signifies breaking the stereotypical alternating current systems. Such a transformation requires a redesign of power distribution network topologies to accommodate multiple applications and devices, thereby maximizing overall efficiency. The Digital Energy Network (DEN) designed here, where microgrids are classified in tiers such as microgrids, nanogrids, and picogrids, also demands customized network design. In cases where high data rate and low power use are crucial, network topology and power distribution have significant interaction. These designs not only streamline operations but also put organizations in a position to further leverage future communication technologies (Banks et al., 2012). Future network topology will also be greatly impacted by increasing reliance on distributed systems and grid computing. Scientific advances in local area networks (LANs) and wide area networks (WANs) overcoming limitations of existing architectures are critical to delivering sophisticated scientific applications and high-performance computing. Prior work indicates that conventional supercomputers continue to dominate due to inefficiencies in geographically dispersed environments, with the discovery of a topology-conscious solution to data communication and processing being essential. Application of new algorithms optimized for lessening communication overhead as well as enhancing data locality greatly improves performance in such environments. This shift towards topology-conscious algorithms not only promises to revolutionize computing capability but also puts the importance of tactically addressing network structure at the forefront in an effort to remain within pace of emerging scientific and technological challenges (Coti et al., 2009) (Figure 10.1).

Overview of Future Trends

The future network topology is poised to be transformed by technological progress and the increased demand for efficient data transfer. With progressive networks, decentralized structure is increasingly clear as a way to deliver more stable and adaptive systems. This is especially useful in the context of the modern electric grid, which has to incorporate smart technology to handle the complexity introduced by renewable energy devices. Their integration not only improves efficiency but also introduces new weaknesses in the grid. In previous analyses, it has been mentioned that a vulnerability analysis would be a source of identification of improvement areas in such networks, particularly with increased application of variable power sources. This growing complexity and interdependence necessitate new network topologies that can enhance system-wide resilience and ensure sustainability against abrupt disruptions (Millis et al., 2019). In combination with the proliferation of smart technologies, network topology is increasingly characterized by the interfacing of Artificial Intelligence (AI) and machine learning. They facilitate superior management of data and decision-making capabilities, eventually leading to superior network performance. With the application of AI capabilities, network engineers can predict traffic flows, maximize resource allocation, and identify automatically anomalies or potential failures in the network. All these preventive measures will enhance the security and reliability of networks, particularly in those sectors that are greatly reliant on seamless communications, such as healthcare and telecommunication. In addition, with more philanthropic activity cutting across sectors, integrative, cooperative solutions in network architecture become a requirement, once again pointing to a future where multidisciplinary network topology solutions thrive in enhancing social performance (Bass, 2013). The final major trend marking the future of network topology is embracing sustainable strategies in infrastructure. As organizations are focusing more on going green, network design also will have to adapt by making green strategies a part of it and minimizing carbon footprints. A move toward clean sources of energy not only impacts the generation of power but even the design of networks that enable energy distribution and management. Consequently, storage capacity emphasis in electric grids, underpinned by vulnerability research, can contribute significantly to network resiliency, especially as the demand for renewable resources increases. Moreover, when humanitarian activities are engaged to fight world issues, such as global warming, public-private partnerships can lead to innovative network solutions that favor sustainability and resiliency. This connectivity of goals among isolated industries is a robust trend in the development of network topologies (Millis et al., 2019; Bass, 2013) (Figure 10.2).

Figure 10.2. *The future landscape of network topology.*

Source: https://stl.tech/wp-content/uploads/2021/10/Banner-Image_Network-Topology.jpg.

10.1. EVOLUTION OF NETWORK TOPOLOGIES

The evolution of network topology has been marked by significant changes as a result of technology growth and evolving user requirements. One of the most important milestones in the evolution was the transition from IPv4 to IPv6. The IPv4 network with exponential growth up to 2001 reached the point where growth plateaued into a linear trend. This change is reflective of a broader movement of network topology development trends, which suggests that developed infrastructure will plateau as it reaches more complete usage. Conversely, IPv6 network, after undergoing its initial slow growth phase, began experiencing explosive growth effects from late 2006. This divergent growth trend reflects an intrinsic shift in internet architecture structure and deployment required to accommodate the increasing connectivity demand as well as the introduction of IoT devices requiring robust network infrastructure (Albert et al., 2010). Recent studies have observed correlations between network structure and information diffusion dynamics that have provided insight into emergent patterns. For instance, the way information packets diffuse through various network structures exhibits a high topology-transport efficiency correlation. Simulations have indicated that topologies affect diffusion properties in the sense that some network structures maximize super-diffusive processes to optimize general performance when transferring data. These discoveries emphasize the significance of not only ensuring strong topology but also ensuring the integration of strong local transport rules harmonious with the global network scheme. These discoveries imply that novel designs in network topology must consider how structural properties interact with packet transportation schemes in ways that enhance functionality and reduce latency (Abate et al., 2003). With advancing network topologies, new paradigms such as Software-Defined Networking (SDN) and network slicing emerge with great potential. The emerging technologies hold the promise of greater flexibility for dynamic adaptation to shifting traffic and user needs. SDN separates the control plane from the data plane, making resource management and allocation more efficient. This separation allows quick deployment and expansion of application-specific services, thus reconfiguring traditional topological models to more dynamic and interactive structures. Network slicing also offers the capability of supporting a multitude of virtual networks on a single physical infrastructure with tailored performance profiles for diverse use cases ranging from mission-critical communications to low-latency applications. These trends portend an age of network topologies evolving into more agile, extensible, and efficient systems that can meet the needs of a more digital society.

10.1.1. Historical Context of Network Topologies

The evolution of network topology is a dynamic tapestry of growth from the early days of computer networking to the complex systems employed today. The introduction of networks in the 1960s with ARPANET employed a very decentralized scheme. This is where a move from point-to-point connections to more complex topologies, which could support the growing number of devices, started. The evolution of these networks highlights a critical paradigm shift in terms of understanding connectivity with the emergence of a number of topological models such as star, bus, and ring topologies. The advent of the internet highlighted the need for flexible and fault-tolerant topologies that were more performing and reliable upon which subsequent designs and developments in network architecture were founded. Knowing about network topologies in the past also involves knowing the importance of metabolic networks in organisms, which can give examples for information networks. Similar to metabolic networks perform crucial functions via numerous pathways, computer network topologies are designed to keep data flow and resource consumption to a minimum. As seen in artificial chemistry models, characteristics such as autocatalytic cycles and hierarchical modules show inherent principles that can be used in computational networks. Metabolic pathways act with a logarithmic trend towards complexity, reflecting the way network designers attempt to do the most with less redundancy. This cross-disciplinary effort challenges further exploration of how biological concepts can inform the design of future computational networks and enrich topology theory richness (Hintze et al., 2010). Furthermore, the historical evolution of network topologies provides insight into future trends in the field. Modern applications, such as the deployment of convolutional neural networks for real-time data analysis, serve to demonstrate the application of historical knowledge to emerging technologies. By circumventing conventional feature extraction techniques and instead adopting end-to-end learning approaches, network architectures are increasingly applying machine learning concepts to optimize operations automatically. These developments undermine earlier assumptions regarding network configurability and efficiency, pointing toward an ongoing need for adaptation. Ahead of us, historical backgrounds such as classification approaches created based on iEEG data underscore the coexistence between networks and data-driven systems, which provide the terrain for the future that is heavily reliant upon intelligent design and adaptive systems (Brinkmann et al., 2018).

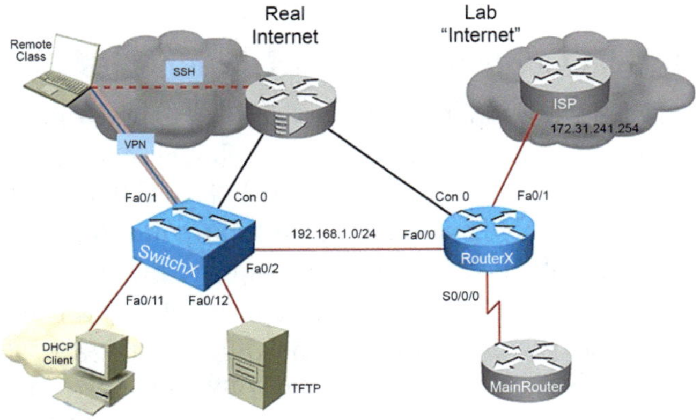

Figure 10.3. *The historical context of network topologies.*

Source: https://www.learncisco.net/wp-content/themes/learncisco/assets/images/icnd1/01-network-diagram.jpg.

10.1.2. Transition from Traditional to Modern Topologies

The transition from traditional network topologies to modern ones is a paradigm shift driven by needs for improved efficiency and flexibility in communications networks. Traditional topologies such as bus and star topologies are typically handicapped by limitations in scalability and fault tolerance, particularly where technology is evolving very rapidly and there is an excessive need for data throughput. With more companies embracing cloud computing, Internet of Things (IoT), and other new technologies, the static infrastructure of traditional topologies proves to be inadequate. On the other hand, today's topologies such as mesh and hybrid networks provide the flexibility needed to suit dynamic workloads as well as higher bandwidth. It is critical that stakeholders become aware of this shift in anticipation of innovative solutions for complex network problems, readying them to capitalize on innovations that redefine connectivity. Emergent network topologies are not only scaling but also enhance the resilience of communication infrastructure. Networks-on-Chip (NoC) is paradigm, and it is becoming critical solutions for semiconductor design in modern times. Traditional interconnect schemes are contradicting complexities arising from higher component densities within ICs, while NoCs enable more scalable design. These networks are designed to enable communication between a high number of small-scale processors, thus overcoming successfully interconnection complexity by traditional silicon approaches. Due to the developing technologies, the non-uniform and three-dimensional networks taking advantage of the design principles of small-world interconnects indicate potential towards improved fault tolerance and communication efficacy, thus paving the way for next-generation adaptive electronics (Teuscher et al., 2007). This ongoing development further influences how developers and researchers come up with and use network topologies. At the same time, the complexity of interconnected environments necessitates advanced modeling instruments that reflect the contemporary interaction complexities. Agent-Based Modeling and Simulation (ABMS) has emerged as an important complex network behavior research method, allowing for systems described by dynamic interactions between independent agents to be simulated. While traditional simulations have been predominantly based on sequential methods, the advent of speculative Parallel Discrete Event Simulation architecture presents an intriguing way to enhance performance. With this novel paradigm of modeling, network designers can more effectively study emergent behaviors of emergent phenomena in novel topological structures, such as NoCs and irregular networks. This blending of sophisticated modeling and modern topology design is critical, allowing researchers to explore complex interactions with reduced computational cost and achieve significant improvements in performance (Sameera et al., 2019).

Therefore, the new trends do not just reflect current trends but also setting the stage for future growth of network architectures and their applications (Figure 10.4).

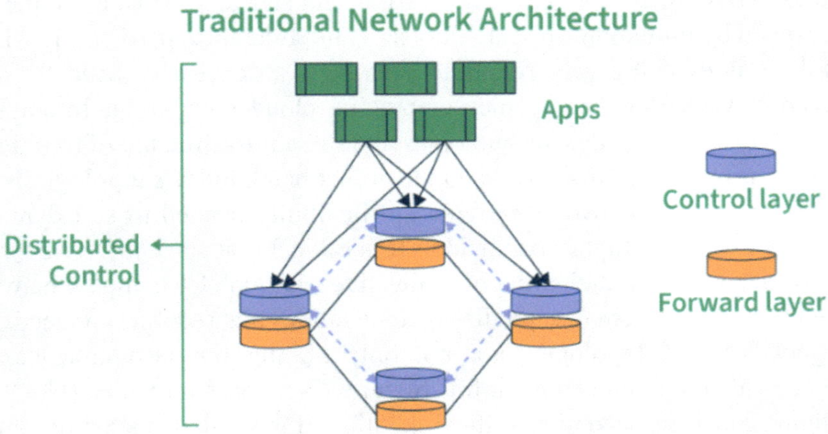

Figure 10.4. *The transition from traditional network topologies.*

Source: https://media.geeksforgeeks.org/wp-content/uploads/20241014180726658038/Traditional-network-architecture.png.

10.1.3. Impact of Technological Advancements

Network topology development profoundly affects data security, transmission, and management. With continuing development in technology, traditional network topologies continue to evolve to accommodate evolving computing paradigms as well as the explosion of data traffic. The integration of intelligent technologies into network equipment has facilitated an interactive and responsive platform, which has spurred innovations such as the move toward wireless Network-on-Chip (WNoC) designs. This transition is particularly important in coping with the requirement for increased efficiency as chip multiprocessors continue to increase in complexity with hundreds or thousands of cores. When WNoC designs emerge into focus, they will improve communication speed and reliability, becoming critical as networks expand to manage future computational and connectivity demands to support more complex applications and services within a robust topology (Millis et al., 2019). Furthermore, increased reliance on intermittent sources of energy in grid networks brings about opportunities as well as challenges that will characterize the topologies of the future. With the generation of electricity from solar and wind energy, the integration of these renewable but intermittent sources of energy demands intelligent grid structures with storage to achieve higher resilience. The most recent vulnerability analysis determines the degree by which well-designed storage can offset the effects of outages on power grid functioning and thus validate the requirement for adaptive network topology. This change in direction toward more intelligent smart technology-based grid networks is a defining change that aims to improve efficiency and sustainability within energy networks. These advances bring to the forefront the critical relationship between network structure and energy distribution, creating a need for resilient architectures that can withstand technological evolution as well as environmental factors (Millis et al., 2019). In addition to increasing resilience and effectiveness, application of new network topologies has deeper significance for data security and management. With growing complexity in networks, such as with edge computing and fog networking, they must be able to handle massive volumes of real-time data with minimal latency. This architectural improvement is significantly reliant on communication protocols capable of handling multicast and broadcast traffic effectively, particularly in distributed networks. The proposed hybrid plans of the new hybrid incorporating the integration of wired and wireless aspects, including those applied to WNoC systems, not only enhance performance but also make data traffic management easier. They are essential in meeting applications' demands for fast data processing and secure communication channels, the way forward suggesting topologies in networks that are designed with adaptability, speed, and security at the core (Cavall et al., 2016).

10.2. EMERGING TOPOLOGIES

The evolution of technology has significantly influenced the evolution of new network topologies that reflect the dynamic nature of applications in the current era. Future topologies, such as multi-microgrids (MMGs), are used to enhance the efficiency and reliability of energy distribution networks using the integration of distributed generation sources. MMGs represent a dynamic and resilient way of handling energy by enabling the change of network topologies based on various operational states. This adaptability is required in order to enhance performance and reduce challenges associated with renewable resources and fluctuating demand. With an increasing number of organizations adopting such innovative configurations, the potential for improving grid resilience creates a center stage, channeling research and development towards optimizing MMG reconfiguration strategies. Worthy of note is that innovation in communication technologies will continue to facilitate this change with enhanced data exchange and business coordination in new topology networks (Hosseini et al., 2025). In the automotive sector, the demand for flexible architecture for military cars illustrates another dimension of new topologies.

The integration of advanced electronics in vehicles necessitates a revolutionary "data bus" network backbone with capability for seamless "universal plug and play" support between various electronic devices. Such designs should be able to support multiple dissimilar data streams like voice, video, control, and diagnostics. This integration provides flexibility and expandability such that military vehicles can be readily reconfigured to accomplish multiple mission profiles without extensive redesign. With these network environments evolving, additional pressure for high-bandwidth, low-latency communication also emphasizes the need for scalable topologies that can support a range of operational demands. Thus, the architecture must provide compatibility and interoperability among existing system elements as well as be flexible enough for future expansion (Murphree et al., 2024). With new topologies continually emerging, communication, control, and power network interaction will be crucial in the design of the next-generation networks. The architecture must guarantee that such networks are asynchronized, and even as additional functionalities are added, they can still operate. This would imply that future topologies ought to incorporate fault tolerance, self-diagnosis, and self-reconfiguration capabilities, which make them strong and reliable. The move towards effective and scalable network topologies addresses not only the performance challenges of increasing data and operational complexity but also positions systems to be in a better position to respond to unforeseen exigencies. Convergence from various fields of emerging new topologies—whether in energy management or warfare—represents a paradigmatic change in network structuring and administration, pushing the boundaries of current technological innovation (Murphree et al., 2024) (Figure 10.5).

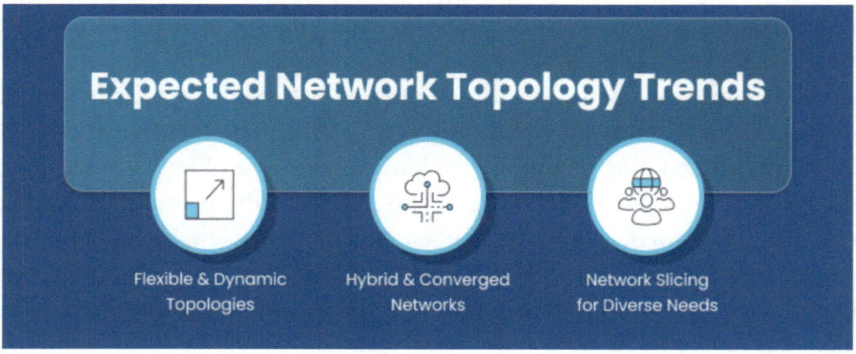

Figure 10.5. *Emerging topologies.*

Source: https://www.motadata.com/wp-content/uploads/2024/08/Blog-Inner-Expected-Network-Topology-Trends.png.

10.2.1. Software-Defined Networking (SDN)

The arrival of Software-Defined Networking (SDN) is a paradigm shift in network control and management topological design. SDN effects centralized control and dynamic traffic through isolation of the data layer from the control plane. This malleability of architecture is particularly timely with networks themselves becoming increasingly complex and demanding more responsive reaction to heterogeneous streams of data. Among the anticipated benefits of incorporating SDN in upcoming network infrastructures is enhanced resource optimization, through smart path calculation techniques. With the utilization of real-time information and algorithms, SDN is able to guarantee routes are optimized and latency minimized, thereby improving the quality of service provided to the end-user.

This emphasizes the importance of incorporating SDN in present designs, creating new solutions for existing networking challenges. With increasing numbers of organizations taking decisions based on data, the integration of cognitive capabilities into SDN takes center stage. Experts predict the use of machine learning and artificial intelligence to extend SDN, making networks capable of modifying themselves automatically in reaction to changing conditions as well as dynamically optimizing resource allocation in real time. This paradigm shift is reflected in conversation around cognitive communications and network structures and indicates direction for how network topologies will emerge. Such cognitive techniques can offer networks increased reliability and fault tolerance, optimally used for mission-critical uses involving uninterrupted service. In addition to improving operational efficiency, cognitive capabilities via SDN may also facilitate sophisticated service-oriented architectures that, apart from enhancing operational efficiency, further enrich the general user experience by performing real-time adjustments based on dynamic demands (Knoblock et al., 2025).

Moreover, recent advances in path computation approaches within the SDN environment are the peak of the actual-world utilization of these trends. Approaches such as Dynamic Shortest Path (DSP) and Hybrid Path Computation (HPC) show the potential for increased network performance by maximizing data flow management. Centralized approaches, taking global network knowledge, and decentralized approaches exhibit varied levels of efficiency in path computation. Notably, the hybrid solutions combine the strengths of both strategies to achieve effective solutions to congestion and routing problems (Bajaj et al., 2023). As SDN continues to develop, the use of these advanced path computation techniques is set to break through critical scalability and interoperability challenges, enabling future network topologies to be resilient and adaptable to increasing demands. The continued evolution and enhancement of these technologies will shape not only the operational environment but also the strategic frameworks employed to guide network growth in the future.

10.2.2. Mesh Networking

Mesh networking has also been a significant topic in the area of network topology of late, particularly with the enhanced requirement for strong, reliable, and extensible mechanisms for communication. In contrast to the traditional hierarchical nature of networks, mesh networking facilitates mutual connection between nodes with the ability to send data along multiple paths. Mesh networking is stronger as, when one faulty link occurs, other paths can redirect traffic easily, allowing connectivity to be unaffected. This robustness is particularly useful for use in rural or disaster areas where infrastructure may be questionable. The explosion of Internet of Things (IoT) devices only serves to underscore the necessity of mesh networks, as it provides the ideal vehicle to host the huge number of devices that are interconnected and require both autonomy and flexibility. As mesh networking continues to grow and develop, its integration with emerging technologies promises great things in the future. For instance, integrating mesh networks with sophisticated data processing features using Machine Learning (ML) and Artificial Intelligence (AI) can significantly improve performance. Such intelligent systems can learn about traffic patterns and dynamically re-route to ensure maximum efficiency with minimal latency. Additionally, the development of Physics-Informed Neural Networks (PINN) is the best example of how innovation can improve network dynamics management. By implementing MINNs in Partial Differential Equations that manage network behavior, the operators would fine-tune their ability to predict congestion and automate parameter calibration to maximize data flow, thus enhancing the efficacy of mesh topologies in complex environments (Cuomo et al., 2022). The social implications of mesh networking also blend with broader tendencies such as the evolution of the Metaverse, which necessitates a new understanding of interconnectedness. As our increasing intermingling of digital presence and real-world experience necessitates, network topologies must also shift accordingly. Mesh networking is appropriate for this intersection, with its facility for the flexibility necessary to support richer user experiences throughout virtual spaces. Merging the hardware technology and software creativity that will play such crucial roles in building the Metaverse will also rely on mesh network flexibility and scalability. This changing landscape demands a rethinking of what we know about connectivity in online spaces, moving away from traditional paradigms in order to address the increasing nuances of our networked reality (Park et al., 2022).

10.2.3. Cloud-Based Topologies

The introduction of cloud-based topologies is a fundamental shift in the topology of network design, driven by calls for increased flexibility and scalability. As enterprises adopt cloud computing platforms in increasing numbers, hierarchical designs are displaced by more flexible designs that can adapt to variable loads. Cloud-based topologies enable distributed computing resources to be pooled and managed across geographical locations, reducing latency and improving data access. Furthermore, integrating edge computing into these topologies allows organizations to compute data close to where it originates, which is critical for applications requiring real-time analytics. This philosophy emphasizes the importance of efficient resource management and servicing orchestration in a multi-cloud environment, ultimately resulting in delivering smooth communication and collaboration between users and devices across disparate geographical areas. The incorporation of Named Data Networking (NDN) within cloud topologies manifests the ongoing shift towards networking solutions to meet contemporary demands. In contrast to traditional IP-based designs, NDN adopts data-oriented paradigms such that content is utilized as the primary unit of exchange. This action corrects the aggravating burden placed on network resources by bandwidth-intensive applications such as video streaming. With the use of name-based routing and content caching, NDN enhances the efficiency of data delivery in accordance with contemporary Internet consumers who keep in touch more with dynamic content. Evolution of NDN, especially as it is combined with cloud architecture, forms the core of the evolution of robust solutions that are capable of handling heterogeneous media streams without aggravating congestion and providing fair access to resources among users, and thus resolving the pressure of consumerization on the one hand and network infrastructure limitations on the other (Zafar et al., 2020). While the future of networking is poised to embrace more next-generation technologies, cloud topologies will have an even bigger role at the intersection of newer paradigms such as Network Function Virtualization (NFV) and 6G networks. Such convergence further encourages the versatility of network design in supporting dynamic resource allocation and service differentiation for numerous applications. NFV, in particular, facilitates the integration of legacy hardware services into cloud-controlled virtual instances, supporting efficient utilization of resources and reduced operation costs. In addition, with the envisioned rollout of 6G networks, integration of ground and satellite networks will drive cloud-based topologies to new paths of speed and complexity. To address the special demands that are associated with it, research on leveraging NDN transmission via terahertz technology is underway. Such advancements are valuable for ensuring high-speed, secure communications across different network environments, thus shaping the future of cloud-based networking solutions (Wang et al., 2023) (Figure 10.6).

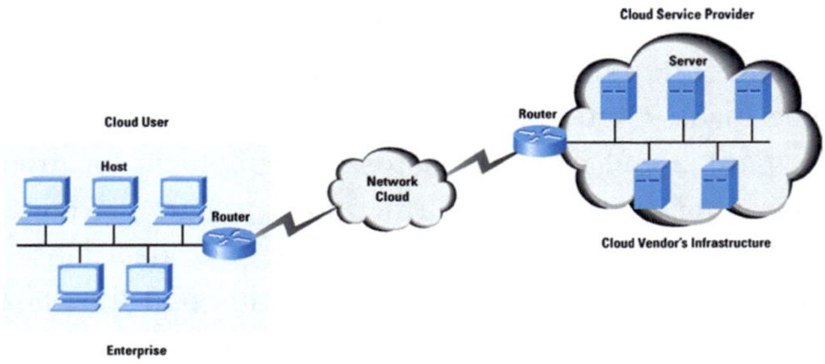

Figure 10.6. *Cloud-based topologies.*

Source: https://www.researchgate.net/publication/356239824/figure/fig1/AS:11431281099213887@1669229549460/Sample-cloud-topology.jpg.

10.3. ROLE OF ARTIFICIAL INTELLIGENCE IN NETWORK DESIGN

The integration of artificial intelligence (AI) into network design has revolutionized the manner in which systems are architected and optimized for performance and reliability. Through harnessing machine learning and deep learning technologies, network architects can analyze massive datasets to identify regions of potential malfunctioning and performance bottlenecks before they become significant issues. For instance, the application of Deep Convolutional Neural Networks (CNN) has been found useful in tasks such as traffic regulation and resource distribution because they can learn and adapt automatically to the traffic dynamics between nodes. The ability of CNNs to recognize complex patterns in real time enables pre-emptive decision-making and hence makes networks self-optimizing and resilient. These innovations are needed for future network architectures that can handle increased bandwidth and connectivity requirements effectively, establishing a foundation for seamless communication in a more digitalized society (Khan et al., 2020). Artificial intelligence is also important in strengthening security features in network architecture, which combats cyber-attacks that infiltrate networks. As networks become more complex and larger, so do the vulnerabilities that hackers exploit. AI can process data from different network sensors and endpoints, detecting abnormal activity that may represent potential attacks. Evolved Plastic Artificial Neural Networks (EPANNs) illustrate this strategy since they evolve and adapt by experience, learning custom responses to new threats. These systems are programmed to automatically detect anomalies, yet also learn from past examples to make subsequent defenses more effective. Thus, incorporating AI into network security not only improves the security of the network in general but also enables organizations to stay one step ahead of the attackers who keep adjusting their strategy (Abbott et al., 2018). This trend indicates the critical need for AI to determine robust and forward-looking network topologies. In the near future, artificial intelligence usage in network designing will further grow at an even faster pace due to the advent of new technologies such as the Internet of Things (IoT) and 5G networks. The development of connected devices requires network designs that are more sophisticated and can change dynamically based on shifting loads in real-time. AI-driven solutions can facilitate smart routing and load balancing, which will efficiently move data traffic within a network. As a result, these technologies can empower the development of more scalable and energy-efficient design, halve operational expenditure while enhance performance. Furthermore, with AI technologies evolving relentlessly, their impact on network design will drive topological innovations, such as self-healing networks that are capable of detecting failures and reconfiguring themselves automatically. Thus, AI is not an add-on but a fundamental driver for new network topology trends that have the capability to bring unparalleled levels of efficiency and reliability.

10.3.1. AI-Driven Network Optimization

Artificial intelligence employed in network optimization heralds a new revolution in network topology, particularly toward coping with the increasing complexity of modern communication networks. AI-driven algorithms enable networks to self-diagnose and adjust automatically to fluctuations in data traffic, leading to more efficient use of resources and reduced latency. For instance, machine learning techniques can predict traffic behavior by scanning past data so that systems can set bandwidth usage and routing practices ahead of time in anticipation of changes in user needs. By eliminating much of the constant human intervention, such automated systems optimize efficiency and lengthen network functional life. The use of smart algorithms marks a move from fixed network topologies to far more dynamic, self-tuning systems, an improvement emphasized by studies citing the effectiveness of AI in solving general problems in wireless sensor networks (Alsheikh et al., 2014). Additionally, AIs application in edge computing plays a large role in optimizing networks, especially with the mainstream popularity of fifth-generation (5G) networks. With the application of cognitive content-centric networking (CCN) techniques, AI can enable real-time processing and data dissemination at points of strategic importance in the network. Such proximity to consumers lowers latency and can handle the massive volumes of data that are common in 5G use cases. Creating a cognitive CCN (C-CCN) enables networks to utilize fog computing, that is, computational resources can be utilized more optimally, enabling context-awareness and traffic optimization. These advancements not only enable more effective content retrieval and better user experiences but also provide the foundation for the development of personalized services, including network acceleration based on individual user need and behavior (Li et al., 2018). The emerging network topology, driven by AI-optimized topology, ultimately provides the promise of unmatched efficiency and user satisfaction. As networks are developed to include various environmental and contextual conditions, they become increasingly resilient to potential disruptions. AI-based traffic offloading and resource management is imperative to ensuring high performance levels in a digital economy that necessitates ubiquity and reliability. Merging AI with network architecture thereby constructs networks with intelligent self-modification capability and thus enhances their functionality. This paradigm shift not only highlights the critical role of technological innovation in network architecture but also lays a foundation for novel solutions to novel problems in networking, such as increasing demands for real-time processing of data and for increased user interaction reliability (Figure 10.7).

Figure 10.7. *AI-driven network optimization.*

Source: https://plat.ai/wp-content/uploads/aiphoto.jpg.webp.

10.3.2. Predictive Analytics for Network Performance

The integration of predictive analytics and network performance management is revolutionizing network topology management in organizations. Traditional methods of network optimization based on closed-form analysis and static models are unable to deal with the complexity of modern-day networks. As the dependence on connected devices increases, so does the need for real-time management platforms. Predictive analytics applies machine learning and data models to understand end-to-end performance as well as application behavior. This move from reactive management to proactive management allows the operators to anticipate problems before they happen, thereby enhancing security and performance of networks. By combining real-time measurement of data and control, networks can be turned into self-optimizing systems that improve operational efficiency and user experience. The growing complexity in the network gives rise to the demand for creative performance management techniques, particularly in network environments where various programs compete for limited resources. Predictive analysis assists network administrators in evaluating massive amounts of data generated by various protocols and devices and transform this information into meaningful data. The necessity of developing algorithms able to detect and label anomalies in real-time cannot be overstressed because offline analysis does not foresee issues before occurrence. Networks must not only respond to already identified issues but also predict them by learning continuously from past records of performance. This shift to intelligent, data-based analytics ensures that networks are able to offer best performance in the presence of dynamic changes in patterns of traffic requirements and security demands, eventually leading to a stronger infrastructure. Moreover, the context in which networks operate is evolving, particularly with the advent of connected things across industries like the automotive industry. The different applications of the network also make it challenging to manage network performance because no single communication technology can fulfill all the requirements optimally. Instead, through the multi-interface approach utilizing predictive analytics, networks have the capability to select the best technology for the context at hand. This method is based on dynamic network interface selection, which optimizes vehicular sensor data transmission by looking forward to channel conditions and queuing transmission accordingly. Such enhancements not only enhance rates and robustness but also demonstrate the potential for predictive analytics to be applied to more efficient network performance. With further development of these paradigms, they hold much promise in shaping the future landscape of network topology in an increasingly interconnected world.

10.3.3. Automation of Network Management

With growing network environments, automation of network management is a critical component in ensuring efficient and dependable operation. Automation enables the monitoring and administration of the network systems at any time, thereby significantly reducing human error and enhancing efficiency in operations. This movement towards automated processes is of utmost significance in safety-critical environments, where the cost of mismanagement can be staggering. Systematic network monitoring is a cornerstone for guaranteeing the operational integrity of distributed systems. Network operators can gain greater insight into network usage and traffic flows through the use of sophisticated monitoring techniques, all of which enables informed decision-making and proactive planning. Lastly, automation is not only a measure of operating efficiency but also a resilience tool in network management, as reflected in existing trends in the sector (Johnson et al., 2012). The Industrial Wireless Sensor Networks (IWSNs) are an excellent example of how tools of automation are being deployed in network management across different industries. IWSNs are seen in industry automation to feed back control and process systems, extending the boundaries of network administration even further. Their inherent advantage—low-cost scalability, flexibility, and capability to self-heal—are made possible by incorporating automated systems that quickly adapt to evolving environments. Although, with such advantages available, the deployment of IWSNs is fraught with serious challenges because of their vulnerability to sophisticated industrial environments. Hence, network automation not only maximizes operations but also addresses problems arising out of the uncertainty of industrial environments. With advanced technology, focus will be given to enhancing protocols and hardware platforms for IWSNs that will probably exhibit new features, highlighting the necessity to further explore automated solutions in this area (Aslam et al., 2018). In the future, the future of network topology is intricately linked to technological advancements in automation processes and technology. As networks evolve, artificial intelligence and machine learning will play an increasingly pervasive role in automating network management functions. The technologies will render systems capable of predicting network needs, maximizing resource usage, and avoiding potential disturbances before developing into full-blown issues. Furthermore, as businesses understand the value of agile and responsive networks, investment in automation will grow exponentially. Automated anomaly detection, for instance, will provide smooth monitoring and feedback on network conditions so that immediate responses can be provided to maintain conditions in the healthiest possible state. Hence, the integration of automation prepares networks not only to face threats in the future but also to leverage leading-edge technologies that enable overall performance to enhance in a more competitive landscape (Johnson et al., 2012; Aslam et al., 2018) (Figure 10.8).

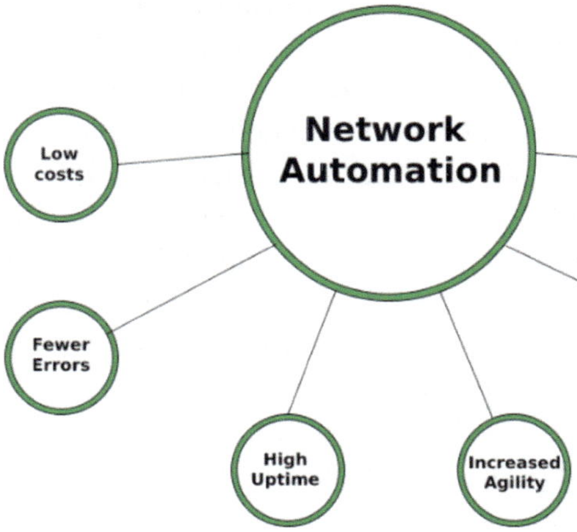

Figure 10.8. *Automation in network management.*

Source: https://media.geeksforgeeks.org/wp-content/uploads/20220825161400/NetworkAutomation1.png.

10.4. SECURITY CONSIDERATIONS IN FUTURE TOPOLOGIES

As networking topologies evolve to keep pace with the greater demands of interdependent systems, security becomes increasingly paramount. Next-generation topologies, particularly those leveraging leading-edge technology like the Internet of Things (IoT), must offer solutions to inherent weaknesses introduced through greater interconnectivity. Multidevice adoption introduces higher attack surface, so robust security structures must be put in place. This is most visibly applicable in the field of healthcare where patient information is highly sensitive and transmitted through IoT devices. Such key concerns as data privacy, unauthorized access, and risks of breaches highlight the need for end-to-end security measures that encompass encryption, authentication mechanisms, and round-the-clock monitoring systems. These problems are not only an additional layer but a core part of design, in which security policies are introduced inside the topology right from the start, thus safeguarding the integrity of the entire network (Rehman et al., 2025). In addition to traditional security approaches, new solutions must address the sophisticated threats brought by new topologies. For instance, free space optical (FSO) communication is emerging as a future technology due to the potential for high data rate and enhanced physical layer security. However, its application has been largely restricted to point-to-point topology due to limitations like beamwidth and line-of-sight. As researchers explore dynamic access points (APs) with FSO communication, the potential for alignment error and natural interference must be carefully assessed. The innovation of advanced technologies such as modulating retroreflectors (MRR) and intelligent reflecting surfaces (IRS) has the potential to enhance the resilience of FSO networks against such vulnerabilities. Besides mitigating against security threats, this new method enhances communication ability, making it a critical factor in future topological evolution (Dabiri et al., 2025). Besides, cooperative models marrying existing security measures to emerging technologies can offer robust solutions to the security concerns brought about by intricate network topologies. Cooperating security models, particularly in IoT-based systems, could not only minimize threats but also facilitate trust among users and stakeholders. As networks increasingly become more interconnected in more sophisticated ways, the need to understand some threat models and patterns of attack cannot be overstressed. Continued research into learning about prospective failure points and bringing in adaptable security plans will be key to the triumph of future topologies. Ultimately, the synergy between emerging technology and comprehensive security plans will determine the operation viability and reliability of the networks that will shape the digital world tomorrow (Rehman et al., 2025; Dabiri et al., 2025).

10.4.1. Vulnerabilities in Emerging Topologies

Topology of the network keeps changing owing to developments in technology, and new paradigms like MANETs and dynamic cloud models emerge. While these developments create unequivocal benefits, they also come with unique weaknesses through which network integrity can be compromised. MANETs, for instance, lack a central control point, rendering them susceptible to all manner of security attacks like black hole and Sybil attacks. Decentralization of these networks usually results in undermined reliability of routing protocols due to the absence of a central authority to stabilize, with which it becomes hard to implement security protocols. Thus, discovery and counteraction to these vulnerabilities are needed to ensure a guarantee of the robustness of new topologies, as any breach in security can incapacitate the operations of the networks, leading to serious operational interruptions. Additionally, the risk-sensitive approach is also crucial in identifying vulnerabilities within new network topologies, for instance, those utilized in cities for snow removal, as viewed through the capacitated arc routing problem (CARP). Current algorithms used for city snow clearing concentrate on road network topology and do not consider the increased risks associated with adverse weather conditions, for instance, snowy pavements. The solutions to these vulnerabilities involve a holistic examination that reorders service priorities by factoring in the added cost of travel needs in winter conditions.

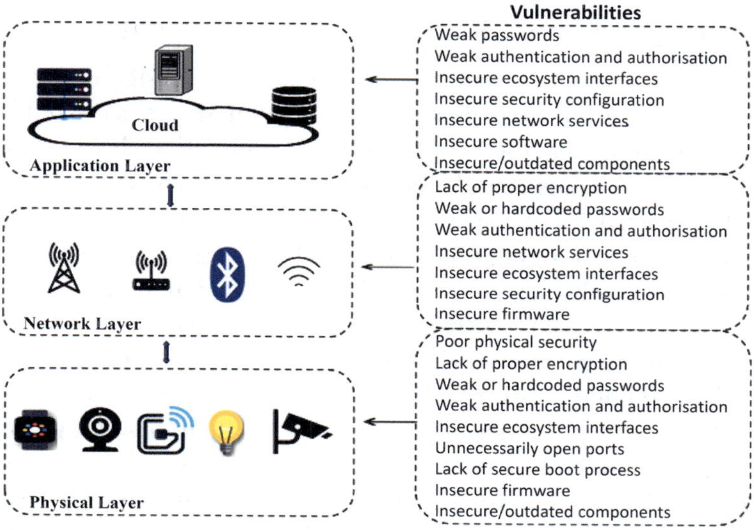

Figure 10.9. *Vulnerabilities in emerging topologies.*

Source: https://www.mdpi.com/electronics/electronics-12-01176/article_deploy/html/images/electronics-12-01176-g001-550.jpg.

The use of a vulnerability-based parallel heuristic algorithm has a practical solution for the minimization of service completion time and sensitivity of the trade-off between operational effectiveness and escalating dispatch times. This paradigm realizes the acute need for cost-benefit analysis on vulnerability assessments as an integral part of overall network planning and operating strategies. With increasingly sophisticated network topologies, integration of security measures into future frameworks is essential. MANETs have been shown, according to newer studies, to be able to use secure communications in spite of their weaknesses through advanced routing methodologies. SAODV and ARAN protocols are but two examples of enhancing data integrity and security, with other innovative solutions proposed consistently to counteract unique vulnerabilities. The future topology of networks will thus be characterized by adaptive security systems that actively respond to evolving threats. With progress along the way of research in this field, the protection of vulnerabilities in new topologies will not only be a guarantor of data integrity but also open space for broader acceptance and usage of these ground-breaking technologies. Enhanced understanding and mitigation strategies will eventually pave the way for a progressively safer and more resilient network infrastructure in service of the continued digital evolution (Figure 10.9).

10.4.2. Strategies for Enhancing Network Security

Among the key forms of enhancement in network security is the adoption of effective encryption methodologies. Encryption serves as a fundamental guard against improper use, ensuring that information being transferred through networks remains confidential and unaltered. As more devices become connected, the need for advanced encryption methodologies becomes even greater. Enhanced encryption, especially in edge computing, not only protects sensitive information but also improves the overall design of network topology. Interweaving encryption algorithms such as AES (Advanced Encryption Standard) and future quantum-resistant algorithms provides a double benefit of data security and building trust between users. This trust is vital for building a safe digital environment, especially with the integration of smart technologies into many applications in network infrastructures, ultimately defining future trends in network topology. Another significant approach to enhancing network security is to put in place strict access control methods. Access control defines who has access to see or utilize resources in a network, which also directly influences the systems' overall exposure to threats. Least privilege principle is critical in adopting, whereby users only have access to what they need for their own job, hence subjecting them to fewer possible security breaches. Secondly, the implementation of multi-factor authentication (MFA) also adds another layer of security to prevent even if credentials are obtained, unauthorized access still cannot be achieved. By implementing such access control mechanisms, organizations will significantly curtail their insider threat and external attacks risks. As networks move toward more decentralized design, building robust access control in scattered nodes and devices is imperative to maintaining security integrity across the realm of modern network infrastructures. Last but not least, ongoing monitoring and vulnerability scanning are essential tools in network security enhancement. The greater the sophistication of the networks, which may involve such add-ons as cloud computing and the Internet of Things (IoT), the more the danger of getting exploited because of vulnerabilities grows exponentially. Real-time monitoring software that tracks traffic patterns can spot irregular activity that indicates breaches, and organizations are able to respond in anticipation. Furthermore, conducting regular vulnerability tests also builds a culture of awareness and preparedness, allowing weaknesses to be identified before being exploited. This is especially critical in the case of evolving threats driven by advancements in smart technology and clean energy sources, where the interdependent nature of systems introduces new vulnerabilities in the need for proper investigation and rapid response techniques in their integration. By performing this, integrating monitoring and assessment into security acts as an assurance that networks are resistant to existing and emerging dangers, as underlined by constant controversies around the vulnerabilities that smart grid technologies and edge deployment introduce (Millis et al., 2019; Baktir et al., 2018).

10.4.3. Blockchain's Role in Network Security

With advances in technologies and the development of network topology, the use of blockchain to improve network security has come to the forefront. This distributed ledger technology not only ensures a secure means of data integrity but also increases transparency in transactions between different networks. Through the use of a distributed design, blockchain eliminates single points of failure and lowers the exposure to cyberattacks. The encryption paradigms of blockchain technology ensure traceability and verifiability of changes in data, making communications in a network more trustworthy overall. From now on, organizations are already beginning to implement blockchain applications in an effort to secure their network infrastructures, preparing the way for future models that will also prioritize security as much as network topology efficiency and scalability. The shift brought by emerging networking technologies such as 5G and the upcoming shift to 6G networks constitutes a new shift in connectivity, and which has blockchain playing a critical role in addressing associated security challenges. Scalability and interoperability issues presented by these new systems necessitate a secure solution to this challenge, which blockchain can provide. By providing a secure two-way communication between infinite devices and systems, blockchain strengthens the security foundation required in future networks. Also, as outlined in existing research, the future and present landscape of 6G networks is estimated to be filled with numerous weaknesses, so it is necessary to integrate blockchain into these frameworks to minimize threats and strengthen defenses against likely attacks (Cheng-Wang et al., 2023). In the context of the metaverse and its far-reaching vision to create a hyper-real virtual world, the security issues introduced are significant. Blockchain technology promises to provide effective solutions for these issues, especially in connection with user data privacy and transaction security in the face of this vast ecosystem's complexities. Highlighted among the discussions on metaverse development is that the inherent nature of such networks—such as their immersive realism and sustainability—poses special security challenges which must be rectified. Therefore, the integration of blockchain within metaverse architecture might make a tremendous difference in enhancing security and making user interactions safe and reliable. By addressing main challenges like scalability and interoperability, blockchain can contribute to constructing secure and resilient metaverse worlds (Wang et al., 2022) (Figure 10.10).

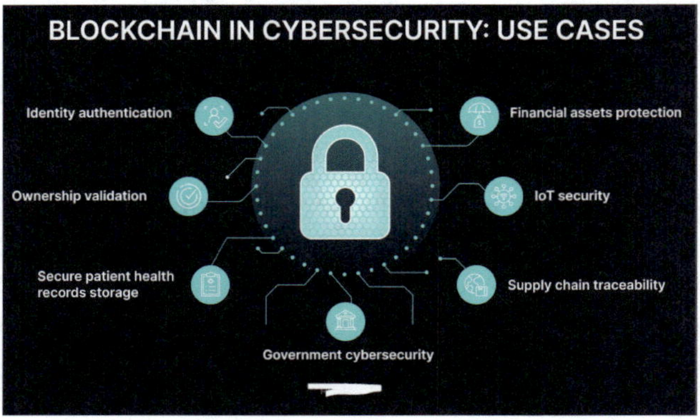

Figure 10.10. *Role of blockchain in network security.*

Source: https://www.psero.com/wp-content/uploads/2024/12/what-are-the-main-use-cases-of-blockchain-in-cybersecurity.jpg.

10.5. INTERNET OF THINGS (IOT) AND NETWORK TOPOLOGY

The Internet of Things (IoT) is transforming the concept of network topology, necessitating shifting to more efficient and dynamic models. With evolving IoT, traditional network topologies such as star, mesh, and tree are being revisited to accommodate the explosion of connected devices. Each device within an IoT ecosystem has unique data patterns and communication requirements, resulting in intricate network designs. Moreover, increased deployment of wireless sensor networks requires focus on the necessity for a versatile topology that optimizes performance and guarantees resilience, particularly where there is limited physical infrastructure. This is the call for future networks to embrace sophisticated architecture that effectively manages connectivity between a heterogeneous range of devices with high levels of service integrity and responsiveness. The intersection of IoT devices is meant to render environments more cognitive, and it is a critical step in the evolution of network topologies (Perera et al., 2018). The evolving paradigm of IoT also brings prominent issues concerning energy efficiency and security within network topologies.

Since resource-constrained devices, that is, wireless sensors, are typical in IoT deployments, energy consumption should be designed to provide a longer lifespan to devices. Effective topological solutions must involve energy-aware protocols that negotiate performance demands versus power consumption. Adding security features—for example, encryption and authentication—unintentionally adds energy loads, so the dynamics of keeping security and efficiency become complicated and uneven in IoT networks. Moreover, threats like denial of sleep attacks are particularly troublesome, particularly when devices are not able to conserve energy due to insecure configurations. Future research must thus reconcile such competing demands by developing innovative topological designs that not only enhance energy efficiency but also enhance network security against emerging risks (Udoh et al., 2019). The interplay between IoT and network topology is also shaping the future of data analysis and real-time decision-making in intelligent ecosystems. As IoT devices become more ubiquitous, they generate huge volumes of data that can be used to draw valuable insights if utilized effectively. Network topologies must change to facilitate seamless data flow with optimized paths of communication to minimize latency. Integrating technologies such as edge computing and fog computing facilitates computation near the data source, lowering the response time and improving the overall user experience. This shift emphasizes the transition away from solely centralized designs to more distributed ones that facilitate IoTs decentralized nature. Ultimately, future trends in network topology will be characterized by an emphasis on interoperability, adaptive communication protocols, and rational data management processes that collectively enhance the functionality of IoT systems (Perera et al., 2018).

10.5.1. Impact of IoT on Network Design

The rapid expansion of the Internet of Things (IoT) has drastically influenced the landscape of the network, presented new challenges and demanded that characterize emerging network topology trends. With increasing numbers of IoT devices going on line, they require a rethinking of traditional network architecture to accommodate increased connectivity requirements and diverse communication protocols. This has resulted in the incorporation of edge computing, which handles data closer to the point where it is generated, reducing latency and bandwidth usage. Consequently, network architectures are shifting towards decentralized architecture marked by geographically dispersed nodes with optimized data flow and processing procedures in various IoT environments. This paradigm is indicative of a core shift in the unique nature and requirements of IoT, indicating that future network architectures will prioritize flexibility and scalability to better support integrated infrastructures. Moreover, the unique requirements of IoT applications, such as those in industrial settings, also illustrate the impact of IoT on network architecture. For instance, the use of Industrial Wireless Sensor Networks (IWSNs) has gained pace since they are cheap, can be scaled, and are easy to implement. The networks enable real-time monitoring and control through environments ranging from manufacturing to infrastructure (Aslam et al., 2018). However, IWSNs are also threatened by security, reliability, and the need for communication protocols that are dependable to a high degree of operation under dynamic and complicated situations.

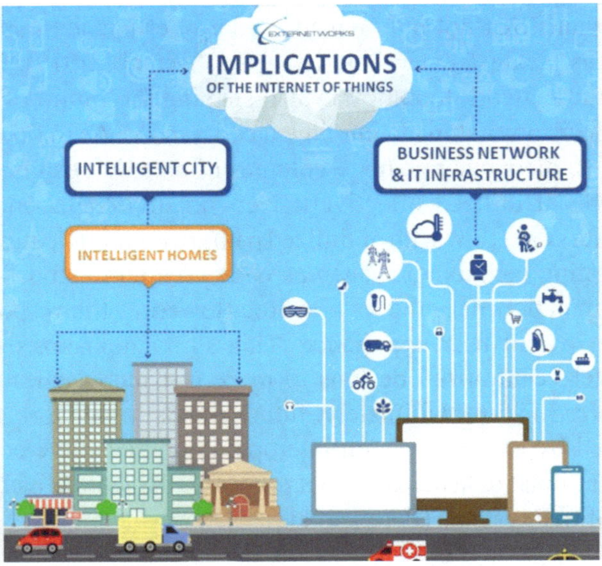

Figure 10.11. *Impact of IoT on network design.*

Source: https://blog.externetworks.com/wp-content/uploads/2016/12/Implications_of_IoT-1-2.jpg.

Thus, designing such a network must take these factors into consideration and hence, there has been topology development that enhances resilience as well as performance and ensures compliance to standards in the industry. This is a pointer to the importance of adaptive architectures that can handle the changing demands of industrial IoT applications. In addition to operational issues, communication band selection for IoT devices also has significant ramifications on network design, most particularly in resource-limited environments. Research indicates that operation in unlicensed bands such as 2400 MHz and 915 MHz bands is a key driver of cost-effectiveness in IoT deployment in smart grids (García Haro et al., 2017). Comparative research indicates that performance can be better in the 915 MHz band in some environments, particularly where the interference from other equipment is minimal (Zhou et al., 2017). These observations compel network architects to consider frequency selection as a fundamental aspect of topology design that not only optimizes overall network performance but also ensures effortless integration and functional compatibility among diverse IoT devices. With more maturity of IoT, upcoming network designs must consider adaptive mechanisms that can optimize performance across different operational environments, thereby making the IoT ecosystem more integrated (Figure 10.11).

10.5.2. Scalability Challenges with IoT Devices

With the ongoing expansion of Internet of Things (IoT) devices, scalability problems become an inherent concern. IoT devices' inherent nature, including limited processing capacity and constrained energy resources, contributes to the challenge of managing large networks efficiently. For instance, as devices multiply, network resource requirements expand, leading to bottlenecks that compromise performance. Traditional network architectures, commonly based on static addressing and routing, are not designed to support the changing dynamics of IoT ecosystems. If left uncorrected, this inflexibility can precipitate subpar service performance, increased latency, and decreased reliability, essentially negating the potential benefits of IoT integration in integrated network infrastructure. Additionally, the implementation of Software Defined Networking (SDN) can yield promising measures to counteract these scalability issues, though with certain challenges. While SDN provides a means to centralize control and optimize network efficiency through programmability, applying it in low-power IoT environments is fraught with challenges. High control message overhead leads to performance degradation, and things get worse particularly in those networks that are resource-constrained. Current work indicates that optimizations are necessary to restrict this control traffics impact without impairing interoperability with existing protocols, as evidenced through the introduction of light frameworks such as {\\\\mu}SDN, whose objective is to reduce control overhead while ensuring QoS for critical network flows. Optimization solutions for these issues are important in opening up the way to scalable IoT deployments. In the Smart Grids scenario, the scalability issue is raised even more, particularly due to the fact that these networks involve an enormous amount of IoT devices. Technological progress of Smart Grid enabled by IoT enables greater energy control and information gathering. Parallel to that, these are accompanied by the necessity to manage thousands of sensors, actuators, and smart meters distributed over different physical and logical networks. Thus, connectivity, automation, and very efficient tracking mechanisms emerge as indispensable. The complex interdependence of devices in this setup calls for advanced network topologies that can gracefully accommodate fluctuations in both device counts and data loads. With the increasing use of IoT in Smart Grids, studies toward overcoming the many issues associated with these scalability issues must address how to solve to ensure to offer reliability and efficiency in energy supply and management networks to create strong and sustainable frameworks for future power grids (Baddeley et al., 2018; Copeland et al., 2019).

10.5.3. Integration of IoT with Existing Topologies

The integration of the Internet of Things (IoT) into current network topologies is a revolutionary shift in the way devices communicate and interact. By bridging the physical and digital divide, IoT enables devices to collect and share information, initiating enhanced decision-making processes and operational efficiency. The implementation of IoT across various industries employs big data analytics to provide critical insights that guide business enhancements, for instance. Though the promise of IoT is captivating, it generates consumer doubt about the veracity of the benefits anticipated. As indicated in various studies, the success of IoT depends on the extent to which these systems can interconnect with traditional infrastructures to bring about a seamless integration that maximizes performance and reliability as it addresses weaknesses in network security and data privacy (Perera et al., 2018). In addition, the advent of smart grid technologies is a prime example of the technical realization of IoT on deployed topologies that has revolutionized the energy system. The conventional power grids, usually prone to inefficiencies and one-way information flow, are getting transformed into Smart Grids (SGs) that leverage IoT devices for monitoring, control, and information exchange between consumers and providers in real time. Such change makes energy exchange bi-directional, allowing dynamic response devices to track consumption patterns and fluctuations in demand. Because IoT allows interconnectivity between devices, it can lower wastage and enhance energy supply reliability. The integration of IoT in the design of Smart Grids is an indication of the necessity to implement novel network topology strategies in a bid to meet the growing demands of modern energy systems in addition to legacy challenges (Copeland et al., 2019). Lastly, the future of network topology in the case of IoT integration also relies on scalability and flexibility. As more devices get connected, the currently deployed networks must scale in a manner that accommodates additional endpoints without sacrificing efficiency. New technologies such as edge computing and cloud computing provide means of load distribution for data processing and storage closer to the devices, hence reducing latency and bandwidth concerns. This not only enhances performance but also allows network management to scale with increasing complexity brought by IoT devices. With organizations set to the future, integrating IoT into existing topologies must be aimed at designing adaptive architectures that enable responsiveness to change and realizing the full potential of networked systems, thereby enabling the smart cities and facilities of the future (Figure 10.12).

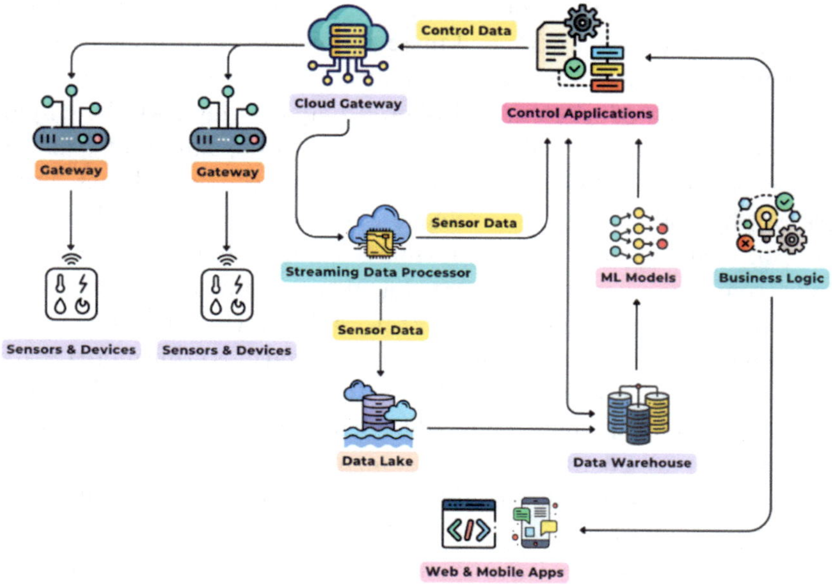

Figure 10.12. *The integration of the Internet of Things (IoT) within existing network topologies.*

Source: https://www.mdpi.com/applsci/applsci-14-07104/article_deploy/html/images/applsci-14-07104-g001.png.

10.6. FUTURE OF WIRELESS NETWORK TOPOLOGIES

Wireless network topologies have future enhancements in store as the demand for greater efficiency and speedier data movement continues to grow. Traditional NoC architecture faces scalability challenges due to the increasing number of processing cores in multiprocessor systems. The introduction of Wireless Network-on-Chip (WNoC) architecture is a paradigm shift where all the cores utilize a shared broadband channel to maximize communication efficiency. This architecture is proposed to be utilized for enhancing low latency as well as broadcast and multicast traffic support, essentially to enhance existing wired NoCs. Through integration of WNoC systems, researchers hope to overcome the performance limit offered by conventional designs, thus providing future multiprocessor architecture a path towards better scalability and communication efficiency in a vast number of cores (Cavall et al., 2016). With wireless technology advances, virtual network embedding into wireless multi-hop networks is a critical topic of concern. Traditional solutions have been centered on wired and cellular networks, and there remains a gap in strategic physical resource allocation in wireless environments. This is especially so given the pervasive expansion of wireless multi-hop networks, which will be employed in sharing resources between different sectors and groups of users. Addressing this issue, novel embedding algorithms are being considered that optimize the use of physical substrates to achieve optimal use of physical substrates, ensuring efficient resource allocation while responding to the unique challenge of wireless environments. These emerge together with the overall trend towards network virtualization, which allows for several heterogeneous architectures to be present and operate over shared infrastructures, and thus bring more flexibility and efficiency into the network topologies (Ok et al., 2012). Looking ahead, hybridized topological architectures blended with advanced virtualization methods are set to control the development of future wireless networks. WNoC systems merged with effective virtualization techniques will not only accommodate increasing bandwidth requirements and lower latency but also provide greater reliability in data transmission. All these technologies combined provide a possibility to develop adaptive topologies of networks that enable the systems to adjust dynamically to various loads of users and working conditions. This adaptability enables the creation of self-optimizing networks that allocate resources wisely depending on real-time analysis, which will improve overall performance. The trajectory of wireless network topologies thus is innovation towards a time when high-level connectivity and transmission rate of data are the main agenda (Cavall et al., 2016; Ok et al., 2012).

10.6.1. Evolution in 5G Technology

The introduction of 5G technology is a significant milestone in the history of mobile communication systems, which addresses the increasing demands for higher data rates, lower latency, and better connectivity. With its launch, 5G has introduced revolutionary transformations to various sectors, with promises of unprecedented user experience and new business opportunities. At the center of driving 5G lies the ability to support a large number of connected devices, which leads it to extend the Internet of Things (IoT) universe. As IoT devices become increasingly common, the need for robust network infrastructure comes to the forefront, paving the way for creative applications which range from smart cities to automated production lines. However, amidst all these advancements, 5G also faces several challenges, such as network security and effective management of frequency spectrum, which require ongoing research and collaboration across academic and industry domains to ensure viable deployment and integration with existing network architectures (Cheng-Wang et al., 2023).

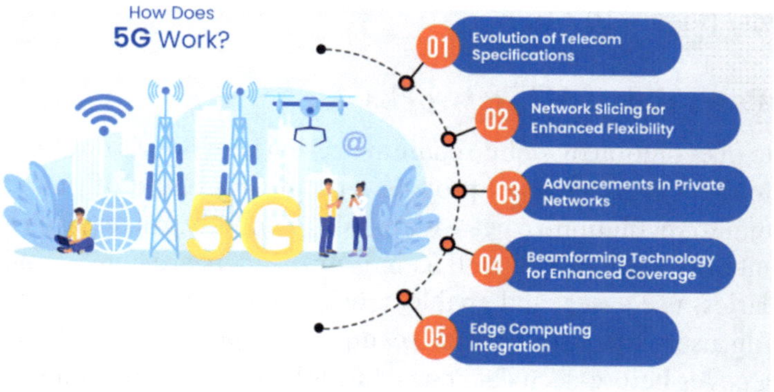

Figure 10.13. *Advancements in 5G technology.*

Source: https://www.veritis.com/wp-content/uploads/2024/05/How-Does-5G-Work.jpg.

As the technology world evolves, the transition from 5G to 6G is already underway, which calls for a close examination of the future of the network topology. Studies are examining how 6G will transform communication paradigms through emphasis on embedding artificial intelligence (AI) and machine learning to optimize network performance. The technologies are likely to improve network efficiency by creating self-optimizing systems that auto-allocation resources in real-time in line with actual requirements. On top of that, the expected development of holographic and terahertz communications in 6G will render bandwidth capacities exponentially higher, significantly improving user experiences. The transition is important to empower next-generation networks to accommodate the complex and demanding applications that next-generation networks will be required to serve, necessitating network topology to develop to effectively handle greater loads of data and user connections (Cheng-Wang et al., 2023). In addition to technological advancements that bring about changes, the rollout of 5G and its evolution into 6G will significantly influence the designs of network topologies. Industry 4.0, which is automation and data exchange in manufacturing technology, is greatly reliant on the rollout enablers like IoT that directly gain advantage from advances in mobile communications. The co-evolution of Industry 4.0 and 5G encapsulates the influence of network topography on smooth interactions among disparate connected devices. Additionally, the integration of wireless sensor networks (WSN) in industrial operations reflects the necessity to enhance network reliability as well as security. Since companies more and more automate and embrace connectivity, future network structures will need to emphasize scalability, interoperability, and resiliency in a bid to fight security challenges that accompany increased connectivity (Figure 10.13).

10.6.2. Potential of 6G Networks

As the rate of evolution of mobile communication networks is now going beyond 5G technologies, 6G networks provide a promising future of innovation with the potential to revolutionize network topology entirely. As research and debate on 6G continue, academia as well as industry leaders are converging to define its boundaries, use cases, and enablers. 6G is anticipated to not only enhance the existing user experience but also surpass its predecessor's limitations by providing never-before-seen data rates, lower latency, and a still more extensive range of applications. This convergence of technological advancements heralds an era in which networks will be more entrenched and empowered to enable diverse industries, ranging from healthcare to smart cities, hence demonstrating the transformative potential of 6G networks in shaping future network topologies (Cheng-Wang et al., 2023). The rollout of 6G will largely coincide with the advent of novel applications and services leveraging its advanced features further in creating network topologies. For instance, the incorporation of extended reality within the metaverse enhances the demand for high-speed, reliable networks, and 6G can potentially fulfill these demands considerably. With growing popularity in direct user interactions with virtual spaces, network design will have to be enhanced to support hyper spatiotemporal and immersive experiences. This necessitates a shift toward decentralized frameworks and edge computing methodologies, thereby enhancing system resilience, and reducing latency. As these technologies advance, the potential for networks to be made more scalable and flexible is heightened, opening doors for a future generation of network topology based on efficiency, security, and human-centered design (Wang et al., 2022). Examining the potential of 6G networks requires an in-depth understanding of the challenges and avenues of open research concerned. While the 6G vision encompasses higher performance, all-around integration of all technologies, and stronger security mechanisms, actual deployments have several challenges to address. Network privacy, data processing, and interoperability among numerous future technologies are a few of the issues that need to be addressed in order to facilitate effective deployment. The most critical aspect will be the potential of artificial intelligence and machine learning in optimizing network performance and solving complex issues. As much as debate around 6G continues, it is crucial for researchers and practitioners to participate in collaborative expeditions that not only define the technology's boundaries but also provide the foundation for solving its in-built challenges, with the ultimate promise of successfully achieving the potential brought about by 6G networks (Cheng-Wang et al., 2023) (Figure 10.14).

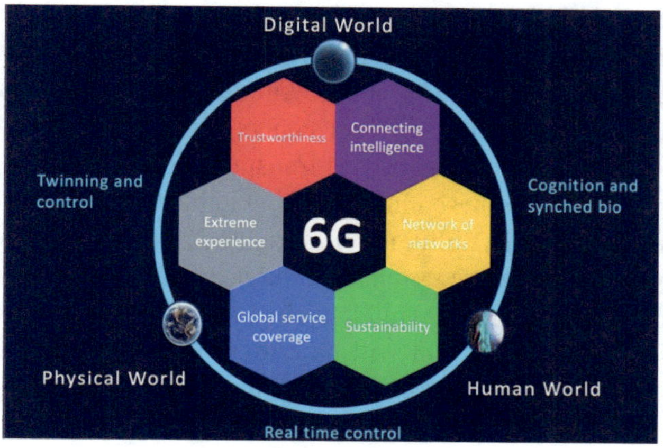

Figure 10.14. *Potential of 6G networks.*

Source: https://theunitedindian.com/images/6G-04-12-24-E-blog1.jpg.

10.6.3. Implications for Urban and Rural Connectivity

The rural and urban future of connectivity also has strong connections with new network architectures that ensure carefree integration within various geographical landscapes. As more Next Generation Access Networks (NGANs) get rolled out, the importance for rural communities in particular is particularly noteworthy. Rural broadband connectivity can be enhanced to encourage economic growth through access to digital content and e-shopping websites. These advances are significant since, in addition to bridging the digital divide, they also enhance local business entrepreneurship and access to education and healthcare services. Further, the techno-economic value of deploying such networks underscores the necessity of transforming regulatory frameworks to support sustainable rural development, ensuring that technology benefits reach even the most isolated regions (Gonzalez et al., 2011). The concept of polycentric spatial development emerges as a vital model in understanding connectivity implications for both rural and urban locations. By producing numerous interconnected nodes, the concept is capable of enhancing functional connectivity between cities, thereby driving regional economies. For the case of Europe, polycentricity enables efficient distribution of resources along with fostering coordination between central cities and small towns. Such economic activity diffusion not only maximizes local linkages but also facilitates the transfer of knowledge and resources to achieve sustainable urban development. Such interconnection can enhance the resilience of both urban and rural landscapes to allow them to thrive even in the face of international economic change (Thierstein et al., 2025). As network infrastructure evolves, the consequences for urban and rural connectivity become more complex, necessitating holistic approaches to managing development. The intertwining of various communication technologies into a polycentric system can potentially enhance not just the efficiency of information exchange and transportation but also inclusiveness. Policymakers, by utilizing these innovations, are able to create an economy that is environmentally friendly, culturally vibrant, and sustainable. The new trends in network topology therefore emphasize the importance of responding to the unique challenges of rural areas while enabling urban regions to take advantage of connectivity. This equilibrium will be critical in establishing an integrated and sustainable future that is responsive to the needs of diverse populations (Thierstein et al., 2025).

SUMMARY

Network topology development, particularly in the era of increasing reliance on smart technologies and renewable energy networks, underscores the clear need for extensive vulnerability analyses. In the new era of the interconnectedness of vast electrical grids, the integration of such networks with sustainable energy sources presents genuine challenges. According to a vulnerability analysis through numerical experiments, storage solutions are able to make networks more resilient to disruptions, especially in systems where there is excess renewable generation. Such a finding means that as networks become increasingly sustainable in operation, future thinking will be needed to ensure that they become resilient against possible failures and vulnerabilities to maintain continuity and security of operations (Millis et al., 2019). To the future, integration of these resilience strategies will be paramount in dealing with risks in modern electric grid operations. Aside from their implications on energy networks, wireless networking technologies are at the forefront of shaping communication between devices in various applications. Market demand fluidity calls for organizations to establish strong foundations for integrating innovative wireless applications into their business models. The model proposed aims at organizing the necessity of aligning organizational processes with the developing capabilities of technology in order to make optimal use of the potential of cellular networks. Alignment is necessary not only to enhance efficiency of operations but also for promoting adaptability in responding to evolving market trends. With investment in that infrastructure that supports mobile networking, organizations place themselves in a position to take advantage of new opportunities, ultimately leading to expansion and even more competitive advantage in a more connected world (Coster et al., 2009). The future of network topology overall is subject to the influence of both integration with renewable energy and development in mobile technologies. Both sectors reveal the multi-dimensional challenges and prospects for this technological shift. The vulnerability of electrical grids to disconnection emphasizes the need for sustained enhancement of resilience, particularly against the backdrop of climate change and variable energy supply. Concomitantly, however, the flexibility enabled by mobile networking technologies emphasizes the necessity for planning models that are robust enough to accommodate evolving market dynamics. It is essential for industry players to understand and implement these concepts in crafting robust and innovative networks that will be the pillars upon which future growth and dependability will be built in a globalized economy. As these trends are in development, careful study and forward thinking will be the main drivers in establishing network configurations and functionalities in the energy and communication arenas.

With network topology evolving further, several significant trends have emerged that are shaping its future. Decentralization of network architecture is one of them, where a movement is inherently being connected with the rise of distributed ledger technologies (DLT), which have begun to reshape how data and resources are managed on networks. DLT provides prospects for increased security and synchronization for wireless communications, particularly in Internet of Things (IoT) applications. With the use of DLT, networks are capable of delivering higher coordination and reliability through consensus mechanisms, thus enabling a more secure environment for fog-Radio Access Networks (RAN). This paradigm shift not only reveals the move to secure communications but also the opportunity for greater resource usage in different places and consequently more flexible and dynamic network topology. For data centers, trends suggest new requirements for low-cost and saleable networking infrastructures. With web applications proliferating at even faster rates, data center topology research has gained momentum, showcasing the limitations of traditional networking models. The standard reliance on ToR and EoR switches, linked with core switches in between, has contributed too often to bandwidth oversubscription, thus limiting overall network performance. More recent studies of advanced topologies such as Fat-Tree, DCell, and BCube hold the promise of optimizing interconnects in these massive infrastructures. These new topologies support the requirements of today's applications and thus enhance the agility and reconfigurability of data center networks. Where additional demands are placed, it is evident that the use of these new topological models will become crucial to the data-centric reality of survival of the network systems. Further, the integration of DLT into network topology not only is revolutionizing security aspects, but it also is expanding the scope of fields of application of networking technologies. As illustrated, DLT can have implications beyond security, including computing and connectivity over networks. The ability to prevent collisions in grant-free uplink access with DLT is one example, and it can make networks more efficient and effective. This wide-ranging impact of DLT illustrates the flexibility of decentralized systems and how they can potentially encourage all things about networking, from managing applications to coordinating resources. As research continues to develop, the interactive dynamics between these emerging trends and the foundational concepts of network topology will give us answers that will reshape communication systems in new and unprecedented ways, further solidifying DLTs position as an architecting block for future network infrastructure.

REFERENCES

1. Abadal Cavallé, S., Alarcón Cot, E. J., Cabellos Aparicio, A., González Colás, J., et al. (2016). Scalability of broadcast performance in wireless network-on-chip. https://core.ac.uk/download/81578757.pdf (accessed on 9th September 2025).
2. Abar, S., Borshchev, A., Campillo, X. R., Holcombe, M., Richmond, P., Sales, C. M., Schelling, T. C., et al. (2019). An agent-based simulation API for speculative PDES runtime environments. https://core.ac.uk/download/196295620.pdf (accessed on 9th September 2025).
3. Abate, A., Arenas, A., Tadić, B., Broder, A., Dorogovtsev, S., et al. (2003). Information super-diffusion on structured networks. http://arxiv.org/abs/cond-mat/0307670 (accessed on 9th September 2025).
4. Abbott, A., Abraham, A., Allis, D., Alpaydin, E., Anderson, B., et al. (2018). Born to learn: The inspiration, progress, and future of evolved plastic artificial neural networks. https://core.ac.uk/download/162581731.pdf (accessed on 9th September 2025).
5. ACM, Nemoto, K., Itoh, K. M., Van Meter, R., Szymanski, T., Thaker, D. D., & Munro, W. J. (2007). Arithmetic on a distributed-memory quantum multicomputer. http://arxiv.org/abs/quant-ph/0607160 (accessed on 9th September 2025).
6. Albert, R., Barabási, A. L., Quoitin, B., Chakrabarti, D., Dorogovtsev, S., Eddy, N., et al. (2010). Phase changes in the evolution of the IPv4 and IPv6 AS-level Internet topologies. https://core.ac.uk/download/1865377.pdf (accessed on 9th September 2025).
7. Alsheikh, M. A., Lin, S., Niyato, D., Tan, H. P., et al. (2014). Machine learning in wireless sensor networks: Algorithms, strategies, and applications. https://core.ac.uk/download/35456291.pdf (accessed on 9th September 2025).
8. Amin, R., Rojas, E., Aqdus, A., Ramzan, S., Casillas-Pérez, D., & Arco, J. M. (2021). A survey on machine learning techniques for routing optimization in SDN. *IEEE Access, 9*, 104582–104611. https://www.semanticscholar.org/paper/8d011b87bd0cb74bba7c177a0947b786503de023 (accessed on 9th September 2025).
9. Aslam, N., Cao, Y., Hussain, S., Khan, Z., et al. (2018). A critical analysis of research potential, challenges and future directives in industrial wireless sensor networks. https://core.ac.uk/download/96885354.pdf (accessed on 9th September 2025).
10. Baddeley, M., Nejabati, R., Oikonomou, G., Simeonidou, D., et al. (2018). Evolving SDN for low-power IoT networks. https://core.ac.uk/

download/210511154.pdf (accessed on 9th September 2025).

11. Baianu, I. C., & Glazebrook, J. F. (2010). Categorical ontology of complex systems, meta-systems and theory of levels: The emergence of life, human consciousness and society. https://core.ac.uk/download/pdf/332869.pdf (accessed on 9th September 2025).
12. Bajaj, P., Sabharwal, M., & Saxena, M. C. (2023). Exploring path computation techniques in software-defined networking: A review and performance evaluation of centralized, distributed, and hybrid approaches. https://core.ac.uk/download/588567618.pdf (accessed on 9th September 2025).
13. Baktir, C., Ersoy, C., Ozgovde, A., Sonmez, A., et al. (2018). Addressing the challenges in federating edge resources. http://arxiv.org/abs/1803.05255 (accessed on 9th September 2025).
14. Banks, G., Counsell, J., Johnston, J., Stewart, R., et al. (2012). Beyond power over Ethernet: The development of digital energy networks for buildings. https://core.ac.uk/download/9039489.pdf (accessed on 9th September 2025).
15. Bass, S. (2013). The philanthropic landscape in the United States: A topology of trends. https://core.ac.uk/download/75779050.pdf (accessed on 9th September 2025).
16. Brinkmann, B., Eberlein, M., Hildebrand, R., Hoffmann, T., et al. (2018). Convolutional neural networks for epileptic seizure prediction. https://core.ac.uk/download/236377961.pdf (accessed on 9th September 2025).
17. Copeland, R., Crespi, N., Rehmani, M. H., Saleem, Y., et al. (2019). Internet of Things-aided smart grid: Technologies, architectures, applications, prototypes, and future research directions. http://arxiv.org/abs/1704.08977 (accessed on 9th September 2025).
18. Coti, C., Agullo, E., Dongarra, J., et al. (2009). QR factorization of tall and skinny matrices in a grid computing environment. https://core.ac.uk/download/50029042.pdf (accessed on 9th September 2025).
19. Cuomo, S., Schiano Di Cola, V., Giampaolo, F., Rozza, G., Raissi, M., & Piccialli, F. (2022). Scientific machine learning through physics–informed neural networks: Where we are and what's next. *Journal of Scientific Computing, 92*. https://doi.org/10.1007/s10915-022-01939-z (accessed on 9th September 2025).
20. Dabiri, M., Hasna, M., Althunibat, S., & Qaraqe, K. A. (2025). UAV-based dynamic FSO access networks: Technological comparison, design considerations, and future directions. *IEEE Wireless*

Communications, 32, 247–253. https://www.semanticscholar.org/paper/b01e22a8f68fe2f89a6af2ba68797ce1a0cc3876 (accessed on 9th September 2025).

21. De Coster, R. (2009). A business planning framework for WiMAX applications. https://core.ac.uk/download/335901.pdf (accessed on 9th September 2025).
22. Feamster, N., & Rexford, J. (2017). Why (and how) networks should run themselves. http://arxiv.org/abs/1710.11583 (accessed on 9th September 2025).
23. Feijoo Gonzalez, C. A., Gómez Barroso, J. L., & Ramos, S. (2011). An analysis of next generation access networks deployment in rural areas. http://oa.upm.es/13112/ (accessed on 9th September 2025).
24. García Haro, J., García Sánchez, A. J., García Sánchez, F., Martínez Sandoval, J., et al. (2017). Evaluating the more suitable ISM frequency band for IoT-based smart grids: A quantitative study of 915 MHz vs. 2400 MHz. https://core.ac.uk/download/322906294.pdf (accessed on 9th September 2025).
25. Hamdi, M. (2013). Keynote speaker: Massive data centers for future cloud computing applications. https://www.semanticscholar.org/paper/2d4c083af99b9d33561fa01366de050c9ef7a95a (accessed on 9th September 2025).
26. Hintze, A., Ricardo, A., Varma, A., Burgard, A. P., Kamp, A. V., Papp, B., et al. (2010). Signatures of arithmetic simplicity in metabolic network architecture. https://core.ac.uk/download/pdf/8395421.pdf (accessed on 9th September 2025).
27. Hosseini, S., Gharehpetian, G., Mozafari, S. B., & Vatani, M. (2025). A survey of networked multi-microgrids reconfiguration strategies: Challenges, opportunities, future directions and case studies. *2025 6th International Conference on Optimizing Electrical Energy Consumption (OEEC)*. https://www.semanticscholar.org/paper/58bca179a5aeee25a14e012c05c048a35e18691f (accessed on 9th September 2025).
28. Huang, G., Liu, Z., van der Maaten, L., & Weinberger, K. Q. (2017). Densely connected convolutional networks. https://doi.org/10.1109/cvpr.2017.243 (accessed on 9th September 2025).
29. Jagadish, J., & Rukmini, S. (2019). Design and evaluation of secure routing schemes in ad hoc wireless networks. *International Journal of Creative Research Thoughts*. https://www.semanticscholar.org/paper/b5cbcc079aa20a07eaa32796875566ab28302f74 (accessed on 9th September 2025).

30. Johnson, C. W., Pezaros, D. P., & White, K. J. S. (2012). Increasing resilience of ATM networks using traffic monitoring and automated anomaly analysis. https://core.ac.uk/download/9400729.pdf (accessed on 9th September 2025).
31. Khan, A., Qureshi, A. S., Sohail, A., Zahoora, U., et al. (2020). A survey of the recent architectures of deep convolutional neural networks. http://arxiv.org/abs/1901.06032 (accessed on 9th September 2025).
32. Khan, W. A., Chung, S. H., Awan, M. U., & Wen, X. (2019). Machine learning facilitated business intelligence (Part II). *Industrial Management & Data Systems, 120*, 128–163. https://doi.org/10.1108/imds-06-2019-0351 (accessed on 9th September 2025).
33. Klaß, M., Pillmann, J., Sliwa, B., Wietfeld, C., et al. (2018). Exploiting map topology knowledge for context-predictive multi-interface car-to-cloud communication. http://arxiv.org/abs/1807.01042 (accessed on 9th September 2025).
34. Knoblock, E. J. (2025). Cognitive communications and networking technology infusion study report. https://core.ac.uk/download/pdf/211016405.pdf (accessed on 9th September 2025).
35. Kuo, P., Mourad, A. A. M., & Ahn, J. (2018). Potential applicability of distributed ledger to wireless networking technologies. *IEEE Wireless Communications, 25*, 4–6. https://www.semanticscholar.org/paper/211b7ecbd804c3155927a078f9c9afd94b522cce (accessed on 9th September 2025).
36. Lei, I., Lin, S., Xie, B., & Liu, L. (2020). A vulnerability-based vehicle routing approach for solving capacitated arc routing problem in urban snow plowing operations. *Mathematical Biosciences and Engineering: MBE, 18*(1), 166–182. https://www.semanticscholar.org/paper/1d0b714aeef6d65c5a353f48f3b3aee67bb1809f (accessed on 9th September 2025).
37. Li, G., Li, J., & Wu, J. (2018). Fog-enabled edge learning for cognitive content-centric networking in 5G. http://arxiv.org/abs/1808.09141 (accessed on 9th September 2025).
38. Majid, M., Habib, S., Javed, A. R., Rizwan, M., Srivastava, G., Gadekallu, T. R., & Lin, J. C. W. (2022). Applications of wireless sensor networks and Internet of Things frameworks in the Industry Revolution 4.0: A systematic literature review. *Sensors, 22*, 2087–2087. https://doi.org/10.3390/s22062087 (accessed on 9th September 2025).
39. Millis, M. (2019). Vulnerability analysis of modern electric grids: A mathematical optimization approach. https://core.ac.uk/download/215464251.pdf (accessed on 9th September 2025).

40. Murphree, J., Weil, R., & Wootton, J. (2024). Emerging trends in intra vehicle networks for data, control and power distribution. *SAE Technical Paper Series*. https://www.semanticscholar.org/paper/db9f28e09d6c8cf89f1b81b09b2cd1e9f76c055d (accessed on 9th September 2025).

41. Ok, J., Park, S., Shin, B., Yi, Y., et al. (2012). Embedding of virtual network requests over static wireless multihop networks. http://arxiv.org/abs/1207.1878 (accessed on 9th September 2025).

42. Park, S., & Kim, Y. G. (2022). A metaverse: Taxonomy, components, applications, and open challenges. *IEEE Access, 10*, 4209–4251. https://doi.org/10.1109/access.2021.3140175 (accessed on 9th September 2025).

43. Perera, C., Chen, F., Suciu, G., Hashem, I. A. T., Xu, L. D., Belgaum, M. R., Sun, Y., et al. (2018). Challenges of Internet of Things and big data integration. http://arxiv.org/abs/1806.08953 (accessed on 9th September 2025).

44. Reddy, Y. M., Raj, V. H., Thethi, H., Gupta, S., Maan, P., & Ghani, R. H. (2023). Low Earth Orbit (LEO) satellite networks: A new era in global communication. *2023 10th IEEE Uttar Pradesh Section International Conference on Electrical, Electronics and Computer Engineering (UPCON), 10*, 1563–1568. https://www.semanticscholar.org/paper/50dce8f9addb6ff2994470c1ea5b5a0d474c4d61 (accessed on 9th September 2025).

45. Rehman, M., Lu, S., Heyat, M. B. B., Iqbal, M. S., Parveen, S., Hayat, M. A. B., Akhtar, F., et al. (2025). Internet of Things in healthcare research: Trends, innovations, security considerations, challenges and future strategy. *International Journal of Intelligent Systems, 2025*. https://www.semanticscholar.org/paper/c7e971787f125e6b6516ba3bdec34fc6a44d317d (accessed on 9th September 2025).

46. Teuscher, C., Das, R., de Micheli, G., Di Caro, G., Lawniczak, A. T., Lawson, J., Levitan, S. L., et al. (2007). Nature-inspired interconnects for self-assembled large-scale network-on-chip designs. https://core.ac.uk/download/37766445.pdf (accessed on 9th September 2025).

47. Thierstein, A., Kruse, C., Glanzmann, L., & Grillon, N. (2025). Polycentricity and metropolitan governance: A Swiss case study. https://core.ac.uk/download/pdf/7046540.pdf (accessed on 9th September 2025).

48. Udoh, E., & Udoh, E. (2019). An energy aware and secure MAC protocol for tackling denial of sleep attacks in wireless sensor networks. https://core.ac.uk/download/305119264.pdf (accessed on 9th September 2025).

49. Wang, C. X., You, X., Gao, X., Zhu, X., Li, Z., Zhang, C., Wang, H., et al. (2023). On the road to 6G: Visions, requirements, key technologies, and testbeds. *IEEE Communications Surveys & Tutorials, 25*, 905–974. https://doi.org/10.1109/comst.2023.3249835 (accessed on 9th September 2025).
50. Wang, X., Li, T., Xu, K., & Li, Z. (2023). Space information network virtualized communication design of terahertz interface. *2023 3rd International Symposium on Computer Technology and Information Science (ISCTIS)*. https://www.semanticscholar.org/paper/5eda857a13d529442eb31b4b8de2eb5c5ed09564 (accessed on 9th September 2025).
51. Wang, Y., Su, Z., Zhang, N., Xing, R., Liu, D., Luan, T. H., & Shen, X. (2022). A survey on metaverse: Fundamentals, security, and privacy. *IEEE Communications Surveys & Tutorials, 25*, 319–352. https://doi.org/10.1109/comst.2022.3202047 (accessed on 9th September 2025).
52. Zafar, H., Abbas, Z., Abbas, G., Muhammad, F., Tufail, M., & Kim, S. (2020). An effective fairness scheme for named data networking. *Electronics*. https://www.semanticscholar.org/paper/4c4bd10baffcf0a87c32eb0c7f824ab66990fbc7 (accessed on 9th September 2025).WW

INDEX

D

E

F

L

M

N

O

P

Q

R

S

T